THE
ARMED FORCES
OF
WORLD WAR II

UNIFORMS, INSIGNIA
& ORGANISATION

A LITTLE, BROWN BOOK

This edition published 2001
by Little, Brown and Company (UK)

© 2001 Little, Brown and Company (UK)

This book is adapted from
The Armed Forces of World War II
© Little, Brown and Company (UK)

ISBN 0-316-85897-8

Production by Omnipress, Eastbourne
Printed in Singapore

Little, Brown and Company (UK)
Brettenham House, Lancaster Place
London WC2E 7EN

Andrew Mollo would like to thank Philip Buss whose advice and consultancy have been invaluable. Grateful thanks are due to Christopher Barbarski, Eric Lefêvre, David Littlejohn, Laurie Milner, E.W. Jørgensen, Guido Rossignoli, D.M. Sekulich, P. Simonsen, René Smeets, Kari Stenman, Glen Sweeting, Thorkild Tønnesen, François Vauvillier, Paul Verheye, Ernesto Vitetti.

Malcolm McGregor would like to express his sincere gratitude to the individuals and institutions listed below for help and information generously provided during the preparation of the figure drawings and in the course of his researches into the material for the rank insignia charts. While giving credit to those whose contributions have helped to make the illustrations in this book as accurate as possible, he owns that any errors or omissions are his alone.

The staff of the Photographic Department of the Imperial War Museum, London, without whom it would surely have been impossible to carry out the work in this particular fashion; Reading Room of the Imperial War Museum, London; Belgian Embassy, London; Musée Royal de l'Armée, Brussels; Royal Norwegian Embassy, London; Norwegian Naval Museum, Horten, Norway; Greek Embassy, London; General Air Staff, Athens; Dept. of Army History, Hellenic Army Headquarters, Athens; Royal Danish Embassy, London; Mariners Bibliotek, Copenhagen; Inga Fl. Rasmussen, Tøjhusmuseet, Copenhagen; Chief of Defence, Denmark; South African Embassy, London; Chief of the SADF, Republic of South Africa; Finnish Embassy, London; General Headquarters Finnish Defence Forces, Helsinki; New Zealand High Commission, London; Ministry of Defence, Wellington, New Zealand; Ministry of National Defence, Taiwan, Republic of China; Sikorski Institute, London; Museums of the Royal Corps of Transport, Aldershot; Lieut-Col Howard Cole; Marshal of the Royal Air Force Sir Neil Cameron GCB CBE DSO DFC past Chief of the Defence of Staff, London; Major A.J. Donald RM, Royal Marines Museum, Southsea, Hants; Royal Naval Museum, Portsmouth; Royal Air Force Museum, London; National Maritime Museum, London; Gurkha Museum, Aldershot; Black Watch Museum, Perth, Scotland; Museum of the Corps of Royal Military Police, Chichester, Sussex; Ian V. Hogg; Commander Maitland-Thornton OBE RNVR, Mons; Frank Steff; Brian L. Davis; Mrs R.A. Rigg; Christopher Barbarski; Royal Netherlands Embassy, London; Stephen Bosley of Coldstream Military Antiques, Amersham, England.

Picture Acknowledgements
The uniforms of the Allied forces were painted by Malcolm McGregor, who also painted the plates of rank insignia. Pierre Turner painted the uniforms of the Axis Forces. The organisational diagrams were drawn up by Adrian Gilbert and Michael Hodson. The largest single source of photographs for the book has been the collection of Andrew Mollo himself (Historical Research Unit), and we were also fortunate in being able to use the resources of the Robert Hunt Library. These apart, the photographs came from the following organisations and individuals: Associated Press; Australian War Memorial; Bibliothèque Nationale, Paris; Bundesarchiv, Koblenz; Communist Party Picture Library; Etablissement Cinématographique et Photographique des Armées, Paris; Imperial War Museum; Musée de la Guerre, Vincennes; National Maritime Museum; Novosti; PAV; J. Piekalkiewicz; Signal; Sikorski Institute, London; US Air Force; US Army; US Coast Guard; US Marine Corps and US Navy. For their help in drawing up the table of ranks, the publisher would like to thank the embassies of the following nations: Belgium, Bulgaria, Denmark, Finland, France, Germany, Hungary, Japan, Netherlands, Norway, Poland and Russia.

CONTENTS

INTRODUCTION

With the publication of this volume I have at last produced the sort of book about which I dreamed as a boy of five, when I first became interested in military uniform at the end of World War II. Living as I did near Aldershot – home of the British Army – I saw so many men and women in uniform that my childish curiosity led me to ask what a particular uniform or badge signified.

The postwar period when men and women all over Europe were gratefully shedding their uniforms, was a pretty bleak one for anybody trying to satisfy such an unusual interest. There were no lavishly stocked model shops, no book shops offering rows of titles ranging from the armies of Byzantium to those of NATO. The only military books available were the Times and Hamilton illustrated histories of World Wars I and II, and the dreary old regimental histories. So bit by bit I assembled my own scrap books from cuttings and the odd coloured postcard or photograph. Any representation of a soldier, however inaccurate, was gratefully pasted in. While other children were preoccupied with football and cricket I used to demolish the Illustrated London News.

This book has been divided into four main sections, each of which deals with a major theatre of operations. The armed forces engaged in a particular theatre are described under three sub-headings – background, organisation and uniform. The coverage given to a nation is not necessarily in proportion to its size or contribution to the war. The major nations are already well covered in numerous books, but there is very little readily available in the English language on the smaller nations.

The uniform text is perforce brief, but the running text is complemented by Malcolm McGregor's and Pierre Turner's superb artwork, the detailed captions to the figure drawings, and the 125 black and white photographs. Obviously one has not been able to go into the minutiae so beloved by the expert, but in no other book will be found 266 figure drawings based on contemporary photographs, 39 coloured charts of badges of rank and other insignia, and 11 organisational diagrams.

ANDREW MOLLO

THE WAR IN EUROPE
1939-40

On 1 September 1939 the armed forces of
Nazi Germany began World War II by invading Poland.
Within a year, Denmark, Norway, Holland, Belgium and
France had also been defeated by the German armies
and Great Britain was preparing to resist invasion.
Meanwhile, the Soviet Union had attacked Finland and,
during the winter of 1939–40, the 'Winter War' was fought.
With the notable exception of Nazi Germany, the
organisation of the armed forces which fought these early
campaigns was dominated by memories of the past (most
particularly by memories of World War I) and this was
also the case in the design of uniforms. Most nations
began the war with many formations equipped
with clothing of an earlier epoch; some were
in a process of transition (the British Army,
for example) and some wore World War I
uniforms designed for other
nations' armies.

GERMANY
ARMY

On 16 March 1935 Adolf Hitler re-introduced conscription and announced to the world the formation of a German air force. Needless to say this brought the restrictions imposed on the size and the strength of the German armed forces to an abrupt end. The next four years saw the rapid expansion of the German Army; a transformation from General Seeckt's *Reichswehr* into Hitler's *Wehrmacht*.

In September 1939 the German Army went to war with forces which, although well trained in the latest concepts of mechanised warfare, had gained little combat experience except in the Spanish Civil War; and that had been very limited. Much of the specialised motorised equipment had yet to reach the field armies and so all the non-panzer and non-motorised divisions still travelled on foot and relied mainly on horses to haul their equipment and artillery.

Whatever the shortcomings in quantity and quality of equipment, German human material was of the best. The Versailles Treaty, which had limited the *Reichswehr* to one hundred thousand men, was turned to advantage, in that only the best personnel were retained in a completely professional army. There was even a surplus of soldiers to man the armed police forces of the various German states (*Landespolizei*), and these were later to be incorporated in the Army when conscription was re-introduced. There was, in addition, a vast pool of semi-trained manpower in the para-military formations of the Nazi Party.

Apart from the conscripts the German Army needed to attract volunteers who would make a career in the Army. To achieve this, terms of service were made more attractive, smart new uniforms introduced and well-equipped modern barracks constructed. At the same time attempts were made to break down much of the traditional petty authoritarianism of the Army, while retaining and even

elevating the privileged position of the German soldier in society. The soldiers of the *Wehrmacht* set themselves very high professional standards so that when they went to war in 1939, they did so with enthusiasm and the strong conviction that they were the finest soldiers in the world.

Hitler's main problem with the Army came from certain senior officers who opposed his aggressive foreign policy and held conservative views on the conduct of war, but these men had little influence. Their opposition was always hesitant, and affected by their approval of Hitler's modernisation programme, while they would always be bypassed or replaced if they proved too troublesome. The German Army of World War II was in general a loyal, obedient and confident instrument of the Nazi dictator.

ORGANISATION In March 1939 the operational control of the Armed Forces was unified under the *Oberkommando der Wehrmacht* (OKW) whose chief was *Generaloberst* (Colonel-General) Keitel.

1

2

3

The management of the Army was the responsibility of the Army High Command, the *Oberkommando des Heeres* (OKH), which included the General Staff, although it was the Supreme Commander, Adolf Hitler, who was increasingly to take over the day-to-day running of the war.

In 1939 Germany was divided into 13 geographical districts known as *Wehrkreise*, each of which was a depot for a

Left: Staff officers of the 7th Panzer Division (commanded by Erwin Rommel) discuss their plans during the campaign of the spring of 1940. The officer in the centre, holding the map, is wearing the older pattern field cap, without chinstrap, and the badge on his left breast pocket is the tank badge for the Spanish Civil War. The officer on the left wears the side cap.

Below: Typically well-equipped German infantry of the first year of the war. The helmets were still shiny at this early period, and displayed the national colours. The sergeant (on the right) carries an MP28 sub-machine gun, and the two soldiers have sacks of grenades slung round their shoulders.

number of divisions and formed a 'home-base' for their regiments. On mobilisation there were 51 active divisions:
39 infantry divisions (including four motorised);
5 panzer divisions (plus a panzer brigade);
4 light divisions;
3 mountain divisions.
When Germany mobilised, the system was rapidly expanded to include 16 reserve, 21 territorial (*Landwehr*) and 14 so-called *Ergänzangsdivisionen* divisions. During 1939–40 the number of panzer divisions was doubled (mainly by 'converting' light divisions) so that there were 10 such divisions by the spring of 1940.

For the Polish Campaign the OKW created two army groups: Army Group North (divided into 2 armies each of 3 corps) consisted of 1 panzer division, 1 mixed Army/SS panzer division, 2 motorised divisions, 16 infantry divisions and a cavalry brigade. Army Group South (10 corps in 3 armies) consisted of 4 panzer divisions, 4 light, 21 infantry and

1 Captain, General Staff, German Army, 1939

As an officer on the General Staff this captain wears crimson stripes (Lampassen) on his breeches and crimson piping on his shoulder straps and cap. A particular feature of the staff officers' uniform was the collar patches (Litzen) where the bars were given a quite distinctive pattern of embroidery. Those officers permanently attached to OKW wore gold embroidered collar patches. In the German Army staff officers were held in high regard and played an important part in the conduct of operations.

2 Colonel-General, German Army

Eduard Dietl, an Austrian, became a legend in his lifetime when his leadership helped save the German Army from disaster during the Norwegian campaign. Shown here in the uniform of a mountain-troop commander, he wears a piped service tunic (without mountain troop insignia) and a mountain cap with the silver national emblem and the 'edelweiss' on the left side of the cap. At this time there was no piping around the crown. On his right breast pocket is the highly prized and rarely awarded Army mountain guide badge. Other decorations are the Knight's Cross of the Iron Cross awarded to him in May 1940, the bar to the Iron Cross 1st Class, and a wound badge. Befitting a commander of mountain troops, Dietl wears mountain boots and puttees.

3 NCO, German Army, 1939-40

This German infantryman wears a combat uniform typical of the early period of the war. The field-grey blouse with dark blue collar and stone grey trousers were soon to be discontinued, while the collar and trousers of uniforms being manufactured were of field-grey cloth. His non-commissioned officer rank is indicated by the aluminium lace around the collar and on the shoulder straps, and as a section leader, (Gruppenführer) in charge of ten men he is armed with an MP38 sub-machine gun.

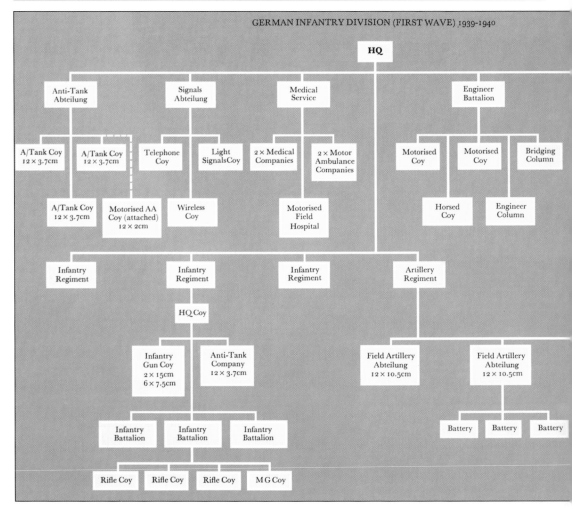

GERMAN INFANTRY DIVISION (FIRST WAVE) 1939-1940

HQ

Anti-Tank Abteilung | Signals Abteilung | Medical Service | Engineer Battalion

A/Tank Coy 12 × 3.7cm | A/Tank Coy 12 × 3.7cm | Telephone Coy | Light Signals Coy | 2 × Medical Companies | 2 × Motor Ambulance Companies | Motorised Coy | Motorised Coy | Bridging Column

A/Tank Coy 12 × 3.7cm | Motorised AA Coy (attached) 12 × 2cm | Wireless Coy | Motorised Field Hospital | Horsed Coy | Engineer Column

Infantry Regiment | Infantry Regiment | Infantry Regiment | Artillery Regiment

HQ Coy

Infantry Gun Coy 2 × 15cm 6 × 7.5cm | Anti-Tank Company 12 × 3.7cm | Field Artillery Abteilung 12 × 10.5cm | Field Artillery Abteilung 12 × 10.5cm

Infantry Battalion | Infantry Battalion | Infantry Battalion | Battery | Battery | Battery

Rifle Coy | Rifle Coy | Rifle Coy | MG Coy

3 mountain divisions. Two of XVII Army Corp's infantry divisions were Slovak, while attached to XIII Army Corps was the motorised SS infantry regiment *Leibstandarte* (Bodyguard Regiment) *Adolf Hitler*.

The most important formation in the German Army was the division which could be one of five basic types: infantry, motorised infantry, panzer (armoured), light and mountain. Infantry divisions had been raised in *Wellen* (waves) and the divisions of each wave varied to some extent in size, organisation and equipment carried, depending upon their purpose and the availability of men and materials. The 35 divisions formed as part of the original 'wave' had a total strength of nearly 18,000 men each while

those of the next wave were about 15,000 men strong. Divisions formed in the third and fourth waves had considerably less artillery support than the earlier formations. The infantry division comprised three infantry regiments (each of approximately 3,000 men) and one artillery regiment plus supporting divisional units as illustrated in the diagram. Contrary to the practice in most armies, the engineer battalion and the reconnaissance *Abteilung* (the *Abteilung* was a unit of varying size, between the regiment and the company, battery or squadron. It approximated to the British battalion, artillery regiment or tank regiment) were combat units, and, being equipped with flamethrowers and anti-tank guns, often led assaults on enemy positions. Another feature of the German

Army was the decentralisation of heavy weapons within the division so that each regiment had its own anti-tank and infantry gun company.

The infantry regiment possessed its own headquarters with a staff company and signals, bicycle and engineer platoon. In the infantry battalion there were three rifle companies (about 180 men with an anti-tank rifle squad); a machine-gun company with three machine-gun platoons (12 men and two heavy machine guns each), and a heavy mortar platoon of three sections each with 19 men and two 8.1cm mortars. The division of the battalion into one machine-gun and three rifle companies was the pattern in the first wave divisions while in later waves there were four 'mixed' rifle

companies. The firepower of a regiment was as follows:
26 heavy machine guns;
85 light machine guns;
18 × 8.1cm mortars;
27 × 5cm mortars;
12 × 3.7cm anti-tank guns;
6 × 7.5cm infantry guns;
2 × 15cm infantry howitzers.

The artillery regiment was divided into three field artillery *Abteilungen* each with three four-gun batteries of 10.5cm gun-howitzers. The medium artillery *Abteilung* was originally a non-divisional unit attached to the artillery regiment, but later became an integral part of first wave divisions.

In addition to the divisional artillery which could vary in type and organisation

from one division to another, both armies and corps had at their disposal additional batteries of medium and heavy artillery. These batteries could range in size of calibre from the dual-purpose 8.8cm gun to the massive 60cm self-propelled howitzer known as a *Karl Mörser*. Most of the heavy anti-aircraft batteries were under Luftwaffe control but could be allocated to the Army for specific operations.

Motorised infantry divisions were intended to keep up with fast-moving panzer divisions, and so they were completely equipped with motor vehicles. For the Polish campaign there were four motorised infantry divisions, each of three infantry and one motorised artillery regiment, but after this campaign they lost their third infantry regiment as more panzer divisions were formed.

The panzer division during the Polish and French campaigns consisted of two tank regiments of two battalions each of four companies with 32 tanks each. This gave a total of 561 tanks including reserves and staff vehicles, although on mobilisation tank strength was usually below establishment with an average of about 320 vehicles. The division was equipped with a combination of Mark I and II light tanks (armed only with machine guns and 2cm cannon), Czech 38(t) tanks and a few heavier Mark III and IV tanks. Each division had two fully motorised infantry regiments which were later to be re-designated as *Panzergrenadiere*. The reconnaissance battalion was equipped with armoured cars and motorcycles, and

the division also had its own motorised signals battalion and other services. The success of the German armoured formations lay not in the quality of their vehicles (which were in some respects inferior to those of their opponents during the campaigns of 1940) but in a superiority of organisation and tactical ability which enabled them to be the cutting-edge of the Army.

The original light divisions, formed in 1937–8, were motorised cavalry formations which varied in organisation but usually comprised a light tank battalion, one or two cavalry rifle regiments (each of two or three battalions) a motorised artillery regiment (24 × 10.5cm gun howitzers); an anti-tank battalion (36 × 3.7cm, 12 × 2cm guns) and a motorised reconnaissance battalion or regiment equipped with armoured cars. As a divisional organisation they were undergunned and underarmoured and following the Polish campaign the light divisions were uprated to panzer divisions. In late 1940 four infantry divisions were redesignated as 'light' divisions although their organisation was still basically that of an infantry division.

The three mountain divisions were organised on lines similar to those of the standard infantry division although in the field organisation varied according to circumstances. A typical establishment would be two infantry regiments, each divided into three battalions; the battalion comprising five companies. In keeping with their ostensible role they had a high proportion of lightweight and easily manageable equipment. The artillery regiment had two *Abteilungen* of eight 7.5cm guns each, one *Abteilung* of eight 10.5cm guns and one *Abteilung* of eight 15cm guns. The anti-tank *Abteilung* comprised 24 motorised 3.7cm guns and was strengthened by the two regimental anti-tank companies which each had a strength of nine 3.7cm and three 4.7cm guns. In mountainous or rough country the mountain divisions proved a success; their flexible structure (based upon the battalion as opposed to the regiment) as well as first class training made them formidable opponents and provided them with an élite status within the German Army. In open terrain, when faced by conventionally armed formations, their lack of heavy firepower told against them, however.

By 1939 there was only one cavalry formation left in the German Army, the 1st Cavalry Brigade (although it should be emphasised that the employment of horses for a variety of duties was widespread and remained so throughout the war). The brigade was composed of two mounted cavalry regiments and a battalion of mounted artillery. The regiments were divided into four cavalry squadrons and one 'heavy' squadron

(6 × 8cm mortars, 4 × 7.5cm guns) with a combined strength of about 1400 men each. Even in blitzkrieg warfare there was still a place for cavalry: on 25 October 1939 the Brigade was redesignated the 1st Cavalry Division and reinforced in December with the 2nd Cavalry Brigade.

The decisive but hard fought victory over Poland (losses were 10,600 killed, 30,000 wounded and 3400 missing) surprised the world, and Hitler was able to brush aside the few remaining voices of caution within the German military establishment. Germany transferred her forces to the West in preparation for the invasion of France. By May 1940, the number of divisions in the German army was as follows:

129 infantry divisions;
4 motorised infantry divisions;
4 light motorised infantry divisions;
10 panzer divisions;
3 mountain divisions;
1 cavalry division.

In addition the *SS-Verfügungstruppe* (from April 1940, known as the Waffen-SS) provided three motorised infantry divisions and a brigade. There were now

Above right: Mountain troops in 1940. Skis were not standard issue, but were used when appropriate. The NCO in front has tinted goggles, and wears non-regulation ski boots.

Below: A group of motorcyclists, about to listen to a gramophone they have found. The man on the left and the soldier kneeling have waterproof coats; the others wear standard greatcoats.

over two-and-a-half million men under arms in the German Army, of which the Waffen-SS contributed about 100,000.

For the invasion of France the German Army was organised into three army groups: Army Group A (von Rundstedt) with 45½ divisions including 7 panzer; Army Group B (von Bock) with 29½ divisions including 3 panzer, and Army Group C (von Leeb) with 19 divisions. Army Group C held a defensive position against the Maginot Line while the main offensive was launched by Rundstedt's Army Group A in the Ardennes with a subsidiary invasion of Holland and Belgium undertaken by Army Group B.

From 9 April (when German troops invaded Denmark and Norway) to the armistice with France on 25 June, the German Army confirmed the superiority of its organisation and tactics. Losses in Norway were 5636 men; the invasion of France and the Low Countries cost 27,074 killed, 111,034 wounded and 18,348 missing.

UNIFORM The field-grey uniform of the German Army was a development of that worn during World War I. The final version was introduced in stages from 1935 onwards.

In the Army there were two kinds of uniform: that issued by the state, and that provided by the wearer either at his own expense or at the expense of the state. During peacetime and in the first year of the war, officers often continued to wear tailor-made uniforms in the field, but since these were impractical, uncomfortable and costly to replace, they increasingly wore issue uniforms with officers' badges of rank.

The basic field-grey uniform was standardised throughout the Army and its principal components were the steel helmet, side cap, field-blouse, greatcoat, trousers and marching boots. Mountain troops received the same uniform but the side cap was replaced by a mountain cap, and the trousers and boots by long baggy trousers gathered at the ankle, elasticated puttees and mountain boots. Mounted personnel were not only to be found in the cavalry, but in the many units which still relied on horses for transport or reconnaissance. They were given breeches lined with leather and heavy riding boots.

A special black uniform for crews of enclosed armoured vehicles was also introduced in 1935. It consisted of a black padded beret which served as a crash helmet, short double-breasted jacket and long baggy trousers. This uniform, which was at first only to be worn when on duty with the vehicle, was both practical and popular. Its black colour, offset by a silver death's head badge, was dramatic and contributed in no small way to the *esprit* of this young arm; and so it was extended to crews of self-propelled guns who received a field-grey version at the beginning of 1940.

Generally speaking the German clothing industry had achieved miracles in keeping pace with the expansion of the Army and the German uniform was a rare combination of tradition and modernity, comfort and smartness. Even so there were not enough uniforms to go round and the vast stocks of uniforms found by the Germans in Austria, Czechoslovakia, and Poland were sorted, stored, stripped of national emblems and issued to German conscripts to compensate for shortages.

INSIGNIA The primary method of identifying rank in the German Army was by means of the system of shoulder straps which not only showed the wearer's rank, but his arm of service, formation and status. In addition, officers were distinguished by their head-dress (peaked cap with silver chin cords and side cap with silver piping) and brown leather equipment. All non-commissioned officers wore the basic soldiers' uniform (unlike many European armies modelled on the French system where NCOs wore the officers' uniform), but were identified by silver lace on their tunic collar and shoulder straps. Soldiers wore their badges of rank on the left sleeve.

The arm of service was indicated by various colours (golden yellow in the cavalry, for example, as illustrated in the insignia chart) which appeared as piping on the peaked cap, chevrons on the front of the side cap, stripes on the collar patches, and as piping and underlay on the shoulder straps.

Medals and decorations were comparatively rare at the beginning of the war, being restricted to World War I awards, long service awards, political awards, and decorations awarded for service in the Spanish Civil War. It was, however, characteristic that the Germans continued to wear decorations in action, although this singled them out as targets for snipers.

GERMAN ARMY INSIGNIA

Collar Patches

Shoulder

Field Marshal · Colonel-General (I) · General of Infantry (II) · Lieutenant-General · Major-General · Colonel (Infantry) · Lieutenant-Colonel (Mtn. Troops) · Major (Cavalry) · Captain (Panzers) · Lieutenant (Transport Supply) · 2nd Lieut (Artillery)

Collar Patches

Shoulder

Arm Patches

Infantryman (Private to Staff L·Corp) · Staff Lance-Corporal · Senior Lance-Corporal · Lance-Corporal · Private 1st Class · Artillery Snr Sgt (early pattern)

Camouflage Clothing Arm Patches

Staff Sergeant (Panzers) · Sgt-Major (Panzer Grenadiers) · Senior Sgt (Motor Recce) · Sergeant (Engineers) · Corporal (Signals) other units and formations of the embryonic Waffen-SS participated in the Polish Campaign alongside German Army units, thereby gaining valuable experience. Immediately behind the advancing armies came units of the German Labour Service (*Reichsarbeitsdienst*) which repaired bridges and roads under the supervision of Army engineers. Electricity, gas and telecommunications were restored by the Technical Emergency Service (*Technische Nothilfe*), while in the newly-occupied towns and villages traffic was controlled and roads kept clear for the armed forces by the special Traffic Regulating Service (*Verkehrs-Erziehungsdienst*) of the National Socialist Motor Transport Corps (NSKK).

Internal security and the full horror of the Nazi regime were ruthlessly imposed by special mobile units of the German Police (*Einsatzkommandos*) who arrested or executed a long list of people considered too dangerous or unworthy to live under the 'new order'.

As German regular troops were withdrawn from Poland, garrison duties were taken over by SS *Tokenkopf* (Death's Head) Infantry Regiments and battalions of German Security Police (*Schutzpolizei*).

UNIFORM The *SS-Heimwehr Danzig* had field-grey Waffen-SS uniform with the death's head on the right collar patch and a black cuff-band on the left cuff with *SS-Heimwehr Danzig* in silver letters. The Danzig *Landespolizei* wore a police green uniform, but instead of the German national emblem, they wore a death's head on the peaked cap and on the right side of the steel helmet. Both the NSKK and the *Reichsarbeitsdienst* had khaki uniforms and wore the NSDAP armlet on the left sleeve. The Technical Emergency Service had a black uniform but men attached to Army units were issued with field-grey uniforms.

AIR FORCE

The creation of the first German Air Force (Luftwaffe) as an independent branch of the German armed forces was announced in March 1935, although, in fact, a semi-clandestine build-up had taken place before this under the cover of the German Air Sports Association (*Deutsche Luftsportverband* or DLV). Soon after Hitler's seizure of power, Hermann Göring was appointed first postwar Air Minister. By the time the existence of an Air Force was made public it already had about 1000 aircraft and 20,000 officers and men. Expansion and the replacement of obsolete aircraft with the very latest models took place very rapidly and

4 Lieutenant, German Police, 1939

Shown here is the standard service dress for officers of the so-called order police (Ordnungspolizei). During the war police battalions were used as garrison troops in occupied territories, while others were conscripted into the Army to act as military policemen. Rank is indicated by the Army-pattern shoulder straps for commissioned ranks. The usual weapon with this order of dress was an automatic pistol although swords were still worn for ceremonial occasions.

5 Private, SS Police, 1940

The combination of Army collar patches and SS national emblem on the left sleeve is rather unusual, but this rifleman is from the SS Polizei-Division whose personnel were drawn from the German police. The uniform is basically that of the German Army (field-grey tunic, boots and trousers) while the helmet is the 1935 model as issued to the barracked units of the police All ranks continued to bear police rank titles and used the military salute. The rifle is the Mauser 98K, a five-shot weapon which was becoming obsolete by 1939; the grenade is the Stielgranate 24. The rifleman also carries a gas mask and camouflage cape.

PARA-MILITARY UNITS

Para-military units played an important part in the campaign of 1939, and in the creation of those tensions which the Germans used to justify their invasion of Poland. Despite its status as a Free City, German 'tourists' were introduced into Danzig during the summer of 1939, and on 18 August came the public announcement of the formation of the German-sponsored *SS-Heimwehr Danzig* (Danzig Home Defence SS). It was organised like a German infantry battalion but with four rifle companies as well as a machine-gun and infantry-gun company, a signals and engineer platoon and two anti-tank platoons. Its strength was 42 officers and 1,500 men and it was fully motorised.

In September the Danzig *Heimwehr*, together with the Danzig Police, took part in the attack on the Polish controlled Post Office, and in the assault on the Westerplatte fortress. After the Polish campaign the battalion was disbanded with its personnel going as cadres to other SS units.

In addition to the Danzig *Heimwehr*

by 1937 the Luftwaffe was able to test its modern aircraft and tactical theories in the Spanish Civil War.

In March 1938 German aircraft were used to transport troops during the annexation of Austria (which resulted in the incorporation of the Austrian Air Force into the Luftwaffe), and in September German airborne troops took part in the occupation of the Sudetenland. When the Luftwaffe went to war in September 1939 it was a well equipped and highly trained force, which had been created to perform a specific role as conceived by the *Wehrmacht* strategists, who saw it as an adjunct to land warfare. To perform its tactical role, the Luftwaffe had pioneered Army/Air Force co-operation, developed effective dive-bombing techniques in support of ground forces, and perfected the transport of troops and supplies by air. In addition it had taken over from the Army its experimental parachute troops and had radically improved the techniques by which troops could be landed in the combat zone by parachute and glider. But when Germany's lightning and unexpected successes took on larger implications, the Luftwaffe, so well adapted to a close-support role, was unable to provide the long-range bomber force necessary to strike effectively at British and Soviet industry and communications.

Below: The fighter ace Adolf Galland climbs out of his Bf 109. He is wearing the fighter pilot version of the 'Mae West' life-jacket.

6

7

ORGANISATION Control of the Luftwaffe was exercised by the Luftwaffe High Command (*Oberkommando der Luftwaffe* or OKL) which had under its command four Air Fleets (*Luftflotten*) with their headquarters in Berlin (No.1), Brunswick (No.2), Munich (No.3), and Vienna (No.4). The administration of the Air Fleets was carried out by the Air Region (*Luftgau*) headquarters which were based on various airfields. The fighting forces were formed into flying corps (*Fliegerkorps*) which were made up of a number of different types of flying unit according to the role that they had to play. The main unit within a *Fliegerkorps* was the *Geschwader* (no exact British equivalent existed). Each *Geschwader* had a staff unit and three or four groups (*Gruppen*) of three or four squadrons (*Staffeln*) of 10 to 12 aircraft each. The three types of *Geschwader* were *Jagdgeschwader* (single-seater fighters), *Kampfgeschwader* (bombers) and *Stukageschwader* (dive bombers).

The aircraft strength of a *Geschwader* was 90 to 120 aircraft, which included a

6 General, German Air Force, 1939
This air force general wears parade dress, which is basically the service dress with an aiguillette and full-dress belt. The primary means of identifying rank are the collar patches and shoulder straps, and in common with all general officers he wears gold buttons and badges and white stripes (Lampassen) on his breeches. During the war the wearing of the aiguillette and full-dress belt was discontinued, while the sword was usually replaced by a pistol.

7 Senior Sergeant, German Air Force, 1939
During the summer months (30 April to 30 September) before the war, officers and non-commissioned officers could wear a cap with white top and white trousers and shoes, while officers could also wear a white tunic. After war broke out, the white-topped cap continued to be worn in Italy, the Mediterranean, southern Russia, and occasionally in Germany. On the figure shown here, rank is identified by the lace on the collar and shoulder straps and the metal wings on the collar patch. The scarlet arm-of-service colour identifies him as an anti-aircraft artilleryman and the badge on the left cuff shows that its wearer is a qualified armourer.

staff flight of four aircraft for the commander (*Kommodore*) and his adjutant, the staff major and the operations officer or '1a' as he was known.

Luftwaffe personnel numbered about 1,500,000 men at the beginning of the war: this included the large figure of 900,000 in the anti-aircraft artillery, 25,000 headquarters and administration staff, 50,000 aircrew and other flying personnel, 100,000 in air signals, 60,000 construction personnel and 80,000 in maintenance and supply, while the remainder were undergoing training.

The Luftwaffe forces ranged against Poland on 1 September 1939 were divided into two air fleets. *Luftflotte* 1 was based in Pomerania, and *Luftflotte* 4 in Silesia. There were also two independent commands, the 2nd Air Division and the Air Command for Special Purposes (*Fliegerführer z.b.V.*). Aircraft strength was about 850 bombers and dive-bombers and 400 fighters. In the first two days of the campaign these forces completely destroyed the Polish Air Force. When the campaign came to an end the Germans had lost 285

aircraft and 734 airmen killed, wounded and missing. It had been a striking demonstration of air power.

The X *Fliegerkorps* played a vital role in the invasion of Norway and Denmark. Its three principal tasks, which had to be carried out in close co-operation with the Army and Navy, were to secure air superiority, capture airfields so that transport aircraft could land troops and supplies, and lastly to prevent the Royal Navy from interfering with German naval operations. These tasks were reflected in the make-up of the forces used. Over half the available thousand aircraft were transports, while over one quarter were bombers.

For the campaign in the West the Luftwaffe deployed 3,902 aircraft. Colonel-General Kesselring commanded *Luftflotte* 2 with I, IV and IX *Fliegerkorps* in support of General von Bock's Army Group B. Colonel-General Sperrle commanded *Luftflotte* 3 with II, V and VIII *Fliegerkorps* in support of General von Rundstedt's Army Group A. For the Battle of Britain which followed the

8 Major, German Air Force, 1940

This Luftwaffe officer wears a beige canvas one-piece flying suit (issued for summer use), over which is worn a life jacket, coloured yellow for air-sea rescue. Rank is denoted by the special flying uniform badge which was worn on the upper sleeve of flying uniforms and overalls. A bomber commander, this major is kitted out in a flying uniform typical of those worn during the Battle of Britain.

9 NCO, German Air Force, 1940

The teamwork which existed between the ground crew and the pilots who flew the aircraft contributed much to German success in the air. This non-commissioned officer wears a black twill side cap and black cotton drill overall. His rank group is indicated by the grey lace on the overall collar.

10 Senior Sergeant, German Air Force, 1940

This NCO of flying troops wears the side cap (Fliegermütze) and flying blouse (Fliegerbluse) which was a garment originally introduced for wear under flying suits. The first pattern had no national emblem nor pockets, but had twisted cord in the arm-of-service colour around the collar. Originally the Fliegerbluse was issued to flying personnel only but it became popular throughout the Luftwaffe.

Above: Mountain troops who have just made an emergency drop clamber out of their parachute clothing at Narvik in 1940. The NCO removing his 'bone sack' and the two soldiers in the foreground wear mountain troop caps, but probably wore paratroop helmets (one of which is in the picture) for the drop itself.

11

AIRBORNE FORCES

The formation of parachute troops began almost simultaneously in both the German Army and Air Force. On 1 October 1935, General Göring's personal guard regiment, which originally had belonged to the Prussian Police, was transferred to the Luftwaffe as the General Göring Regiment. At the same time volunteers from the regiment were sent to Altengrabow training ground where the formation of the Luftwaffe's parachute rifle regiment was taking place.

In Spring 1936 the Army established an experimental staff with 15 officers and 80 other ranks, which was to become the Army's parachute rifle battalion. During the occupation of the Sudetenland the battalion came under the tactical command of the Luftwaffe, and on 1 January 1939, the battalion was transferred to the Air Force. From then on the Luftwaffe assumed total responsibility for the recruitment, training, equipment and operational control of parachute troops, and Germany became the only country in which parachute troops were exclusively part of the Air Force. Although paratroops were part of the Luftwaffe, the other component element of Germany's airborne forces, the air landing troops, remained as part of the Army. Air landing troops were infantry soldiers trained in the skills of rapid airborne landings (as indeed their name suggested) and equipped with a number of specialised lightweight weapons.

defeat of France, the two air fleets mentioned above were joined by Colonel-General Stumpff's *Luftflotte* 5 in Norway.

The strength of the two air fleets based in France was as follows (with the numbers of aircraft serviceable and ready to fly in parenthesis):

809 (650) Bf 109 fighters;
250 (170) Bf 110 fighter-bombers;
316 (250) Ju 87 (Stuka) dive-bombers;
1130 (770) bombers.

The air fleet in Norway played a minor part in the Battle of Britain deploying these serviceable aircraft: 70 Bf 109 fighters, 30 Bf 110 fighter-bombers and 95 bombers.

Despite poor strategic handling of the Air Force by Göring during the Battle of Britain, the Luftwaffe aircrews conducted a gallant and skilfull campaign against their British opponents. Indeed, in terms of tactical skill the British had much to learn and copied a number of German flying techniques and formations most notably the *Schwarm* formation (four planes flying as two pairs) instead of the 'Vic-3' (three planes in a 'V' formation).

Losses during the Battle of Britain are difficult to calculate, but were probably about 1700 fighters and bombers.

11 Paratroop NCO, German Air Force, 1940

This uniform was originally developed in the German Army which organised the first unit of parachute troops. The cut-down helmet had a thick sorbo-rubber lining and could be worn with a cloth cover. The overall or 'bone sack' was made of cotton duck material and was worn over the field equipment. The trousers were field-grey (not grey-blue as often shown in postwar illustrations) and had special pockets on the side of the thighs to hold a knife, field-dressing and other necessities. Elbow pads (not shown), knee pads and padded gloves were all necessary to help avoid injury during landing as the RZ1 parachute was rather primitive.

In July 1938 Major-General Student was transferred to the Luftwaffe from the Army, to undertake the development of the parachute troops, but by the time the Germans went to war in September 1939, the 7th Airborne (*Flieger*) Division was still in the process of formation.

After a winter spent in further specialist training an air landing corps was formed from the 7th Airborne Division and the 22nd Infantry Division.

Germany's parachute troops played a small, though successful, role in the Norwegian campaign which included the relief of General Dietl's beleaguered command at Narvik. Some of the 'paratroopers' dropped during this operation were mountain soldiers who had undergone a seven-day parachuting course. The invasion of Holland and Belgium in 1940 saw the most spectacular triumph of this new arm when paratroops under the command of Major-General Student captured the modern Belgian fortress of Eben Emael and the bridges over the Albert Canal, the key points in the line of Belgian fortifications.

The parachute division was similar in organisation to the infantry division with two or three parachute rifle regiments each of three battalions; an artillery

regiment of two *abteilungen* equipped with 10.5cm recoiless guns and an anti-tank battalion armed with airborne 5cm guns or lightweight 7.5cm guns.

UNIFORM Members of the German Air Sport Association began to wear a blue-grey uniform in 1933, and since this organisation was to provide much of the cadre for the new German Air Force, it was both logical and economical that this existing uniform should form the basis of the new Luftwaffe uniform, which appeared in public for the first time in March 1935.

The blue-grey uniform resembled that of the British Royal Air Force. Headgear consisted of a peaked cap with artificial mohair band, and a side cap; the tunic was worn open with shirt and tie, with

either matching long trousers and black shoes or breeches with high boots; the greatcoat was also worn open and was double-breasted. The basic cut of the uniform was the same for all ranks, but whereas officers' uniforms were made of smooth cloth, issue uniforms were made of a coarser wool.

One of the most comfortable and popular items of clothing was the so-called *Fliegerbluse*, which was a short jacket with concealed buttons and no breast pockets. It was designed to be worn under the flying suit, but was also often worn by aircrew instead of a flying suit or flying jacket.

Working dress was either the natural-coloured cotton drill uniform, or black working overalls. Officers also had a lightweight version of their service tunic or

GERMAN AIR FORCE INSIGNIA

Collar

Shoulder

Flying/Field Arm Patches

| Reichs-marschall | Field Marshal | Colonel-General (I) | Air Force General (II) | Lieutenant-General | Major-General | Colonel (General Staff) | Lieutenant-Colonel (Flying) | Major (Signals) | Captain (Medical) | Lieutenant (Construction) | 2nd Lieut (Artillery) |

Collar

Gen's Breast Eagle

Off's Breast Eagle

Shoulder

Flying/Field Arm Patches

Pilot's Badge

| Staff Sgt (Construction) | Sergeant-Major (Flying) | Senior Sergeant (Arty) | Sergeant (Arty-'H. Göring') | Corporal (Signals) | Staff L-Corporal (Medical) | L-Corporal-Major (Air Security) | Senior L-Corporal (Flying) | Lance-Corporal (Arty) | Private (Signals) |

flying blouse, designed for everyday wear in warm weather, or for wear when working in an office.

At the beginning of the war flight clothing consisted of a beige linen flying helmet and one-piece overall, while in cold weather there were both lined and unlined leather flying helmets and suits. Flying boots were made of black leather and suede and were lined with lambswool.

Paratroops wore standard Luftwaffe uniform with a yellow arm-of-service colour since they were classified as flying troops. But as the first parachute troops had been formed by the Army, it was the Army that developed the special jump uniform. The first type included a cut-down version of the standard M1935 steel helmet, a loose-fitting olive-green smock which was designed to be worn over the equipment, and long field-grey trousers which were tucked into soft leather rubber-soled lace-up boots. When the Army parachute rifle battalion was transferred to the Luftwaffe this experimental uniform underwent further development in the Luftwaffe, and was to become the model for the uniform of the British airborne forces.

INSIGNIA While the Luftwaffe retained Army rank titles and rank badges in the form of Army shoulder straps, it also introduced two new systems of badges for wear on the collar patches and on the flying suit. Luftwaffe general officers were further distinguished by white lapels on the undress jacket and greatcoat, and white stripes (*Lampassen*) on the breeches and trousers.

Arm of service was indicated by the colours (*Waffenfarben*) which appeared on the head-dress, on the collar patches and shoulder straps, and on the collar piping.

A large percentage of Luftwaffe personnel were skilled tradesmen and they wore a badge on the lower left sleeve with an emblem which indicated their particular skill. Aircrew specialists wore a winged badge whereas ground crew wore circular ones.

NAVY

The Treaty of Versailles strictly limited the size of the German Navy and forbade the design or construction of submarines, aircraft carriers, naval aircraft or heavy coastal artillery. The displacement of new vessels was limited to 10,000 tons.

Hitler chose to ignore the restrictive terms of the treaty, but was also anxious to remain on good terms with England. On 18 June 1935 the Anglo-German Naval Treaty was signed and while this limited the strength of the German

12

13

12 Admiral, German Navy, 1940
Admiral Rolf Carls was Commanding Admiral of the Baltic Sea Fleet. As shown here, he wears a peaked cap with double row of embroidered oak leaves, and a greatcoat with blue lapels. Rank is indicated by the two pips of the shoulder straps. He was awarded the Knight's Cross of the Iron Cross on 14 June 1940.

13 Lt.-Commander, German Navy, 1940
This Korvettenkapitän wears the standard naval officers' service dress: a peaked cap with single row of gold embroidered oak leaves on the peak and a reefer jacket with rank distinction lace on the cuffs. Decorations are the ribbon to the Iron Cross 2nd Class, Iron Cross 1st Class and below that a wound badge in black.

Navy to 35 per cent of that of the Royal Navy, it permitted Germany to have submarines and all the other types of ships forbidden her under the Treaty of Versailles. An ambitious programme of ship-building (the 'Z' plan) was set under way in 1937, and by September 1939 the German Navy comprised:

2 old battleships;
2 battlecruisers;
3 pocket battleships;
3 heavy cruisers;
6 light cruisers;
22 destroyers;
20 torpedo boats;
59 U-boats.

ORGANISATION The German Navy was divided into three basic arms under the command of a leader (*Führer*) or flag officer. The capital ships came under the direct control of the *Oberkommando der Kriegsmarine* (OKM) and then the group commands (*Gruppenkommandos*). The flotillas of minesweepers, patrol boats, coastal defence ships and auxiliaries of all types and sizes came under the naval security section. The third arm, which was to pose the greatest threat to the Allies at sea, was the submarine command.

Volunteers and conscripts underwent their basic training in regiments (*Schiffs-tammregimenter*), while petty officers

14   15   16

14 Petty Officer, German Navy, 1939
This sailor wears pre-war walking-out dress, which fell into disuse after the first two years of the war. For security reasons, the cap tally with the name of the ship (Panzerschiff Deutschland) was soon replaced by a standardised model, bearing only the word Kriegsmarine. *Petty officer rank is indicated by the gilt metal badge on the left sleeve and the rank distinction lace on the cuff. The lanyard shows that the wearer is a marksman.*

15 Seaman, German Navy, 1939
Illustrated is the pre-war summer parade dress as worn between 30 April and 30 September. The white cap cover, the tally with the name of the ship and white shirt (Bluse) were not officially worn during the war, although sailors on leave in Germany did sometimes ignore regulations. With this and other orders of dress the trousers were usually worn rolled-up (as in illustration number 16).

16 Seaman, German Navy, 1940
This rating in landing rig wears the 1935 pattern steel helmet, a pea-coat, and standard German Army field equipment. Sailors equipped like this took part in the capture of the Westerplatte fortress during the Polish campaign and fought in Norway. The rifle is the Mauser 98K.

(*Unteroffiziere*) received their training in NCO battalions (*Marineunteroffizierlehrabteilungen*). A pool of trained personnel was held in reserve units for assignment as and when required. The German and occupied foreign coastlines were defended by coastal artillery and anti-aircraft artillery battalions. There were no marines as such and personnel for combined operations or assignments on land were drawn either from the ship's company, or from the training and reserve units. By May 1941 the strength of the Navy had reached 404,000 in all ranks.

Unlike most of the other great navies, the *Kriegsmarine* did not have its own aircraft. An Air Force general was attached to OKM and was responsible for providing the Navy with its requirements in the air. The *Führer der Marineluftstreitkräfte* was Major-General Geissler and both his aircraft and men were carefully selected for the special tasks they had to carry out.

The war began with both remarkable success and significant failures. U-boats gained their first important victories

(sinking the British vessels *Courageous* and *Royal Oak*), and magnetic mines presented the British with a nasty if only temporary shock. Naval units played an important part in the capture of the Polish coastal fortress at Westerplatte near Danzig: German ships safely transported German forces to Norway and German submarines threatened Britain's maritime life-lines. But in doing so the Germans lost three valuable capital ships and ten destroyers. The decisive battles of the sea war were still to come.

UNIFORM The German uniform of World War II was basically the uniform introduced in 1848 for the Prussian Navy, and was based on that of the British Royal Navy. There were three main types of uniform: navy-blue, white for summer and tropical wear, and field-grey for land-based personnel. There was a whole range of protective clothing for extreme conditions ranging from the severe cold of the Arctic to the heat of the Mediterranean.

The basic uniform for officers, petty officers and cadets is illustrated by figure

13 while the regulation greatcoat is shown by figure 12, although it shows the pattern with blue lapels which was worn only by flag officers. Ratings wore the cap with blue or white top; the white top was discontinued at the beginning of the war. This cap fell into general disuse except as walking-out and full-dress head-gear. During the war the most common type of head-dress for all ranks was the side or boarding cap. The basic uniform for ratings in wartime is shown in figure 15. Petty officers wore a cap with black peak and chin strap, a double-breasted reefer jacket with shoulder straps, white shirt, black tie and long trousers with black shoes.

Sailors serving in land-based units or in landing parties wore standard Navy uniform depending on the season or climate but with a steel helmet and Army personal equipment, as well as trousers rolled up to mid calf and worn outside

Left: Günther Prien, the U-boat commander whose sinking of the Royal Oak *was an early success for the Kriegsmarine. He wears the white cap cover typical of U-boat commanders and, again in keeping with U-boat tradition, his reefer jacket is battered and old.*

the marching boots. From 1938 personnel in naval artillery units, NCO training battalions and, later on, members of the Naval Air Spotting Company were issued with a field-grey uniform which closely resembled that of the German Army except that all buttons, badges and lace were in gilt or yellow, as opposed to grey and silver.

INSIGNIA Officers were identified by the pattern of embroidery on the cap peak, the number and width of the gold lace rings on the reefer cuffs, or by the shoulder straps on the greatcoat and field-grey uniform. Petty officers and cadets wore their rank badges in the form of shoulder straps on the reefer, while ratings wore chevrons on the upper left sleeve of the jumper and pea-jacket. (See rank insignia chart.)

There was no arm-of-service designation as such in the Navy, but the special skills and trades held by ratings were identified by the badges worn on the upper left sleeve. Administrative officials wore silver buttons, badges and lace. On the field-grey uniform, officers displayed their branch-of-service colour and badge on the Army-pattern shoulder straps.

GERMAN NAVY INSIGNIA

Cap Peaks

Shoulder

Cuff

| Admiral of the Fleet | Admiral (Comndr of Fleet) | Admiral | Vice-Admiral | Rear-Admiral (Engineering) | Commodore | Captain | Commander | Lt-Cmdr (Ordnance) | Lieutenant | Lieutenant (II) | Sub-Lieutenant (Coastal Artillery) |

Shoulder

Collar Patches
Arm Patches

| CPO (I) (Writer) | CPO (II) (Mechanic) | Petty Officer (I) (Boatswain) | Petty Officer (II) | Petty Officer (III) | Petty Officer (IV) | Leading Seaman (I) (8yrs exp.) | Leading Seaman (II) (6yrs exp.) | Leading Seaman (III) (4½yrs exp.) | Leading Seaman (IV) | Able Seaman | Ordinary Seaman |

POLAND
ARMY

The Polish national Army came into existence after World War I, and, like all the armies of the newly-independent states which emerged at this time, it was equipped from the dumps of the vanquished. Not until 1937 was a programme of modernisation undertaken, and when war came two years later, the Polish Army was still basically obsolete; but although lacking in modern equipment and under poor strategic direction, the Polish Army fought bravely.

In 1939, as Europe moved towards war, the Polish government ordered partial mobilisation in March and August, and then, on 30 August 1939, general mobilisation was declared. Along her western frontiers Poland deployed seven armies and a tactical group which accounted for over half her infantry divisions and nearly three-quarters of her cavalry brigades. The remainder of the Army was in the process of formation and was to be used as reinforcements and operational reserves.

At dawn on 1 September 1939 German forces swept into Poland in the first blitzkrieg of the war. For 36 days the Polish armed forces put up a bitter resistance, despite their lack of modern weapons and equipment, and yet the lack of any real understanding of modern warfare (from grand strategy to minor tactics) by the Polish Army made defeat inevitable. Casualties were high: 66,300 killed, 130,000 wounded and over 400,000 prisoners-of-war.

ORGANISATION The President of the Republic was the Commander-in-Chief of an army of 1,500,000 soldiers. Its frontline strength of 1,000,000 men was organised in:
39 infantry divisions (including 9 reserve divisions);
11 cavalry brigades;
2 motorised brigades;
a variable number of infantry brigades.

Armament comprised 4500 guns and mortars, 2000 anti-tank and 3000 anti-aircraft guns.

The infantry division comprised three regiments of infantry and a regiment of light or field artillery plus the usual divisional services which included a reconnaissance unit with a company of TKS tankettes. In a small number of active divisions a heavy artillery group (of 105mm guns and 155mm howitzers) was included.

Line infantry and mountain rifle regiments had a regimental staff, three

17   18

infantry battalions, an administrative company, a pioneer platoon, and a signals company. They had an establishment strength of 1900 officers and men armed with Mauser M29 rifles or 9mm M38 pistols. Support weapons were:
90 light machine guns (Browning M28);
36 heavy machine guns (Browning M30);
27 light mortars;
6 heavy mortars;
2 field guns;
9 anti-tank guns.

Polish infantry regiments were poorly equipped, both in quality and quantity of artillery support weapons, compared to their German counterparts. The Polish reliance on offensive tactics only exposed more cruelly this weakness.

The various types of artillery were field, mountain, horse, heavy, extra

Left: Polish cadets at a pre-war torchlit review. This photograph shows particularly well the 'zigzag' collar embroidery on Polish uniform, (which had its origin in the collar markings of the Polish troops of the Napoleonic armies) and the design of the Polish helmet. The leather equipment is of the German pattern.

heavy, and anti-aircraft. A field artillery regiment had a staff, a signals troop and three batteries each of three troops of four guns (24 × 75mm M1897/17 and 12 × 100mm Austrian M14 howitzers).

Artillery was mostly horsedrawn with the exception of the anti-aircraft guns which were motorised. Mountain artillery had the same basic organisation except that a regiment had no signals section. The 65mm and 75mm mountain guns were carried on horseback, while the 100mm howitzer was drawn by a two-wheeled cart and two horses. At all levels, the Polish army was short of artillery, a weakness particularly marked in the larger formations which rarely possessed a full complement of heavy guns.

The Polish Army had a small tank force but the Polish High Command had little experience in the handling of tanks with the result that in 1939 Polish armoured units were soon overwhelmed by the German panzers. In 1939 the Polish armoured forces consisted of:
170 11-ton 7TP light tanks (armed with a 37mm Bofors gun);
50 Vickers six-ton tanks;

67 Renault FT-17 light tanks (of World War I vintage);
about 700 TK/TKS tankettes and 100 armoured cars.

In addition there were 53 Renault R-35 light tanks which did not take part in the fighting and were withdrawn to Romania.

Characteristic of the Polish army was the size and prestige of the cavalry. There were 210 squadrons, consisting of three regiments of light cavalry, 27 regiments of lancers and 10 regiments of mounted rifles. The 11 cavalry brigades were intended to play an important strategic role, although in fact they were unable to do so (partly because they were badly positioned at the outbreak of hostilities) and they proved extremely vulnerable. Pride in the cavalry tradition (many troopers continued to carry lances) and personal bravery were unavailing against the apparatus of modern war.

The organisation of the cavalry brigades varied somewhat but normally conformed to the pattern given in the diagram overleaf. There were either three or four cavalry regiments; a large battery of horse artillery and a rifle battalion as

17 Colonel, Polish Army, 1939
The commander of the 7th 'Wielkopolski' Mounted Rifles wears the standard officers khaki service dress with the traditional square-topped czapka. The regiment is identified by the colour of the cap band and the pennant-shaped collar patches. On the left breast pocket he wears the regimental badge of the 7th Mounted Rifles above that of his former reigment, the 1st Mounted Rifles. The medal is the Virtuti Militari, an award for gallantry.

18 Trooper, Polish Army, 1939
This trooper wears the French 1915 model Adrian steel helmet which was standard issue in mounted units, and a sheepskin coat which was designed to be worn instead of the long double-breasted greatcoat in very cold weather. The rifle is the German Mauser 98K.

19 Private, Polish Army, 1939
This modern-looking uniform was standard throughout the infantry, although it had not always reached the other arms. The arm-of-service colour (dark blue for infantry) appears on the collar patch, and the badges of rank on the shoulder straps. Equipment is similar to the German pattern but made greater use of cheaper webbing equipment. The rifle is the Polish version (the M29) of the German Mauser.

20 Tank crewman, Polish Army, 1939
Crews of armoured vehicles wore special clothing originating in France which consisted of a cut-away helmet for motorised troops and the three-quarter-length leather coat. They also wore a one-piece khaki overall. The distinctive insignia of armoured troops were the orange and black triangular collar patches. The helmet is the French pattern for motorised troops, which existed in many variations and was used in many countries.

19   20

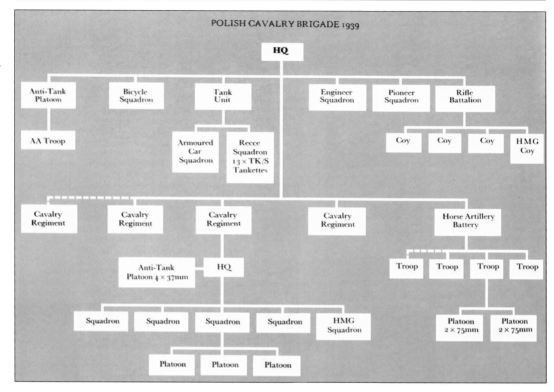

POLISH CAVALRY BRIGADE 1939

well as the normal brigade services, including a small tank unit. At full strength a four-regiment brigade had 6911 men and 273 officers. Support weapons were:

16 × 75mm guns;
18 × 37mm anti-tank guns;
2 × 40mm anti-aircraft guns;
2 × 81mm mortars;
9 × 50mm mortars.

UNIFORM The uniform of the Polish Army was originally introduced in 1919, gradually improved and standardised in the 1920s and modified again in 1935; it was this uniform that was worn in the brief 1939 campaign. The uniform was highly standardised and existed in five basic patterns: for officers, dismounted personnel, mounted personnel, mountain troops and armoured vehicle crews.

The basic service dress for officers is illustrated by figure 17. For undress occasions the breeches and boots were replaced by long khaki trousers with stripes and black leather undress ankle

boots. The greatcoat for all ranks was khaki, single-breasted with a large pointed fall collar, and had matching pointed shoulder straps and turn-back cuffs with tab and two buttons. Cavalry wore very long greatcoats which almost touched the ground.

Infantrymen and all dismounted personnel wore the uniform illustrated by figure 19. With orders of dress not requir-

ing the steel helmet, soldiers normally wore a khaki side cap, or a soft version of the square-topped *czapka*. Personal equipment was based on the German pattern. Mounted personnel wore the basic khaki uniform but retained the French *Adrian*-pattern steel helmet, and were issued with riding breeches and high boots. The units forming the 11th Carpathian Mountain Division had two distinctive items of

Right: The band of the 7th Lubelski Lancers mounted on greys. The troopers are unmistakably Polish in their long greatcoats and czapkas.

uniform. The first was a circular khaki felt hat, not unlike the British steel helmet in shape, and the second a long khaki cape which was worn over the left shoulder.

Personnel in armoured units wore the basic khaki uniform but when serving with their armoured vehicles they wore either a black beret or the French-pattern tank helmet (as in figure 20) and a one-piece khaki overall and brown leather gauntlets. Officers had a three-quarter-length black leather coat with black cloth collar and shoulder straps.

INSIGNIA Rank badges were worn on the head-dress and on the shoulder straps (see insignia chart). General officers were distinguished by silver zigzag embroidery on the cap band, collar patches, shoulder straps and cuffs, and by dark blue stripes on the breeches and long trousers.

Arm-of-service and regimental colours appeared on the cap band and collar patches, which were in the form of lance pennants for all cavalry and armoured

units, while those for all other units followed the shape of the collar points in the French manner. These were sometimes adorned by a small white metal badge which identified special appointments, trades, or units.

AIR FORCE

The Polish Air Force dated in embryonic form from the end of World War I; from even before Poland gained her independence. In December 1918 Polish airmen who had served in the French, Austrian and Imperial Russian air forces swore allegiance to the Polish Republic. In September 1919 a Commander-in-Chief was appointed and a re-organisation undertaken which established the Air Force as a part of the Army, and not an independent service.

Between 1 and 6 September 1939 the Air Force was able to put up a coherent air defence, but was soon completely overwhelmed by both the quantity and quality of German aircraft, and disorganised by the surprise strafing of the

airfields at the onset of offensive operations. Further re-organisations and change of bases only added to the breakdown of organisation and supply, and lack of fuel and liaison made further resistance virtually impossible, although isolated units continued to attack German ground forces whenever they could.

When Poland capitulated on 5th October she had lost 327 machines, while 98 were evacuated to Romania.

ORGANISATION The Air Force was commanded by the Aviation Commander with the rank of general, who was directly subordinate to the Ministry of Military Affairs. At the end of 1937 an Air Staff was formed within the General Staff, but it was to act independently of the Aviation Commander.

In the Spring of 1939 an operational plan was undertaken which entailed a re-grouping of aircraft into two formations. The bulk of the aircraft were distributed amongst the individual armies along the German border and formed the Army Air Force while a central reserve

21 Captain, Polish Air Force, 1939

This captain wears the 1936 pattern service dress with rank badges on the front of the cap and on the shoulder straps. The Air Force version of the national eagle is displayed on the cap. On his left breast he wears the Pilot Observer (combat) badge which was issued in 1928 for aviators with dual qualifications although in 1933 the badge was superseded by two separate qualification badges. The dagger, which was identical to the pattern worn by tank officers, was worn with most orders of dress.

22 Lieutenant, Polish Air Force, 1939

In the summer months, crews of enclosed aircraft wore this one-piece overall which was made of undyed linen. A special version of the badges of rank was worn on the left sleeve; the two-star badge illustrated is that of a lieutenant. In common with the flying crew of many nations, this officer wears his own scarf, to prevent his neck chafing against the rough overall cloth. He wears the standard leather flying helmet with goggles.

23 Sergeant-Major, Polish Air Force, 1939

As working dress this staff sergeant wears a sensible and practical working uniform. The only insignia to be worn on this dress were the badges of rank which appear on the beret and shoulder straps.

was held back under the control of the Commander-in-Chief and was known as the Dispositional Air Force. Each army had from three to seven squadrons of reconnaissance, light-bomber and fighter planes acting in a localised ground-support role. The Dispositional Air Force comprised 145 aircraft, organised in:
1 pursuit brigade of 5 fighter squadrons;
one bomber/reconnaissance brigade of 8 squadrons;
1 observation squadron;
4 liaison squadrons.

On 1 September 1939 the frontline strength of the Polish Air Force was 433 aircraft: 59 fighters, 154 bombers, 84 observation machines with negligible armament, and 36 liaison aircraft.

UNIFORM The military aviation of the Polish Army began to replace its Army uniforms with a blue-grey design in 1936. The new uniform was to be worn by all officers and regular NCOs by 1 April 1938.

The service dress for officers is illustrated by figure 21; the greatcoat was grey, double-breasted and with two rows of three white metal buttons. Generals, staff officers and cadets wore the same badges on the greatcoat collar as on the tunic collar. The tunic for other ranks was worn with closed collar and matching pantaloons or long trousers.

Working dress was officially as shown in figure 23, although more typical working dress was probably a crumpled pair of overalls. In warm weather an unlined beige flying suit as illustrated by figure 22 was worn, and in colder weather both a lined and unlined leather flying suit, or a three-quarter-length black leather French-pattern flying coat.

INSIGNIA   Rank badges were worn on the head-dress (peaked cap and beret), on the shoulder straps of the tunic and greatcoat, and on the upper left sleeve of the flying suit.

Certain categories of officers wore white metal badges on the tunic and greatcoat collar. Medical officials wore cherry coloured cloth as backing to their rank distinction braid on the peaked cap, and as lace on the tunic cuffs and trousers. Administrative officials wore royal blue as their arm-of-service colour.

21

22

23

POLISH AIR FORCE INSIGNIA

Officer's Cap Badge

Peaked Cap Band Insignia

Pilot's Badge

| General | Lieutenant-General | Major-General | Colonel | Lieutenant-Colonel | Major | Captain | Lieutenant | 2nd Lieut |

Peaked Cap Band Insignia

Flying Uniform Insignia

Beret Insignia

Shoulder

| Warrant Officer | Sergeant-Major | Sergeant | Lance-Sergeant | Corporal | Lance-Corporal | Major | Captain | Sergeant-Major | Sergeant-Major |

POLISH NAVY INSIGNIA

Officers' Chinstraps

Shoulder

Cuff

| Admiral | Vice-Admiral | Rear-Admiral | Captain (Engineers) | Commander 6 yrs exp (Coastal/Rivers) | Commander (Technical) | Lt.-Cmdr (Administration) | Lieutenant | Sub-lieut. |

| Warrant Officer | Chief Petty Officer (I) | Chief Petty Officer (II) | Petty Officer (Ordnance Artificer) | Leading Seaman (I) (Stoker) | Able Seaman (Diver) | Ordinary Seaman (Unqualified) |

NAVY

At the Treaty of Versailles Poland was granted some ninety miles of Baltic coastline. The great port of Danzig (Gdansk) was declared a Free City, so the Poles had to construct a large modern naval complex at Gdynia to the west of Danzig. Fortifications with coastal artillery were built at Westerplatte and Hel.

The 180-man garrison of the naval fortress at Westerplatte resisted German air and sea bombardment and attacks from German naval landing parties until forced to surrender on 13 September. The

24 Able Seaman, Polish Navy, 1939
This able seaman wears the standard 'square rig' of the Polish Navy. The cap tally reads: Marynarka Wojenna. *Rank is indicated by the stripe on his sleeve under the non-substantive badge (RT for* Radio Technik). *The equipment, rifle (Polish 7.92mm Wz29) and gaiters were worn by guards of honour.*

24

Above: A Polish seaman with white-topped summer cap surrenders at Westerplatte.

defence of the Hel Peninsula continued until 1 October when ammunition ran out; 3200 soldiers and sailors were taken prisoner, and they left behind over 200 dead and wounded.

At sea the Polish Navy had four destroyers, five submarines, one mine-layer, six minesweepers and two gun-boats. On the eve of the German invasion three of the destroyers and the submarines were ordered to sail to England. After a difficult and dangerous voyage the destroyers and two submarines reached Leith in Scotland on 1 September 1939. The three remaining submarines were unable to break out of the Baltic Sea, and were interned in Sweden.

ORGANISATION The flag officer commanding the Polish Fleet was Vice Admiral J. Unrug. The main naval ports were Gdynia, Oksyvie and Rozewie. In 1939 the strength of the navy was about 400 officers and 4000 ratings. There were no marines as such in the Polish Navy, but there was one naval infantry regiment.

UNIFORM Polish Navy uniforms were very similar to those worn in most other navies, and were based on regulations issued in 1920, 1922, 1927 and 1930.

The uniform for officers is illustrated in the photograph, while cadets and chief petty officers wore the same basic uniform with special rank distinctions (see insignia chart). In hot weather these ranks could wear a white cap cover, white tunic with stand collar, long white trousers and white canvas shoes.

Ratings wore the uniform illustrated by figure 24, although personal equip-

ment and white gaiters were only worn by landing parties or on ceremonial occasions. In cold weather sailors and petty officers had a three-quarter-length pea-coat, while they also received a white uniform for summer and tropical wear. Working dress was a white American-pattern hat and off-white linen jumper and trousers. Petty officers wore a peaked cap and a single-breasted blue tunic with stand collar, patch pockets and five buttons on the front of the tunic.

INSIGNIA Rank was indicated by the number and width of the gold lace stripes on the cuffs and shoulder straps of officers, chief petty officers and petty officers. Officers also had rows of gold braid on the cap peak (gold zigzag embroidery for admirals), and tiny five-pointed gold stars on the chin strap so that it was possible to tell the rank of an officer by looking at his cap. This was useful since Navy personnel often wore protective clothing which did not display badges of rank.

From 30 November 1938 corps and branch colours appeared as backing or 'lights' (the coloured cloth which appeared between the rows of rank distinction lace on the cuffs and shoulder straps). Seamen wore trade and speciality badges in red on the upper left sleeve, while petty officers had yellow badges.

Below: Serving with the Royal Navy after the defeat of Poland, the ratings in this photograph are still wearing Polish caps under their duffle coats.

FINLAND
ARMY

During the autumn of 1939, fearful of the eastward expansion of Nazi Germany, the Soviet government made overtures to Finland for an exchange of territory which would push back the border in the Karelian Isthmus (to make Leningrad more secure) and demanded a long-term lease on the Baltic port of Hanko. The Finns refused, and on 30 November 1939 the Red Army crossed the Finnish border.

The Finnish army was one of the smallest in Europe and the Red Army expected little opposition. But the Soviet invasion found the Finns well prepared; and they turned to their advantage the sub-zero temperatures and deep snow which in any case favoured a defensive. The main Finnish defence, the Mannerheim Line, held until 12 February 1940, although once it was breached there was no alternative but to sue for peace. For an army which never exceeded 200,000 men, Finnish losses were very high: 25,000 killed and 45,000 wounded.

There was talk of Allied intervention since the Soviet Union had signed a non-aggression pact with Hitler's Germany, but the only country to make a sizeable contribution was Sweden which provided weapons, a squadron of aircraft and two battalions of infantry. Volunteers from a number of countries including Norway, Italy, Britain and the United States of America were formed into a volunteer battalion, but it was not ready in time to take part in the fighting.

ORGANISATION Although capable of forming 12 divisions, Finland only had nine at the outbreak of war, and these were sadly lacking in motor transport, communications equipment, anti-tank guns, and automatic weapons. The armed forces were maintained by a small regular cadre which relied on an annual intake of conscripts to complete its numbers. In peacetime, conscripts served for one or one-and-a-half years depending on the arm of service. On completion of conscription the Finnish soldier passed into the reserve in which he remained until the age of 60, when he joined the ranks of the militia.

The country was divided into nine Military Districts, each of which was expected to field a division as well as to provide depots, installations, and facilities to enable the Army to mobilise rapidly.

The organisation of a division consisted of a divisional staff, three infantry regiments, an artillery regiment and companies of signals and pioneers. The artillery regiment comprised 36 guns of various calibres, all of them pre-1918 models and many unsuitable for modern warfare. Although a number of 120mm mortars had been ordered, none had been delivered by the outbreak of war and so the division had only eighteen 81mm mortars, clearly insufficient when compared to the hundred or so mortars of a Soviet division. The supply of automatic weapons was rather better, there being 250 Suomi sub-machine guns and 116 machine guns per division. At full strength a division had 14,200 men.

In addition to the nine divisions of infantry there was an independent cavalry brigade which was made up of a staff, two cavalry regiments, a rifle battalion (mounted on bicycles) and a horse artillery battery.

There was little reserve artillery and the whole field Army possessed only 100 Bofors 37mm anti-tank guns and no anti-aircraft guns at all. The Army had had only minimal experience of tank warfare; but the densely wooded terrain of southern Finland reduced the role of the

25

26

25 Marshal, Finnish Army, 1940
As the only person of that rank in the Finnish Army Marshal Mannerheim's uniform was by definition unique. The badges on the shoulder straps are the Finnish lion in silver and above that the regimental badge of the Uusimaa Dragoons, Mannerheim's old regiment. Rank is not indicated on the collar in this illustration but would otherwise consist of crossed batons and three lions in gold on a silver background (see insignia chart). Suspended from his neck is the Mannerheim Cross of the Cross of Liberty, an award for outstanding gallantry and merit in wartime. On the left sleeve is a Civil Guard badge.

26 Captain, Finnish Army, 1939
Germany had played a leading role in the development of the Finnish Army after World War I and the field-grey M1936 uniform illustrated here has a distinctly German cut. The officer's sheepskin coat and other forms of protective clothing were normal winter issue to the Finnish Army. His winter field cap has a fur-lined peak and flaps which could be turned back; the peak being fastened by the blue and white national cockade and the gilt Finnish lion, the badge of regular Army officers. Arm of service and rank are denoted by the collar patch: a deep green patch with grey frame for the infantry and three brass roses for a captain.

tank to that of infantry support. Some 30 Vickers light tanks had been supplied but they played only a minor part in this infantry war.

There were few medical supplies and communication was at best rudimentary: there was no wireless system and the Army had to rely on field telephones and when that failed a system of runners. This deficiency was particularly serious given the great distances that had to be covered by the beleaguered Finnish Army and, in addition, effective artillery support for the infantry was impossible without radio.

Despite these problems the Finnish Army had two great advantages: firstly, a thorough knowledge of the land in winter weather conditions; and secondly, vastly superior human material which expressed a fierce determination to resist the foreign aggressor. These two qualities came together in the crack battalions of ski troops — men experienced in cross-country skiing and able to cover long distances silently and more quickly than troops equipped with any other form of transport. In particular, the *Sissi-Joukkeet* (guerrilla ski troops) operated behind enemy lines, and proved a considerable thorn in the side of the Red Army.

Below: This Finnish sniper in the Karelian forest wears a snow-camouflage suit and is armed with a rifle with telescopic sights. Snow suits such as the one shown here were merely a thin cloth smock (with hood) and loose over-trousers worn on top of normal winter clothing.

UNIFORM The Finnish Army uniform which was worn throughout World War II was introduced in 1936, and was basically the same for all ranks.

Head-dress consisted of a peaked field cap, although senior officers still continued to wear the old stiff cap with embroidered peak. The tunic was single-breasted with stand-and-fall collar, matching shoulder straps, and six buttons in front. The pleated breast patch pockets had a flap and button, while the side pockets had a flap only. All ranks wore matching breeches and high black leather boots.

To operate in the severe winter, troops received sheepskin caps and coats, white snow camouflage clothing and various types of special footwear which included felt boots. During the Winter War the Finns made use of clothing and equipment captured from the Red Army, but the importation of military equipment from all over the world meant that the Finnish Army suffered from a lack of standardisation which was only partially remedied by the Germans in 1940–41.

INSIGNIA Rank was indicated on the tunic collar patches, and by the rank distinction lace on the greatcoat cuffs. On the raincoat and other types of winter and protective clothing, rank distinction lace appeared on a patch which was buttoned onto the cuffs. Other ranks wore chevrons on the shoulder straps.

The principal methods of indicating arm of service were the colour of the collar patches and the yellow metal badges which were worn on the shoulder straps. In the Imperial Russian tradition (Finland had been part of the Russian Empire until 1917) most formations, units, staffs and establishments had a distinctive metal badge which was worn on the left breast pocket.

AIR FORCE

The Finnish Air Force was not an independent arm but formed part of the Army under its own commander. The Air Force was based on the British model with many instructors and some aircraft being supplied by Great Britain. At the beginning of the war, however, the Air Force was much below establishment and had practically no reserve. The front-line strength was 200 aircraft, but only 108 were operational. Personnel consisted of some 2500 men.

The Air Force was organised as follows: 1st Flying Regiment (ground support, dive bombing and reconnaissance): 4 squadrons each with 3 flights of 4 aircraft (a total of 48 aircraft);

27

27 2nd Lieutenant, Finnish Air Force, 1940

During the war Air Force officers wore a combination of the blue and the grey service uniform; as does this lieutenant. Apart from his blue cap he can be identified as an Air Force officer by the colour of his collar patches and the winged propeller badge on the shoulder straps. Rank is shown by the single rosette on the collar patch. This officer does not wear the white metal flying badge on his left breast pocket, and so he is not a qualified pilot. Breeches tucked into high boots were a very common item of Air Force clothing.

2nd Flying Regiment (fighter defence): 2 squadrons each with 3 flights (a total of 46 aircraft);
3rd Flying Regiment (bombing and long-range reconnaissance): 2 squadrons each with 3 flights (a total of 16 aircraft).

In addition, 2 squadrons for naval reconnaissance, the Air Combat School, and 3 Operational Training Regiments functioned as independent units.

Despite its inherent weaknesses, the Finnish Air Force fought hard and

FINNISH ARMY/AIR FORCE INSIGNIA

Peaked Cap Badge: Air Force Officers | Cap Badge Officers | Cap Badge NCOs | Cap Badge ORs | Cap Badge Offs & NCOs (worn with other badges) | Pilot's Badge (Breast Pocket)

Collar / Greatcoat Cuff

Marshal of Finland | General (Infantry) | Lieutenant-General (Jägers) | Major-General (Cavalry) | Colonel (Artillery) | Lt-Colonel (Coastal Artillery) | Major (Engineers) | Captain (Air Force)

Collar

Lieutenant (Signals) | 2nd Lieut (Armour) | Sergeant-Major (Guards) | Senior Sgt (Service Corps) | Sergeant (Infantry) | Lance-Sergeant (Cavalry) | Corporal (Artillery) | Other Ranks (Air Force)

FINNISH NAVY INSIGNIA

Admiral (Summer) | Capt., Cmdr. Lt-Cmdr | Junior Officers | Petty Officers | NCOs | Junior 'Officials'

Shoulder / Cuff

Admiral | Vice-Admiral | Rear-Admiral | Captain (Engineers) | Commander | Lieutenant-Commander | Lieutenant (Medical) | Sub-Lieut | Ensign (Music) | Reserve Ensign | 'Official' (Lieut) | Cap Badge Senior 'Official'

Shldr Strap P.O.

Cuff and Arm

W.O. 1st Class (I) (Machinist) | W.O. 2nd/3rd Class (II/III) (Torpedoes) | W.O. 4th Class (IV) (Signals) | C.P.O. (Sergeant-Major) | P.O. (I) (Mines) | P.O. (II) (Supply) | P.O. (III) (Medical) | Leading Seaman (Gunnery) | P.O. (Radio) Conscript | Leading Seaman Conscript | C.P.O. (Admin.) | P.O. (Admin.)

inflicted heavy losses on the Red Air Force, claiming 208 victories. Its own losses were 62 combat aircraft and 72 men.

UNIFORM A branch of the Army, the Finnish Air Force did not originally have a special uniform. Eventually a dark blue service dress was introduced for officers, but during the war the most common uniform was that worn by the Army, although items of the blue and grey uniform were sometimes worn together.

Flying clothing consisted of a one-piece unlined overall and leather flying helmet and gloves. Crews of open aircraft and bombers were equipped with fur-lined flying suits and boots, and with fur mittens.

INSIGNIA Army badges of rank were worn on Army uniforms and a special pattern of gold lace stripes was worn on the lower sleeves of the blue (Air Force) uniform.

The Air Force arm-of-service colour was blue and this appeared on the collar patches of Army uniforms. The Air Force emblem was the winged propeller which was worn on the

Below: Wearing a winter flying-suit and fur mittens, this Finnish aircrewman is better equipped than were many of his colleagues. But the cold was such that very few sorties could be flown and action was rare for the flyers.

shoulder straps. Qualified pilots wore a white metal badge on the left breast pocket.

NAVY

The President of Finland was Commander-in-Chief of the armed forces, while one of his deputies was chief of the Navy. Under him was the chief of the Coastal Defence Fleet, who, in time of war, came under the operational command of the Army. The strength of the Navy in 1939 consisted of 396 officers and 3613 other ranks.

The greatest problem faced by the Finnish Navy was the shortage of ice-free ports. Apart from three ports on the Murmansk coast, in winter all other ports were seldom ice-free and often completely frozen.

To carry out its principal task of coastal defence, the Finnish Navy had at its disposal 3 gunboats, 30 minelayers and minesweepers, and a number of motor launches and auxiliaries. There were also seven motor torpedo boats of British and Italian design, and five modern submarines. The largest units of the fleet were two heavily armed and armoured coastal defence ships each with a crew of 300 men. The Lake Ladoga Flotilla comprised 20 vessels of various types, but most of these were scuttled or handed over to the Soviet Union in 1940. The Naval Air Force comprised four squadrons including one torpedo bomber squadron.

Severe winter conditions hampered naval activity during the Winter War, although some Finnish submarines operated in the approaches to the Gulf of Bothnia. Coastal batteries (there were two regiments of coastal artillery) did, however, play a significant role in the defence of Finnish territory.

UNIFORM The Finnish Navy uniform was very similar to that of the British Navy. Officers and chief petty officers wore a peaked cap, reefer jacket with white shirt and black tie, long trousers and black shoes. The greatcoat was double-breasted with two rows of six buttons.

Petty officers and ratings wore a square rig and a blue cap with long tally on which appeared the name of the vessel or installation in gold lettering, a jumper with blue denim collar, bell-bottomed trousers and black shoes. In cold weather sailors wore a double-breasted pea-coat.

In very cold weather officers wore a black astrakhan cap and all ranks received special cold- and foul-weather clothing. In hot weather officers wore a

28 Seaman, Finnish Navy, 1939
Over his standard 'square rig' this sailor wears one of the various types of protective clothing issued to members of the Finnish Navy. This outfit is made of water-repellent canvas and is lined with fleece. He is also equipped with a rudimentary radio-telephone apparatus.

white uniform while petty officers and ratings wore the white cap cover.

Personnel serving on shore installations or in the coastal artillery wore Army uniforms – often the obsolete 1922 pattern – with Navy head-dress and rank badges.

INSIGNIA Officers wore rank distinction lace on the cuffs and on the greatcoat and white tunic shoulder straps. Other ranks wore chevrons on the upper left sleeve.

The branch or corps of officers was identified by the colour which appeared as 'lights' between the rank distinction lace. Petty officers had gold while conscripts had red branch of service badges above their rank chevrons.

SOVIET UNION
ARMY

During 1939–40, the Soviet armed forces were undergoing a period of transition. New weapons and tactical ideas were being developed, but misguided and often stultifying central control meant that there was little sense of initiative or responsibility, and important advances in any sphere were often left in isolation. The excellent progress made in tank construction, for instance, was counterbalanced by the absence of an effective radio-communication system, without which tanks were severely restricted.

The baleful influence of Stalin over the Soviet armed forces during the 1930s culminated in the purges of 1938 which decimated the officer corps. Almost inevitably, the most able and outspoken officers were destroyed by the purges and this was a significant factor in the poor performance of the Red Army in the Winter War against Finland in 1939. It has been estimated that Soviet casualties were about 200,000 men during this short campaign.

At the time little or nothing was known in the West about the Red Army of Workers and Peasants. Some twenty

Below : General T. F. Shtykov inspects the weapons of his troops on the Leningrad Front. The men are all well furnished with winter clothing.

29

30

29 Marshal of the Soviet Union, Red Army, 1940

Marshal S. K. Timoshenko was commander of the Kiev Military District and Commander-in-Chief of the Soviet forces during the war against Finland. He wears the new grey parade uniform which had been introduced in July 1940 for generals and marshals as part of a gradual process of enhancing the status of senior Red Army officers. Rank is denoted by the cap badge, collar patches and sleeve insignia. Timoshenko's decorations are (from top to bottom): the Gold Star of a Hero of the Soviet Union; two Orders of Lenin; three Orders of the Red Banner, and the Red Army 20th anniversary medal.

30 Private, Red Army, 1939

The private is wearing a cloth helmet (the budionovka or shlem) named after the Russian Civil War cavalry commander Budenny, which was found to be unsatisfactory and during the Winter War against Finland began to be replaced by the fur cap with earflaps. The colour of the cloth star and the raspberry red collar patches identify his arm of service as the infantry. Rank badges appeared on the collar patches only. Equipment is rudimentary but effective and (apart from the gasmask in its canvas bag) was the same as that worn during World War I. The rifle is the Moisin-Nagant 7.62mm M1930.

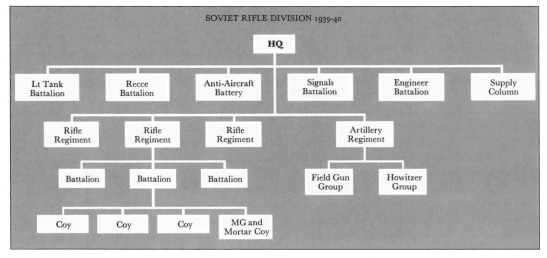

SOVIET RIFLE DIVISION 1939-40

HQ

Lt Tank Battalion · Recce Battalion · Anti-Aircraft Battery · Signals Battalion · Engineer Battalion · Supply Column

Rifle Regiment · Rifle Regiment · Rifle Regiment · Artillery Regiment

Battalion · Battalion · Battalion · Field Gun Group · Howitzer Group

Coy · Coy · Coy · MG and Mortar Coy

years of isolation had veiled much of what went on in the Soviet Union.

ORGANISATION Overall control of the Red Army was exercised by the People's Commissariat for Defence and the Commander-in-Chief, First Marshal of the Soviet Union K. E. Voroshilov. Decisions were reached in consultation with the Council for Work and Defence, and the eighty-member War Council. Directly subordinate to Voroshilov's Commissariat was the General Staff which was divided into seven departments: operations, organisation, railways, intelligence, mobilisation, anti-aircraft defence and topography. Four deputies were responsible for armaments, land, air and sea forces.

The Army was essentially a standing army which was run by a professional cadre, but it relied on conscription for the mass of its personnel. Men were liable for military service for a period of 22 years from the age of 20 to 41. A conscript served three to four years, depending on his arm of service, in the active or cadre troops, after which he entered the active reserve. From the age of 27 to 35 he was part of the 1st Reserve, and from 35 to 41 part of the 2nd Reserve. The peacetime strength of the army was estimated at 1,800,000 men, while mobilised strength could be as high as 11,000,000.

The Soviet Union was divided into 13 military districts and 2 military commissariats. Each had under its command separate heavy artillery, motorised mechanical corps, aviation, engineer and technical troops as well as all the Field Army units and installations under its jurisdiction. The Field Army consisted of: 35 rifle (infantry) corps (about 100 rifle divisions including 23 Territorial divisions); 7 cavalry corps (32 cavalry divisions); 12 independent cavalry divisions; 5 tank corps (10 tank brigades); 1 motorised rifle brigade.

A rifle corps comprised three to four rifle divisions, a regiment of corps artillery, pioneer, bridging and signals battalions and a squadron of aircraft.

The Soviet rifle division of 1939 had an establishment strength of nearly 19,000 men and was in theory well equipped with supporting arms. As can be seen in the diagram, the Soviet division was a 'combined arms' force capable of undertaking most tasks at divisional level. In practice, however, a chronic shortage of trained manpower prevented the technical and mechanical elements working effectively with the result that the division was little more than a formation of riflemen with artillery support.

The division was, in theory at least, lavishly supplied with artillery, with 12 × 152mm and 28 × 122mm howitzers, 42 × 76mm and 54 × 45mm guns, and over 100 mortars of various calibres ranging from 50 to 120mm. A novel feature was the inclusion of a battalion of T-26 light tanks and armoured cars but they proved ineffective during the fighting in Finland and were withdrawn.

A rifle regiment had a strength of about 2900 officers and men, armed with 7.62mm Moisin-Nagant rifles and M1933 Tokarev pistols. Support weapons were:

81 light machine guns (7.62mm Degtyarev);

58 heavy machine guns (7.62mm Maxim);
6 infantry guns;
6 anti-tank guns.

Great importance was attached to artillery and the Red Army experimented with large groups capable of delivering massive barrages on given targets, a method which was to be fully exploited during the later stages of World War II.

Artillery was organised in 140 light artillery regiments each with a regimental staff, staff battery, anti-aircraft battery and three to four battalions each with three to four batteries of three or four guns each. There were 35 heavy corps artillery regiments with tractor-drawn 150mm guns and howitzers, and 20 artillery regiments held in reserve for use by the Supreme Commander. Anti-aircraft artillery battalions were also motorised and equipped with guns ranging from 40mm Vickers M18s to the 105mm Leningrad M1934.

During the inter-war years Soviet industry began to deliver increasing numbers of armoured fighting vehicles which the Red Army, partly under British influence, had decided to concentrate into large independent armoured formations.

These tank formations (which became an independent arm of the Red Army) were based around either the mechanised brigade (three battalions of 32 T-28 tanks, a battalion of reconnaissance – BT-7 and BT-8 – tanks, and a motorised machine-gun battalion) or the tank brigade (four battalions of T-28 tanks). This was in addition to the battalion of T-26 tanks which formed part of some infantry divisions, the BT-7 tanks which were issued to mechanised units in cavalry formations, and the T-35 tanks which made up the strength of the heavy tank brigades held as Army reserve troops. But experience during the Spanish Civil War and the disastrous showing of armoured formations in unsuitable and sub-zero conditions in Finland led to the abandonment of this progressive development in favour of the French practice of splitting-up tanks amongst the infantry as mobile gun platforms.

Another new concept developed by Soviet military planners was the use of troops and equipment transported by air and dropped by parachute. During large-scale manoeuvres in the Kiev military district in 1935–6 a complete rifle division with all its supporting arms was dropped by parachute. Even light tanks, slung underneath heavy bombers, were dropped from tree-top level without parachutes. But this was merely an exercise, and in the politically unstable days of the late 1930s the techniques of airborne warfare were not developed further by the Red Army. Although the Germans were impressed few others seem to have seen the significance of this novel form of warfare.

The Soviet Union placed great reliance on cavalry because of vast distances, poor

Below: A Soviet machine-gun team training on the M1910 Maxim, an old but reliable weapon which was in widespread use. They are wearing the shlem *and standard-issue greatcoat.*

road and rail communications and the inability of Soviet industry to provide vehicles for all of such a huge army. In 1937–38, for example, large-scale cavalry formations, able to operate as independent forces, had been created as a 'strategic cavalry'.

A cavalry corps consisted of a corps staff, three cavalry divisions, and corps troops. The cavalry division comprised: divisional staff;
2 brigades (each of 2 regiments);
2 motorised rifle battalions;
1 horse artillery regiment;
1 armoured car (or tank) battalion;
pioneer and signals squadron;
supply unit.
The cavalry regiment comprised:
regimental staff;
5 squadrons of sabres;
1 machine gun squadron (mounted in carts);
1 artillery battery (76mm guns);
pioneers, signals and chemical troops;
baggage train.

UNIFORM   The Soviet Union maintained the largest Army in Europe, and in order to keep it supplied with uniforms and personal equipment, Soviet industry could only produce tried and tested designs. Many of the basic patterns of clothing had been designed at the beginning of the century at the time of the Russo-Japanese War, and had proved themselves during World War I. Westerners often describe Russian uniform as cheap and shabby, and refer to a lack of standardisation. In fact, the traditional Russian uniform had a certain rugged smartness when well worn, and since everything was manufactured in state factories the degree of standardisation achieved was never equalled in any other Army.

The basic uniform consisted of a flat 'Japanese-style' peaked cap, a khaki shirt in traditional cut but with stand-and-fall collar, which was worn outside the trousers. Breeches were either of a matching colour or dark blue. High boots were increasingly replaced by ankle boots (often of American manufacture) and puttees. This basic uniform was worn throughout the year, but in winter all ranks wore a long grey greatcoat (*shinel*) and grey cloth pointed helmet (*shlem*).

In addition to the basic items described above officers had a superior quality shirt, with piping, which was made of cotton for summer and wool for winter wear. The greatcoat was made of good quality cloth with piping and brass buttons. At the end of 1935 officers had received a new single-breasted tunic

31

31 Colonel, Red Army, 1939
As part of a general smartening-up process, and to enhance the importance of the tank arm within the Red Army, a new steel-grey service dress was introduced in December 1935. During the war tank troops wore the standard khaki uniforms but occasionally an officer continued to wear his grey peaked cap. There is no confirmation that other ranks received steel-grey service uniforms.

which could be worn with either breeches and boots or long trousers and shoes.

In the 1930s the armoured troops became one of the most prestigious arms of the Red Army, and this status was reflected in a new steel-grey uniform which was introduced in 1935 as an undress and full-dress uniform. In the field officers wore the standard Army uniform or the special protective clothing issued to crews of armoured vehicles. This clothing consisted of a leather helmet fitted with padded ribs, a one-piece black overall and leather driving gauntlets.

Soviet insignia is examined in the section on the Eastern Front.

AIR FORCE

Throughout the 1920's and 1930's the Soviet Government made enormous efforts to build up a large modern air force, but the difficulties in finding suitable designs and the machines and materials to mass produce aircraft were enormous.

To overcome the lack of pilots and mechanics the government poured money into the voluntary organisation *Osoaviakhim* (Society for the Support of Defence, Aviation and Chemical Defence). Soon after its formation in 1927 it had a membership of three million which had grown to 13 million by 1936. Aero clubs were set up to provide pilots, mechanics and para-chutists, and until 1940 all Red Air Force volunteers came from this source. Shortages of instructors, training aids and aircraft meant that the standard attained was very low, however, and it was finally decided to select Air Force recruits from the annual military draft.

Between 1935 and 1937, 3576 aircraft, including a large proportion of four-engined bombers, were produced, but as the numbers increased so effectiveness decreased because the technical standard of the aircraft industry was falling behind developments in more advanced industrial nations.

The Red Air Force had its first practical experience in the Spanish Civil War and this resulted in certain organisa-tional and operational changes, but it was the traumatic experience of the Winter War against Finland (in which some 1000 Soviet aircraft were lost) that really showed up the alarming shortcomings in training, tactics and equipment. Red Air Force commanders were not ignorant of these defects but the purges of 1937–1938, which removed many senior com-manders, meant that the remedies under-taken were not necessarily the most effective.

ORGANISATION The Soviet govern-ment not only had to overcome technical and manpower problems in the construc-tion of an air force, it also encountered difficulties in its organisation. Soviet military doctrine considered air power as an adjunct to land warfare and so the Air Force continued to be part of the Army. But by 1937 the Air Force had grown in size and importance to such an extent that it was decided that an Air Force representative should be admitted to the State Commissariat for Defence.

The Air Force of the Red Army (VVS-RKKA) was, however, divided into two basic components. The first was

Above: A group of Soviet pilots, preparing for take-off. They are wearing leather flying coats, fur-lined helmets and goggles.

the Air Force of the Red Army which consisted of fighter and ground attack regiments under the direct control of a Military District (later Front). The second component was the Long-Range Bomber Force which was at the disposal of the State Commissariat of Defence for tactical deployment on any front when necessary.

In April 1939 a thorough re-organisa-tion within the Air Force took place. The largest formation was now the air division, which comprised between four and six air regiments (formerly brigades). Each regiment consisted of about 60 aircraft with additional reserve planes (usually about 40 aircraft).

There were three types of Air Regi-ment:
bomber regiments with four squadrons of 12 aircraft each;
fighter regiments with four squadrons of 15 aircraft each;
ground attack regiments with four squadrons of 15 aircraft each.

The squadron was divided into wings (*Zven 'ya*) of three aircraft.

The Air Force attached to a Military District or Front included a number of fighter and bomber regiments, while mixed regiments with both bomber and fighter components were attached to army corps, which also retained their own reconnaissance squadrons.

UNIFORM As members of the Red Army, Air Force personnel wore Army uniforms. Following the French custom, however, a dark blue uniform was introduced in 1935 for wear as a dress and undress uniform. Items of the blue uniform continued to be worn with khaki clothing during the war, because of the shortage of uniforms in the war-time Soviet Union.

The basic pre-war flight clothing for fighter pilots was a fur-lined leather flying helmet and double-breasted brown leather coat. In warm weather pilots of enclosed aircraft wore their service uniforms. Bomber crews wore either an unlined one-piece black overall or a fur-lined one-piece flying suit, with soft fur-lined flying boots which could cover the thighs, but were often worn with the tops folded down to give the appearance of fur leggings (as in figure 32).

NAVY

As a land power the Soviet Union did not look upon the Red Navy's role as a strategic one. Its main tasks, therefore, were the patrolling of territorial waters, the protection of shore installations, the support of land forces, and the provision of vessels and personnel for amphibious operations.

ORGANISATION The head of the Red Navy, the Chief of Naval Forces, was directly subordinate to the People's Commissar for Defence, and acted as the latter's deputy and adviser on all naval matters. The Navy was divided into the Fleet, including the Underwater (submarine) Fleet, the Naval Air Force, and Coastal Defence.

Conscripts in the Navy usually served for five years in one of the four fleets (Baltic, Northern, Black Sea and Pacific), or in one of the flotillas which operated in the seas and lakes of the Soviet Union. The Red Navy did not have a special force of marines, but used its ratings – who had all undergone basic infantry training in the fleet depots – for combined operations when necessary. The strength of the whole Soviet Navy in 1939 was estimated at 40,000 men of whom 22,000 were serving at sea.

The fleet involved in the war against Finland was the Baltic Fleet. At the beginning of the war the fleet was operationally subordinated to the Leningrad Military District, and comprised the following:

2 battleships;
2 cruisers;
21 destroyers and torpedo boats;
52 submarines;
41 motor torpedo boats;
13 minelayers, minesweepers and auxiliaries;
2 escort and patrol boats.

Added to this were the small craft of the Lake Ladoga Flotilla.

32 Pilot, Red Air Force, 1939
Over his service uniform this pilot of a Tupolev SB-2 bomber wears a one-piece fur-lined flying suit, on which he carries his equipment: including pistol, map case and parachute harness. The thigh-length fur-lined flying boots were often worn turned down as illustrated. The extreme cold of the Russian winter made such warm clothing a vital necessity.

33 Seaman, Red Navy, 1939
This Red Fleetsman on guard duty wears the standard naval cap and the greatcoat which had replaced the pea-coat (bushlat) in cold weather. The cap tally translates as 'Northern Fleet'. Over his right shoulder he carries a gas mask in a canvas bag. The rifle is the Moisin-Nagant M1930 rifle with bayonet fixed in reserve position.

Above: Cadets of the Naval School parade in Red Square. As this was a ceremonial occasion, the cadet in the foreground carries a whistle, traditionally used to pipe officers on board ship.

The extreme winter weather restricted naval operations and activities were limited to providing artillery support for land operations, and providing personnel for landing operations in the Gulf of Finland and on the Karelian Isthmus.

UNIFORM Uniform in the 'Muscovy Fleet', as the Red Navy was sometimes called, followed the standard international naval pattern, but incorporated two unusual features: it was the only navy in which the sailor's traditional square rig was worn with the petty officer's peaked cap, and in which the sailor's uniform combined both the colours blue and black.

The officers' black uniform consisted of peaked cap, reefer jacket with white shirt and black tie, black trousers and black leather shoes. The black greatcoat was double-breasted with two rows of six gilt metal buttons. Ratings wore a dark blue jumper (*flanelevka*) and black bell-bottom trousers. The cap had a long ribbon or 'tally' on which appeared the name of the ship in gilt cyrillic letters.

Warrant officers (*mishman* from the English midshipman) and chief petty officers wore the officer's uniform with a special cap badge, while petty officers with more than five years' service wore the peaked cap with sailor's uniform.

32   33

35

DENMARK
ARMY

The German pretext for the occupation of Denmark, was to protect her from attack by Britain, and so German troops were ordered to make the take-over as peaceful and friendly as possible. In fact Danish casualties were only 12 airmen, 11 soldiers and 3 frontier guards killed.

The German authorities allowed the King and government to exercise limited power, while all questions relating to the occupying power were the subject of negotiation between the two parties. The Danish forces were to continue to exist, but in much reduced circumstances, with a total strength not exceeding 3300 men. These consisted of the Royal Life Guards, trained conscripts and conscripts required for maintenance and repair work. In addition there were a number of reserve officers and NCOs undergoing training in the Army Officers' School.

Relations between the two countries deteriorated, however, and the Germans imposed restrictions which in November 1942 banned Danish soldiers and the wearing of military uniform from Jutland. The Danish Army was then concentrated in Sjaelland and the Island of Funen. The final act came in August 1943 when the Germans took the Danish garrison by surprise and disarmed it after a short fight. Thereafter all Danish military personnel were made prisoners-of-war, and the armed forces disbanded.

ORGANISATION The Danish Defence Act of 1937 set up a peacetime establishment of two divisions, an independent anti-aircraft and engineer regiment, an army air force, the Bornholm garrison, a transport battalion and a general headquarters.

In peacetime the regiments and battalions were no more than a small administrative staff responsible for the training of the annual intake of 6599 conscripts who were allocated as follows: 4340 to the infantry, 465 to the Life Guards, 374 to the cavalry, 1120 to the artillery, and 300 men to the engineers. On 8 April 1940 there were 6600 conscripts with eleven month's training service with the colours, as well as a further 2050 non-combatants. During the German invasion part of this force was on leave, while a further seven per cent were unfit for duty.

The Sjaelland Division had its headquarters in Copenhagen and consisted of the Life Guards, the 1st, 4th and 5th Infantry Regiments, the Guards Hussars, the 1st and 2nd Field Artillery Regiments, the 13th Anti-Aircraft Battalion and an engineer battalion.

The Jutland Division had its headquarters in Viborg with the 2nd, 3rd, 6th and 7th Infantry Regiments the infantry pioneer regiment, the Jutland Dragoon Regiment, the 3rd Field Artillery Regiment, the 14th Anti-Aircraft Battalion, and the 2nd Engineer Battalion.

The establishment strength of an infantry regiment was 3000 all ranks who were armed with Krag-Jørgensen M84/24 rifles and Bayard M1910 pistols.

34 **35**

34 Staff Officiant, Danish Army, 1940

This warrant officer has been issued with the old 1864 model black greatcoat, which was the same for other ranks but without the turn-ups on the cuffs. As well as the M1923 steel helmet, he carries a khaki field cap (with the national cockade just visible on the front) tucked into his Sam Browne belt. The two gold rosettes on the brown silk shoulder straps indicate his rank. Below his old-style black greatcoat, the warrant officer is probably wearing the new khaki uniform. Although most other ranks had not been issued with the new colour, many NCOs and officers had purchased khaki uniforms privately.

35 Private, Danish Army, 1940

Although the 1915 pattern grey wool clothing was outmoded by 1940 it was still worn by the rank and file, and trousers turned over the boots were a characteristic feature of Danish uniform. This private is equipped with a haversack and below that the 1926 gas mask; an entrenching tool with a knife bayonet attached, and the Danish M1923 steel helmet. Armament consists of a Danish M1889/10 8mm rifle with ammunition pouches strapped onto the belt.

36 First Lieutenant, Danish Air Force, 1940

Apart from the pilot's wings, this uniform was worn by both Army and Air Force officers. On the officer's pattern cap is the national cockade and below that the badge for junior officers. The uniform is the khaki M1923 pattern worn with a Sam Browne belt. Rank is denoted by the gold star (of an officer) on the collar and the two five-pointed stars (of a first lieutenant) on the grey silk shoulder straps. The breeches are tucked into the standard pattern high polished boots.

Above: The crew of a Danish anti-aircraft gun undergoing training. This photograph shows the shape of the Danish helmet extremely well.

The supporting arms of the regiment consisted of:

256 light machine guns (Madsen M24);
32 heavy machine guns (Madsen M29);
24 horse drawn machine guns (Madsen M29);
24 heavy mortars;
6 horse-drawn anti-tank guns (37 mm Bofors).

An artillery regiment consisted of a staff, and four battalions each of three batteries. Artillery pieces used were Krupp 75 mm field guns, Schneider 105 mm guns and Schneider 50 mm howitzers.

UNIFORM In 1940 Danish Army uniform was in the process of change, and a new khaki uniform with brown leather equipment and footwear was replacing the old uniform with its black leather equipment and footwear. Denmark's neutrality and peacetime economies meant that the changeover only took place slowly, and when the Germans invaded in April 1940, they encountered soldiers dressed in both grey and khaki uniforms with a mixture of brown and black equipment. Generally speaking officers and regular NCOs wore khaki, but the bulk of the Army and in particular conscripts wore grey tunics and greatcoats, light blue trousers, and black leather equipment.

The khaki uniform consisted of a single-breasted tunic with stand-and-fall collar fastened with six bronzed buttons and pleated patch pockets. The great-coat was double-breasted with two rows of six buttons and a large fall collar. Trousers were worn rolled half way up the calf outside the leather lace-up field boots. The new M1923 (1937) pattern steel helmet had a distinctive shape and had the Danish coat of arms on the front. When the helmet was not needed all ranks wore a khaki side cap.

The Royal Danish Life Guards had a field uniform in the same cut, but it was made in a grey-green cloth, not dissimilar to the German field-grey, and later in the war this uniform was adopted by the German-sponsored Schalburg Corps.

INSIGNIA Rank was indicated by the number, width and colour of the lace and braid on the side cap, and the shoulder straps. Corporals wore yellow lace chevrons on the sleeves.

For arm-of-service identification, certain categories of commissioned ranks wore gilt metal badges on the tunic collar, while other ranks wore an enamelled badge above the right breast pocket.

AIR FORCE

The Air Force, which formed part of the Army, consisted of two battalions, one of which was based on Jutland, and the other on Sjaelland. On the morning of

9 April 1940 the Air Force order-of-battle was as follows:

1 squadron with 13 interceptor aircraft;
1 squadron with 8 interceptors and 2 reconnaissance aircraft;
1 squadron with 11 reconnaissance and 1 training aircraft;
1 squadron with 14 reconnaissance aircraft and an autogiro;
the Air Force School with 18 training aircraft.

Following the German disbandment of the remaining Danish armed forces in August 1943, a number of Danish pilots made their way to Sweden where they began to train on Swedish aircraft (Saab B-17s). It was planned to form an air support unit for the Danish Brigade in Sweden, but this plan was not completed before the end of the war.

UNIFORM Air Force personnel wore Army uniform, although officers do appear to have preferred an open version of the khaki service tunic. Qualified flying personnel wore embroidered 'wings' on the right breast.

NAVY

The King of Denmark was Commander-in-Chief of the armed forces while actual command of the Navy was exercised by the Naval Minister, Vice-Admiral H. Rechnitzer, who was also responsible for all coastal defences. The personnel of the Navy in 1940 was about 1500 men, and the main base was at Copenhagen. The Navy comprised:

12 coastal defence ships;
17 motor torpedo boats;
9 submarines;
14 minesweepers;
6 minelayers;
several fishery control vessels.

The Naval Air Service had at its disposal sixty-four aircraft, but only two of these were shipborne.

Despite warnings of an imminent German attack on 4 April 1940, no warlike preparations were made for fear of providing provocation. When it was reported that large numbers of German warships and transports were sailing in Danish waters through the 'Great Belt', Danish ships were ordered not to open fire unless fired upon. As the German ships were not resisted there was no fighting and no ships were sunk at sea.

The Danish Navy continued to exist under the German occupation and even undertook some local minesweeping, but it was not long before relations between the two countries deteriorated to such an extent that the Danes prepared to sail their ships to Sweden, or scuttle them. On 29 August 1943, following the failure of German attempts to negotiate the surrender of the sovereignty of the Danish Navy, 31 vessels were scuttled.

UNIFORM Danish Navy uniform, as worn during World War II, was originally introduced in the 1870s and amended in 1909 and 1932.

Officers, chief petty officers and petty officers wore a peaked cap, reefer jacket with white shirt and black tie, matching navy-blue trousers, and black

Right: A Danish rating in square rig, the basic uniform of the Navy.

Below: A Danish Navy flyer wearing basic uniform under his harness. His rank (sub-lieutenant) is shown on the cuffs.

shoes and socks. The navy-blue greatcoat was double-breasted, and here the Royal Danish Navy departed from the established practice and officers wore rank distinction lace on the greatcoat cuffs, instead of on the shoulder straps.

Ratings in square rig wore the standard sailor's cap with a circular cockade in the national colours on the right side, and a blue jumper worn outside bell-bottomed trousers. Under the jumper was worn a white shirt with blue denim collar edged with three white lines, and a black scarf. In summer all ranks wore a white cap cover and there were white versions of both officers' and ratings' uniforms.

INSIGNIA The rank group was indicated by the cap badge, and the rank by the number of bands and width of the rank distinction lace on the cuffs of officers and chief petty officers. Ratings and petty officers wore their rank badges on the upper sleeve.

For arm-of-service distinction, officers serving in special branches such as the reserve or coastal artillery wore a letter ('R' with anchor or 'K') inside the 'curl' of the rank distinction lace, while other branches were identified by coloured backing or 'lights' which appeared between the rank distinction lace. Naval aviators wore the letter 'F' (*Flyver*) in the 'curl' and gold-embroidered wings on the breast.

DANISH ARMY/AIRFORCE INSIGNIA

Forage Cap Officers and Cornets
Forage Cap Officiants and Sgts
Forage Cap Other Ranks

Cap Badge General Rank
Cap Badge Senior Officers
National Cockade
Cap Badge Junior Officers/Officiants
Cap Badge NCOs/Cornets

Pilot's Wings

General | Lieutenant General | Major-General | Colonel | Lieutenant-Colonel | Captain | Captain (II) | Lieutenant | Lieut of Reserves | 2nd Lieut

Corps Officiant | Staff Officiant | Senior Officiant | Officiant | Cornet | Sergeant-Major | Sergeant | Corporal | Lance-Corporal | Helmet Badge

DANISH NAVY INSIGNIA

Peaked Cap Badge Admirals
Peaked Cap Badge Senior Officers
Peaked Cap Badge Junior Officers

Admiral (on White Jacket) | Admiral | Vice-Admiral | Rear-Admiral | Commodore (Paymaster) | Captain (Engineers) | Commander (promoted before 1937) | Commander (Flying) | Lieutenant Commander (Medical) | Lieutenant | Sub-Lieut (Engineers) | Sub-Lieut (Coastal Arty)

Peaked Cap Badge Midshipman and CPOs
Cap Badge Petty Officers
National Cockade

Senior Midshipman | Midshipman (Engineers) | C P O (I) (Coastal Arty) | C P O (II) (Radio) | C P O (III) (Paymaster) | P O (I) (Torpedoes) | P O (II) (Steward) | Cadet | Able S'man (Volunteer 1st yr.) | Able S'man (Volunteer 2nd yr.) | Able S'man (Volunteer 3rd yr.) | Able S'man (Conscript)

39

NORWAY
ARMY

In 1939, after more than a hundred years of peace, Norway did not possess a large standing army and her government considered that effective national defence against a major power was impossible. The Soviet Union's invasion of Finland in 1939 was a severe shock, and during the winter a sizeable Norwegian force was established in northern Norway. After the Soviet Union signed an armistice with the Finns in March 1940, however, the force was disbanded. When the Germans invaded on 8 April, the Norwegian Army was only partially mobilised and in the process of training new recruits. But despite these disadvantages, Norway put up a stubborn fight and it was two months before the

country was completely overrun and the British, French and Polish contingents evicted. The government finally capitulated on 9 June 1940. Despite bitter fighting casualties had been light; the Norwegians lost just 1335 killed and wounded. Small contingents of Norwegians managed to escape to England, while others crossed into Sweden.

ORGANISATION King Haakon VII was Commander-in-Chief of a basically territorial army, which when fully mobilised, was to have had a strength of about 100,000 men. A small cadre of regular officers and NCOs was responsible for running the Army and for the training of conscripts.

The country was divided into six Military Districts or Commands with their headquarters in Halden, Oslo, Kristiansand, Bergen, Trondheim and

Harstad. Each Command was initially expected to field a brigade, later to be expanded to a division and garrison and ancillary troops.

An infantry division comprised a staff, two or three infantry regiments, and either a field artillery regiment, or a mountain artillery battalion. The 2nd Infantry Division in Oslo included the Royal Guard and a cavalry regiment. The 5th and 6th infantry divisions had, in addition, a pioneer and flying battalion.

An infantry regiment had a strength of 3750 men armed with Krag-Jorgensen M1894 rifles. Some regiments had a bicycle company for reconnaissance duties, which in winter became a ski troop. Support weapons consisted of:
96 light machine guns (6.5mm Madsen);
36 heavy machine guns (Colt-Browning M29);
8 heavy mortars.

37 Lieutenant, Norwegian Army, 1940
This infantry officer wears the basic 1934 pattern service dress with rank distinctions appearing on the kepi and on the collar, while arm of service is identified by the design of the buttons and the colour of the piping on the kepi, tunic collar, cuffs and trousers. In very cold weather officers and men often wore various kinds of sheepskin coats and other types of protective clothing over this uniform. In his holster he carries the M1914 service pistol, and the pouch on the left holds three magazines for the same weapon.

**38 Corporal,
Norwegian Army, 1940**
The soldier depicted here wears the winter version of the service dress tunic, which was sufficiently baggy to allow plenty of warm clothing to be worn underneath. His soft cap with earflaps was known as a 'Finnmark' cap. The trousers are worn tucked into thick knitted socks over which he wears canvas gaiters (both these items proved popular with the inadequately equipped German soldiers). On his pack is the obsolete dark-blue overcoat which was still worn in 1940. The rifle is the 6.5mm Krag-Jorgensen M 1894. The old-pattern red piping is worn.

37

38

Field artillery regiments had three battalions of two or three batteries of four guns. The first and second battalions were equipped with Kongsberg 120mm field howitzers, while the third battalion acted as a reserve with three batteries of Ehrhardt 75mm M1901 field guns. All artillery pieces were horsedrawn.

The anti-aircraft regiment was motorised and equipped with Madsen 20mm heavy machine guns, and Kongsberg 75mm M1932 anti-aircraft guns.

UNIFORM The grey-green uniform of the Norwegian Army was originally introduced in 1912. The uniform was highly standardised and the same for all ranks. The basic uniform for officers and other ranks is illustrated in figure 37, but additionally there was a side cap with piped flap and two patterns of steel helmet. The first helmet was the British Mark 1 which was being replaced by the Swedish civil defence helmet (designated M1931 by the Norwegians). In 1935 an oval stamped badge bearing the Norwegian lion was issued for wear on the front of the helmet.

Over the tunic, which existed in three patterns, a double-breasted water-repellent grey-green cotton-duck jacket

Left: Three Allied soldiers evacuated from Norway: from left, a French chasseur alpin, a British infantryman and a Norwegian officer.

NORWEGIAN ARMY/AIR FORCE INSIGNIA

General · Lieutenant-General · Major-General · Colonel · Lieutenant-Colonel · Major · Captain

Lieutenant · 2nd Lieutenant · Officer Candidate · Sergeant · Corporal

Cap Badges

Generals · Officers · N.C.O.s · Privates

Observer's Badge · Pilot's Badge

without insignia was often worn.
Norwegian officers and men also wore
sheepskin coats and other items of civilian
winter clothing.

INSIGNIA Rank distinction lace
appeared on the kepi, tunic collar and
greatcoat shoulder straps, while NCOs
had rank distinctions on the cuffs.

Arm of service was indicated by the
colour and design of the uniform buttons.

AIR FORCE

By midday on 9 April 1940, the German
armed forces had occupied nearly all the
airfields and seaplane bases south of
Narvik, and most of Norway's semi-
modern fighters (Gloster Gladiators) had
been destroyed in the defence of Oslo on
the opening day of the German invasion.
Thereafter, the Air Force took little part
in the fighting.

The Air Force was organised in three
flights (one each of fighters, bombers and
reconnaissance aircraft) with a total of
76 aircraft and 940 men, and was intended
to play a ground-support role.

UNIFORM Air Service personnel wore
Army uniforms with a bright green
arm-of-service colour as piping on the
kepi, side-cap, tunic, greatcoat and
trousers. The silver buttons bore a
horizontal propeller and a crown.

INSIGNIA Rank distinction lace
appeared on the kepi, tunic collar and
greatcoat shoulder straps. NCOs wore
their rank badges on the cuffs. There
were also distinctive patterns of cap
badge for NCOs, officers and generals.

There were no branch or arm-of-
service badges as such, but pilots and
observers wore silver-embroidered wings
on the right breast.

NAVY

On 8 April 1940, the day before the
German invasion, 5200 officers and men
were serving in the Navy and its Air
Service. Despite the fact that the bulk of
the vessels of the Norwegian Navy were
obsolete, they gave a good account of
themselves, during the hostilities with
Germany. Indeed, during the fighting
most of them were put out of action or
sunk. There were initially 113 vessels,
comprising:
2 small armoured cruisers;
10 minelayers;
7 destroyers;
3 large 'Trygg' class torpedo boats;
14 torpedo boats;
9 submarines;
8 minesweepers;
9 patrol boats;
49 vessels converted to patrol boats.

Only 13 of these made British ports
after capitulation.

NORWEGIAN NAVY INSIGNIA

39

Above left: A Norwegian pilot, wearing the side cap, breeches and high boots. His rank (lieutenant) is shown on his collar, and the wings on his right breast signify a pilot's qualification.

Above: Norwegian sailors in exile in Britain. This photograph is particularly interesting in that it shows the national differences in the standard naval uniform. The sailor in the right foreground is wearing Norwegian uniform; the others have British clothing. The inspection is by King Haakon.

On 22 April 1940, while fighting was still in progress, the Norwegian Government decided to requisition the whole Norwegian merchant fleet still under its control. 1000 ships (totalling 4,000,000 tons) manned by 30,000 seamen were saved for the Allied cause, and played an indispensable part in the Battle of the Atlantic.

In addition to the fleet there were coastal fortifications armed with guns of various calibres at Oscarborg, Oslofjord, Kristiansand, Bergen and Agdenes, which were manned by 308 officers and 2095 other ranks.

The Norwegian Naval Air Service had been formed as early as 1915, and because of its small size necessarily played only a limited role in the war against Germany.

Some Navy aircraft did, however, fly to northern Norway after the initial German attack, and they continued to operate from there until fighting ceased on 7 June 1940.

UNIFORM The uniform worn during the 1940 campaign was based on the regulations of 1907, and in most respects conformed to the standard international pattern.

Officers, cadets and petty officers (quartermasters) wore a peaked cap, double-breasted reefer jacket with white shirt and black tie, matching blue trousers and black shoes. The greatcoat was double-breasted. Ratings wore the uniform illustrated in figure 39, over which, in cold weather, they wore a double-breasted pea-coat. The winter head-dress for officers was a black astrakhan cap on which was a special pattern of cap badge.

INSIGNIA Rank was indicated by the pattern of cap badge for admirals, officers, chief petty officers, quartermasters, cadets and petty officers. As in other Scandinavian navies, conscripts had special insignia. Rank distinction

39 Seaman, Norwegian Navy, 1940
This Dekksmann wears Norwegian Navy 'square rig' with his rank badge on the left sleeve. On the cap tally appears the legend, Den KGL Norske Marine ('Royal Norwegian Navy'). He carries a 6.5mm Krag-Jørgensen M1894 rifle and ammunition pouches.

lace appeared on the reefer cuffs and on the greatcoat shoulder straps. Ratings wore their rank badges on the upper left sleeve.

As arm-of-service distinctions, officers in certain branches were identified by the shape of the 'curl' on the rank distinction lace, or the absence of a 'curl', and the colour of the 'lights' between the rank distinction lace. Chief petty officers had gold badges while other petty officers and ratings wore red branch badges above their rank badges.

Naval Air Service personnel wore naval uniform while qualified flying personnel wore gold-embroidered wings on the right breast. Ratings wore their uniform with special branch and trade badges incorporating wings and the letter 'A' on the upper left sleeve.

Netherlands
Army

During World War I Holland's neutrality had been respected and during the inter-war years her government saw fit to reduce spending to an absolute minimum.

Germany's warlike stance, and warnings from well-informed sources failed to alert the Dutch government to the strong possibility that this time her neutrality would be violated. Thus it was not until April 1940 that the Dutch armed forces were mobilised. Some German officers who had misgivings about invading a neutral country informed the Dutch of the exact date of the invasion, and Dutch forces were placed on an alert from early morning on 10 May 1940. Despite the warning and many valiant acts of self-sacrifice, the German invasion was over in five days and Holland was forced to capitulate. After the war the Dutch command was blamed for this poor performance, but in fact there was little the Dutch could have done in the circumstances. The German High Command was impressed by the tenacity of the Dutch Army but it had neither the equipment, nor the appropriate training and experience to put up much more than a token resistance against the invading forces.

Many Dutchmen avoided German capture and eventually reached England, where they continued their struggle.

ORGANISATION The Army consisted of a small professional cadre of 1500 officers and 6500 other ranks which was responsible for maintaining the military establishment, and for the training of the annual intake of 60,000 conscripts, who were eligible for eleven months military service between the ages of 20 and 40. The field army on mobilisation numbered 114,000 men, or, including reserves, 270,000 all ranks.

The country was divided into four army corps based on Amsterdam, Arnhem, Breda and Amersfoort. An army corps comprised a corps staff, two infantry divisions, one or two heavy artillery regiments, one independent artillery battalion, and a signals and reconnaissance battalion. In addition, there was a light brigade (consisting of a staff, signals battalion, armoured car squadron, cyclist regiment, two hussar regiments and one horse artillery regiment) and an anti-aircraft brigade with staff and two anti-aircraft regiments.

An infantry regiment had a strength of 2691 all ranks armed with Mannlicher M9 rifles and FN 9mm pistols. Support

40

41

weapons consisted of:
72 light machine guns (Lewis M20);
36 heavy machine guns (Schwarzlose MO8/15);
6 heavy mortars;
4 anti-tank guns.

UNIFORM A grey-green uniform was introduced in 1912, but the colour soon underwent a change, so that by the outbreak of war in 1940 the colour was almost identical to German field-grey. The issue uniform was simple, but outdated in the sense that the cut was still tight and restricting, and the full lining made it hot in summer and difficult to dry when wet. In 1937 the uniform underwent certain modifications which made it more practical. The stiff stand collar became a softer stand-and-fall pattern, exterior pockets were added, breeches were introduced for mounted personnel, and a new comfortable side cap became the basic form of head-dress. Before the outbreak of war the regulars wore a black dress uniform when not on active duty, while cavalry and horse artillery retained vestiges of their former full-dress uniforms.

40 Lieutenant-Colonel, Dutch Army, 1940

An officer of infantry cyclists, this lieutenant-colonel wears standard service dress with the side cap which was introduced in 1937 to replace the kepi (finally abolished in the spring of 1940). Badges of rank based on the Austrian pattern are worn on the collar (two stars and a bar for a lieutenant-colonel) and his arm of service is shown by the blue (infantry) piping and the bicycle wheel on the collar. On the 'Sam Browne' belt he wears a Belgian 9mm FN pistol with two extra magazines in the pouch.

41 Corporal, Dutch Army, 1940

This infantryman wears the 1912 pattern 'grey' uniform and the standard Dutch steel helmet with the 'Lion of Nassau' badge. Just before the war a more comfortable pattern of tunic was introduced with stand-and-fall collar and no piping, but it was not issued in any great numbers before the German invasion. Rank is indicated by the chevron on the sleeve and arm of service by the green piping and the horn badge on the collar. The trade badge on the left sleeve is that of a pistol marksman. The rifle is the 6.5mm Mannlicher M1895 model. The Dutch uniform, as shown here, was quite distinctive, mainly because of its combination of a unique helmet (the only equivalent was in the Romanian Army), an old-fashioned cut and the green colour.

The Dutch issue tunic had a stand or stand-and-fall collar, seven matt bronzed buttons in front, two slash breast pockets with pointed flap and button, and round cuffs. The shoulder straps, which were stitched down, ended in a roll which prevented the equipment from slipping off the shoulders.

The greatcoat was double-breasted with a large fall collar, two rows of five metal buttons, turn-back cuffs, slanting slash side pockets with rectangular flaps, and a half-belt at the back fastened with three buttons. There were no shoulder straps or piping on the greatcoat.

In 1940 head-dress consisted of the side cap or steel helmet. The stiff shako fell into disuse in spring 1940, although some officers continued to wear it. The side cap was introduced in 1937 and was piped in arm-of-service colour for other ranks, or metallic braid for officers.

All unmounted other ranks wore matching knickerbockers and puttees, while officers, warrant officers and NCOs wore matching breeches (sometimes piped) and black riding boots or ankle boots and leather gaiters. Gloves were of brown leather or grey-green wool.

Crews of enclosed armoured vehicles

Below: A Dutch mortar team in action. The photographer has managed to capture the bomb leaving the weapon. The equipment of the nearest infantryman includes gas-mask, knapsack, bedding-roll and an old-fashioned sword-bayonet.

wore a brimless helmet and a one-piece grey overall.

Officers and warrant officers wore a brown leather waistbelt with a brass two-pronged buckle and leather cross-strap. On the right they usually carried the Belgian 9mm FN short automatic pistol in a brown leather holster.

INSIGNIA General officers were distinguished by a special peaked cap, gold-embroidered oak leaves on the tunic collar and two rows of crimson piping on the breeches. All officers had gold braid piping on the side cap, and badges of rank on the tunic and greatcoat collar. Other ranks wore sleeve badges of rank.

Arm of service was identified by the colour of the piping on the side cap, tunic collar and cuffs and breeches of officers and warrant officers. The rank distinction lace worn on the sleeves by NCOs and men was edged in arm-of-service colour. Some units and formations wore a metal badge on the left of the side cap.

AIR FORCE

In 1937 the Dutch government, alarmed by Germany's warlike stance, embarked on a programme of limited expansion and re-organisation of the Army Air Force. The Air Force remained part of the Army but became a semi-independent arm to which was added, in November 1938, anti-aircraft artillery, searchlight sections and air observer corps; and the whole was designated Air Defence Command.

In May 1940 the active element of the Army Air Force was divided into two air regiments, the first consisting of four fighter squadrons, one bomber and one reconnaissance squadron, and the second consisting of four reconnaissance wings and two fighter squadrons.

It was decided to replace the obsolete aircraft then in service (Fokker DVII fighters and Fokker CL and CV two-seater reconnaissance planes), and orders were sent out for 36 Fokker DXXI single-seater fighters, 36 Fokker GIA twin-engined fighters, 16 Fokker TV bombers and (from the United States) 18 Douglas DB-8A-3N attack bombers. A further 23 Curtiss Hawk 75A single-seat fighters were also ordered but these were not delivered by the invasion.

On 10 May 1940 the Army Air Service had 139 operational aircraft at its disposal, although not all of them were the newer types. Nearly all of these were destroyed as a result of the German surprise attacks on Dutch airfields. Personnel losses were about 8000 which included 500 men taken prisoner.

42

**42 2nd Lieutenant,
Dutch Air Force, 1940**

This 2nd Lieutenant wears an Army officers' uniform, privately purchased and made out of whipcord, as opposed to the coarse and darker cloth of the issue uniform. He also wears the obsolete but handsome kepi which was occasionally still worn in 1940. The colour of the piping and the badge on the collar identify him as an airman, while the metal 'wings' on his left breast show he is a qualified pilot. Fighter pilots usually wore a leather flying helmet and a three-quarter-length double-breasted leather coat, with rank badges on the collar.

UNIFORM AND INSIGNIA Air Force personnel wore Army uniforms with blue piping and an embroidered badge consisting of a radial engine and twin-bladed propeller on their collars. Qualified pilots and observers had a gilt metal badge which was worn on the left breast of the tunic and greatcoat.

Flying clothing was of the French pattern and consisted of a leather flying helmet or a steel helmet and double-breasted leather jacket. The rank stars in metal were affixed to the collar.

43 Leading Seaman, Dutch Navy, 1940
This leading seaman wears the standard 'square rig'
of the Royal Netherlands Navy. The cap tally with
the legend Koninklijke Marine *('Royal Navy')*
in Gothic lettering began to be replaced by one in
block lettering at the beginning of the war. He wears
infantry equipment and carries a 6.5mm Mannlicher
M1895 rifle.

NAVY

Before the War the Dutch Navy in
European waters was intended primarily
for local coastal defence and mine-laying
work in the North Sea; its most powerful
units were stationed in the Dutch East
Indies. By 1939, however, new warships
were being constructed which were
suitable for both the Far East and Europe.

In May 1940 the Chief of Naval Staff
and Commander-in-Chief of Naval
Forces was Vice-Admiral J. Th. Furstner.
Personnel was about 11,750 men including
Marines. The vessels consisted of:
4 cruisers;
8 destroyers;
23 submarines;

7 escort and patrol vessels;
5 motor torpedo-boats;
28 mine-sweepers.

The Navy played a limited if
courageous role in the battle for Holland.
Ships patrolled the coastline giving supporting fire to land forces, and in one
unique instance a Dutch ship shelled a
beach on which German troop-carrying
aircraft were landing. Small craft assisted
by transporting troops and supplies.

When defeat became inevitable, Dutch
ships ferried troops across the sea, and
20,000 men reached Britain.

The bulk of the Dutch Navy's aircraft
were stationed in the Dutch East Indies,
although in May 1940 it disposed of 44
seaplanes and 30 training aircraft in
Holland. The Naval Air Service carried
out a number of reconnaissance missions
and shot down one modern German
fighter, but by 13 May there was hardly a
serviceable aircraft left.

On Tuesday 14 May, the day of the
Dutch capitulation, the last six seaplanes
at Veere left for France, and during the
course of the day were followed by any
machines able to fly. During the campaign in Holland the Naval Air Service
had lost 18 seaplanes at their moorings,
and all the trainers on the ground.

UNIFORM The uniform worn during
World War II was governed by regulations which came into force in April 1933.

The uniform for officers followed the
standard pattern, although instead of a
greatcoat issue wear was a frock coat
with rank distinction lace on the cuffs.
The uniform for ratings is illustrated by
figure 43, although the illustration shows
the old-pattern cap tally, which was
replaced at the beginning of the war by
one with block lettering. The Dutch
sailor also had a double-breasted pea-
coat with brass buttons.

For all ranks there were white uniforms
for summer and tropical wear which
included white covers for the standard
head-dress, and a white sun helmet or
straw panama hat.

INSIGNIA Officers and warrant officers
wore rank distinction lace on the cuffs
and on the shoulder straps of the white
tunic. Senior petty officers wore their
rank badges on the cuffs of the blue
uniform, and on the collar patches of the
Marine Corps (grey-green) and tropical
uniforms. Ratings wore cuff rank badges.

Officers wore their arm-of-service emblem in the centre of the cap badge and
on the reefer jacket collar. Speciality
insignia was worn on the upper left
sleeve. Naval aircrew wore gilt metal
'wings' on the left breast.

MARINES

On 10 May 1940, the *Korpsmariniers*
(originally formed in 1665 and in action
against the English in 1667) was stationed
in Rotterdam.

The Rotterdam garrison included one
hundred trained conscripts 1st Class, one
hundred 3rd Class, and one hundred
with only three months' service. At the
naval depot there were a further 150
Marines, 90 conscripts and 600 new
recruits. Despite their small number and
lack of training, the Marines fought
stubbornly against German parachute
troops both on the Zuider Zee and in
defence of the Maas bridges at Rotterdam, until, on 14 May 1940, they surrendered together with all other forces in
Holland.

UNIFORM AND INSIGNIA The field-
dress of the Dutch Marine Corps was
that of the Army, but during the German
invasion in May 1940 the Marines wore
the M1928 steel helmet painted black
with a white metal foul-anchor on the
front and a navy-blue double-breasted
greatcoat with brass buttons. Rank
badges were worn as on the Navy uniform.

Below: Marines of the Rotterdam garrison
marching through the town, wearing their double-
breasted greatcoats. The man on the right is
wearing both sword and pistol.

NETHERLANDS ARMY/AIR FORCE INSIGNIA

Collar Patches

General | Lieutenant-General | Major-General | Colonel (Air Force) | Lieutenant-Colonel (Artillery) | Major (Air Force) | Major (Reserve) (Voluntary Motor Corps)

Captain (I) (Grenadiers) | Captain Adjutant (II) (Air Force) | 1st Lieutenant (I) (Cavalry) | 1st Lieutenant Adjutant (II) (Air Force) | 2nd Lieutenant (Jagers) | Warrant Officer (infantry) | Other Ranks (Air Force)

Cuff

Greatcoat Collars

Sergeant-Major (Infantry) | Senior Sergeant (Jagers) | Quarterm't'r (top) & Sergeant (Air Force) | Corporal | Private 1st Class

Lieut-General | Colonel | Warrant Officer

Pilot's Badge | Observer's Badge

NETHERLANDS NAVY INSIGNIA

Peaked Caps

Shoulder

Cuff

Admiral of the Fleet | Admiral | Vice-Admiral | Rear-Admiral | Captain | Commander | Lieutenant-Commander | Lieutenant | Sub-Lieut

Tropical Uniform Insignia *Arm* *Collar Insignia*

Shoulder

Cuff

Warrant Officer | Chief Petty Officer | Petty Officer 1st Class | Leading Seaman (Seam'n Branch) | Leading Seaman (Other Branches) | Able Seaman (I) | Able Seaman (II) | Line Engineers | Aviation Medical

47

44

45

BELGIUM
ARMY

In 1914 neutral Belgium had been suddenly attacked by the German Army and had experienced four years of trench warfare. After the German occupation of the Rhineland in 1936 the country was again jolted into awareness of impending danger. National service was extended from 8 to 12 months, the military budget increased by 15 per cent, and new fortifications were constructed. But this could not conceal the fact that military thinking had not progressed beyond the trenches of World War I. Armour, for example, was only considered an offensive weapon, and Belgium, whose Army had a purely defensive role, had no tank units. Belgium fielded 22 divisions against the invading forces of Army Group B in 1940, and the tenacity of the Belgian infantry at first surprised the Germans. Nonetheless, the Belgian army was on the point of collapse within two weeks of the invasion, and on 28 May the last units surrendered. After 18 days of fighting, casualties were 23,350 killed and wounded.

ORGANISATION The 100,000-strong Belgian Army under its Commander-in-Chief, King Leopold, was basically a standing army but one which relied on conscription for its annual intake of recruits. Its strength on mobilisation was in the region of 550,000 men, which for a small country of eight million people was a remarkable feat.

The country was divided into three army corps areas based on Brussels,

44 Colonel, Belgian Army, 1940

This colonel of the 1st Infantry Regiment is wearing typical service dress and boots with leggings. The regimental number appears on the shoulder straps. The uniform is very similar to that worn by British field officers of the same period and was introduced in 1915 (the original officers' tunic had a stand collar). The arm of service is shown by the crown on the cap (surmounted by the Belgian national cockade) and the red collar patches with blue piping. The swagger stick and jodhpurs add a final British flourish to this typical Belgian colonel.

45 Sergeant, Belgian Army, 1940

This sergeant, identified by the diagonal silver bar on his sleeve, wears the 1915 model French Adrian steel helmet with the Belgian lion on the front. His arm of service (the infantry) is indicated by the colour of the collar patches and the crown on his shoulder straps. The regimental number is worn on the left sleeve, but this was often removed before going into action for security reasons. The spray of flowers, the petites cloches de Mai indicates that it is Labour Day: 1 May 1940. The rifle is a Belgian 7.65mm Mauser M1889, a copy of the more famous German model, a reliable bolt-action weapon which was used in both World Wars.

Below: Belgian soldiers take a rest by the roadside as a British lorry passes on 13 May 1940. The troops are carrying all the personal equipment they will need in action.

Antwerp and Liège, a cavalry corps in Brussels, an army artillery brigade in Antwerp, the Ardennes Rifle Corps in Namur, as well as three independent frontier bicycle battalions, six infantry divisions, and two cavalry divisions.

The army corps comprised a staff, two infantry divisions, one corps artillery regiment, and one pioneer regiment.

An infantry division had a staff, and three infantry regiments. Each regiment had 3000 men armed with Mauser M35 rifles. The support weapons of a regiment were:
108 light machine guns (Browning M30);
52 heavy machine guns (Maxim M08);
108 light mortars;
9 heavy mortars or infantry guns;
6 anti-tank guns.

The corps artillery regiment had four battalions each with two batteries. Transport was partly horsedrawn and partly motorised. The corps' guns were 16 Schneider 155mm M17 field howitzers, 8 Schneider 105mm M13 guns and 8 Cockerill 120mm M32 field guns.

Just before the war there was a rapid attempt to improve mobility and one of the two divisions in the Ardennes Rifle Corps and the two cavalry divisions received motor vehicles. The Motorised Cavalry Corps had a staff, two cavalry divisions, one corps artillery regiment

and a bicycle pioneer battalion. A cavalry division had three mixed regiments each with a battalion of cavalry, a battalion of motorcyclists, an armoured car squadron, and a training squadron.

UNIFORM During World War I, the Belgian Army adopted khaki uniforms mainly because Britain was the only country providing sufficient new uniforms to replace the obsolete coloured ones then in use.

The Belgian soldier of 1939, however, had a predominantly French appearance which was emphasised by the *Adrian* steel helmet and the habit of wearing the greatcoat skirts folded back. In complete contrast, the officers looked British, especially after 1935 when an open tunic for wear with collar and tie was introduced.

The Ardennes Rifles Corps wore a variation on this basic style: a green beret with boar's head badge, a shortened version of the greatcoat and long leather leggings. Mechanised troops received either a fibre helmet of Belgian design, or the French steel helmet for motorised troops, both of which were adorned in front with a lion's head. In addition mechanised troops received a leather jacket and breeches with long leggings, or a one-piece khaki overall.

INSIGNIA Rank distinctions appeared on the peaked cap, side cap, and on the collar patches and shoulder straps. Other ranks also wore their rank badges on the cuffs.

The primary means of identifying the arm of service was the colour of the collar patches and the collar patch piping. In addition there was an extensive range of yellow metal badges which appeared on the head-gear, collar patches and on the shoulder straps. Finally, a number of staff and administrative functions were identified by embroidered badges on the collar patches and also sometimes on the front of the peaked cap.

AIR FORCE

On 1 March 1920 an air force was formed as part of the Belgian Army. From its beginning until the outbreak of war the Air Force was plagued by a shortage of modern aircraft. While developing its own fighter (the Renard R-36), Belgium imported aircraft from England and the USA.

When the Germans invaded only 180 of the 234 aircraft were operational, and most of these were obsolete. All but one of the few modern Hurricanes were destroyed on the ground at Schaffen before the Belgian aircraft could disperse.

BELGIAN ARMY INSIGNIA

Peaked Cap Bands

Generals | Colonel (Artillery) | Senior Officers (Carabiniers) | Junior Officers (Engineers) | Warrant Officers (Light Regt)

Collar

Lieutenant-General | Major-General | Colonel (Artillery) | Colonel (Ardennes Rifles) | Lieutenant-Colonel (Grenadiers) | Major (Light Regt.) | Captain-Commandant (I) (Infantry) | Captain (II) (Frontier Cyclists) | Lieutenant (Transport) | 2nd Lieut (Carabiniers)

Collar / Cuff

W.O. 1st Class (I) (Mtd Chasseurs) | W.O. (II) (Cyclist Carabiniers) | Sergeant-Major | Senior Sergeant | Sergeant | Corporal | Private 1st Class | NCO's Collar Patch and Shoulder Strap (1st Infantry Reg) | Officer's Greatc't Collar and Shoulder Strap (Lt. Ardennes Rifles)

ORGANISATION In May 1940 the
Aéronautique Militaire was grouped to-
gether with the Observer Service and
Anti-Aircraft Artillery to form the Terri-
torial Air Defence (*Défense Aéronautique du
Territoire* or DAT).

The Belgian Air Force consisted of
three regiments: the 1st an observation
and Army co-operation unit; the 2nd a
fighter regiment, and the 3rd a reconnaissance and bombing regiment. In
addition there was one auxiliary regiment with ancillary and refuelling
companies.

The 1st Air Regiment comprised six
squadrons, with a total of 62 serviceable
machines. The 2nd air regiment also had
six squadrons and totalled 79 aircraft.
The 3rd Air Regiment totalled 41 aircraft
in four squadrons. Each flying squadron
had a complementary anti-aircraft
squadron (*Escadrille de Parc*).

UNIFORM There were two basic uniforms in the Air Force. The first was
that of the Army of which the Air Force
was a branch. The second was a blue-
grey air force uniform which was introduced for wear by the regular cadre of
flying personnel. This situation was
further complicated by the continued
wearing of regimental uniform by a
number of Air Force officers.

The blue-grey uniform is illustrated
by figure 46. In addition there was a
peaked cap with black band and black
peak and a double-breasted, blue-grey
greatcoat. More common than the
breeches and boots were long blue-grey
trousers with black shoes.

INSIGNIA Rank badges on the blue-
grey uniform were the same as those
worn on the khaki uniform.

The arm-of-service colour which
appeared on the collar patches of khaki
uniforms was bright blue with red piping.
Enamelled squadron badges were worn
on the right breast pocket.

NAVY

By the end of the 19th century, the
Belgian Navy had virtually ceased to
exist, and it was not until the end of
World War I that attempts were made to
re-form this tiny force. During the inter-war years this
tiny force was once again disbanded
because of lack of funds, and it was only
on 15 September 1939 that the *Marine
Korps* (later *Corps de Marine*) was again
established.

In November 1939 conscripts with
previous naval experience were transferred from the Army to the *Corps de
Marine* which then had a theoretical

46   47

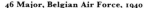

46 Major, Belgian Air Force, 1940
*As a pilot in the 2nd Air Regiment the major wears
the blue-grey service uniform of the regular flying
branch. All other officers in non-flying branches and
reserve pilots serving in the Army continued to wear
Army uniform. Rank badges appear on the collar
patches, 'wings' on the left sleeve, and the squadron
badge on the right breast pocket.*

47 Pilot, Belgian Air Force, 1940
*Typical of all flying clothing was the one-piece
overall which was issued in a number of different
colours, including white. The tartan silk scarf was
to protect the neck from chafing against the overall
collar when scanning the sky for enemy aircraft, and
the parachute is that of a fighter pilot.*

*Right: Belgian sailors in 1940. On the left is a
lieutenant (his rank shown by the two stars on the
greatcoat collar and the two bands on the cap) and
on the right a petty officer second class (recognisable
as such by the two bars on the cuff and the cap). The
seaman's cap is of the French pattern, with pompom
on the top and cord fastened around the cap rather
than under the chin. He is heavily laden, a sign
that the German victory was by now inevitable,
and he is about to be evacuated.*

strength of 30 officers (mainly Army reservists with merchant marine experience), 98 petty officers, and 513 petty officers second class and ratings. These were to provide the personnel for a headquarters and 1st Squadron at Ostende, 2nd Squadron at Zeebrugge, 3rd Squadron at Antwerp, and a replacement and training squadron.

Vessels consisted of small coastal craft armed with one 47mm gun and two machine guns, while other vessels were requisitioned from their civilian owners. Some large wooden trawlers were used as minesweepers. There were two coastal guns – one in Antwerp and the other in Zeebrugge – which were manned by Army crews.

During the German invasion, the Navy lost about a quarter of its personnel, while a number of survivors found their way to England. By May 1943 the Belgian section of the British Royal Navy had seven ships and about 350 men.

UNIFORM New regulations for Belgian Navy uniform were published in January 1940, and so any alterations to existing uniforms were only beginning to percolate through the Navy when Germany invaded.

The Belgian uniform followed the 'international' model, but also bore marked similarities to that of the French Navy. Officers and petty officers wore a peaked cap, reefer jacket with white shirt and black tie, long trousers with black shoes and a double-breasted greatcoat.

Quartermasters and ratings wore a blue cap with light blue woollen pompom on top and cap tally with *Marinekorps* in gold. The blue jumper had a blue denim collar edged with three white lines. The pea-coat was double-breasted with two rows of five brass buttons.

INSIGNIA Here the Belgian Navy departed from convention in two respects. Because the Naval Corps was basically a branch of the Army, officers and chief petty officers wore black collar patches piped in light blue on which they wore Army rank badges. Officers and chief petty officers also wore rank distinction lace on the peaked cap in the French manner. In 1940 the seaman's cap legend was changed to read just *Marine*.

BELGIAN AIR FORCE INSIGNIA

Cap Bands: Officers

Collar

| Lieutenant-General | Major-General | Colonel | Lieutenant-Colonel | Major | Captain Commandant (I) | Captain (II) | Lieutenant | 2nd Lieut |

Cuffs

Collar

| Warrant Officer 1st Class (I) | Warrant Officer (II) | Sergeant-Major | Senior Sergeant | Sergeant | Corporal | Private 1st Class | Pilot's Wings Officers (top) Non-officers (btm) |

BELGIAN NAVY INSIGNIA 1939

Officer's Cap (Lieut)   Warrant Officer's Cap   Other NCO's Cap   Seaman's and Quartermaster's Beret

MARINE KORPS

Cap Bands

Cuff

Collar

| Colonel | Lieutenant-Colonel | Major | Captain-Commandant (I) | Captain (II) | Lieutenant | 2nd Lieut | Warrant Officer | Petty Officer 1st Class (I) | Petty Officer 2nd Class (II) | Petty Officer 3rd Class (III) | Leading Seaman |

FRANCE
ARMY

France emerged from World War I with considerable military prestige, but the Army and indeed the whole nation were exhausted. After the experiences of World War I, there was considerable weight of opinion and political pressure behind the view that a strategy based upon a solid defensive line accorded best with the demands of modern warfare and the needs of the country. The result was the construction of the fortress complexes of the Maginot Line, which absorbed a great deal of the defence budget. The French military establishment had its critics, and there was a small but vociferous school of thought which condemned the reliance on static fortifications. The French Army, based on conscription, was of variable quality; reserve divisions especially were often considered a liability, and observers, including the British General Brooke, were shaken by their insubordination and slovenly appearance.

The French Army was mobilised on 1 September 1939: about 5,000,000 reservists were to be added to the standing army of 900,000 men. The *drôle de guerre* (Phoney War) and bitter winter, however, added to the low morale of the armed forces. On 10 May 1940 the German offensive began by outflanking the Maginot Line in an advance through the Ardennes region, a move totally unexpected by the Allies. Once knocked off balance France never recovered and despite brave and sometimes effective counter-attacks, German tactics, troop training, morale and much military equipment proved decisively superior. After a campaign lasting less than two months France was forced to sue for peace and an armistice was signed on 22 June 1940.

Under the terms of the armistice, in the unoccupied zone of France those forces that remained intact were rapidly demobilised except 100,000 men who were to maintain order (*l'armee de l'armistice*). The French fleet and colonial forces were to remain intact for the time being. Total casualties amounted to 290,000 men killed or wounded and 1,900,000 taken prisoner.

A large number of men had succeeded in escaping to the colonies, however, and many had been evacuated to England.

There was one redeeming feature in this massive defeat: the performance of the French forces on the Italian border, where 185,000 men (in three divisions and various garrison forces) under

Above: The crew of a French Char B1 tank pose for the camera above the 75mm gun which was the tank's main armament. They are wearing the typical helmets and leather clothing of armoured troops.

Below: A French soldier prepares to fire a Hotchkiss M1914 machine gun. This is a good close-up of the standard-pattern helmet. The letters 'RF' on the grenade stand for République française.

48 Major, French Army, 1940
The old-style closed tunic with badges of rank appearing on the front of the side cap (bonnet de police) and on the cuffs is worn here by a battalion commander. The arm-of-service colour and his corps number appear on the collar patches, while each regiment (here the 46th Infantry) also had a metal badge which was worn on the right breast pocket. As a field officer who traditionally rode a horse, he wears breeches and boots with spurs. The medal ribbons are for the Croix de Guerre 1914–1918 (red and green), and the Dardanelles campaign (white and green).

49 Private First Class, French Army, 1940
This artilleryman is wearing walking-out dress with a blue-black kepi and a tunic (the vareuse*) which came in a number of different patterns, with seven, six and finally five buttons. An alternative tunic in gabardine was designed for summer wear. In 1938 the old breeches were beginning to be replaced by knickerbockers for dismounted personnel. The gas mask is the ANP 1931 model. The artillery arm is identified by the colour of the kepi and collar patches on which the regimental number of the 182nd Artillery Regiment also appears. The badge on the left sleeve is as worn by armourers.*

50 Sergeant, French Army, 1940
This sergeant of motorised troops wears the protective clothing typical of the tank arm. He carries the padded M35 helmet under his arm, and is wearing the tank beret, which bore the tank badge (crossed cannon and a medieval helmet). The leather coat and trousers gathered at the ankles (pantalon cachou) were standard issue. His rank badge is on the jacket front, and his unit markings, on the collar (for the 2nd BCC), are green; grey was more normal.

General Olry completely halted the Italian attack of 20–25 June at a cost of 37 killed, 42 wounded and 150 missing.

ORGANISATION In May 1940, the French Army on the north-east front, which stretched from Switzerland to the North Sea, was divided into the 1st and 2nd Army Groups and the 7th Army. These forces comprised:

63 infantry divisions (of which 30 were regular);
7 motorised infantry divisions;
3 armoured divisions;
3 light mechanised divisions;
5 cavalry divisions;
13 fortress divisions.

The general reserve comprised a further 17 infantry, 2 motorised and 3 armoured divisions.

The backbone of the French Army was the infantry which, apart from increased firepower, was in organisation and training, very similar to that of World War I, and still relied on horse transport to a great extent. The basic French infantry division had provided a model for those of many other countries, and

consisted of a divisional headquarters, three infantry regiments, two artillery regiments, and a reconnaissance group of four squadrons: headquarters, motor-cycle, horse and weapons. The support elements of the division included two companies of engineers, a telegraph and a radio company, two baggage trains (one horsedrawn, one motorised), an artillery park and a medical group. The divisional anti-tank unit comprised a company of twelve 25mm anti-tank guns and a battery of 47mm guns, and was attached to one of the Infantry Regiments. The full complement of a division was 17,000 men and 500 officers.

Each regiment possessed a head-quarters company, a weapons company (six 25mm guns, two 81mm mortars and three gun carriers), a supply company and three infantry battalions making a total of about 3000 men and 80 officers armed with Ruby or Starr 7.65mm pistols and Lebel rifles of various models. The battalion comprised a headquarters section, three rifle companies (190 men divided into a headquarters and four rifle sections) and a machine-gun com-

pany made up of one gun section (two 25mm guns and two 81mm mortars) and four machine-gun sections each with four heavy (Hotchkiss M14) machine guns. The smallest unit in the Army was the group of 11 men equipped with a light (Châtellerault M24/29) machine gun; three groups making a rifle section. Total support weapons of a regiment comprised:

112 light machine guns;
48 heavy machine guns;
9 light mortars;
8 heavy mortars;
9 infantry and anti-tank guns.

In May 1940 France had over 3000 tanks, and in terms of numbers, quality and firepower they were generally superior to those employed by the Germans. Tactically, however, the French were definitely inferior, and with one or two exceptions the handling of this valuable force was uninspired and wasteful. The basic armoured unit was the tank battalion, comprising a staff, three tank companies and a reserve company (in all, some 45 to 60 tanks). There were 39 tank battalions in 1940 and for tactical

48

49

50

purposes they were twinned to form tank battalion groups. At the outbreak of war only five battalions had received the latest tanks (the D-2 and B-1 models) while the rest still retained a variety of modern and semi-obsolete types. In addition to the battalion groups there were also 11 independent tank companies.

Between January and May 1940, four reserve armoured divisions were formed and placed at the disposal of the General Headquarters. Each division was formed from a *demi-brigade* (two battalions) of Char B tanks, two battalions of Hotchkiss light tanks, a battalion of motorised rifles, a regiment of tractor-drawn artillery (two groups of 105mm guns), and engineer, aviation and service units. These divisions absorbed a number of the above-mentioned tank battalions and companies.

Armoured fighting vehicles were also to be found in the cavalry divisions undergoing mechanisation, in five light cavalry divisions which were also still not completely mechanised, and in the reconnaissance groups. All these formations combined horsed cavalry, motorcycle troops, armoured cars, tanks, and infantry mounted in cross-country vehicles. Finally there were the three light mechanised divisions each of which had two regiments of tanks, a squadron of armoured cars and motorcycles and a regiment of motorised infantry (*Dragons portés*). However, it should be pointed out that not all of these formations had received all their equipment by May 1940, and many were still being formed.

French cavalry, although in the process of motorisation, still represented a large mounted force. Apart from the cavalry in the mechanised brigades and light mechanised divisions, there were also regiments of *Cuirassiers, Dragons, Dragons portés, Chasseurs à Cheval* and *Hussards*. In May 1940 the three remaining cavalry divisions were partially motorised and formed into light mechanised divisions and light cavalry divisions.

Troops from Algeria, Morocco and Tunisia counted as part of the metropolitan army, and North Africans made a large contribution to the French Army. The 12 North African infantry divisions were each composed of three infantry regiments and one artillery regiment. They included regiments of the French Foreign Legion, *zouaves*, and Moroccan, Algerian and Tunisian *tirailleurs* (light infantry).

Three Brigades of *spahis* from Algeria and Morocco fought with distinction before retreating to the unoccupied zone of France. A *spahi* brigade had a strength of some 80 officers, 2200 other ranks (of whom 930 were French), 2000 horses and 150 motor vehicles.

French colonial troops came under the control of a special directorate of the Ministry of War, and were stationed partly in the colonies and partly in France. Their commandant had the status of regional commander and was appointed Senior Commandant of Colonial Troops in France. The designation of formations as 'colonial' meant either that it had been raised in France to serve in the colonies, or that it was composed of native troops from the French Empire.

In May 1940 there were nine divisions of colonial infantry, while in the 102nd Fortress Division there was a *demi-brigade* each of Indochinese and Malagasy machine gunners helping to man the Maginot Line. In addition a number of metropolitan divisions had been brought up to strength by the addition of non-metropolitan regiments.

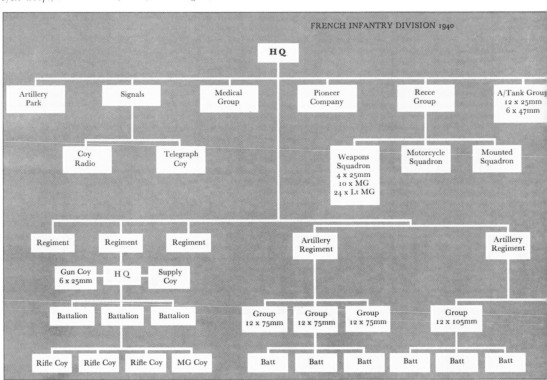

FRENCH INFANTRY DIVISION 1940

UNIFORM Twenty years after its introduction, the old 'horizon blue' gave way to khaki when in 1935 this became the standard colour of French Army uniforms. Previously only the colonial and African troops had worn khaki. In the years leading up to World War II, a number of modifications to existing uniforms were made, and completely new items of clothing and equipment were introduced, but these had not reached all troops by the summer of 1940.

Officers either continued to wear the old closed tunic, or the new open pattern illustrated by figure 52. In the field, generals wore a plain khaki kepi with metal rank stars on the front. The greatcoat was single-breasted, with five or six buttons in front and low fall collar with pronounced points, and turnback greatcoat was single breasted, with five cuffs. In undress uniforms officers could wear long khaki trousers with brown piping and stripes.

The basic field uniform for other ranks is illustrated by figure 51. Other forms of head-dress were the khaki side cap and the khaki beret for fortress troops. One of the main variations on the field

51

52

51 Corporal, French Army, 1940

This corporal of the 24th Infantry Regiment wears the 1926 model of the Adrian helmet (which had its shell stamped from one piece of manganese steel), the 1938 model single-breasted greatcoat, and the ANP 1931 model gas mask. The rest of his equipment, including the Lebel ammunition pouches, waterbottle, haversack and pack are the standard issue originally introduced in World War I. The carbine is the 8mm mousqueton M92/16. This carbine was not a very good weapon, with its difficult bolt action and a tendency to jam.

52 Lieutenant-General, French Army, 1940

This divisional general wears service dress with the new open tunic which replaced the closed model worn by the infantry officer, figure 48. On active service generals usually wore a plain khaki kepi with metal stars on the front according to rank. Rank is identified by the embroidery and braid on the kepi and the stars on the cuffs. All officers, including generals, were entitled to wear five different types of uniform, and the kepi was worn with all except the field clothing.

Left: One of the North Africans serving in France – a Moroccan tirailleur with an impressive array of medals and decorations.

uniform was worn by mounted personnel in cavalry, horse artillery and horse-drawn supply trains. They received a single-breasted greatcoat and riding breeches, while their footwear consisted of ankle boots, spurs and leggings.

Rifles (*chasseurs à pied*) and mountain rifles (*chasseurs alpins*) wore a distinctive dark-blue uniform, although they retained the khaki infantry greatcoat for winter field wear. The head-dress was a dark blue beret.

The winter of 1939–1940 was particularly severe and the French soldier found his uniform inadequate for the temperature which sometimes reached minus 20 degrees centigrade. Winter clothing had to be improvised by the unit or individual and consisted in the main of additional underwear and pullovers. The most common forms of external winter clothing were sleeveless sheepskin coats and gauntlets, rubber boots, and winter camouflage dress.

Members of motorised and armoured formations received the standard uniform but when on duty with their vehicles they wore a special helmet or a black beret, and either the obsolete double-breasted black leather coat or the new single-breasted brown model. Over khaki trousers and puttees they wore khaki drill trousers which fastened around the ankle. In warm weather tank crews usually wore their two-piece working overalls. Motorcycle troops also wore the motorised troops' helmet and a leather coat, or the new 1938 model double-breasted cotton duck jacket, or a waterproof canvas raincoat.

The colonial and African troops serving in France during the 1940 campaign wore standard French Army uniform with certain distinctive features; the Foreign Legion, for example, had the right to wear the white kepi (although it was seldom worn in action) while the *zouaves*, *tirailleurs* and *spahis* wore *chechias* or turbans of different colours. In addition, the Foreign Legion and the *zouaves* wore a blue sash, *tirailleurs* a red sash, and *spahis* a white and red burnous.

INSIGNIA Officers' rank was denoted by the insignia on the sleeves of the tunic and greatcoat and on the kepi and forage cap. On the coat and other over-garments rank insignia was shown by a series of stripes on tabs which were affixed to a coat button. Officers of general rank had gold oak leaves embroidered on the kepi while other officers wore gold and silver lace on the kepi to denote rank. The regimental badge or number was shown on the front of the kepi.

Insignia for warrant officers and NCOs was worn as chevrons and stripes on the arm. Ranks from corporal upwards were entitled to wear a gold or silver chin-strap on the kepi. The colour of the chevrons and numerals and the colour of the collar patch itself identified the unit of the wearer. Infantry and tank troops, for example, had khaki patches; but while infantry had blue chevrons and red numerals, the tank troops usually had grey chevrons and numerals. Artillery had red collar patches with blue chevrons.

AIR FORCE

The French Air Force (*Armée de l'Air*) was formed as an independent service on 1 April 1933. Head of the service was the Air Minister who was also president of the Supreme Air Council which dealt with organisation, co-operation with land and sea forces, supply, training, tactics and equipment.

The air defence of France and her overseas Empire was the responsibility of five Air Regions (Dijon, Paris, Tours,

53

Aix-en-Provence and North Africa) each of which was sub-divided into two Air Districts. The largest flying formations were the air divisions and independent brigades. An air division had two or three brigades each with two or three squadrons. Frontline strength on the eve of World War II was 1200 fighters, 1300 bombers and 800 reconnaissance aircraft, and in August 1939 there were 110,000 personnel of all ranks, a figure which had risen to 150,000 by March 1940.

The Air Force had suffered considerable neglect between the wars, and its performance in 1940, with machines which were in general much inferior to those of the enemy, was not impressive. Indeed, according to French sources, only 420 modern fighters and 31 heavy bombers were serviceable when the Germans struck in May.

Anti-aircraft artillery, except that forming part of the field army, came under the commander of anti-aircraft

Left: French aircrew about to leave on a mission. They are wearing full leather protective clothing, helmets and gauntlets.

artillery in the Air Ministry. On mobilisation a reorganisation took place which divided the anti-aircraft defence of France into the interior and coastal regions. The latter came under the control of the Naval Minister, while the former was organised into five battalions each with three batteries of 75mm guns and a sixth battalion equipped with searchlights. In wartime anti-aircraft artillery also assumed responsibility for barrage balloons.

UNIFORM In July 1934 the Air Force adopted a dark 'Louise-blue' uniform whose origin was to be found in the dark blue uniform worn by the army engineers who had pioneered military aviation before World War I.

The service dress for officers and regular NCOs is illustrated by figure 55. A double-breasted greatcoat with two rows of three gilt metal buttons was often worn over this. Other ranks had a dark steel-grey blouse with a round fall collar which was worn closed but left exposed a blue shirt and black tie. It was worn with matching long trousers

53 Private, French Army, 1940
The French and Polish mountain troops who fought as part of the Allied Expeditionary Force in Norway were dressed and equipped as the figure shown here. This chasseur alpin of the French 5th demibrigade wears the blue chasseur beret and waterproof cotton duck anorak, but for additional warmth he has been issued with a sheepskin jacket which is carried rolled on the rucksack. Armament consists of a pistol and a 7.5mm MAS 36 carbine. Gaiters and skis were standard issue for French mountain troops, although in fact these soldiers had little opportunity to use their skis during the fighting in Norway. Mountain troops of all nations during the war tended to carry more equipment than the average infantryman and this somewhat overburdened figure is no exception.

54 Pilot, French Air Force, 1940
This pilot of a Potez 63/II reconnaissance aircraft wears the standard padded chrome leather flying helmet, one-piece overall, and Chanole parachute with a quick release harness.

55 Sergeant-Major, French Air Force, 1940
Sergeant Duval, air gunner in the GAO (groupe aerienne d'observation) 502, wears the 'Louise-blue' Air Force service dress with badges of rank on the cap and cuffs. The wings on the right breast were worn by all flying personnel, whereas the metal badge on the right breast was worn only by crews of aeroplanes and airships. The badge on the left breast pocket flap is a squadron emblem. This non-commissioned officer wears medal ribbons for the Médaille Militaire (yellow and green), an award for soldiers who had distinguished themselves in war, and the Croix de Guerre (red and green).

54   55

FRENCH ARMY INSIGNIA

Marshal of France
General (I) (Army Commander)
General (II) (Army Corps)
Lieutenant-General (Division)
Major-General (Brigade)
Colonel
Lieutenant-Colonel (Tanks)
Major (Saharan Companies)
Captain (Dragoons)
Lieutenant (Moroccan Spahis)
2nd Lieut. (Foreign Legion)

Chief Warrant Officer (I)
Warrant Officer (II)
Sergeant-Major
Sergeant (Regulars)
Sergeant
Corporal-Major
Corporal
Private 1st Class
Corporal-Major (Tanks)
Corporal (Cavalry)
Pte 1st Cl (Moroccan Rifles)

Sergeant-Major
Sergeant (Regulars)
Sergeant

FRENCH AIR FORCE INSIGNIA

Cap Badges

General (Air Army Commander)
General (Air Corps Commander)
Lieutenant-General (Air Division)
Major-General (Air Brigade)
Colonel
Lieutenant-Colonel
Major
Captain
Lieutenant
2nd Lieutenant

Cap Badges

Chief Warrant Officer (I)
Warrant Officer (II)
Sergeant-Major (Field Uniform)
Sergeant-Major
Sergeant (Regular)
Sergeant
Corporal-Major
Corporal
Private 1st Class
Observer's Badge

and a 'horizon-blue' greatcoat. This obsolete infantry greatcoat began to be replaced in 1937 by the cavalry pattern coat but in 'Louise blue'.

Head-dress consisted of a peaked cap with white cover for summer wear, a black beret for everyday and working wear, and the two patterns of French Army steel helmet (the *Adrian* model of the infantry and the version worn by motorised troops).

The standard canvas flying suit is illustrated in figure 54, but many pilots of single-seater aircraft wore a double-breasted leather jacket.

INSIGNIA Rank was indicated by the embroidery or rank distinction lace on the peaked cap and on the cuffs of officers and warrant officers. On the working cap the rank distinction lace was restricted to an oval patch on the front of the cap, rather than around the circumference of the cap band. Other ranks also wore their rank badges on their head-dress and cuffs. On flying clothing and working dress, rank distinction lace was worn on a cloth patch which was buttoned to the front of the garment.

For arm-of-service distinction, certain branches and sometimes units themselves were identified by an emblem or number which was incorporated in the winged badge which was worn on the front of the peaked cap and on the right breast. Other ranks wore their branch colour in the form of chevrons on the collar patches, while the formation number or emblem was embroidered in orange for other ranks or gold for NCOs.

Pilots of aircraft and balloons and cadet pilots, mechanics and observers wore a distinctive circular white metal badge on the right breast pocket.

NAVY

The Ministry of National Defence co-ordinated the activities of the three ministries representing the armed forces. The most important office of the Ministry of Marine was the Chief of the Admiralty, Vice-Admiral F. X. Darlan. He controlled all operations at sea and was also responsible for coastal defence. His immediate subordinates were the squadron and base commanders.

In January 1937 France began a programme of modernisation and expansion which elevated the French Fleet to fourth largest in the world, although it was considerably smaller than that of her ally, Great Britain.

On 23 August 1939 Navy reservists were called up, anti-aircraft defences manned, and liaison officers were ex-

changed with the Royal Navy. By 1 September 1939 the strength of the French Navy was 160,000 personnel of all ranks.

The deployment of the French Navy on the outbreak of war was as follows:
Indo-China: 2 cruisers, 5 destroyers, 2 submarines, and a number of sloops and river gunboats;
Casablanca: 2 destroyers and 4 submarines to cover the routes between France, Dakar and the West Indies;
Channel: 7 destroyers, plus the equivalent of an Army division for coastal defence;
Bay of Biscay: 3 destroyers;
Mediterranean: In agreement with the British Admiralty the strongest concentration of French vessels was in the Mediterranean where the powerful Italian fleet posed a threat to the vitally important sea routes from France to North Africa and the British routes via the Suez Canal to Gibraltar. The Mediterranean Squadron was commanded by Vice-Admiral R. E. Godfroy and was based at Toulon and Mers-el-Kébir. It comprised 3 battleships, 1 sea-plane carrier, 10 cruisers, 48 destroyers and 53 submarines. The submarine strength reflected France's emphasis on underwater warfare both for fleet work and for the destruction of commercial vessels. The giant *Surcouf* was actually officially designated a 'corsair' submarine;
Atlantic: established at Brest was an independent *Force de Raid* under Vice-Admiral M. B. Gensoul. It was to operate against German surface warships which might try and break out into the Atlantic and was composed of 2 battlecruisers, 1 aircraft carrier, 3 cruisers and 10 destroyers. By concentrating their most modern warships – specially designed to counter the latest enemy vessels – the French Navy had produced the first task force of World War II.

The early war strength of the Fleet Air Arm (*Aéronavale*) was four squadrons of dive-bombers, two of seaplanes and one of flying boats. They were all intended to be shipborne, although the employment of the two rather slow carriers on ferrying duties meant that the aircraft had to be shore-based, apart from those planes mounted on capital ship and cruiser catapults. In 1939, naval aircraft strength was 350 planes.

The Battle of France was fought and lost on land, but the French Navy proved itself a brave and capable force during the combined operations in Norway and during the evacuation of Allied forces from France. As the German Army approached the Channel coast French ships were ordered to leave the

56

56 Petty officer, French Navy, 1940

Shown here is summer parade dress as worn by a petty officer, second class. He is wearing the white cap cover and white trousers; his status as a petty officer is shown by the officers' uniform and the two diagonal yellow stripes on the sleeve (these were sewn to the uniform, whereas on white summer working dress, they were often detachable). He wears a fourragère of the Croix de Guerre on his left shoulder, and the badge of a master gunner or machine gunner on his left sleeve. His medal ribbon is the Medaille d'Orient, awarded to troops who had fought in the French Army of the East during World War I. The rifle, infantry equipment and gaiters were worn by ratings and petty officers with full dress uniform. The rifle is the M92/16 carbine a widely-used although unpopular weapon.

Channel and Biscay ports. Some set sail for England, while the majority headed for the Mediterranean ports of Oran and Mers-el-Kébir, others to Alexandria and some to Dakar in French West Africa.

According to the terms of the Armistice of 22 June, the new (Vichy) French government could retain its warships (which had not been defeated at sea), provided they placed themselves under German or Italian control. This meant in harbours within the Axis sphere of influence rather than under Axis control. Accordingly some 70 to 80 seagoing capital ships, cruisers, destroyers and submarines were berthed at Toulon under Admiral Jean de Laborde (Commander-in-Chief of the French Navy). Most of these ships were scuttled on 27 November 1942.

Meanwhile, following the Armistice, there were two French battleships, ten destroyers, 12 sloops, seven submarines and a number of smaller vessels sheltering in Plymouth, Falmouth, Portsmouth and Sheerness.

At dawn on 3 July 1940, in Operation 'Catapult', British boarding parties wearing carpet slippers stole on board the French ships in British ports and disarmed the surprised French crews, but not without bloodshed.

On 3 July the French Fleet lying in Mers-el-Kébir received the British ultimatum to place itself at the disposal of the British and continue the war against Germany and Italy, agree to be disarmed under British supervision, sink itself, or be sunk. Bad communications with the newly-established Pétain government and the unyielding atmosphere of the

57 Leading Seaman, French Navy, 1940
This leading seaman presenting arms wears parade dress: the standard 'square rig' cap with distinctive red pompom, striped vest and blue collar. (In fact, sailors were often called 'blue collars'.) The cap legend is Maritime Nationale. *White gaiters were only worn with parade dress. The carbine (a modified 8mm Mg2/16) has an Mg2 knife bayonet.*

58 Lieutenant, French Navy, 1940
Lieutenant H. L. G. Rousselot of the submarine Rubis *wears the standard French naval officer's uniform. Rank is indicated by the lace rings on the cap and cuffs. The embroidered passants on the shoulders were originally intended to hold the full-dress epaulettes, but in fact they were never worn on the reefer jacket.*

Left: French ratings on board the Jaguar, *the flagship of the 2nd Torpedo Flotilla, in Gravesend in 1939. They are wearing working rig of natural coloured cotton drill.*

negotiations led to the understandable French rejection of British demands. At 5.54 pm the British Fleet opened fire and in sixteen minutes three French capital ships had been disabled while one capital ship and a number of smaller vessels managed to slip away to Toulon. In this and a subsequent attack the French lost 1297 killed and 351 wounded. At Alexandria, the French agreed to disarm their ships and no lives were lost.

It is now clear that the French had no intention of letting their Fleet fall into German hands, and all British policy succeeded in doing was antagonising the bulk of the French Navy, which resulted in the refusal of most of the French sailors in England to join the FNFL (Free French Naval Forces), and the strengthening of the Vichy French resolve to resist the anti-German Free French landings in Dakar two months later. Ironically the Vichy government continued to pay allowances to the relatives of men serving with the FNFL.

UNIFORM The French Navy uniform of World War II was the result of regulations issued in 1922 (for petty officers) and 1931 (for officers) although the traditional 'square-rig' for ratings originated in 1858.

Service dress for officers is illustrated by figure 58. The greatcoat was double-breasted with two rows of five buttons in front. There was also a double-breasted raincoat which was worn without insignia.

Officers could wear the blue reefer jacket with cap with white cover, white trousers and white canvas shoes, or they could wear the special white summer jacket. There was also a khaki drill uniform for wear on duty in hot climates.

Warrant officers (*officiers mariniers*) and petty officers wore officers' uniform as a full-dress or for walking-out, but on board they usually wore a blue linen working jacket.

Ratings wore the uniform illustrated by figure 57, over which they could wear the double-breasted pea-coat in cold weather. Working dress was either blue or undyed denim, and for summer and wear in hot climates there was a white version of the 'square-rig', or a special white uniform with shorts and sun helmet. There was no special corps of marines, and so sailors serving on land or in disembarkation companies were issued with the Army-pattern steel helmet and navy-blue greatcoat, infantry equipment, and canvas leggings.

INSIGNIA Officers, warrant officers, petty officers and all other ranks entitled to officers' uniform wore their badges of rank on the peaked cap, shoulder straps and cuffs. Ratings wore their badges of rank on the cuffs of the jumper, pea-coat and greatcoat.

Arm-of-service colours appeared on the cuffs and as 'lights' between the rank distinction lace on the cuffs and shoulder straps. Specialist badges were nearly always worn on the upper left sleeve, and on the pea-coat and greatcoat collar.

FRENCH NAVY INSIGNIA

Cap Badges

Shoulder / Cuff

Vice-Adml (Chief of Staff) — Vice-Adml (in Command of Forces) — Vice-Admiral — Rear-Admiral — Captain — Commander — Lieutenant-Commander — Lieutenant — Lieutenant (Junior) — Sub-Lieutenant — Midshipman

Tropical Uniforms

Chief Warrant Officer — Warrant Officer — Chief Petty Officer — Petty Officer (I) — Petty Officer (II) — Leading Seaman — Leading Seaman (II) — Able Seaman — Seaman (Graduate P.O School) — Quarter-master (fourrier) — Upper rt sleeve (Non-P.O.s)

Cap Badge P.O.s — Cap Badge Non-P.O.s — Leading Seaman — Leading Seaman — Able Seaman — Greatcoat Collar (Non-P.O.s)

ARMED FORCES
IN EXILE,
FRANCE 1939–40

POLISH ARMY

Many Polish soldiers, singly or in small groups, had evaded capture or escaped internment after the defeat in 1939, and made their way to France through the Baltic countries in the north, and through Hungary, Romania, Yugoslavia and Italy in the south. The formation of a Polish Army in France had begun in November, 1939, and a large camp was set aside for the Poles in Coetquidan in Brittany. Polish volunteers arrived in a steady stream until they filled camps in no less than three French *départements*.

Gradually an army began to take shape. It was to comprise a headquarters, training establishments, two infantry divisions with a further two in the process of formation, an independent Highland Brigade, and an armoured cavalry brigade: a total strength of some 72,000 men. When the German invasion took place, the Polish Army was only half ready. The 3rd and 4th Infantry Divisions were called upon to provide 12 anti-tank companies to reinforce French divisions, while the 10th Armoured Cavalry Brigade, after only a few days in which to get used to its new equipment was split into two, and a combat group was sent straight into action. The Independent Highland Brigade which had been modelled on the French *chasseurs alpins* – although few of its men knew much about mountains – was shipped off to Norway. In France the 1st Grenadier and 2nd Rifle Divisions sustained heavy casualties before being driven across the border into Switzerland and internment.

From a total of 83,000 men serving in the Polish Forces abroad on 15 June 1940, 24,000 were evacuated to England where they joined 3700 Poles already serving with the Royal Navy and the Royal Air Force, 5000 were in the Middle East, and 50,000 were casualties, prisoners of war, or internees.

ORGANISATION The 1st Grenadier Division and the 2nd Rifle Division had three infantry regiments each, a regiment of field and a regiment of medium artillery, an engineer battalion, pioneer company, reconnaissance unit, signals battalion, radio telegraph company, divisional anti-tank company, two transport companies, a platoon of military police and various services: a total of 16,000 men in each division. The 3rd and 4th Infantry Divisions had only two infantry regiments, although it was planned to add a third at some later date.

The Independent Highland Brigade consisted of two demi-brigades of two battalions each with three rifle and one support company armed with rifles and pistols, supported by fifteen 60mm and fifteen 81mm mortars and 25 anti-tank guns. Its strength was 182 officers, 45 officer cadets (*aspirants*), 742 NCOs and 3809 other ranks.

The 10th Armoured Brigade had been formed from troops of the former Polish Armoured Brigade which, following the Polish defeat, had been interned in Hungary. The men had then filtered through to France in small groups. By June 1940 its strength was 3323 all ranks. It was organised as a tank regiment of two battalions with a total of 90 R-35 tanks, a motorised cavalry regiment of two battalions, an artillery battery of two troops of 105mm guns, and an anti-tank gun troop with 25mm guns, a signals squadron, engineer company and services. In addition there was a detached 'Combat Group' which consisted of 102 officers and 1607 other ranks.

UNIFORM Polish troops in France at first received obsolete French 'horizon-blue' uniforms left over from World War I, but these were gradually replaced by the standard khaki pattern. Those officers who still possessed pre-1939 Polish uniforms tended to wear them off duty. The standard uniform for officers was a side cap, an open single-breasted khaki tunic with khaki shirt and tie, and matching breeches with either brown lace-up boots or high black boots. Equipment was in brown leather, as for French officers.

Other ranks also received a standard khaki field uniform and the Highland Brigade which was sent to Norway was issued with additional mountain troop clothing and equipment. Other forms of head-dress for other ranks were a khaki beret for mountain troops, black beret for armoured troops and the two patterns of the French steel helmet on the front of which were painted the Polish eagle in white.

INSIGNIA Rank badges appeared on the side cap and beret and on the shoulder straps for all ranks. Cloth collar patches in arm-of-service or regimental colours appear to have been rarely worn by anybody other than commissioned officers.

59

**59 Sergeant,
Polish Army, France 1940**

This sergeant waiting to embark at Brest for Norway wears the new pattern French Army uniform complete with knickerbockers (pantalons golfs). Polish rank badges are worn on the shoulder straps, and the Polish national emblem is painted on the front of the 1926-model steel helmet. The leather equipment is of World War I pattern while the rifle is the French Lebel M86/93.

POLISH AIR FORCE

The crews of the 84 Polish aircraft which had been evacuated to Romania in October 1939 were interned, but one by one they managed to reach France, where, by April 1940, 8678 Polish airmen assembled. This number represented almost the complete trained flying and ground personnel of the pre-war Polish Air Force.

Despite shortages of equipment and machines and poor morale it was decided to form one fighter group and one bomber group. On 4 January 1940 the Franco-Polish Air Agreement was concluded: this recommended the formation of two fighter groups, a reconnaissance group and a personnel pool. On 22 February 1940 General Sikorski, Commander-in-Chief of Polish Forces, detached the Air Force from Army control and made it an independent branch of the armed forces. When the Germans invaded France in May 1940 only the Polish fighter groups had become operational, while the other formations were being equipped and undergoing training.

On 19 June General Sikorski appealed to his Polish troops to make their way to England where Polish forces would again be re-formed. Some pilots flew their aircraft to England, while others escaped by ship. By July 1940 some 550 Polish airmen had reached England. During the fighting in France Polish airmen claimed 56 enemy aircraft destroyed for the loss of 11 pilots and 40 aircraft.

UNIFORM Polish Air Force personnel were (after a delay) equipped with the 'Louise-blue' uniform of the French Air Force. On their head-dress (peaked cap or beret) they wore the Polish eagle and their badges of rank. Polish qualification, school, establishment and regimental badges were worn on the French uniform, and rank badges were attached to the shoulder straps.

CZECHOSLOVAK ARMY

Before 1938, the 1,500,000 strong Czech Army was one of the largest in Europe. After the Munich Agreement, Czech soldiers began to leave their homeland, and the first Czech units abroad were formed in Poland. The nucleus of a Czech Army was constituted from about 1000 soldiers and 150 airmen, but it was not long before Poland herself was crushed, and the Czechs were forced to leave Poland; some travelling to the Soviet Union, some to the Middle East and some to France.

At first, the French had insisted that all Czechs serve in the French Foreign Legion, but after France's own entry into the war an agreement was negotiated by the Czech National Committee in Paris to cancel the Foreign Legion obligation.

At the Foreign Legion base at Agde in southern France, the Czechs were formed into the 1st Czech Division, made up of the 1st and 2nd Infantry Regiments. The organisation, equipment and armaments were French, although many of the weapons were leftovers from World War I. During the Battle of France the 1st Regiment (at Coulommiers) and the 2nd (on the Marne) tried to halt the 16th Panzer Division, but had their flanks

Above: Polish pilots wearing French leather equipment, but with Polish badges on the front of their peaked caps.

Below: Polish troops in French uniforms at a camp in England in 1940. They bear the Polish eagle on the French Adrian helmet.

Right: Czech and French airmen in 1940, soon after their evacuation to the United Kingdom. The Czechs are wearing French Air Force uniform with Czech caps and rank badges, and both Czech and French wings on the right breast. The French officer in the right foreground wears French wings, a French formation sign on his left breast and a French cap badge, whereas the man on the far left wears the Czech pilot's badge on his right breast.

60 Lance-Sergeant, Czechoslovak Army, France 1940

This sergeant of the 1st Infantry Regiment wears French Army uniform with Czech badges of rank on the shoulder straps. Both the tunic (vareuse) and knickerbockers are of the new pattern. He is equipped with a French World War I helmet and an 8mm M1892 revolver.

61 Staff-Captain, Czechoslovak Air Force, France 1940

On the French 'Louise-blue' uniform this Czech pilot wears a Czech cap badge and Czech rank insignia on the shoulder straps. On his left breast pocket is the Czech pilots' badge; on the right the French aircraft pilots' badge with French aviation wings above. The medal ribbon indicates an award of the Croix de Guerre for World War II.

60

61

turned and had to fight a rearguard action back across France: they were eventually re-grouped at Narbonne before being evacuated from Selte.

UNIFORM AND INSIGNIA The Czech soldiers serving in Czech units with the French Army wore French Army uniform with Czech badges of rank on the shoulder straps. Graduates of the Officers' Academy wore their graduation badge on the right breast pocket.

CZECHOSLOVAK AIR FORCE

A number of Czech airmen made their way to France, but it was not until France declared war on Germany that it was agreed that the Czechs should serve in the French Air Force. They were distributed between 15 squadrons of fighter and bomber aircraft. On 1 June 1940 a treaty was signed establishing Czech Air Force units to operate in conjunction with the Czech Army in France, and two Czech squadrons began formation. After the fall of France, the airmen were evacuated to Britain.

UNIFORM AND INSIGNIA The Czech airmen with the French Air Force wore the French 'Louise-blue' uniform with a Czech cap badge, rank insignia on the shoulder straps and various flying badges of the former Czech Air Force on the left or right breast pocket.

GREAT BRITAIN

ARMY

On 2 September 1939, the day before England declared war on Germany, a small military advance party was flown to France, and soon after this the British Expeditionary Force began crossing the Channel. By 27 September, 152,031 soldiers, 21,424 vehicles and all the necessary weapons and stores had arrived in France.

A general headquarters was established near Arras while the British I Corps (1st and 2nd Divisions) took their places in the line along the Franco-Belgian frontier east of Lille. As agreed between the British and French governments the BEF came under overall command of the French Commander-in-Chief of the North East Theatre of Operations (General Georges), but the British commander, General Gort, reserved the right to appeal to the British Government if he thought any order given to him might imperil the BEF.

For the next six months little military action took place except a minor, half-hearted French offensive in the Saar region. The BEF trained, consolidated its position, and built up its depots and dumps. From November, by arrangement with the French, one British division at a time served for a short spell under French command on the Saar front to get experience. By the end of April 1940, the strength of the BEF was 394,165 men.

When war did begin in earnest on 10 May 1940 the small British contingent was unable to stem the rapid German advance: within two weeks the BEF was forced back towards the Channel coast and Operation 'Dynamo' – the evacuation from Dunkirk – was put into effect. Largely through the efforts of the French Army in holding back German forces (as well as Hitler's controversial order to halt the Panzers outside Dunkirk) 224,320 British (including 15,850 wounded) and 141,842 Allied soldiers were evacuated. Although Dunkirk was the last act of a major British defeat, the escape from France of over a third of a million trained soldiers was a great achievement and a considerable boost to sagging British morale.

3457 members of the BEF were killed during the campaign in France, and although the British role in the fighting was only a minor one many German soldiers had been impressed by the disciplined performance of the British troops. Adolf Hitler, made this comment on the British Army:

The British soldier has retained the characteristics which he had in World War I. Very brave and tenacious in defence, unskilful in attack, wretchedly commanded. Weapons and equipment are of the highest order, but the overall organisation is bad.

ORGANISATION The King, with the rank of Field Marshal, was the titular head of the Army but actual control of Britain's military strength was exercised by the Army Council, a body established in February 1904. The Council had both civil and military members under its president the Secretary of State for War. The members, whose task was collectively to advise the Secretary of State, were the Parliamentary Under-Secretary, the Financial Secretary of the War Office, the Chief of the Imperial General Staff, the Adjutant-General to the Forces, the Quarter-Master General to the Forces, and one Civil Service member, the Permanent Under-Secretary of State

62 Captain, British Army, 1940

Shown here is a captain of the Grenadier Guards in the BEF. Officers of the five regiments of Foot Guards retained a number of regimental distinctions on their khaki service dress. For instance, instead of the standard 'pips' which denoted rank, the Guards used a system either of miniature stars of the Orders of the Garter (Grenadiers, Coldstream and Welsh Guards), Thistle (Scots Guards) or Shamrock (Irish Guards). This captain still wears the old-fashioned service dress which had largely been replaced by battledress in 1940. The combined belt, cross strap and sword frog was called a 'Sam Browne' after its inventor. The medal ribbon is the British War Medal 1914–1920.

63 Sergeant, British Army, 1940

This Welsh Guards sergeant wears the old khaki service dress with knickerbockers and long puttees, which was in the process of being replaced by the battledress at the beginning of the war. Over the jacket he wears a leather jerkin lined with thick khaki cloth. This item had first been worn during World War I and had proved both popular and practical. The equipment is the 1937 pattern web equipment with the gas mask (on chest) in the 'ready' position. The rifle is the .303 rifle No. 1 SMLE (Short Magazine Lee Enfield), Mk 3.

62

63

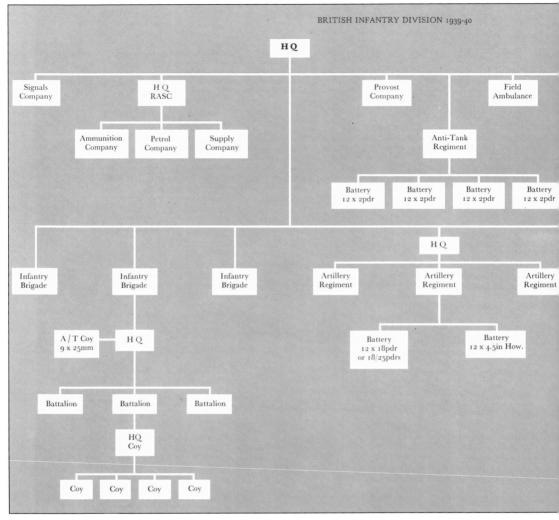

BRITISH INFANTRY DIVISION 1939-40

for War. In addition to their collective responsibility the members of the Army Council were also responsible individually for the operation of their respective departments within the War Office. The Department of the Chief of the Imperial General Staff, for example, contained the Directorates of Military Operations, Military Intelligence, and Military Training, while the Adjutant-General's Department housed the Directorates of Recruiting and Organisation, Mobilisation, and Personal Services. The Chief of the Imperial General Staff as the senior military officer represented the Army on the Chiefs of Staff Committee which reported to the three Service Ministers

and the Defence Committee.

In 1939 the regular British Army had a strength of 227,000 men, inclusive of British troops in India and Burma, and was organised in:
2 regiments of the Household Cavalry;
20 regiments of cavalry of the line;
5 regiments of foot guards;
64 regiments of infantry of the line;
the Royal Artillery;
the Royal Tank Regiment;
auxiliary units and services.

This force was supported by the Territorial Army which had a strength of 204,000 officers and men organised in a field force of nine infantry divisions, one mobile division, two cavalry brigades,

and an anti-aircraft corps of five divisions. During 1939, there was a massive increase in the size of the Territorial Army as it was put on a war footing and by August it numbered 428,000 men. This rapid growth was the result of a surge in volunteer recruitment, the recall of reservists and the imposition in May of compulsory service.

The United Kingdom was divided into six geographical Army Commands, two Independent Districts, and one functional command responsible for anti-aircraft defence. The geographical commands were the Aldershot, Southern, Eastern, Northern, Western, and Scottish Commands, with the London District and

Royal
Engineers

Field
Coy

Field
Coy

Field
Coy

Field
Park
Coy

Divisional
Cavalry
Regiment

Squadron

Squadron

Squadron

the Northern Ireland District. The Commands were divided into a series of areas and zones depending upon the importance and number of troops stationed within them. A General Officer Commanding-in-Chief was responsible for each Command and the overall framework was controlled by the General Headquarters of the Commander-in-Chief, Home Forces.

The troops within each command were organised in corps, divisions, and brigades or as depots and training establishments. In peacetime, Aldershot was the premier Army Command with two regular divisions stationed there, while Southern, Eastern, and Northern

commands each had one regular division. Each Command also contained three or four Territorial Army Divisions which were administered to a large extent by the Territorial County Associations. When hostilities began the Territorial Army merged with the regular Army but all subsequent expansion was based on the Territorials and all recruits whether volunteers or conscripts were deemed to have enlisted in the Territorial Army.

As in all other armies the infantry division was the basic formation of the British Army. Divided into three infantry brigades with three regiments of field artillery and supporting units the division totalled 13,600 men. Despite its relatively small size the British division was exceptionally well equipped, particularly in artillery with 36×18 pounders, 36×4.5 inch howitzers (or converted 18/25 pounders), and 48×2 pounders (or 25mm) anti-tank guns as well as the three brigade anti-tank companies. The divisional cavalry regiment had under its command 28 light tanks and 44 Universal (Bren) carriers. The infantry battalion (33 officers and 780 men) was divided into four rifle companies (each with a headquarters and three platoons) and a headquarters company of six platoons (signals, anti-aircraft, mortar, carrier, pioneer and administration). In wartime the battalion and the brigade were the

Below: British troops in training, using Thompson sub-machine guns and wearing the standard gas-mask which (in spite of fears that gas would be used by the Germans) never saw action.

basic tactical formations; the infantry regiment being an administrative unit.

Besides the field artillery regiments, there were the larger calibre medium and heavy artillery regiments. The medium artillery regiment had a strength of 650 men and two batteries each of eight guns, either 6 inch howitzers or 60 pounders. The heavy artillery regiment (700 men) had one four-gun battery of 6 inch howitzers and three four-gun batteries of 8 inch or 9.2 inch howitzers.

The largest tank formation in the British Army was the armoured division which comprised two armoured brigades, an artillery support group and two motorised infantry battalions. A typical armoured brigade would be made up of three armoured regiments each consisting of a headquarters squadron and three tank squadrons adding up to a total of 52 cruiser tanks, 10 scout cars and 575 men.

UNIFORM At the beginning of the war the uniform of the British Army was undergoing a major change. In 1937 a new field uniform consisting of a baggy waist-length 'blouse' and long baggy trousers gathered at the ankle began to be introduced under the name of 'battledress'. Although impractical and difficult to wear smartly, it was both easy to manufacture and required comparatively little cloth. At the same time a lightweight version made of denim was introduced as a working dress and summer battledress.

64 Lance-Corporal, British Military Police, 1940

'MPs' were well known for the standard of their turn-out and were expected to set an example to their fellow soldiers. The most distinctive features are the arm brassard and the peaked service cap with traditional red top. This lance-corporal (there were no privates in the military police) wears one chevron on the sleeves of his greatcoat, which is the pattern for mounted personnel. He carries a Webley .455 No. 1 Mk 6 revolver.

65 Lance-Corporal, British Army, 1940

As a member of a Highland regiment, this lance-corporal of the Black Watch wears the cut-away version of the service dress tunic which was called a doublet. The head-dress or 'Tam o'Shanter' had a khaki pompom or touri, and instead of a badge the Black Watch wore a red hackle. On the left sleeve is the formation sign of the 4th Infantry Division (evacuated at Dunkirk), lance-corporal's chevron, and proficiency badges of a driver and a rifle marksman. At the bottom of the sleeve are two good conduct chevrons. The kilt is in 'government' or Black Watch tartan. The lance-corporal is armed with a .303 rifle No. 1 Mk 3 with a 1907 Mk 1 bayonet.

While the battledress was being issued soldiers continued to wear the old khaki service dress, illustrated by figure 63. Officers wore their own version which had an open tunic for wear with collar and tie, and pantaloons which tended to look like golfers' knicker-bockers. Mounted officers continued to wear beige cord breeches and brown leather field boots with spurs.

With the introduction of battledress for all ranks the officers' service dress was reserved for more formal occasions. The greatcoat for all ranks was double-breasted, although the old single-breasted pattern for other ranks continued in use. There were no variations of the battle-dress as such, but the blouse could be worn with tartan kilt or trews in those regiments which traditionally wore them.

Officers wore the peaked, service dress cap, the side or field service cap in regimental or corps colours with badge on the left front, or any other form of head-dress prescribed by indivi-dual units, such as the glengarry, Tam o'Shanter or coloured beret. The standard head-dress for other ranks was the khaki field service cap, or stiff khaki peaked cap for those in the Guards or Military Police.

Crews of armoured fighting vehicles wore the black beret and overalls of the Royal Tank Corps, but as more and more cavalry regiments were mechanised an increasing number of colourful and distinctive head-dresses began to adorn the heads of armoured car crews.

INSIGNIA Rank was indicated by the pattern of embroidery on the cap badge for general and staff officers, and by the metal or cloth rank badges which were worn on the shoulder straps by all commissioned ranks. Warrant officers wore their rank badges on the lower sleeves, while other ranks wore theirs on both upper sleeves.

The primary means of identifying corps, regiment, or arm of service in the British Army was the badge which appeared on the front of the peaked cap or beret and on the left front of the field service cap. A reduced version of the same badge was worn on the collar of the service dress jacket. On the service dress tunic for other ranks, the regiment or corps was identified by the buttons and metal shoulder titles. On the battledress all ranks wore cloth formation signs and shoulder flashes below which appeared a strip of cloth in the arm-of-service colour.

THE HOME GUARD

The German invasion of Holland and Belgium focused attention upon the use of paratroops to occupy areas behind the enemy's main defence lines and it seemed highly probable that this form of attack would be employed against Britain. As a precaution Anthony Eden, the Secretary of State for War, broadcast an appeal on 14 May 1940 for fit men between the ages of 16 and 65 to enrol in a military organisation which would be known as the Local Defence Volun-teers (LDV). By 20 May nearly 250,000 volunteers had come forward and by the end of the month the figure had reached 300,000. The force was to be organised in conjunction with the Territorial County Associations and came under the operational command of the C-in-C, Home Forces. On 31 July 1940 the title

Right: Troops of the 13/18th Royal Hussars are briefed by a lieutenant (two pips on his shoulder strap) during an exercise near Arras in October 1939. The men are wearing armoured-vehicle overalls and are armed with the regulation issue Enfield Mk 1* revolver which was worn with the low-slung holster of the tank crewman.

64

65

66

67

68

66 Corporal, British Army, 1940

This corporal of the Hampshire Regiment has the new battledress and a Mk 1 steel helmet with elasticated chin strap. He wears 1937-pattern web equipment with binocular case on his left. As in figure 68 the service respirator is carried on the chest in the 'ready' or 'alert' position. The rubber 'Wellington' boots were not standard issue but were made available in very wet weather to soldiers in the trenches. Below the basic ammunition pouch is a pleated hip pocket which held a field dressing. The rifle is the standard .303 rifle No. 1 Mk 3.

67 Private, British Army, 1940

Over khaki battle dress this private in the 2nd battalion of the East Yorkshire Regiment on duty on the Maginot Line at St François wears a specially manufactured snow suit. Ammunition is carried in a cloth bandolier. The rifle is the .303 No. 1 Mk 3.

68 Other Ranks, British Army, 1940

During the Norwegian Campaign British soldiers were issued with this heavy and uncomfortable 'Tropal' coat which was lined with kapok. For added warmth, the soldier is also wearing a 'balaclava helmet'. His gas mask is in the 'ready' position and the two pouches contain magazines for a Bren gun.

69 Lance-Corporal, Home Guard, 1943
The first volunteers who offered their services in the defence of the British Isles from German invasion had no uniforms and precious little armament. Eventually the light working version of the battle dress – known as demims – was issued together with various patterns and combinations of patterns of equipment. On his side (field-service) cap this lance-corporal wears the badge of the Hertfordshire Regiment, and on the left sleeve the 'Home Guard' shoulder title above HTS (which stands for Hertfordshire) and the battalion number. The medal ribbons are World War I awards including the British War Medal 1914–20 (far left). The web ammunition pouches were specially produced for the Home Guard. On his US Enfield .30 M1917 rifle is painted a red band which indicated that the rifle took non-standard (that is, .30 instead of .303 inch calibre) ammunition.

70 Lance-Corporal, British ATS, 1940
This lance-corporal of the ATS (Auxiliary Territorial Service) wears a privately purchased coloured field service cap; the issue pattern was khaki. The formation sign is that of 1st Anti-Aircraft Division which was heavily engaged in 1940–41 defending London from aerial attack. Since she is attached to the Royal Artillery she wears the RA badge on her left breast.

Above: King George VI inspects Local Defence Volunteers being given Bren gun instruction in July 1940. The men kneeling have LDV armlets just visible on their right arms.

of the force was changed to the Home Guard.

The immediate problem faced by The Home Guard was an acute shortage of arms, uniform and equipment. There were military rifles for only one-third of the Guard and the remainder had to make do for many months with shotguns, sporting rifles, and even golf clubs and home-made pikes. The Home Guard were unpaid and were required for duty and training only after working hours. They were organised as battalions, companies, and platoons but there was no fixed size for these units and a company could be 300 or 400 men strong. Commanders of units were not commissioned officers but holders of appointments and every man whatever his rank was subject to Military Law as a private soldier. The Home Guard was dispersed through the country and each city, town and village had its contingent. Their duties consisted of guarding important buildings, road junctions, railways and factories, and patrolling coastal areas where enemy landings might be made. By the end of July 1940 the Home Guard numbered 500,000 all ranks and during the invasion months of that year its presence and enthusiasm not only helped to inspire the population of Britain but

69

70

also relieved large numbers of regular troops from the distraction of guard and garrison duties.

Some of the American residents of London volunteered for service in the Local Defence Volunteers. They then formed themselves into the 1st American Squadron of the Home Guard which became known as the 'Red Eagles'. Some 128 Americans served in this unit during the whole of World War II, and not only provided their own motor vehicles, but purchased their own 'Tommy Guns'.

UNIFORM At first, Local Defence Volunteers wore their everyday clothes and a khaki armlet on the upper right arm, with the letters LDV in black. Former soldiers, particularly officers, wore their old uniforms although this practice, together with the wearing of insignia of former regiments or corps on Home Guard uniform, was actively discouraged.

As soon as was possible, Home Guard members began to be issued with denims and, later, battledress so that gradually they received the same kit as a serving soldier. Equipment was at first of the so-called Home Guard Pattern with leather waistbelt and straps, web pouches and special pattern water bottle and haversack.

INSIGNIA The first insignia proper to be issued was the 'Home Guard' armlet, and large letters cut from coloured cloth to denote the zone ('S' for South for instance), but these were soon changed to a regional patch above another which bore the battalion number. Home Guard staff attached to district commands wore the formation sign of the command.

A few Home Guard units in coastal areas adopted naval rig on which they wore their Home Guard insignia.

THE AUXILIARY TERRITORIAL SERVICE

Women in uniform, first in the Women's Legion and later in the Women's Army Auxiliary Corps (formed in 1917), had made a significant contribution to Britain's military performance during World War I. As the possibility of war with Germany became more certain in the late 1930s consideration was once again given to the employment of women in the Army. The formation of the Auxiliary Territorial Service received Royal Assent on 9 September 1938 and it was planned to raise 20,000 women volunteers between the ages of 18 and 50

who would be attached in companies to Territorial Army units. Although they wore uniform the women of the ATS were not at this stage subject to military law and they were employed as orderlies, cooks, drivers, and clerks with the official status of camp followers. On general mobilisation the recruitment limit of 20,000 was raised to 40,000 but the only additional tasks entrusted to the ATS were those of signal duties, and all officers and other ranks remained civilians.

In Spring 1940 a number of ATS telephonists and drivers arrived in France for service with the BEF's lines of communication. After Dunkirk the acute manpower shortage brought home to the Army the importance of the role women could play. The establishment of the ATS was raised to 200,000 and in April 1941 its members were given full military status although only a modified form of the Army Act was applied to women.

The area of employment in which women could be used within the Army was expanded to over one hundred occupations including many of the more skilled trades such as service at searchlight, radar and artillery stations. The ATS was not, however, integrated into the Army and it developed its own organisation and administrative system based on platoons, companies, and groups. Platoons contained from 23 to 75 women, two to five platoons made up a

company, and groups were formed of varying numbers of companies with the proviso that each group must have a minimum strength of 250 women. Groups were usually formed geographically to conform as far as possible to the boundaries of the military area in which they operated. By the end of December 1941 the overall strength of the Service stood at 2468 officers and 81,965 other ranks.

ROYAL AIR FORCE

During the inter-war years the British Government tried to maintain an Air Force with a merely defensive capacity, but when, in October 1938, a re-armament programme was initiated it provided for a large expansion of the Royal Air Force, so that it could not only continue to defend Great Britain, but also carry offensive operations into Germany should the need arise. Since the British Government did not wish to get involved in land warfare on the Continent, no consideration was given to providing air support, or for the dispatch of large air forces overseas.

The initial establishment of the BEF, however, included a so-called Air Component of two bomber-reconnaissance

Below: At the cockpit of his Spitfire is the fighter pilot 'Ginger' Lacey who, with a score of 18 aircraft shot down, 6 damaged and 4 probables was Britain's top ace during the Battle of Britain.

71 Airman, RAF, 1939

This airman is kitted out with a thermally insulated jacket and trousers made from glazed sheepskin by the Irvin Parachute Company. A number of these suits were wired for electrically-heated gloves and socks.

72 Aircrew, Royal Air Force, 1939

This member of a Whitley bomber crew wears an 'Irvin Harnisuit' over his service dress. The 'Harnisuit' had an inflatable life-belt and three attachment points for the parachute. He is equipped with a type B helmet and an oxygen mask with a fitted microphone and oxygen tube. The boots are of the 1936 pattern – polished black leather with a sheepskin lining.

73 Officer, Royal Air Force, 1940

Rather unusually this fighter pilot wears his parachute over his officer's service dress. The prized 'wings' are on his left breast. The parachute harness has a quick release device (metal disc) with the parachute release handle to its right. The parachute is the 'seat-type' used by pilots of single-seater aircraft. .

74 Sergeant, Royal Air Force, 1940

Sergeant G. W. Garton wears RAF service dress with silk scarf to prevent his neck from getting sore from continuous scanning of the sky for intruders. The 'Mae West' life jacket is the 1932 pattern which had to be inflated by the wearer and was sometimes painted yellow as an aid to identification by air-sea rescue. He carries a type B helmet with a type D face mask with microphone and wears 1940-pattern flying boots with canvas calves. Sergeant Garton, a Hurricane fighter pilot, commanded 'A' Flight, No. 43 Squadron in 1940 and later became Wing Commander, DSO, DFC.

71

72

squadrons, four fighter squadrons, six Army co-operation squadrons, and two flights of an HQ communication squadron. In addition it was agreed with the French government that an Advanced Air Striking Force of medium bombers from Bomber Command would operate from France, but would not be under the operational command of the BEF. By 27 September 1939 RAF personnel in France numbered some 9392 men.

In January 1940 it was decided to unite the Air Component and the Advanced Air Striking Force under the command of the Air Officer Commanding-in-Chief British Air Forces in France, Air Marshal Barratt.

As soon as possible after its arrival in France, the RAF took part in operations which brought it in contact with German aircraft. Although a number of German machines were shot down, RAF losses were heavy as many of their planes (the Fairey Battles and Blenheims for example) were found to be inadequately armed and ill-suited to combat with modern fighter planes like the Messerschmitt Bf 109.

Britain was anxious not to squander its precious aircraft by using them as a sort of fire brigade at the beck and call of the Allied land forces. The RAF wanted to ensure that its bombers were only used to cause maximum destruction to the enemy, although strategic bombing of targets in Germany was only authorised on 15 May 1940. Fighters based in France and England were to be deployed against the enemy as long as it did not impair Britain's ability to defend herself. On 10 May 1940, 416 of Britain's total number of 1873 first-line aircraft were stationed in France, but on 20 May it was decided to bring back to England the remaining 66 fighters so that they could continue the war from English airfields.

The first phase of the German plan for the invasion of England was to gain control of the air and so during the months of July and August 1940 the RAF prepared its forces for the inevitable battle against the Luftwaffe.

Right: These fighter pilots off duty by a Spitfire can be seen wearing a variety of aircrew clothing including the 1940-pattern flying boots and a sheepskin-lined leather jacket.

73   74

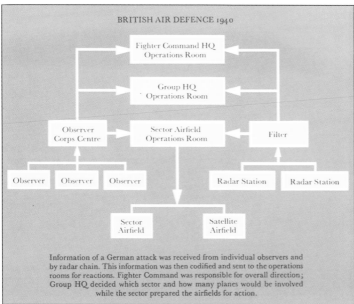

BRITISH AIR DEFENCE 1940

Information of a German attack was received from individual observers and by radar chain. This information was then codified and sent to the operations rooms for reactions. Fighter Command was responsible for overall direction; Group HQ decided which sector and how many planes would be involved while the sector prepared the airfields for action.

The main defence possessed by the British was RAF Fighter Command which was under the inspired leadership of Air Chief Marshal Sir Hugh Dowding. The country was divided into four large areas to be defended by fighter Groups, the most important being 11 Group under the command of Air Vice-Marshal Keith Park. This Group covered London, the Home Counties and south-east England, the fighting areas of the Battle of Britain. Underneath the Group was the sector (nine in 11 Group) which would control anything from two to five squadrons. In some sectors all the squadrons would be based on the one airfield, in others they would be spread out over as many as four airfields. A typical sector was Northolt which was organised as follows:

No. 1 Sqdn – 10 Hurricanes;
No. 275 Sqdn – 13 Hurricanes;
No. 604 Sqdn – 10 Blenheims;
No. 609 Sqdn – 15 Spitfires.

By the end of July the RAF had 530 fighter aircraft ready for combat out of a total of just over 600, with another 289 fighters in reserve.

The RAF had considerable advantages over the Luftwaffe, the chief of these being a flexible command structure which ensured resources were not wasted; an integrated radar system which usually enabled RAF fighter pilots to intercept the German bomber squadrons; and the advantage of fighting over home territory. The margin of the RAF's victory over the German Air Force was slim but it was sufficient to deter the *Wehrmacht* from seriously contemplating an invasion of Britain.

UNIFORM Before the war the RAF uniform was basically the same as that of the Army but in blue-grey, although unlike the Army, all ranks in the RAF had an open tunic which was worn with collar and tie. In 1940 a blue-grey version of the battle-dress began to be issued.

Officers wore the service dress consisting of peaked or field service cap with cloth covered peak, black mohair band and gold-embroidered badge. The tunic was worn open with blue shirt and black tie and long matching trousers with black socks and shoes. The greatcoat was double-breasted with matching cloth belt, and in addition there was both a mackintosh and raincoat.

Other ranks wore the uniform illustrated by figure 75, although the most typical form of head-dress was the field service cap, or stiff peaked cap with metal cap badge. In wartime, RAF personnel were issued with the Mk I steel helmet and 1937 pattern webbing in blue-grey. The

75   76

working dress of ground crews was a field service cap and dark blue or black overalls. Flying clothing is illustrated by figures 71 to 74.

INSIGNIA The RAF was unique in introducing not only a new system of rank insignia, but also a range of special rank titles. Officers wore rank distinction lace on the cuffs of the tunic and on the greatcoat shoulder straps. NCOs wore chevrons on both sleeves of the tunic and greatcoat. Contrary to the practice in most other Air Forces there were no special rank badges for wear on flight clothing.

There were no arm-of-service or branch badges as such, but a number of specialists were identified by special insignia, some of which appear in the illustrations.

ROYAL NAVY

From the outbreak of war the Royal Navy was engaged in action throughout the world. The hunt for the *Graf Spee*, for example, tied up large numbers of British naval forces in the South Atlantic, until the German battlecruiser was scuttled in the River Plate on 19 December 1939. In home waters, the Navy played an important role in the defence of Norway, inflicting heavy casualties on the German forces. The major work of the Navy, however, was the protection of British merchant vessels from the ever-present threat of the German U-boats which, even in the first months of the war, were causing heavy losses.

At the beginning of the War, the Royal Navy was the most powerful in the world. It had the largest number of ships and a network of naval bases and coaling stations around the globe. This massive organisation was directed from offices in Whitehall by the Board of Admiralty. The chairman of the board was officially titled First Lord of the Admiralty and was a political appointee responsible to the cabinet and to Parliament.

Professional expertise was provided by the five Sea Lords, all serving officers in the Royal Navy. The First Sea Lord, Admiral of the Fleet Sir Dudley Pound was responsible for running the Navy's operations throughout the world, and was assisted in this by a naval staff. He was also the Royal Navy's representative on the Joint Chiefs of Staff Committee together with the heads of the Army and Air Force.

Before mobilisation the strength of the Navy was 9762 officers and 109,170 ratings. In January 1939 there were in addition 51,485 men in the Royal Fleet Reserve, 10,038 in the Royal Naval

75 Sergeant, Royal Air Force, 1940

The issue service dress for other ranks in the RAF was identical in cut to that worn by officers, but was made of serge. On the sleeves this sergeant wears three chevrons beneath the eagle badge which was worn by all ranks below warrant officer first class.

76 Leading Aircraftwoman, Royal Air Force, 1940

This leading aircraftwoman wears the women's version of the standard RAF service dress as worn by members of the Women's Auxiliary Air Force (or WAAFs as they were known). The badges on her left sleeve are the RAF eagle above the letter 'A' for auxiliary, the flash for a wireless operator, and the horizontal propeller which was the badge of rank of a leading aircraftman/woman.

77 Chief Petty Officer, Royal Navy, 1940

As this figure is wearing working rig his jacket is single-breasted whereas a double-breasted jacket would be worn on all other occasions. On the jacket collar is the non-substantive trade badge which denotes this CPO as a gunner's mate.

78 Petty Officer, Royal Navy, 1940

The 'square rig' illustrated was the basic uniform for Royal Navy ratings and had provided the model for the uniforms of many of the world's navies. At the outbreak of war the cap tally with name of the ship was officially replaced by one bearing only the letters HMS (His Majesty's Ship) without the ship's name. On his right sleeve is the non-substantive badge which identified the wearer's trade (two stars and crossed guns for gunlayer first class), while on the left sleeve is the substantive or rank badge for petty officer.

77   **78**

Reserve (mainly serving in the Merchant Navy), 2049 in the Royal Navy Auxiliary Sick Berth and Wireless Auxiliary reserves, and 6180 in the Royal Naval Volunteer Reserve.

Royal Navy dispositions in European waters in September 1939 were as follows: Home Fleet (Admiral Sir Charles Forbes) based at Scapa Flow;
7 battleships and battlecruisers;
2 aircraft carriers;
15 cruisers;
17 destroyers;
7 minesweepers and sloops;
21 submarines.

Left: A group of British sailors just recently returned to port illustrate the various types of working dress worn by the Royal Navy during the war.

Right: The commanding Officer (Commander J. G. W. Deneys, DSO) and a group of the crew of the destroyer HMS Vanoc. The various ranks of the ship are clearly shown in this photograph. Seated are the officers and behind them are the confirmed petty officers – wearing peaked cap and single-breasted jacket – and petty officers, while the back row is composed of the ship's ratings.

North Atlantic Command (Rear-Admiral N. A. Wodehouse) – responsible for waters west of Gibraltar:
2 cruisers;
9 destroyers;
2 submarines;
2 minesweepers.
Concentrated in home waters for patrol, escort and striking purposes were:
2 battleships;
5 cruisers;
2 aircraft carriers;
65 destroyers;
12 minesweepers.

Escort vessels served worldwide, while a number of ships of all types were undergoing refit, were in reserve, or being used on miscellaneous duties such as training.

Captains commanded battleships, battlecruisers, cruisers and aircraft

Below: A British sailor on guard duty ashore. He is armed with a rifle and fixed bayonet and equipped with gaiters and standard issue ammunition pouches. Of interest is the cap tally which displays HMS without the ship's name – a wartime security measure.

carriers, which were organised in squadrons of between two and nine ships under a rear-admiral. Eight destroyers, each in the charge of a commander, plus a specially fitted leader commanded by a captain, usually comprised a flotilla. All smaller warships were grouped in flotillas, usually under a captain or commander with subordinate officers commanding individual ships.

Since 1937 (although in practice only since May 1939) the Royal Navy had maintained its own Naval Air Branch under its chief, Vice-Admiral Sir Alexander Ramsey.

The Fleet Air Arm as it was known went to war with 190 aeroplanes in aircraft and seaplane carriers; plus spotter floatplanes mounted on catapults in capital ships and cruisers.

Throughout the war, RAF Coastal Command operated reconnaissance, escort and strike squadrons. From April 1941, they came under the operational control of the Admiralty while remaining part of the RAF.

UNIFORM Royal Navy uniform, which had evolved over many years, became the model for the uniforms of most of the world's navies during the nineteenth century.

The basic uniform for officers consisted of a peaked cap which could be worn with a white cover; double-breasted 'reefer' jacket which was worn with white shirt and black tie; matching long trousers and black socks and shoes. The greatcoat was double-breasted and was worn with brown leather gloves. The uniform for chief petty officers was similar to that of commissioned officers, while the so-called 'fore and aft' rig was also worn by petty officers and other junior ratings who were not members of the seaman branch.

Ratings wore the 'square rig' illustrated by figure 78, but instead of the short winter coat found in some navies, ratings received a single-breasted greatcoat. For everyday work ratings wore a blue boiler-suit, or one of the many other different types of protective clothing. In cold weather ratings received a thick white woollen pullover and sea socks for wear inside rubber boots, a knitted woollen cap comforter and the famous duffle coat. In rough seas sailors wore waterproof clothing, notably the oilskin 'sou'wester' and coat.

INSIGNIA Both flag and senior officers were identified by gold embroidery on the cap peak, while all officers wore rank distinction lace on the cuffs of the reefer jacket or on the greatcoat shoulder straps. Officers in the Royal Naval Volunteer

79

79 Captain, Royal Navy, 1940

This officer wears the traditional double-breasted 'monkey jacket', or reefer, as part of his temperate-climate uniform. Rank is denoted by the four gold rings on the sleeve and by the single row of oak leaves on the cap's peak (the latter piece of insignia was common to the ranks of commander and commodore 2nd class). The captain's arm-of-service colour (the purple 'lights' in between the gold rings) indicates that he is an engineer.

Reserve had 'wavy' rank distinction lace, while Royal Naval Reserve officers had plaited rank distinction lace in which the 'curl' formed a six-pointed star. Seamen and petty officers wore their rank badges on the upper left sleeve, while chief petty officers had three buttons on each cuff and a special cap badge.

For arm-of-service distinction, non-executive officers in civil branches wore 'lights' which appeared between the rank distinction lace. Specialists wore distinguishing badges on the collar if chief petty officers, or otherwise on the right arm.

THE WAR IN
THE MEDITERRANEAN

From June 1940, when Italy declared war
on France and Great Britain, to April 1945, when
the German Army in Italy surrendered, the
Mediterranean Sea was the centre of a series of campaigns,
which involved fighting in North Africa, Ethiopia, Syria,
Iraq, Greece, Yugoslavia, Italy and southern France;
not to speak of the air and sea wars. These campaigns
demanded great flexibility, both in organisation and uniform.
Formations suited to mobile desert warfare were unlikely
to feel at home in the mountains of Greece and Italy, for
example. The same went for uniform, with the added
problem that many nations sent their troops to this
theatre wearing quite unsuitable clothing, which
was modified as the war progressed. And a final
complication was the large number of irregular
units – either outright partisans or *ad hoc*
formations within the regular forces – which
had their own distinctive clothing
and organisation.

ITALY
ARMY

The Italian Army had suffered heavy losses for only limited gains during World War I and in common with the other combatant nations the Army was drastically reduced in size and influence following the 1918 armistice. But the development of the fascist corporate state in the 1920s saw a revival of the influence of the Army. The new leader of Italy, Benito Mussolini, combined an authoritarian approach to domestic affairs with an aggressive foreign policy. The Army was expanded to become the instrument of Mussolini's territorial ambitions. In 1935 Italy invaded Ethiopia, and in April 1939 took over Albania.

Despite Mussolini's grandiose claims, Italy did not possess the capability to wage effective war. The population was apathetic, there was a severe shortage of strategic raw materials and the Army, woefully lacking in the necessary arms and equipment, was insufficiently prepared in the techniques of modern warfare.

Italy's entry into the war – the campaign against France from 10 to 25 June 1940 – was a humiliating fiasco, partly because strategic planning was centred on the Mediterranean, and the General Staff was caught off balance by the directives for an Alpine campaign. The Army suffered over 4,000 casualties in this brief campaign (the French lost just over 200 men).

A further military setback occurred a few months later when an Italian Army of around 160,000 men invaded Greece from the new territorial acquisition of Albania. Much to the surprise of the Italians and, indeed, to the world in general, the Greek Army repulsed the poorly-organised invasion.

East Africa was the scene of further disasters. The Italian Army in East Africa (*Africa Orientale Italiana* or AOI) was impressive on paper with 88,000 Italian and 200,000 colonial troops but there were many weaknesses. The artillery was antiquated and reserves of equipment, supplies and ammunition were so low that the Viceroy and Commander-in-Chief, the Duke of Aosta estimated that in the event of war he could only hold out for six or seven months at the most.

On 19 January 1941 the first British forces invaded Ethiopia and within the space of four months the Duke of Aosta was forced to surrender all his troops to the victorious British.

In Libya, Italy suffered another disaster: eight divisions were destroyed and 130,000 men taken prisoner in Wavell's offensive of 1941. The arrival of the Africa Corps in February 1941 prevented a total collapse but after that the Italian Army played a subordinate role in Axis operations.

Right: Pictured at a review, these Italian troops exhibit the old-style black velvet collar on their uniforms. The officers' lighter uniforms are clearly visible, while the regimental badge is carried on the steel helmets.

84

85

86

84 Private, Italian Army, 1940

The Italian infantryman was as inadequately dressed for the bitter winter campaign of 1940–41 as his Greek adversary, and both sides suffered from exposure. The Italian Army greatcoat was cheaply made of coarse cloth and was not even double-breasted. No special winter clothing was issued and the only soldiers to have even adequate clothing were the mountain troops. Characteristic of the Italian Army were the two ammunition pouches carried at the front of the belt.

85 Colonel, Italian Army, 1940

This colonel commanding the 36th Infantry Regiment in France in 1940 continues to wear the old cordellino uniform with gold wire and rank badges. On the field service uniform the cap badge was usually embroidered in black thread, but this officer continues to wear the gold-embroidered pattern. The madder red backing to the cap and rank badges was only worn by colonels commanding a regiment. The crown and swords on the breast is the badge for promotion due to meritorious service in the field, while above the medal ribbon the metal eagle denotes the colonel as a graduate of a war academy.

86 Private, Italian Army, 1940

The standard field service uniform remained virtually unchanged throughout the war. The knickerbockers were either worn with the woollen socks illustrated or with leather leggings by motorised personnel. The steel helmet is the model 933 which often had a regimental badge in black paint on the front. The green collar patch was worn by the two regiments in the Alpi Brigade (51st and 52nd regiments) whose members sometimes also wore a red tie in memory of Garibaldi. The rifle is the Mannlicher-Carcano M1891. This weapon was obsolete by 1940; even in 1934, during the Abyssinian campaign, there had been complaints about its performance.

Some 99,000 Italians were captured when the Axis forces surrendered in 1943; the North African campaigns had cost Italy the equivalent of 25 divisions.

During the course of the war 20 new divisions were raised but they could not replace the massive losses suffered by the Italian Army. Mussolini's 'crusade against Bolshevism' cost Italy dear; of the 229,000 despatched to the Eastern Front over half became casualties. In Africa as a whole, 27 divisions were destroyed between December 1940 and May 1943. Another 36 divisions were immobilised outside Italy, occupying France or suppressing guerrilla activities in the Balkans. A number of divisions were undergoing retraining and there were only 20 divisions to face the Allied invasion of 1943.

On 25 July 1943, Mussolini was deposed. When Badoglio, the new head of government, agreed to surrender terms with the Allies, the Germans moved swiftly in Operation *Achse*. The Italian Army was ruthlessly disarmed by the Germans (who meted out severe reprisals for the slightest Italian resistance) and ceased to exist as a coherent force.

ORGANISATION The nominal Commander-in-Chief of the Italian Army was His Majesty King Emmanuel III, although most of his responsibilities had been taken over by the Chief of State, Benito Mussolini. Under Mussolini came the supreme command (*Commando Supremo*), an organic staff which functioned through the respective defence ministries (War, Admiralty and Air) via the various high commands (Army Group West, Albania, East Africa, the Aegean and Libya).

All Italian citizens from the ages of 18 to 54 years were liable for military service. The first stage was that of conscript service where the recruit served 18 months with the colours, followed by post-military training which ran from the completion of service until the 33rd birthday. After that date the citizen went into the reserve and could be liable to call-up in time of war until the age of 54. Until 1943 Italy did not suffer from a shortage of manpower; the problem lay in training and equipping her soldiers.

In 1940 over 2,000,000 Italians were under arms, the 73 divisions of the Army being organised as follows:
59 infantry divisions;
6 Alpine divisions;
3 mobile (*celere*) divisions;
2 motorised divisions;
3 armoured divisions.
In addition there were frontier guard troops whose number was estimated to be equivalent to nine divisions. Although an impressive total on paper, few of the divisions had their full complement of men and equipment.

While the division was the basic formation in the Italian Army a number of troops were organised at corps or army level essentially to act as higher formation reserve units.

The Italian infantry division was known as a 'binary' division (*divisione binaria*) because it was based around two infantry regiments. From 1 March 1940 an MVSN Legion of two battalions was attached to most of the divisions, partly to increase the manpower of the division but also to include fascist troops within regular army formations. The infantry division comprised:
divisional headquarters (336 men);
two infantry regiments (3279 men each);
mortar battalion (435 men);
pack gun company (241 men);
divisional artillery regiment (2769 men);
engineer battalion (440 men);
Blackshirt legion (1693 men).
This was in addition to the divisional services and in some instances a reserve infantry battalion. The division totalled about 13,500 men at full strength.

The infantry regiment was normally composed of three rifle battalions, although a few regiments had as many as five battalions. The armament of the regiment included:
24 heavy machine guns;
108 light machine guns;
6 × 81mm mortars;
54 × 45mm mortars;
8 × 47mm guns.

The infantry battalion with an establishment strength of 876 men was divided into a headquarters company, three rifle companies (156 men sub-divided into a headquarters platoon and three rifle platoons each of two sections) and a support arms company of two machine gun platoons (four heavy machine guns each) and two 45mm mortar platoons (nine mortars each).

The two Blackshirt battalions were organised on the same lines as the regular battalions but with less men (700 each). The legion had a support arms company comprising two machine-gun platoons (each with three guns) and two 81mm mortar platoons (each with three mortars).

The artillery regiment consisted of a regimental headquarters; a horsedrawn 100mm howitzer battery; a horsedrawn 75mm gun battery; a 75mm park howitzer battery and a mechanised 20mm anti-aircraft troop. Each battery comprised three troops of four guns each; the anti-aircraft troop being divided into four two-gun sections.

The mortar battalion consisted of three 81mm mortar companies (six mortars each) and the gun company had eight 47mm guns divided into four platoons.

The engineer battalion consisted of a pioneer company and a telegraph and radio-telephone company.

Although each division had direct control of most of the heavy support weapons it would need, the armament and equipment of the Italian division compared unfavourably with its British counterpart. Whereas the Italian divisional artillery regiment could only muster 36 antiquated medium-calibred guns, the British division possessed 72 modern, mixed-calibre guns and howitzers. Another weakness (especially in North Africa) was the heavy reliance on horse transport.

A number of infantry divisions were designated mountain infantry divisions, being partially adapted for conditions in rough and mountainous country. The only organisational difference compared to the standard division was in the artillery regiment, which comprised three

Right: Prisoners wearing the uniform of the fascist MVSN militia queue for daily rations near Addis Ababa. Their uniform is standard Italian Army issue, with the exceptions of the silver fascio on each collar patch and sleeve rank chevrons in black.

ITALIAN INFANTRY DIVISION 1940-43

87 Sergeant, Italian African Police, 1942

This sergeant of the Polizia Africa Italiana wears standard Italian Army tropical uniform consisting of side cap (bustina), jacket or sahariana, breeches and leather leggings for motorised personnel. Distinctive insignia are the cap badge and blue aiguillette. He carries a 9mm Beretta M38A sub-machine gun.

88 Lieutenant, Italian Army, 1940

This infantry lieutenant in Sidi Azeis in August 1940 wears typical tropical dress. On the front of his side cap (the bustina) is the infantry cap badge with the regimental number in the centre of the grenade. The shoulder straps bore two stars for a lieutenant, while the collar star was common to all arms and ranks.

89 Carabinieri Private, Italian Army, 1942

The Royal Carabinieri was the senior arm of the regular Army with fine traditions and hand-picked men. In addition to their military tasks Carabinieri also carried out military police duties. Distinctive insignia was the exploding grenade cap badge over a tricolour in national colours and special collar patches. The bandolier was only issued to mounted or motorised personnel.

87   88   89

75mm howitzer batteries each of three troops, the guns of which could all be transported in horse-drawn wagons or on pack animals. Despite the high proportion of pack animals the personnel of these divisions were not specially trained in mountain warfare.

The real mountain troops were the Alpini divisions whose personnel – drawn from Italy's Alpine regions – was of superior quality; well trained in mountain warfare they were expert in the handling of pack artillery.

The Alpine divisions differed in organisation from the regular infantry formations in that the regiments had their own detachments of artillery, engineers and ancillary services which were affiliated to them on a permanent basis from the divisional organisation. This made the regiment reasonably self-supporting and capable of independent action for considerable periods of time; often an essential requirement in mountainous terrain. If necessary, battalions and even companies could be detached from their parent units to be combined with units of artillery to form semi-independent *raggruppamenti*.
The division consisted of:
divisional headquarters (388 men including an anti-tank platoon);
two Alpine regiments (4757 men each);
divisional artillery regiment (1710 men);
mixed engineer battalion (341 men);
chemical warfare company (234 men);
two reserve battalions (766 men each);
divisional services (medical and supply sections and a transport column, a total of 1500 men).

The Alpine regiment was composed of headquarters company, which included a platoon of flamethrowers, three Alpine battalions and regimental services (consisting of a medical platoon, field hospital, supply platoon and transport unit). Each Alpine battalion (1267 men at full strength) was formed from three Alpine companies (340 men divided into three rifle platoons and a machine gun platoon) and a headquarters company. The firepower of the regiment was as follows:
27 heavy machine guns;
81 light machine guns;
17 40mm mortars;
12 81mm mortars;
27 flamethrowers.

The artillery of the Alpine division consisted of two 75mm howitzer batteries, each of three four-gun troops, which were all transported on pack animals. The two batteries were split between the two Alpine regiments, with the three troops of the battery being allotted to each of the Alpine battalions. The reserve or complement battalions were similarly divided between the Alpine regiments.

During 1942 attempts were made to increase fire-power and mechanisation within the Army. Additionally a new, more flexible organisational structure was introduced. The 'North Africa 1942' division was made up of two infantry regiments, an artillery regiment, a mixed engineer battalion and medical and supply sections. The infantry regiment could vary considerably in size being based around the company which was organised as follows:
headquarters section (15 all ranks);
rifle platoon (35 all ranks, six LMGs);
machine gun platoon (23 all ranks, three HMGs);
light gun platoon (24 all ranks, three 20mm guns);
anti-tank platoon (36 all ranks, three 47mm guns).
Two to four of these companies formed a battalion and two or three battalions (plus a regimental headquarters company and a 81mm mortar company) formed a regiment. A regiment of three battalions

90 Sergeant, Italian Army, 1941
The bersaglieri *were an élite corps of riflemen formed by Luciano Lamarmora during the Italian Risorgimento. The traditional cockerel feathers usually adorned the round black hat worn by the* bersaglieri *but during the war they were equally proudly worn on the steel helmet and solar topee. This sergeant of the 6th Regiment wears standard tropical clothing with leather leggings for motorised personnel. The carbine is the 7.35mm M91 with folding bayonet.*

91 Alpine 2nd Lieutenant, Italian Army, 1943
This officer wears a mixture of uniform and equipment typical of wartime. The distinctive head-dress was a felt hat with eagle feather and a woollen pompon on the left side. The colour of the pompon identified the battalion. The cap badge is a black eagle over crossed rifles and hunting horns. The tunic is the pre-1940 pattern with detachable shoulder straps. In addition to his pistol he carries a Moschetto M38/42 sub-machine gun with folding bayonet, and so he also has to wear other ranks' equipment with ammunition pouches to hold the clips.

of four companies would have a strength of just over 2000 men.

The artillery regiment was composed of one or two 12-gun 100mm batteries, two 12-gun 75mm batteries and an 8-gun 20mm troop. Some regiments were equipped with a battery of German 8.8cm guns. The regiment was mechanised to a higher degree than previously, although few units had their full complement of motor vehicles.

In order to increase mobility a number of infantry divisions were in theory fully mechanised although they retained a good proportion of animal transport. Known as lorry-borne or motor transportable divisions they were organised as a normal infantry division except that they had a larger complement of mortars and were without the Blackshirt Legion.

Those motor transportable divisions in Africa were upgraded to become motorised divisions 'North Africa' type. In spite of their name they were not fully motorised, relying on other non-divisional sources for transportation. They had a strength of 6800 men and were organised as follows: two infantry regiments each with two infantry battalions (580 men each) and a support and anti-tank battalion (anti-aircraft company, anti-tank company, mortar company and

Below: Italian Alpini, *pictured during a break in operations, wearing white snow camouflage. The soldier on the right displays the eagle feather and pompom on his helmet; the former identifies him as a member of the crack Alpine divisions, while the colour of the latter would identify the battalion to which he belongs.*

machine gun company); a standard artillery regiment; a light tank battalion (an HQ section of seven tanks, and three companies of 13 tanks each); a divisional support and anti-tank battalion; and a mixed engineer battalion.

The motorised division proper was similar in organisation to the 'North Africa' type but it included a regiment of *bersaglieri* – a unit of élite riflemen – which brought up the divisional strength to 9216 soldiers. The *bersaglieri* regiment had 1827 men and was constituted as follows:
headquarters company;
motor cycle company;
two lorry-borne *bersaglieri* battalions;
support and anti-aircraft battalion.
Each *bersaglieri* battalion had a headquarters company, two rifle companies and a support and anti-tank company.

The mobile (*celere*) divisions were old cavalry formations that had undergone some degree of mechanisation. They were designed to operate in a reconnaissance or support role; fire-power being sacrificed for mobility. The division, with an overall strength of 7739 men, comprised:
two cavalry regiments (878 men each);
a *bersaglieri* regiment (2727 men);
bersaglieri motor cycle company (178 men);
anti-tank company (155 men, 8 × 47mm guns);
divisional artillery regiment (1523 men);
light tank group (312 men);
mixed engineer company (366 men).
Divisional services were provided by a medical and a supply section and a motor transport group with 218 vehicles.

The horse-mounted cavalry regiment was divided into two squadron groups (each sub-divided into two 150-man sabre squadrons) and a machine gun squadron armed with 12 heavy machine guns. The *bersaglieri* regiment was equipped with bicycles and comprised an HQ and three battalions of 850 men each.

The light tank group had a headquarters of nine tanks and four squadrons each with a tank for the squadron commander and three platoons of four tanks.

The vulnerability of the mobile division was quickly exposed and attempts were made to mechanise the formations fully, but shortages of trained personnel and equipment prevented this.

Pre-war the armoured divisions were armed only with light tanks and were incapable of providing the armoured spearhead that the panzer formations did for the German Army.

During the course of the war the armoured divisions were reorganised with the introduction of a better medium tank (*Carro Armato* M13/40), self-propelled guns and heavier divisional support weapons. Nevertheless the Italian armoured division could not compare equipment-wise with its British counterpart. The division comprised:
tank regiment;
artillery regiment;
divisional support and anti-tank battalion;
mixed engineer company;
bersaglieri regiment,

The tank regiment normally had three, although sometimes there could be as many as five, tank battalions. Each battalion had a strength of 457 men and 55 tanks armed with 47mm guns and was divided into a headquarters company, a reserve company of six to eight tanks and three tank companies.

The mechanised artillery regiment was organised as follows:
2 twelve-gun 75mm batteries;
1 eighteen-gun 105mm battery;
1 eight-gun 90mm battery;
2 ten-gun armoured batteries of self-propelled guns mounted on M13/40 tank chassis.
In addition there was a troop of 47mm anti-tank guns and three anti-aircraft troops armed with 20mm guns.

The divisional support and anti-tank battalion had the same organisation as the motorised division, 'North Africa' type and the *bersaglieri* regiment had the standard motorised division organisation.

Although the Italian Army did not employ airborne troops in the spectacular manner of their Axis partner two parachute divisions were raised. The organisation of these formations was broadly similar to that of the Alpine division, the parachute regiments including units of all divisional supporting arms and services enabling them to act in an independent role.

The division was divided into two parachute regiments, each of four battalions, and an artillery regiment of two batteries which was split up amongst the parachute regiments. The parachute battalion (comprising a headquarters unit and three parachute companies) had a strength of 326 men and was well-armed with 54 light machine guns and 62 semi-automatic rifles. At divisional level there was a motor cycle company, an 81 mm mortar company and in addition an engineer company.

The Alpine and *bersaglieri* regiments were often of the highest quality but most of the infantry formations were poorly-equipped, and badly supplied. The Italians tended to subordinate the infantry to other arms; and Italian soldiers were never convinced of the necessity or righteousness of their involvement in the war.

Italian military doctrine stressed the primacy of the offensive, the defensive being considered as a temporary expedient prior to launching a rapid counter-offensive. In reality, however, Italian attacks were seldom pressed home with much conviction: in 1940 the Greek Army considered that Italian assaults would grind to a halt if contained for only 20 minutes. Despite popular myth the Italian soldier did not lack bravery, what he lacked were the arms and equipment necessary for modern warfare.

COLONIAL TROOPS

As an imperial power Italy employed colonial troops in a number of capacities. The best troops for desert warfare were the *Sahariani* who were completely mechanised, having their own complement of motorised artillery. Most of Italy's colonial troops were poorly armed and untrained for modern warfare.

In Libya the Royal Corps of Libyan Troops was raised consisting of infantry and cavalry units. The two infantry divisions were destroyed in the fighting of 1940–41 and were only partially re-formed, existing only as administrative depots. The cavalry was organised in groups of squadrons consisting of a headquarters and four squadrons of 150 men each.

The motorised saharan troops (*Compagnia Sahariana*) consisted of six companies organised as follows:
a headquarters platoon;

92

two or three machine gun platoons;
an anti-tank platoon;
a reconnaissance section of two to three *Ghibli* aircraft.
The strength of the company comprised 147 men, 20 motor transport vehicles, eight heavy machine guns and two 47 mm anti-tank guns.

Camel-mounted troops were employed by the Saharan Command for desert patrol purposes and consisted of two companies, each of 280 men, four machine guns and 12 automatic rifles.

UNIFORM Despite the fact that the Italian Army had developed a comfortable and practical uniform as far back as the wars of the *Risorgimento*, the first grey-green uniform introduced in 1909 included two very uncomfortable and impractical features – a stiff high collar and puttees.

The 1934 amendments to the 1931 dress regulations introduced a tunic with open collar for wear with shirt and tie. This fashion had been adopted during World War I by the *Arditi* (commandos) and

then taken over by the Fascist Militia. As soon as war came the trend was towards simplification and removal of the difference between the uniforms of officers and men.

The standard uniform for other ranks was made of a coarse dark grey-green cloth, while officers continued to wear uniforms made of a much lighter shade of twill (*cordellino*). The issue tunic had four patch pockets and a cloth belt fastened with two grey-green buttons. The old collar in black or facing colour was replaced by one in grey-green. The shirt and tie were also grey-green but some regiments wore a red or blue tie, and the *Carabinieri* retained their black tie on certain occasions. The greatcoat was single-breasted although a double-breasted version for officers and mounted personnel continued to be worn. Dismounted personnel wore baggy trousers with either puttees or black leather leggings if serving in motorised or tank units. Mounted personnel wore breeches with leather leggings.

Head-dress included the side cap or

92 Paratroop Captain, Italian Army, 1942
This captain wears the special helmet and camouflage smock introduced in 1942. The badge of rank is worn on the front of the camouflage smock, as well as on the front of other types of leather, camouflage and waterproof clothing. The sub-machine gun is the Beretta M38A, which was usually only issued to special troops.

93 Tankman, Italian Army, 1941
The special clothing worn by Italian tank crews was based on the French model and consisted of overalls, crash helmet and threequarter-length leather coat. The distinctive insignia of Italian armoured troops were the blue collar patches with red double flame for tank troops, and white double flame for units equipped with tankettes.

94 Corporal, Italian Colonial Army, 1942
This corporal of the Gruppi Sahariana wears the white full-dress jacket with sirical trousers. The coloured sash indicated the service group (the 3rd), while the rank badge on the right sleeve is the pattern introduced in 1939 when Libyans were granted Italian nationality. The equipment is the standard pattern adopted in 1920 by all desert troops.

95 Corporal, Italian Colonial Army, 1940
This corporal from Italian East Africa wears the uniform prescribed by the 1929 regulations. The head-dress was called a tarbusc and its tassel identified the battalion (VI Eritrea) as did the coloured sash. The rank chevrons were worn on the left sleeve above three stars which indicated ten years' service. The rifle is the Mannlicher-Carcano M91/38.

93 **94** **95**

bustina which was supposed to have replaced the peaked cap on active service, the 1933 model steel helmet, the grey-green felt hat with feather for *Alpini* (see figure 91), and the dark crimson fez with light blue tassel which was worn by the *bersaglieri*. In 1942 a new *bustina* with peak, like that worn by the Africa Corps, was introduced and found particularly suitable for wear in hot climates.

Special clothing was issued to personnel in motorised and tank units (see figure 93) which consisted of a black leather helmet with neck flap and a double-breasted black leather jacket. Parachute troops received a very practical collarless grey-green jacket cut like a *sahariana* and long baggy trousers worn gathered at the ankle. At first the *bustina* was to have been worn with this uniform but it was soon replaced by a grey-green beret. Parachute troops were also the first to wear camouflage clothing.

Italian soldiers in the colonies had two uniforms in the same basic cut as the grey-green ones, but in khaki cloth or khaki drill depending on the season. Also in use

was the bush jacket or *sahariana* which was equally popular in the German and Italian forces. Also popular were shirts and shorts worn with sandals. The basic head-dress was the sun helmet with arm-of-service badge in brass mounted on a circular cockade in the national colours on the front.

Officers had two basic uniforms. Service dress was a khaki version of the grey-green uniform, which with few additions could be worn as a full-dress. Head-dress was a khaki or white *bustina* which later was manufactured with a peak. Officers serving with colonial battalions in East Africa were permitted to continue wearing their arm-of-service badge of origin on their head-dress. The sun helmet was also made in khaki and white versions.

The field service dress was basically a shirt, *sahariana*, shorts with woollen socks and ankle boots or sandals, or breeches and brown leather boots. Officers serving in *meharisti* (units mounted on dromedaries) or saharan units also wore a white *sahariana* and loose baggy trousers: a practical and comfortable outfit.

INSIGNIA In the Italian Army rank badges appeared on the head-dress, shoulder straps, sleeves, cuffs, and on the front of various kinds of protective clothing. Officers and warrant officers wore rank distinction lace on their peaked cap band and on the left side of the *bustina*, and in the form of chevrons on the left side of the *Alpini* hat. On the temperate weather greatcoat and on the tunic rank badges were worn on the cuffs, but on the tropical jacket, *sahariana* and shirt they appeared on detachable shoulder straps. Other ranks wore small rank chevrons on the upper left sleeve of the tunic and greatcoat.

The rank badges of indigenous non-commissioned officers and men in colonial units consisted of red chevrons on a black cloth ground which were combined with stars according to length of service. On certain types of head-dress each rank chevron was represented by a star. (As illustrated in figure 95.) Those officers serving in the Army's colonial units wore the standard pattern rank badges. A badge worn on the front of most kinds of head-dress, including the steel helmet, identified the wearer's unit or arm of service. During the war this form of distinction became less common.

Collar patches appeared in regimental or arm-of-service colours, while certain arms had so-called 'flames' with one, two or three points. Other units had an emblem. The five-pointed star was common to all soldiers.

The colour of the bolero and sash of North African troops varied according to battalion, squadron or arm of service, whereas the sash worn by East African troops identified the arm of service. The *Penne di Falco* (colonial cavalry of the AOI) wore a wide sash of a tartan pattern in their squadron group colour around their *tarbusc*.

On the upper left sleeve was also worn a metal or cloth divisional shield on which appeared the number and name of the division, while the colour of the shield identified the type of division (red for motorised, blue for infantry and green for Alpine).

FASCIST MILITIA 1939–43

Roughly equivalent to the German Waffen-SS was the Italian Fascist Militia (*Milizia Volontaria Per La Sicurezza Nationale* or MVSN) more popularly known as the 'Black Shirts'. This fascist para-military organisation was formed in 1922 by Mussolini from the bands of ex-servicemen known as *Squadristi*.

The Commanding General of the MVSN was Mussolini himself while executive command was exercised by a chief-of-staff, who, during wartime, came under the command of the Italian Army. In imitation of the old Roman Army the MSVN adopted antiquated designations for its organisation:
Zona (Division);
Gruppo (Brigade);
Legion (Regiment);
Coorte (Battalion);
Centuria (Company);
Manipolo (Platoon);
Squadra (Section).

Ranks were similarly arranged: a *Console* commanded a regiment, and a *Centurione* a company. A Legion was composed of 3 cohorts and a cohort had 3 centuries.

The Militia was organised into 14 Zonal Commands (roughly equivalent to Army Corps areas), and there were 133 Legions each with two battalions (one of men aged between 21 and 36 and a second territorial battalion with men up to the age of 55). The average strength of a legion was intended to be 1300 men, but legions were usually understrength for one reason or another. Total strength at the outbreak of war was estimated at 340,000 men.

At the beginning of the war three Black Shirt divisions were formed, while a number of battalions went to reinforce infantry divisions. Black shirts had served in Abyssinia and Spain, and fought on all the World War II fronts Italy engaged in. The remaining Militiamen served as Army auxiliaries or in the special Militias: these were the Railways, Port, Post and Telegraph, Forestry, Anti-Aircraft and Coastal Defence, Frontier and University Militias. With the collapse of the Fascist regime the MVSN was disbanded.

ITALIAN ARMY INSIGNIA

Peaked Cap Bands

Field Service Cap Insignia

Cuff

Marshal of the Empire / Marshal of Italy / General (Army) / General (of Army Corps Cmdng Army) / General (Army Corps) / Lieutenant-General (Division) / Major-General (Brigade) / Colonel / Lieutenant-Colonel / Major / 1st Captain (I) / Captain (II)

Peaked Cap Bands

Field Service Cap Insignia

Cap and Arm

Cap Badge Marshals & Gens.

Cuff

Shoulder

1st Lieut (I) / Lieut (II) / 2nd Lieut / Cadet / Warrant Officer 1st Class (I) / Warrant Officer 2nd Class (II) / Warrant Officer 3rd Class (III) / Sergeant-Major / Sergeant / Corporal-Major / Corporal / Cap Badge Lt- & Major-Gens.

UNIFORM From June 1940 members of the MVSN Legion serving with the Italian Army wore standard grey-green uniform and its variations such as the khaki drill worn in the tropics. However, the Fascists retained the black shirt, black collar patches with the silver *fascio* and the black fez with tassel. Badges of rank were also basically the same as those worn in the Army except that a lozenge-shaped loop replaced the Army oval loop on the uppermost bar. Titles were different and echoed those of the legions of ancient Rome. Each of the three Black Shirt divisions had a distinctive black armshield which was worn on the upper left sleeve.

96 Corporal, MVSN

The fascist militia uniform was basically that of the Italian Army although MVSN men were distinguished by black shirts and black ties (hence the name Blackshirts). This corporal wears medal ribbons of the Crown of War Merit, Ethiopian Campaign, Volunteer in Spain, and ten years' service in the MVSN. The special dagger was a distinctive part of Blackshirt uniform.

96

AIR FORCE

On 24 January 1923 the Italian Royal Air Force (*Regia Aeronautica*) was formed as an independent arm, separate from the air services of the Army and Navy and in 1925 the establishment of an Air Ministry put the new service on a secure footing. During the inter-war years the Italian Air Force was held in high regard: Italian planes were technically advanced, and her Air Force commanders, who included the aerial theorist Giulio Douhet, were considered to be amongst the most progressive and imaginative in Europe. And yet by 1940 the Air Force was in decline.

Having built up a modern air force in the 'twenties and 'thirties, Italy did not develop it further with the result that at the outbreak of war Italy's front-line planes were largely obsolescent. During the course of the war attempts were made to replace the Fiat CR-32 and CR-42, the mainstay of Italy's fighter arm, but the industrial and technical weakness of the country failed to produce a plane in sufficient quantities that remedied the Italian problem of poor armament and a weak power-plant.

A further serious problem facing the Air Force was the defence of Italy's colonial possessions and its over-commitment in fulfilling Mussolini's grandiose designs.

Following the declaration of war on 10 June 1940, the Italian Air Force engaged with its French and British counterparts throughout the Mediterranean. Initially the Italian Air Force did reasonably well but with the introduction of the RAF's Hawker Hurricane towards the end of 1940 the balance of forces was tipped to the Allies' advantage.

During the October of 1940 Mussolini despatched an expeditionary force to Belgium in order to take part in the Battle of Britain. But once pitted against RAF Fighter Command on its home ground, the mixed Italian fighter/bomber force was badly mauled and was retired to defensive duties. A further expeditionary force was sent against the Soviet Union in the August of 1941 as part of the 'Crusade against Bolshevism'; the net result of which was to stretch Italian resources and to deny desperately needed aircraft to the Mediterranean Fronts.

In the Mediterranean the Air Force was engaged in the aerial assault on Malta and in supporting the Army in Libya. The failure to knock out Malta and prevent British convoys from traversing the Mediterranean made possible the build-up of British forces in North Africa and ultimately ensured the defeat of the out-numbered Axis forces in the autumn of 1942.

In Italian East Africa the Air Force provided the Army with reconnaissance and ground support services. The sides were fairly evenly matched, but the Italian Air Force was worn down in a battle of attrition. Italian pilots fought on to the bitter end until the last aircraft was shot down on 24 October 1941.

Mounting aircraft losses during 1941 and 1942 were not met by increased aircraft production, and Germany eventually took over the brunt of the aerial war in North Africa, the Italian Air Force concentrating on reconnaissance and supply duties as well as the defence of the homeland from the increasing attacks of Allied bomber forces.

The collapse of the Axis forces in North Africa in May 1943 and the massive build-up of Allied aircraft put the Italian Air Force on the defensive. Despite valiant efforts the Air Force was unable to stem the tide of Allied material supremacy. On 8 September, with the signing of the armistice, the *Regia Aeronautica* was no more.

The Italian Air Force had begun the war with nearly 2000 operational aircraft ready for combat and with almost the same number in reserve. By the September of 1943 the Air Force numbered 1200 aircraft of which about half were serviceable.

ORGANISATION In 1940 the Italian Air Force was divided into four Territorial Air Zones which covered metropolitan Italy and five overseas Commands. While the Air Force was an independent service within the Italian armed forces there was an Army air force of 37 squadrons which was attached directly to the ground forces as well as a Navy air service of 20 squadrons of sea-planes and flying-boats and ten squadrons of transport aircraft.

There were 12,000 pilots and aircrew, 6100 non-flying officers and 185,000 other ranks in the Air Force in 1940.

The basic tactical unit was the squadron (*squadriglia*) which had a strength of around nine aircraft with another three in reserve, although bomber squadrons usually had only six front-line planes. Occasionally the squadron might be broken down into two sections (*sezzione*) which could act in a semi-independent role.

Two or three squadrons formed an air group (*gruppo*) and two or more groups would form a wing or *stormo*, the basic tactical formation within the Air Force. Two or three wings would on occasion combine to form an air brigade which in turn with another brigade would form an air division. The largest formation in the

97 Air Marshal, Italian Air Force, 1940

Air Marshal Italo Balbo wears a combination of tropical and temperate uniform. On the cap is the elaborately embroidered greca which was the distinctive mark of general officers and marshals. Badges of rank also appear on the shoulder straps of the saharaina. One of the most popular figures in the Fascist movement, Balbo was accidentally shot down and killed by Italian anti-aircraft fire near Tobruk shortly after the declaration of war in the summer of 1940.

98 Major, Italian Air Force, 1940

The one-piece white flying suit was typical of the war in East and North Africa, although the white jacket of the two-piece flying suit was often worn with khaki drill shorts or other types of trousers. Badges of rank appear on the cuffs and the squadron badge on the left breast.

99 Major, Italian Air Force, 1942

This torpedo-bomber pilot wears a leather flying helmet and a flying jacket over his service dress. His rank badges are worn on the cuffs of the flying jacket and on the left breast is the metal badge of the torpedo bombardiers.

Air Force was the air fleet which consisted of two or more homogeneous fighter or bomber air divisions.

The forces within the Territorial Air Zones based in Italy were organised as follows:

Northern Zone – seven wings of bombers and three wings (plus one group) of CR-42 fighters;

Central Zone – three wings of bombers and two wings and a group of fighter planes;

Southern Zone – five bomber wings and one fighter wing as well as an autonomous fighter group and dive-bomber group;

South-Eastern Zone – one wing of night-bombers and float-planes and a group of obsolescent CR-32 fighters.

The largest of the overseas commands was that based in Libya and comprised four bomber wings; a fighter wing and three other fighter groups; and two groups plus two squadrons of colonial reconnaissance aircraft. The heavy losses incurred by the British offensive in January-February 1941 entailed a full-scale reinforcement of the Italian Air Force in North Africa.

Italian air strength in North Africa reached its peak in October 1942 with the following operational groups:
seven groups of MC-202 fighters;
five groups of CR-42 fighters;
one group of Ju 87 Stuka dive-bombers;
one group of Z-1007 bombers;
two groups of SM-79 bombers.

The shortage of spare parts and aviation fuel severely reduced the efficiency of the Italian Air Force in North Africa which by early 1942 had, in effect, become sub-ordinate to the Luftwaffe.

The Air Force in Italian East Africa was divided into three Commands:
Eritrea – ten bomber squadrons and three fighter squadrons;
Central Ethiopia – nine bomber squadrons, two fighter squadrons and one ground-attack squadron;
Southern Ethiopia – three bomber squadrons.

All told there were 338 aircraft spread throughout East Africa, of which 187 were with operational units.

97

98

99

ITALIAN AIR FORCE INSIGNIA

Peaked Cap Bands

Shoulder

Cuff

Air-Marshal | General (Air Army) | General (of Air Sqdn Cmdng Army) | General (Air Squadron) | Lieutenant-General (Division) (Services) | Major-General (Brigade) | Colonel | Lieutenant-Colonel (Commissariat) | Major | Captain (Fitter) | Lieutenant | 2nd Lieut (Engineers)

Cap Band W O s

Arm

Cap Badges
Gen. of Air Sqdn to Marshal *(left)*.
other Officers *(right)*

Flying Branch 'Passants

Generals

Senior Officers

W O (I) (Medical) | W O (II) (Flying)

W O (III) (Wireless) | W O (IV) (Mechanic) | Sergeant-Major | Sergeant | Corporal-Major (1st Aircraftman) | Corporal (Leading Aircraftman) | Pilot's Wings | Observer's Wings | Junior Officers

The Italian Army's invasion of Greece was supported by the Albanian Air Command (one bomber and one float-plane wing; plus one SM-79 bomber group, a group of ground-attack planes and two fighter squadrons) and the Italian South-Eastern Zone. With reinforcements this brought Italian strength to 380 planes against 149 Greek aircraft, although the Greek Air Force was itself being reinforced by RAF fighter and bomber aircraft. Throughout the early months of 1941 there was a constant battle between the Italian Air Force and the RAF and Greek Air Force to gain control of the skies; the conflict only being resolved by the German invasion of Yugoslavia and Greece in April 1941. Units of Italian aircraft remained in Greece until 1943 with the responsibility of attacking Allied shipping in the Aegean and eastern Mediterranean.

Although there had been occasional bombing raids on Italy by RAF Bomber Command, it was only in 1942, with the development of the successful long-range four-engined bomber, that the industrial centres of northern Italy came under any sustained attack from aircraft based in England.

Three groups of night-fighters were formed and a number of radar-equipped Messerschmitt Bf 110 and Dornier Do 217J aircraft were supplied from Germany but without a proper ground control system, an effective defence proved impossible. Fortunately for Italy, the main brunt of the Allied strategic air offensive was directed against Germany.

The loss of North Africa brought most of the Air Force back to Italy in order to defend the homeland against the expected Allied invasion. On 10 July 1942 – the date of the Allied invasion of Sicily – there were 165 aircraft on the island itself as well as units from the Italian Southern Zone. Although a transport ship was sunk on the first day of the invasion Italian losses were heavy. Allied air superiority over the battle-ground wore the Italian Air Force down. Many aircraft were destroyed on the ground by the Allies while the remaining serviceable aircraft were overwhelmed.

UNIFORM The uniform of the Italian Air Force was basically the same as that of the Army, but it was manufactured in grey-blue cloth. There were minor differences in cut, such as the pocket flaps which were three-pointed as opposed to straight. The side cap was a special model with a pleat in the crown, while airmen wore narrower pantaloons and puttees. Officers tended to wear long trousers and black shoes more often than their colleagues in the Army.

At the beginning of the war some of the frills disappeared: the shoulder straps and full-dress belt were abandoned, as was the coloured backing to the rank distinction lace which indicated the branch of the wearer.

The flying helmet was made of brown leather and there were two types of flying suit in general use. The winter model was lined and made of brownish olive-green material, whereas the summer one was made of white linen. Both types were manufactured in a one- or two-piece version. The Air Force parachute unit, *Arditi dell Aria*, had a grey-blue version of the Army parachute uniform on which was worn Air Force rank badges.

INSIGNIA Non-commissioned officers and men wore the same rank badges as their counterparts in the Army. Officers wore Army rank distinctions on the peaked cap and on the cuffs, but on the cuffs the loop was replaced by a diamond. The embroidered *greca* for general officers was in gold. On tropical jackets and shirts rank badges were worn on grey cloth shoulder straps.

During the war, the branch of service was identified by a small circular badge at the bottom of the cap badge. Other ranks wore a metal version of the same badge on their shoulder straps. This badge was also embroidered in gold wire on the grey cloth passants worn on both shoulders of the tunic and greatcoat by officers.

Pilots and observers wore gilt metal wings on the left breast above the medal ribbons, while aircrew wore a number of different badges on the left breast pocket. These badges were awarded in three classes for exceptional performance of duty.

NAVY

Mussolini hoped that the *Regia Navale* would play an important part in any Mediterranean war. He saw control of the sea (*Mare Nostrum* – Our Sea – was how he described the Mediterranean) as an essential prerequisite for expanding his empire into Nice, Corsica, Tunis and the Balkans. Italian naval building accelerated during his tenure of power, and by June 1940, the Navy comprised:
4 battleships;
8 heavy cruisers;
14 light cruisers;
128 destroyers;
115 submarines;
62 motor-torpedo boats.

There were also 4 battleships fitting out. The personnel of 4180 officers and 70,500 ratings was expanded rapidly on mobilisation, until there were, on average, 190,000 men serving at any time between 1940 and 1942.

The surrender of the French fleet in June 1940 seemed to offer a great opportunity to the *Regia Navale*; one of its main rivals had been removed at a stroke. But although the main Italian vessels were modern, fast and well-armed, and (in spite of graceful lines) had considerable armoured protection, the Italian vessels were overborne by the might of the British Royal Navy. Early defeats at Taranto and Matapan, although not crippling in themselves, confirmed British superiority; the absence of both radar and

a proper fleet air arm were considerable handicaps; and a shortage of fuel proved a progressively crippling brake on operations. Only the small attack craft lived up to expectations, in many brave and successful actions.

From June 1940 to September 1943, the Navy lost one battleship and 13 cruisers, out of total losses of 339 ships of all types, and 24,660 men.

ORGANISATION The supreme commander of the Italian armed forces and Minister of Marine was Benito Mussolini, but executive control was exercised by the Under-Secretary and Chief of Naval Staff (*Supermarina*) Admiral Domenico Cavagnari. Commander-in-Chief of the Fleet was Admiral Campioni. Departments of the Ministry of Marine and the Naval Staff undertook the customary responsibilities of the admiralty, with one exception. The Ministry of Marine submitted design requirements to a separate department which catered for the needs of all three services. Examples of this were the battleships *Littorio* and *Vittorio Veneto*, projected by General Umberto Pugliese, whose team supervised the arrangements for their construction by Ansaldo at Genoa and CRDA at Trieste.

The Navy was organised in two squadrons with torpedo-boats, submarines, training and reserves forming four main sub-divisions.

When Italy entered the war on 10 June 1940, the *Regia Navale* was disposed as follows.

The Taranto Command, which included Messina and Augusta, comprised:
2 battleships in divisions of 2 to 4 vessels, each commanded by a divisional rear-admiral. Several divisions were grouped together under a vice-admiral;
44 destroyers and torpedo-boats in divisions of 2 to 4 vessels;
22 submarines;
16 motor torpedo-boats in flotillas;
2 minelayers;
4 escort and patrol boats.
The Venice (Adriatic) Command including Brindisi and Bari comprised:
8 destroyers and torpedo-boats;
4 submarines;
16 motor-torpedo boats;
1 escort and patrol boat.
La Spezia Command including Cagliari consisted of:
21 destroyers and torpedo-boats;
36 submarines;
26 motor-torpedo boats;
1 minelayer;
3 escort and patrol boats.
The Naples Command consisted of:
4 cruisers;
18 destroyers and torpedo-boats;

Above: The wartime grey-green working rig of the sailor on the left contrasts with his companion's more formal square rig.

11 submarines;
6 motor torpedo-boats;
3 minelayers;
1 escort and patrol boat.
The Sicily-Libya Command, which included Syracuse, Palermo, Tripoli and Tobruk, consisted of:
1 cruiser;
24 destroyers and torpedo-boats;
26 submarines;
12 motor torpedo-boats;
2 minelayers;
3 escort and patrol boats.
The Dodecanese (Leros) Command comprised:
6 destroyers and torpedo-boats;
8 submarines;
20 motor-torpedo boats;
1 minelayer.
The Red Sea (Massawa) Command (which was destroyed in April 1941) comprised:
9 destroyers and torpedo-boats;
8 submarines;
5 motor-torpedo boats;
4 escort and patrol boats.
There were 1235 Italian merchant ships, totalling 3,448,453 tons.

The Navy lacked aircraft, and was dependent on the Air Force for protection and reconnaissance. This was an unsatisfactory state of affairs; co-operation was poor, and although the torpedo-bombers and reconnaissance aircraft of the *Regia Aeronautica* were effective, high-level bombers did not have much success against ships at sea.

The Navy did possess a small, antiquated air arm, the *Aviazione per la Regia Marina*, which was dispersed among the various commands, and it was clear that a fast aircraft carrier was required. *Aquila* was converted from a liner, but she was not ready by the time the armistice was signed.

This lack of close air support was particularly serious because of Italy's problem of supplying her forces in North Africa. Land-based fighters, including the deadly Stukas, could not prevent aerial, surface and submarine harassment of Axis Mediterranean convoys. Each handful of German and Italian merchantmen had to be escorted by two or three destroyers and torpedo boats, which suffered grievous losses: 85 of the escorts were sunk while only 33 were built from dwindling stocks of raw materials, or captured from defeated navies.

There were few specialist escort vessels. It had been hoped that a combination of minefields (most warships except the very largest were equipped for minelaying) and defensive patrols by major surface units and submarines would seal off the Adriatic and Tyrhennian Seas, forming two corridors of sea power from Italy to North Africa and the Dodecanese. Meanwhile a smaller number of warships was to be employed against French and British communications.

The construction of smaller corvette-size escorts was begun and 32 were completed but, five had been lost by 8 September 1943. As the war progressed, however, experience and the installation of German detection equipment accounted for the loss of at least another 19 British submarines.

The Italian Navy did have one great advantage: it was the only fleet with continuous peacetime experience of fast attack craft. The MAS-boats (torpedo-armed motor boats or anti-submarine motor boats) were equipped with non-tumbling gyros which enabled their torpedoes to be dropped from light racks, and were driven by Isotta Fraschini petrol engines.

The tradition of attack in small craft was the basis of the most successful of all formations in the Royal Italian Navy: *Decima Flotiglia MAS* (10th MAS Flotilla) formed in August 1940 under *Capitano di Fregata* Vittorio Moccagatta. There was a Surface Division, commanded by *Capitano di Corvetta* Giorgio Giobbe and an Underwater Division under the leaderships of *Capitano di Corvetta* Prince Junio Valerio

Borghese: under the Republic he ran the whole flotilla. Their weapons were explosive motor boats (delivered by destroyers), guided two-man torpedoes (launched from submarines) and small charges (carried by free-swimming frogmen).

Overcoming early misfortunes and, on occasion, suffering high casualties, they wrecked the cruiser HMS *York* in Suda Bay, disabled the two battleships HMS *Queen Elizabeth* and *Valiant* at Alexandria, and conducted a two-year campaign against shipping at Gibraltar. This last was undertaken secretly, operating from Spanish territory, with the assistance of the Italian Naval Consul. Threat of such attacks added to the strain on the defenders of all Mediterranean anchorages.

100 Submarine Commander, Italian Navy, 1943

In contrast to the formally dressed Naval Officer in figure 101, this submarine commander wears a very unorthodox outfit, the only regulation part of which is the peaked cap. The windcheater is worn with sports shorts and seaboots and sea socks.

Italian submarines and MAS boats also operated outside the Mediterranean. From January 1941 onwards a total of 32 submarines joined Admiral Dönitz's U-boats in the Atlantic. Although they accounted for the loss of about a million tons of Allied shipping, their large conning towers and slow surface speed made them unsuitable for wolf-pack attacks on convoys. Several were later converted for use as undersea blockade runners between the Far East and Europe.

Meanwhile six midget submarines had been transported overland to the Black Sea, becoming operational on 19 June 1942. They lay in wait off the Crimean coast for Soviet vessels attempting to supply the besieged town of Sevastopol or

101 Ranking Lieutenant, Italian Navy, 1942

This officer wears standard officers service dress with peaked cap and 'reefer' jacket. Rank is indicated by the bands around the cap, the bars and 'curl' on the cuff and by the 'passants' on the shoulder (these are shown in more detail in the rank insignia chart).

100   101

102

103

104

102 Seaman, Italian Navy, 1941

This rating wears the basic 'square rig' of the Italian Navy in the correct manner. On the cap tally appears the legend, Regia Marina in gold letters. On the back of his blue denim collar are two five-pointed white stars.

103 Seaman, Italian Navy, 1942

This seaman operating out of Bordeaux is serving on a submarine, hence the dolphin badge on his left breast. This practical uniform in Army grey-green with black beret was introduced for submarine crews during the course of the war and was only to be worn on board ship.

104 Sergeant-Major Italian Marine Infantry, 1942

This is basically the same uniform as worn by the submariner but in the version for marines with pantaloons and puttees. The distinctive badge of the marines was the Lion of St. Mark which was worn on the cuffs, while the badges of rank appear as inverted chevrons on the sleeve. The web equipment was made under contract in Britain by the Mills company. The dagger is similar to the pattern worn by the Fascist Militia. Although only of ceremonial value the wearing of these weapons was widespread in the Italian armed forces.

interfere with German convoys, but with no success. Ten MAS-boats of the 4th Flotilla also accompanied the midget submarines to Yalta; they sank one submarine and blew the stern off the 8800-ton cruiser *Molotov*.

Another four MAS-boats served on Lake Ladoga in northern Russia from the summer of 1942 to June 1943, and were subsequently handed over to the Finnish Navy. In September 1943, all surviving Italian vessels in the Black Sea, at Bordeaux, and in the Far East, were seized by the Romanians, Germans and Japanese.

At the time of the Italian Armistice in September 1943, all *Regia Navale* warships were ordered to make their way to Allied ports. Some were already at sea, but others had to fight their way out of German control. Only a small number preferred to remain in the service of Mussolini and the newly-declared Italian Socialist Republic: the Navy had strong Royalist traditions and felt no loyalty to the Fascist regime. Its personnel braved the Luftwaffe dive-bombers rather than surrender to the Germans.

UNIFORM The uniforms of the Royal Italian Navy were based on the regulations published in February 1936. Typical officers' service dress is illustrated in figure 101. In the summer months or in tropical waters officers wore a white cap cover and single-breasted white tunic trimmed with white lace.

Petty officers wore the same blue uniform as officers but the white tunic was simpler having open patch pockets and no lace trimming.

Ratings wore the square rig illustrated in figure 102 and were also issued with a three-quarter-length pea-coat. In the summer they also wore a white cap cover and shirt with blue denim collar and cuffs.

During the war, and particularly in small vessels such as submarines dress was varied and informal. Officers continued to wear their peaked cap or a peaked field cap, on the left side of which there was a reduced version of the rank badge. Overalls, windcheaters, shirts of various colours and pullovers were worn in conjunction with items of regulation uniform. A simpler version of the working rig in grey-green is illustrated in figure 103.

Marine officers wore grey-green Army uniform with Naval rank distinctions on the cap and cuffs. Other ranks wore the uniform illustrated in figure 104. In North Africa Marines wore a khaki drill uniform which was similar in cut to the grey-green version.

INSIGNIA Officers wore rank distinction lace on the peaked cap and on the cuffs. On the greatcoat, white tunic and tropical jackets officers and petty officers wore rank badges on shoulder straps. Commissioned warrant officers wore officers' uniforms with rank distinction lace on the cuffs surmounted by a small metal branch badge. Petty officers and ratings wore the same rank badges as Army non-commissioned officers on the sleeves.

Only line officers were entitled to wear a curl on the rank distinction lace on the cuffs, while those in other branches had a branch colour appearing in the centre of the cap badge, as backing to the rank lace on the cap and cuffs, and as piping on the passants and shoulder straps. Ratings wore their branch badges above their rank chevrons on the sleeves.

ITALIAN SOCIAL REPUBLIC 1943–1945

ARMY

On 12 September 1943 German paratroopers liberated Mussolini and six days later the Italian Social Republic was formed on the side of the Germans against the Allies and the Kingdom of the South.

The formation of an army in a war zone was not easy. The Germans refused to release the 600,000 men they had taken into captivity on 8 September, but did allow the recruitment of 13,000 volunteers from amongst the prisoners. By March 1944 the Fascists had 60,000 men.

Between September and November 1944 the first four divisions which had been sent to Germany for equipping and training, returned to Italy. They fought alongside the Germans throughout the rest of the Italian Campaign.

UNIFORM In the beginning the uniforms of the Army of the RSI were basically the same as those worn prior to

8 September 1943. However, all monarchistic symbols were removed from the insignia and the five-pointed star was replaced by a Roman sword within a wreath of laurel which became the symbol of the RSI.

At the end of 1944 new dress regulations were issued which attempted to Germanise Italian uniform, but the general situation and lack of supplies meant that these regulations never really came into force, and only a few senior officers ever actually wore them. The RSI was far too busy fighting for survival against the Allies and the internal threat posed by the partisans to worry too much about new uniforms.

Uniform became a very mixed combination of the classic *sahariana* with anoraks, camouflage clothing, and the new collarless parachutist's jacket. The old grey-green tunic was often rebuttoned in the German style. Typical were the long baggy trousers fastened at the ankle and worn with ankle boots and rolled woollen socks, or pantaloons with puttees or leggings. Both officers and men contributed to the confusion by adopting the

ITALIAN NAVY INSIGNIA

Peaked Cap Bands

Shoulder

Cuff

| Admiral of the Fleet | Admiral | Vice-Admiral (di Armata) | Vice-Admiral (di Squadra) | Rear Admiral (di Divisione) (Construction) | Rear-Admiral (Naval Ordnance) | Captain (Commissariat) | Commander (Medical) | Lieutenant-Commander | Lieutenant/ Ranking Lt. | Lieutenant (II)/ Ranking Lt. (II) | Sub-Lieutenant |

Peaked Cap Bands

'Passants' for Blue Uniforms

Shoulder

| W.O. 1st Class (I) (Yeoman) | W.O. 2nd Class (II) (Radio) | W.O. 3rd Class (III) (Gun Pointer) | Petty Officer (I) (Fire Control) | Petty Officer (II) (Torpedoman's Mate) | Leading Seaman (I) (Gnr. 4th Sqdn) | Leading Seaman (II) (Signals. 1st Sqdn) | Able Seaman (Artificer Fireman. 3rd Sqdn) | Sub-Lieut and Lieut (II) |

Admirals

Lieutenant to Capt.

W.O. (I)

W.O. (II)

W.O. (III)

105 Militiaman, Legion Tagliamento, Italian Social Republic, 1944

Typical of the type of para-military uniform to be seen on the Fascist side at the end of the war was this outfit worn by a Legionary 'M' (Mussolini) of the Republican National Guard (GNR). The black head-dress was similar to the pattern worn in dark red by the bersaglieri. The Legion badge, a silver fascio on a red letter 'M', was worn on the collar of the black shirt or on black collar patches. Equipment is a mixture of Italian and German. The belt is Luftwaffe, the grenades German, the dagger is the standard MVSN pattern, and the sub-machine gun is the Beretta M38. This weapon had been widely used before 1943, and proved very popular with RSI para-military forces and partisans alike, because it was well made and reliable.

106 Major-General, Italian Social Republic Air Force, 1944

The service dress is still that which was in use before September 1943, but with new-pattern peaked cap. The gladi have replaced the stars on the collar. In his button-hole is the ribbon of the Iron Cross 2nd Class; German decorations were still being worn by Fascist troops.

Above: Italian troops loyal to Mussolini celebrate the fact with some Germans in October 1943. A variety of uniforms are on show: the German on the right in peaked cap, for example, is in tropical uniform, with the distinctive badge on the cap front. In the centre, an Italian officer is standing next to another German in tropical gear. The Italian soldiers are wearing various elements of the standard uniform, including the shirt, jacket, shorts, trousers and cap.

most disparate and eccentric styles of dress. The peaked *bustina* was widely worn alongside the *alpini* hat and the *bersaglieri* fez.

INSIGNIA Rank insignia was moved from the cuffs to the shoulder straps, but the new pattern of rank insignia prescribed in the September 1944 regulations was never introduced. The original divisions which were equipped and trained in Germany adopted German rank insignia for other ranks as a practical measure to enable German training personnel to recognise the rank of Italian non-commissioned officers and men, but on their return to Italy German rank badges were usually removed. New coloured badges and collar patches were also introduced to identify arm of service.

PARA-MILITARY FORCES

The *Guardia Nazionale Repubblicana* was formed on 24 November 1943 to replace the MVSN which had been found to be unreliable. The GNR, composed of ex-members of the *Carabinieri* Militia (which had also been disbanded for having shown

105

106

107 Major,
Italian Social Republic Air Force, 1944

The badge on the cap is the new pattern and the lace around the cap band denotes his rank. The jacket is the sahariana, *on the collar of which are worn the* gladi *of the Social Republic armed forces. On his left breast he wears pilot's 'wings' and Italian medal ribbons as well as the Iron Cross and the ribbon for the Iron Cross 2nd Class.*

108 Private,
Italian Social Republic Marine, 1944

This bearded marine wears the special grey-green uniform originally introduced for Army parachutists. The Lion of St. Mark is no longer worn on the cuffs but on the collar patches which also bear the gladio. *He is armed with a Beretta M38 sub-machine gun.*

109 Seaman,
Italian Social Republic Navy, 1944

This seaman wears Naval square rig with web equipment (originally manufactured in England for RIN) and steel helmet with the second pattern anchor painted on the front. On the back of the blue collar the star was replaced by a white gladio.

allegiance to the King) and former members of the Italian African Police, was called upon to carry out both military and civil police duties.

With the constitution of the Social Republic ex-members of the old Fascist squads (*Squadristi*) reappeared and began to scour the country looking for 'traitors'. Pavolini, secretary of the National Fascist Party, wanted to use the squads in the war against both the resistance and the partisans, and so on the 26 July 1944 the Black Brigades were formed as the armed force of the Fascist Party. Notorious for their ferocity in the service of the German security forces (SS and Police), the Black Brigades represented all the best and worst elements of the Social Republic – decorated heroes, child mascots, common criminals, opportunists and idealists.

UNIFORM The National Guard retained the collar patches and black shirt of the former Militia (MVSN), but adopted a pair of red letter 'M's (Mussolini) instead of the *gladio*.

The Black Brigades (*Brigate Nera*) had in theory the simplest of uniforms consisting of black beret, black shirt and grey-green tunic or woollen sweater. Trousers were grey-green or khaki depending on season. In reality they appeared in an amazing array of extravagant and irregular uniforms and insignia of personal invention whose common denominator was the skull and crossed bones and mottoes involving death.

AIR FORCE

The Air Force of the RSI was formed on 27 October 1943. Its creation was due to the efforts of Lieutenant-Colonel 'Iron Leg' Botto, a man noted for his great organisational talents and firmness in respect of both restless pilots and the Germans. Following the armistice, the Germans had requisitioned aircraft and equipment as well as pilots and technicians. Botto managed to get most back, but his clashes with General Wolfram von

107

108

109

110

Richthofen and German attempts to
incorporate the RSI Air Force into the
Luftwaffe meant that the Air Force did
not become operational until October
1944. In the period January 1944 to
April 1945 it succeeded in shooting down
240 Allied aircraft, mostly B-17 and B-24
bombers.

The main strength of the RSI Air
Force was in fighter and torpedo aircraft.
There was a bomber squadron but for
political reasons it was sent to the Eastern
Front. Torpedo aircraft operated against
the Allied Fleet in the Mediterranean

from March 1944, and in June of that
year took part in the bombing of
Gibraltar.

After September 1943 the uniform of
the Air Force of the Italian Social
Republic remained virtually unchanged
except that the star was replaced by the
gladio.

NAVY

Few Navy personnel joined Mussolini's
MAS Flotilla instructed German K-men
in the employment of small battle units
and worked with them in attacks on Allied
shipping (which by then had prepared
routine precautions against them). There
were about a dozen MAS-boats and
midget submarines in Fascist service:
most ex-Italian vessels were manned by
the *Kriegsmarine*, however. The Fascist
Navy only reached a twentieth the size of
the Co-Belligerent Fleet.

The uniforms of the Navy of the Italian
Social Republic underwent few changes.
The crown was removed from the cap
badge and replaced by a winged bird and
the stars were replaced by the *gladio* on
the collar of both the reefer and sailor's
blue jean collar. Rank distinction lace on
the cap band was replaced by different
patterns of chin cords which were blue and
gold for junior and gold for senior officers.
The traditional sailors' cap fell into disuse
and was replaced by a blue beret with a
small gilt metal anchor on the front, and
from 1943 Republican Marines began to
receive the grey-green parachute troop
uniform as illustrated in figure 108.

ITALIAN
CO-BELLIGERENT
FORCES

On 28 September 1943 the first military
unit of the Kingdom of the South was
constituted as the First Motorised Combat
Group (*1. Raggruppamento Motorizzato*)
with a strength of 295 officers and 5387
men. Its first action was in the Cassino
sector at Monte Lungo, and did much to
remove Allied distrust of Italian soldiers
fighting on their side.

Following service with the American
5th Army and re-organisation the *Raggruppamento* was transferred to the Polish
Army on the extreme left of the British
8th Army.

On 17 April 1944 the formation, now
22,000-men strong, assumed the name
Italian Liberation Corps (*Corpo Italiano di
Liberazione*). The continuous influx of
volunteers made it necessary to form
further formations, but for political

reasons what had now become divisions
were still called combat groups. Each
Gruppi di Combattimento had two infantry
and one artillery regiment, a mixed
battalion of engineers, two sections of
Carabinieri and services totalling 400
officers and 9000 men.

The first six of these groups entered the
line at the beginning of 1945, but
political considerations still meant that
the Allies underscored the part played by
Royalist troops in the victory in Italy.

The Italian Navy played an important
role once the armistice was signed.
Altogether five battleships, eight cruisers,
33 destroyers, 39 submarines, 12 motor
torpedo-boats, 22 escorts and three minelayers of the *Regia Navale* formed a Co-
Belligerent Force. There were an additional four squadrons of seaplanes from
the *Regia Aeronautica*. The Italian C-in-C
established his headquarters at Taranto,
but three cruisers were soon detached to
help hunt blockade runners in the South
Atlantic. Other vessels were assigned to
various tasks in the Mediterranean after
undergoing refits and repairs. One of the
force's most significant contributions
during this period was its cooperation in
the rehabilitation of Italian harbours. At
the same time, Italian frogmen joined
British human-torpedo teams in sinking
two cruisers and the aircraft carrier
Aquila lying disabled in German-occupied
ports.

The other major element of the Italian
forces on the Allied side was, of course,
the partisans; but they were unstandard-
ised in organisation and uniform.

UNIFORM At the beginning the grey-
green or khaki Italian uniforms continued
to be worn with the insignia of the House
of Savoy on the breast. The lack of
supplies of all sorts, partly due to Allied
bombing and partly as a result of German
requisitioning forced the Italians to adopt
Allied uniform and equipment. The
choice was for English uniforms on which
the Italian insignia was to remain unchanged. Even the *Bersaglieri* and the
Alpini attached their respective feathers
to the British Mk. 1 steel helmet. Since it
was necessary to differentiate the Italians
from the rest of the Allied troops, a
rectangular badge in the Italian national
colours was introduced for wear high on
the left sleeve. The emblem of the combat
group was printed in black on the white of
the Italian *Tricolore*. Officers moved their
rank badges from the cuff to the shoulder
straps.

The uniforms of the Royalist Air Force
and Navy did not undergo any great
changes.

GREECE

ARMY

From 1935 until the German invasion, Greece was a constitutional monarchy under King George II, but the actual power was in the hands of her dictator-President General Metaxas.

The Greek armed forces, like most of those of the smaller nations, suffered from a shortage of modern weapons and motor transport. However, the mountainous frontier with Albania was ideal for defensive fighting, and the natural sturdiness of her soldiers proved too much for the Italian forces which invaded on 28 October 1940. The outnumbered Greek forces were able not only to contain the Italian attack, but force the invaders back into Albania, where, with the British aid in men and *matériel*, they were able to hold them until the Germans invaded from Yugoslavia on 6 April 1941. This attack, by the best army in Europe, overwhelmed the Greek defences, and despite bitter resistance the Germans forced the Greek Army in eastern Macedonia to capitulate and the Allies to retreat. On 20 April the Greek Epirus Army surrendered and on 22 April the Allies began their evacuation of Greece.

ORGANISATION The Commander-in-Chief of the Greek Armed Forces was General Papagos and the control of the Army was exercised by a General Headquarters and five Army Corps areas.

In 1940, just before the Italian attack, Greece mobilised her armed forces. The field army was organised in two Army Groups, six general headquarters, six infantry and nine mountain divisions, four mountain brigades and one cavalry division. At the outbreak of war the Army numbered 430,000 men, but losses were heavy and some 60,000 men were killed, wounded or missing after the winter fighting.

In March 1941, shortly before the German invasion, the Greek Army, under four army high commands and three general headquarters, comprised:
5 infantry divisions;
14 mountain divisions;
1 infantry brigade;
1 motorised division;
1 cavalry division.

In March 1941, total strength was 540,000 men, but this included 50,000 recruits with only one month's training. The German invasion cost the Greeks 15,700 battle casualties; about 220,000 Greek soldiers were taken prisoner, but released soon after.

The army corps each consisted of two

to four infantry or mountain divisions. I, II, III, IV Corps were each supported by a heavy artillery regiment of 7 batteries (8×85mm, 8×105mm and 12×155mm guns) while V Corps had 4×85mm guns, 4×105mm guns and 4 static six-inch guns. Each corps also had its own anti-aircraft support of 88mm, 37mm and 20mm guns.

An infantry division consisted of three infantry regiments, a regiment of divisional artillery and ancillary units. The mountains divisions were particularly important given that the Greek Army, woefully deficient in modern equipment, preferred to fight in the mountains. The mountain divisions were organised on the same basis as the infantry divisions, but with rather less artillery. Mountain and infantry divisions were 12,000-strong.

The 56 regiments of infantry each consisted of a regimental staff, reconnaissance platoon, HQ platoon, staff company, and two battalions each with battalion staff, three rifle companies and one machine-gun company. Regimental strength was about 58 officers and 1100 men. The main weapon was the Mannlicher-Schönauer M1903/14 rifle. Support weapons comprised:
36 light machine guns (Hotchkiss 8mm);
8 heavy machine guns (St Etienne M07);
4×81mm mortars;
2×65mm mountain guns.

The crack infantry of the Greek Army were the *Evzones*. Originally formed as light infantry during the war for independence at the beginning of the 19th century, these highlanders became part of the regular army in 1833. In 1940 they served in light regiments and in the Royal Guard.

Divisional artillery for the mountain divisions consisted of four batteries (in the Greek Army a battery consisted of four guns) of 75mm mountain guns, and two batteries of 105mm guns. Infantry divisions had nine batteries of 75mm field guns. Each Army Corps had its own allocation of heavy artillery (see above) and there were, in addition, 12 batteries of heavy artillery for use with the field army.

Since the artillery was equipped with either French, German or Czech guns Britain was unable to supply ammunition, and stocks in America were soon exhausted, so all the British could do was supply the Greeks with Italian *matériel* captured in Libya.

In addition to the line infantry and mountain regiments there were a number of battalions and companies for island and land frontier defence, as well as a number of mobile and static machine gun units. When the British landed in Greece

III

in March 1940 they were dismayed to find that many divisions existed in name only. One division of recently-assembled troops had a strength of just six battalions, and its transport was limited to the commander's motor car and five trucks, while the 'motorised' division had been formed from 2000 recently conscripted garage hands. It had only 24 light Italian and Dutch tankettes, some Italian lorries, a few British Bren Gun Carriers, and some motor cycles and motor cars.

There were two regiments of cavalry each with four sabre squadrons, a machine gun troop with 12 machine guns and a squadron with four 81mm mortars. A third regiment, in the process of motorisation, consisted of four squadrons equipped

112 Lieutenant, Greek Army, 1941

The kepi is the pre-war model with rank distinction lace. Rank badges were worn on the shoulder straps, while the black collar patches indicate artillery. As a mounted officer this lieutenant wears riding breeches and boots. In addition to his 'Sam Browne' belt he carries binoculars and a map case.

113 Lieutenant-Colonel, Greek Army, 1941

The service dress worn by this officer was almost identical to the British model with metal rank badges on the shoulder straps. The Greek Crown above an enamel cockade in the Greek national colours was worn on most head-dresses. The arm of service was denoted by the dark red gorget patch with yellow grenade for infantry officers.

114 Private, Greek Army, 1941

This Evzone wears the Greek steel helmet over his side cap and a coarse compressed goat-fleece cape over his service dress. Instead of the more typical pantaloons and puttees this stalwart wears the tight pantaloons, stockings and footwear, which were the military version of the native dress of the Greek mountain dwellers. Again, the enamel cockade is clearly visible on the cap.

with armoured cars, one machine-gun troop, one squadron with 81 mm mortars and a mounted machine-gun troop with three machine-gun companies each with 12 machine guns, and a sabre troop. These three regiments together with a battery of mountain artillery, a pioneer squadron and a radio squadron were formed into an independent brigade and played an important role in the defeat of the Italian invasion.

Apart from this large formation, there were mounted forces serving as reconnaissance units with the Army Corps and infantry divisions; these reconnaissance battalions consisted of two squadrons, a machine-gun company or section, and (for the corps units) a mortar section.

The Greek Army had put up a stout resistance to the forces of the Axis, and Greek partisans were to prove a redoubtable foe for the Germans.

UNIFORM Greek Army uniform had developed along British lines and the service dress for officers illustrated in figure 113 differed only in so far as

officers wore collar patches, and on the khaki peaked cap general and field officers had gold embroidery on the peak. The greatcoat for officers was double breasted and was also worn with collar patches and shoulder strap rank badges.

Other ranks' uniforms were made of coarse khaki cloth and were also similar in cut to the British khaki service dress. In fact uniforms supplied by Britain were worn complete with buttons bearing the British coat of arms. The uniform consisted of side cap, tunic, single-breasted greatcoat, and pantaloons worn with puttees and ankle boots. Mounted personnel wore breeches and riding boots or leather leggings.

A distinctive uniform based on Greek national dress was worn by the crack *Evzones* who formed the Royal Guard. On active service the more extreme features such as the pleated kilt and shoes with woollen pompoms were, of course, replaced by the more practical uniform worn by the other dismounted soldiers.

There were two steel helmets in general use in the Greek Army. The first was the

112   113   114

GREEK ARMY INSIGNIA

Cap Peaks

Shoulder

Marshal | Lieutenant-General | Major-General | Colonel | Lieutenant-Colonel | Major | Captain | Lieutenant | 2nd Lieut

Collar Patches

Shoulder

Warrant Officer (Artillery) | Sergeant-Major (Infantry) | Sergeant (Artillery) | Corporal (Cavalry) | Lance-Corporal (Engineers) | Lance-Corporal (Reserve) | Generals | Other Officers (Patch in arm-of-service colour) | Gen Staff Officers

British Mk. 1 pattern, which was in the process of being replaced by a Greek model similar to the Italian helmet.

INSIGNIA Officers wore rank badges on the shoulder straps of the tunic and greatcoat, while non-commissioned officers wore chevrons on the sleeves. Those for regulars were in gold or yellow lace and were edged in the arm-of-service colour, while the chevrons for conscripts were silver and unedged.

The arm-of-service colour appeared on the collar patches and as edging to the rank chevrons of regular non-commissioned officers.

AIR FORCE

The Greek Air Ministry was responsible for the air services maintained by the Greek Army and Navy. There was no independent Air Force as such. The Army air service was small with just 250 officers and 3000 men. Many of the pilots had undergone their training in England, and although outnumbered first by the Italians and then by the Germans, the air service put up a stubborn resistance in the campaigns of 1941.

Right: Greek Air Force groundcrew in service dress talk to an RAF pilot. Both the side and peaked caps are being worn.

In 1940 the combined strength of the Army and Navy air services was as follows:
44 fighters (including Polish P.Z.L.24s, Gloster Gladiators and a few Hurricanes);
46 bombers and reconnaissance planes;
16 general purpose aircraft;
20 flying boats (Fairey IIIs and German Do 22s).

When the Germans invaded in April 1941 only 41 combat aircraft were still operational.

The Army air service was organised in three flying regiments each of two squadrons, based on rather primitive airfields in Athens, Candia, Drama, Joannina Larissa, Salonica, Tanagra and Thebes. Its primary role was to provide air support for ground operations, but by

January 1941 casualties and lack of spares had practically grounded it, and so the Greek command had to appeal to the RAF to switch its emphasis from bombing Italian lines of communication to providing air support to ground forces.

UNIFORM The grey-blue service dress for officers is illustrated in figure 115, although on active service officers appear to have preferred wearing breeches and high boots. The side cap and the greatcoat were, like the rest of the uniform, modelled on the British RAF pattern. Other ranks wore a grey-blue version of the khaki uniform with side cap, single-breasted tunic, pantaloons and puttees and ankle boots.

Flying clothing consisted of the usual leather flying helmet, goggles, and fleece-lined leather flying jacket which was worn over the service dress or overall.

INSIGNIA Officers wore rank distinction lace on the cuffs, while general officers had two and field officers one row of gold embroidered oak leaves on the cap peak. Other ranks wore Army-pattern rank badges on the sleeves. There were no arm-of-service colours as such, but qualified pilots wore embroidered 'wings' over medal ribbons on the left breast.

NAVY

The executive commander of the Navy was the Chief of the Admiralty, Admiral A. Sakellariou. Under him were 6300 regular naval officers and men and 11,000 reservists and the following vessels:
1 old armoured cruiser built in 1905/06;
2 old light cruisers;
4 old destroyers;
4 Hidra Class (Italian) destroyers;
13 old torpedo boats;
2 motor torpedo-boats;
6 submarines.

The Greek Navy suffered its first loss on 15 August 1940, before the opening of hostilities, when the minelaying cruiser *Helli* was alleged to have been sunk by an Italian submarine. On the outbreak of the war two months later the Navy's first task was to ensure the safe passage of thousands of Army reservists recalled to the colours from the numerous Greek isles. At the same time the Navy patrolled the coast of Albania and provided artillery support.

German entry into the Greco-Italian war was heralded by aerial attacks which destroyed a number of Greek warships. On 21 April 1941 the Greek government decided to evacuate the mainland, and the port of Salamis was blown up as the last ship carrying Allied troops left. 29 warships and auxiliary vessels were

115 Wing Commander, Greek Air Force, 1941
Air Force officers with the rank of Squadron Leader and above wore a row of gold-embroidered oakleaves on the cap peak. Rank distinction lace on the cuffs followed the Navy pattern and had a diamond shaped 'curl' on the upper row. The embroidered wings are worn on the left breast above the ribbons.

116 Able Seaman, Greek Navy, 1941
This seaman in parade dress is dressed like a 'matelot' in the British Royal Navy. The inscription on the cap tally reads, B. Naytikon. The red chevron on his arm indicates his rank and the torpedo badge his speciality. He is armed with an M1903/14 rifle.

sunk – a very high proportion of the pre-war Navy.

UNIFORM Greek naval uniform followed the international pattern, and like the uniforms of the other branches of the armed forces, followed closely the British style.

Officers wore the peaked cap with or without white cover and a gold-embroidered cap badge on the front. The reefer jacket had rank distinction lace on the cuffs and was worn with long trousers and black shoes. In the summer months or in tropical waters officers wore a white tunic with stand collar, white trousers and

the standard-issue white canvas shoes.

Petty officers wore a similar uniform to that worn by officers, but had a special cap badge.

Ratings wore the uniform illustrated in figure 116, and a white version in tropical waters. The leggings were the same webbing pattern as worn in the British Royal Navy but the waistbelt and leather ammunition pouches were as issued to the Greek Army.

Officers wore rank distinction lace on the cuffs and on the shoulder straps of the greatcoat and white tunic. Petty officers and ratings wore their rank badges on the upper sleeve.

GREEK AIR FORCE INSIGNIA

Cap Peaks

Cuff

| Air Marshal | Air Vice-Marshal | Group Captain | Wing Commander | Squadron Leader | Flight Lieutenant | Flying Officer | Pilot Officer |

Cuff / **Arm**

| Warrant Officer | Flight Sergeant | Sergeant | Senior Corporal | Corporal | Flying Off (Khaki drill shoulder strap) |

Cap Badges Officers (left) Other Ranks (right)

Pilot's wings

GREEK NAVY INSIGNIA

Cap Peak: Flag Officers

Captain to Lt. Commander

Capt. to Lt. Comndr (legal branch)

Capt. to Lt. Comndr (other branches)

Cap Badge: Officers

Shoulder

Cuff

| Admiral of the Fleet | Admiral | Vice-Admiral | Rear-Admiral (Engineers) | Captain (Construction) | Commander | Lieutenant-Commander (Aviation) | Lieutenant (Supply) | Lieutenant (II) (Reserve, Medical) | Sub-Lieut (Volunteer Reserves) |

Cap Badge: Petty Officers

Arm

| Chief Warrant Officer (Telegraphy) | Warrant Officer (Electrician) | C.P.O. (Ordnance Artificer) | P.O. (I) (Boatswain) | P.O. (II) (Marksman Gunnery) | P.O. (III) | Leading Seaman (Signals) | Able Seaman (Machinist) |

101

YUGOSLAVIA
ARMY

The titular head of the armed forces was the King. At the end of March 1941 a group of Army officers overthrew the Regent Prince Paul and declared Crown Prince Peter King, although technically he was under age. This coup was seen abroad as a spontaneous patriotic rejection of the unpopular alliance with Germany although the coup had been planned long before negotiations for the alliance began. The Germans immediately prepared to invade.

When the Germans attacked at 5.15 am on 6 April 1941, from bases in Bulgaria, the Yugoslav Army (including some 400,000 recent draftees) was spread out along 1800 miles of border. The front soon crumbled and on 9 April further massive attacks were launched from Austria and Hungary. Two days later the Italians and Hungarians joined in the fray. By 13 April organised resistance was coming to an end and on 17 April 1941 Yugoslavia capitulated. 6028 officers and 337,684 other ranks were captured by the Germans.

ORGANISATION Yugoslavia had a standing army and the male population was liable for military service from the age of 20. The first one and a half years was done in the active army, followed by 18 years in the reserve, and a final ten years in the reserve of the reserve army. The peacetime strength of the Army was 148,000 and mobilised strength approximately 1,400,000 men.

The Army was divided into five army corps with headquarters in Neusatz, Sarajevo, Üskup, Agram and Nis. They comprised:

16 infantry divisions;
1 independent guards division;
2 cavalry divisions;
32 regiments of artillery (a total of 90 battalions and 213 batteries);
6 regiments of engineers;
various supporting arms.

An army corps consisted of a headquarters and three or four infantry divisions; an infantry division had a headquarters, two to four infantry regiments, one or two artillery regiments or an independent artillery battalion and technical troops. Two infantry divisions were organised slightly differently and were classified as mountain divisions. The infantry regiments were 2400 men strong, and their support weapons were 168 machine guns and four infantry guns.

The guards division had a headquarters, one infantry regiment and one

117   118

117 1st Captain, Yugoslav Army, 1941

This officer wears the standard service dress of the Royal Yugoslav Army. The rank badges take the form of Imperial Russian shoulder boards. On the front of the side cap is an oval enamel cockade in the national colours over which is superimposed the gilt metal cypher of King Peter I. The arm-of-service colour appears on the collar and as piping on the tunic cuffs. Shoulder boards indicated not only the rank of the wearer, but his arm-of-service (infantry) and in this case his regimental number. The aiguillette was the badge of an ADC. The breeches were also striped in arm-of-service colour.

**118 Senior Sergeant,
Yugoslav Army, 1941**

This non-commissioned officer in the Yugoslav artillery wears the issue version of the uniform worn by the officer in figure 117. Unlike the officers' uniform, the shoulder straps for other ranks did not follow the Russian pattern. Arm-of-service colour appears as collar patches and as piping on the shoulder straps. The wearing of the officers' belt by senior non-commissioned officers and warrant officers was a custom copied from the French. Non-commissioned officers did not, however, have the metal cypher of King Peter over the national cockade on the cap front.

119 Private, Yugoslav Army, 1941

This soldier wears the old Serbian World War I uniform which was in the process of being replaced by a new single-breasted tunic. The steel helmet is the French Adrian pattern with Yugoslav coat of arms on the front. He is armed with a Yugoslav 7.9mm M1924 rifle which was actually the Czech ZB made under licence in Yugoslavia. The ZB was widely used by central European armies.

119

cavalry brigade and one field artillery regiment; cavalry division had a headquarters, two cavalry brigades, one bicycle battalion, one battalion of horse artillery, and an engineer unit.

The invasion of Yugoslavia had obliged Hitler to postpone the invasion of the Soviet Union by one vital month. The Germans were so anxious to redeploy that the task of rounding-up, disarming and demobilising the Yugoslav Army was incompletely carried out. Thousands of Yugoslav soldiers, perhaps as many as 300,000, retained their arms and either went home or joined bands of soldiers in the mountains. It was these men and their officers who, as the Yugoslav Army in the Homeland, were the first to raise the banner of resistance in German-occupied Europe.

UNIFORM In 1941 the uniform of the Royal Yugoslav Army was basically that of the Serbian Army in World War I. Although new uniforms were being gradually introduced, many soldiers still wore the obsolete pattern. The colour of the issue uniform was a brownish grey, while officer's uniform, made of superior quality cloth, were a greener, lighter colour.

The typical service dress for officers is illustrated in figure 117. The greatcoat was double-breasted with two rows of six buttons, matching collar, turn-back cuffs. The uniform worn by all other Army ranks consisted of a French *Adrian* steel helmet with stamped metal Yugoslav coat of arms on the front, side cap with cockade in the national colours on the front, tunic, greatcoat and pantaloons worn with puttees and ankle boots. There was a more comfortable and practical uniform for mountain troops which included a loosely cut tunic and long baggy trousers gathered at the ankle. Crews of armoured fighting vehicles wore the French helmet for motorised troops and a brown leather double-breasted jacket.

INSIGNIA All ranks wore their rank badges on the shoulder straps. The shoulder straps for officers were based on the Russian Tsarist model, although the stars were similar to those used on German shoulder straps. Another unusual feature was the imitation gold and silver lace

Far left: Men of the Belgrade 'Iron Regiment' on the march. Uniform consists of the double-breasted tunic, French-pattern helmet, trousers and puttees. The officer saluting is distinguishable as a 2nd lieutenant by the single pip on his shoulder board.

Left: A Yugoslav tank commander wearing the early version of the French helmet for motorised troops which was standard issue.

YUGOSLAV ARMY INSIGNIA

Field Marshal | General of Army | Lieutenant-General (Division) | Major-General (Brigade) (Artillery) | Colonel (General Staff) | Lieutenant-Colonel (Cavalry) | Major (Infantry)

Cap Badges

1st Captain (I) (Engineers) | Captain (II) (Artillery) | Lieutenant (Administration) | 2nd Lieut (Cavalry) | Sgt-Major 1st Class (Cavalry) | Sgt-Major 2nd Class (Artillery) | Sgt-Major 3rd Class (Infantry) | Senior Sergeant (Administration) | Sergeant | Corporal | Officers (1st Pattern) | Officers | NCOs

stamped out of metal. There was also a special system of rank badges for wear on raincoats, anoraks and other kinds of protective clothing.

Arm-of-service colours in the form of piping appeared on the head-dress, tunic, greatcoat and trousers and on the shoulder straps and collar patches on the greatcoats. Regimental and academic badges in metal were worn on the breast pockets of the tunic.

AIR FORCE

The Army Air Service, which included balloon companies and the anti-aircraft artillery, came under the Minister of War. In 1938 the Air Force was organised in three brigades with a total of 14 bomber, eight fighter and 21 reconnaissance flights. Aircraft strength was estimated at 500 with a further 300 reserve and training aircraft. These totals included 30 Italian Savoia-Marchetti bombers, 70 Dornier Do17Ks and 50 Bristol Blenheims. 73 fighters were German Bf 109Es (although only 46 were serviceable when war broke out) and 40 were Hurricanes.

Pitted against the might of the Luftwaffe the Yugoslav Air Force had little chance and by 13 April 1941 had almost ceased to exist.

Personnel strength in the flying branch was 980 officers, 1600 non-commissioned officers, 720 air gunners and 7500 other ranks.

Right: King Peter of Yugoslavia, in exile with some of his officers. They are mainly from the Air Force, with pilots' badges on the right breast.

UNIFORM The grey-blue uniform of the Royal Yugoslav Air Force was introduced in 1938 and consisted of peaked cap, side cap, open tunic with patch pockets which was either worn with long matching trousers and black shoes, or matching breeches and black high boots. In the summer months officers and senior regular non-commissioned officers could wear a cap with white cover and white version of the service dress tunic.

The other ranks' version of the uniform was similar to that worn by officers but was of poorer quality and cut, with trousers or pantaloons and puttees.

The Corps of Anti-Aircraft Artillery had slightly different uniforms although technically belonging to the Air Force. The colour was grey blue but the officer's tunic was in black velvet and the cuffs were piped in black. Badges of rank were only worn on the shoulder straps.

YUGOSLAV AIR FORCE INSIGNIA

Peaked Caps

Shoulder

Cuff

General of Army	Lieutenant-General (Division)	Major-General (Brigade)	Colonel	Lieutenant-Colonel	Major	1st Captain (I)	Captain (II)	Lieutenant	2nd Lieut

Shoulder

Sgt-Major 1st Class	Sgt-Major 2nd Class	Sgt-Major 3rd Class	Senior Sergeant	Sergeant	Corporal	Cap Badge: Officers		Pilot's Badge	Observer's Badge

YUGOSLAV NAVY INSIGNIA

Shoulder

Cuff

Admiral	Vice-Admiral	Rear-Admiral	Captain	Commander	Lieutenant-Commander (Construction)	Lieutenant 1st Class (Engineers)	Lieutenant 2nd Class (Gunnery)	Sub-Lieut 1st Class (Administration)	Sub-Lieut 2nd Class (Flying)

Shoulder

Arm

C P O 1st Class	C P O 2nd Class	C P O 3rd Class	Petty Officer (I) (Qtrmstr)	Petty Officer (II) (Radio)	Leading Seaman (Stoker)	Cap Flag Officers	Cockade Other Ranks	Cap Senior Officers

105

120

**120 Captain,
Yugoslav Air Force, 1941**

The service dress followed the usual pattern although badges of rank appeared in both the traditional Army manner on the shoulder boards, and on the cuffs. Flying personnel were distinguished by an eagle worn above the lace on the cuffs, while qualified pilots wore a metal badge on the right breast. The decoration is the Yugoslav Order of the White Eagle.

INSIGNIA All ranks wore their rank badges on the shoulder straps, while officers also wore rank distinction lace on the cuffs. Field officers had one and general officers two rows of gold embroidery on the cap peak. General officers also wore five-pointed stars in the French manner on the cuffs of the tunic and greatcoat.

The Air Force was divided, as far as arm-of-service distinction was concerned, into four branches. Flying personnel wore a gold-embroidered bird with outstretched wings above their rank distinction lace on the cuffs and qualified aircrew

wore a metal badge above the right breast pocket. Ground personnel did not have the bird emblem on the cuffs. Engineering officers had red lights to the rank distinction lace on the cuffs and on the shoulder straps, and instead of the bird they had a triangle within a circle on the cuffs. Anti-aircraft officers had crossed cannon barrels surmounted by a bird on the cuffs and a black arm-of-service colour.

Yugoslav cap badges and qualification badges continued to be worn on British Royal Air Force uniform by members of the Royal Yugoslav Air Force serving with the Allies in the Middle East.

NAVY

The Yugoslav Navy, under the command of Vice Admiral Marjan Polić, had an active strength at the beginning of the war of 625 active officers and 5700 men with a further 400 reserve officers and 900 men. Because of its small size the Navy was not expected to carry out offensive operations, but to provide support for land operations. It comprised:
1 training cruiser;
1 Yarrow Class destroyer;
5 destroyers;
6 old torpedo boats;
2 submarines;
6 mine sweepers;
2 old motor torpedo-boats.

The Navy was quickly overwhelmed in the Balkan Campaign with only one submarine and a few smaller craft escaping to join the Allies, while those craft still afloat in or near harbours were taken over by the Italians.

UNIFORM Navy uniform corresponded to the international pattern. Officers wore the peaked cap, double-breasted reefer, long trousers with black shoes and double-breasted greatcoat. In the summer months officers wore a white cap cover and open single-breasted jacket.

Ratings had the standard square-rig with soft cap bearing a cap tally with '*Ratna Mornarica*' in Cyrillic letters below an oval cockade in the national colours. In winter, ratings wore a double-breasted pea-coat.

INSIGNIA Ratings wore inverted white tape chevrons on the left sleeve, while petty officers had blue cloth shoulder straps on which they wore their rank badges. Officers wore both shoulder boards and rank distinction lace on the reefer cuffs, while shoulder boards only were worn on white jacket and greatcoat.

Ratings wore red trade badges above their rank chevrons. Officers wore small white metal branch badges on the shoulder boards, while branch colours appeared both there and as lights between the rank lace on the cuffs.

Yugoslav personnel serving with the British Royal Navy wore Royal Naval uniform with the Yugoslav cap badge where applicable and sometimes 'Yugoslavia' on both sleeves at shoulder height. Shoulder boards were worn only on greatcoat and white jacket.

Below: Yugoslav cadets on the bowsprit of the training vessel Jadran. *Although rather posed (the ship is entering Portsmouth in 1939) the photograph shows standard 'square rig' well.*

GERMANY
ARMY

German involvement in the Mediterranean theatre began early in 1941 with the arrival of the Luftwaffe and Rommel's Africa Corps in North Africa, and was to continue until the final surrender in 1945. The Germans fought campaigns in three major areas: in Yugoslavia and Greece in 1941; in North Africa, 1941–43, and in Sicily and Italy, 1943–45.

YUGOSLAVIA AND GREECE, 1941

In order to secure his southern flank for the invasion of the Soviet Union Hitler forced Yugoslavia's Prince Regent Paul into the Axis alliance, but when he was overthrown by anti-German patriots in Belgrade, Hitler ordered the invasion of Yugoslavia and the expulsion of the British from Greece.

Operation *Marita*, the invasion of Yugoslavia, was launched on 6 April 1941 (after a mere ten days of preparation) and was a complete success; for the loss of 558 men the Yugoslav Army was completely destroyed, and over 300,000 men taken prisoner. Simultaneously, five divisions of List's 12th Army invaded Greece and by the end of April the country lay in German hands, although losses here were rather higher, at just over 5,000. The Wehrmacht's victory in the Balkans was due to the imaginative handling of armoured and airborne forces against the armies of a disorganised enemy.

ORGANISATION The German forces stationed in the Balkans were organised in two armies and a panzer group: 2nd Army (von Weichs) based in Hungary consisted of four corps:
LII Corps – two infantry divisions;
LI Corps – two infantry divisions;
XXXXIX Corps – one light infantry and one mountain division;
XXXXVI Motorised Corps – one motorised division and two panzer divisions.

12th Army (List) and 1st Panzer Group (von Kleist) based in Romania and Bulgaria were deployed as follows:
XXX Corps – three infantry divisions;
XVIII Corps – two mountain and one panzer division;
XXXX Motorised Corps – one infantry division, one motorised brigade (SS *Leibstandarte Adolf Hitler*) and one panzer division;
XI Corps – one infantry and one mountain division;
XIV Motorised Corps – one motorised and two panzer divisions;

XXXXI Motorised Corps – one motorised infantry regiment (*Grossdeutschland*), one motorised brigade (Hermann Göring) and one motorised division (SS *Das Reich*).

One corps of three infantry and one panzer division was held in reserve while a further three panzer divisions were under the direct control of OKH.

It can be seen from the list above that the corps was a very flexible structure, which could be composed of a variety of different formations to suit local needs: XVIII Corps, for example, was composed of two mountain divisions and one panzer division, specifically for operating in difficult terrain.

The divisional organisation of the German Army was much the same as it had been in 1940 with the exception of the panzer formations which were reorganised to include a better balanced infantry element, to avoid the problem encountered in France in 1940 when unsupported tank units raced on ahead of the foot-slogging infantry. The panzer division now had one tank regiment, two motorised infantry regiments and stronger supporting units which included self-propelled anti-tank guns and artillery. It was 15,600 men strong and had an establishment strength of 211 tanks. The Mark III and IV tanks now formed the striking force of the panzer division.

NORTH AFRICA, 1941–43

General Rommel arrived in Tripoli on 12 February 1941 and two days later the first units of what was to become the celebrated Africa Corps (*Deutsches Afrikakorps* or DAK) began to disembark.

The German commander launched an offensive against the British almost immediately with the newly-constituted 5th Light Division and two Italian divisions. Despite initial success the Axis forces were held by the British: this offensive was the prelude to a series of attacks and counter-attacks launched by both the British and Axis over the following eighteen months.

The Africa Corps built up a fearsome reputation in mobile warfare because its flexible combination of tanks, anti-tank guns and infantry proved too sophisticated for its British opponents. Compared to the Eastern Front, however, the battles in the desert were small-scale affairs: in January 1942, Rommel attacked from El Agheila with just 84 German medium and heavy tanks, and in May 1942 he had just 40 of the main battle tank, the Mark IV. The build-up of British strength and Rommel's failure to secure a decisive victory led to the defeat of the Axis forces at El Alamein

121

121 Major-General, German Army, 1942
Generalmajor Freiherr von Esebeck was commander of the 15th Panzer Division from 1940 to 1943. As shown here, he wears issue tropical uniform with the peaked cap from his temperate uniform; a typical mix. His decorations are the Knight's Cross, 1939, bar to the Iron Cross 1st Class, Iron Cross 1st Class 1914 and Tank Assault Badge in silver. The collar patches were common to all general officers, and the specific rank was only displayed on the shoulder straps.

in October 1942 and their retreat from the desert.

After the landing of Allied forces in French North Africa (Operation 'Torch') the German High Command began to pump men and materials into Tunisia but this strategically mistaken move came too late to effect the outcome of the campaign, the net result being to ensure the capture of over 100,000 unwounded veteran German soldiers. Total Axis losses in the North African campaigns were around 620,000 men, over a third of whom were Germans.

122

123

122 Infantryman, German Army, 1943

This machine gunner wears the tropical uniform issued to German troops serving in the so-called Adriatic Coast Line which stretched from Trieste to the Greek Isles. As a machine gunner he carries on his belt a pouch containing tools and an anti-aircraft sight for his MG43 machine gun, and an automatic pistol.

123 Officer, German Army, 1942

This officer wears the tropical field cap, bleached almost white by the sun, and goggles to protect his eyes from the clouds of dust thrown up by vehicles moving in the desert. The greatcoat is the standard pattern which was usually worn with shoulder straps to identify the wearer's rank. The web belt is the special pattern for officers, with round buckle.

124 Sergeant-Major, German Army, 1942

This NCO in the Military Police (Feldgendarmerie) wears standard Africa Corps uniform with the duty gorget and cuff-band which were the distinctive badges of the military police. The gorget with its luminous national emblem and chain led its wearers to be known as 'chained dogs' (Kettenhunde). The arm-of-service colour was orange which appeared as a chevron on the field cap and on the shoulder straps.

125 2nd Lieutenant, German Army, 1942

This tropical version of the side cap was issued to crews of armoured fighting vehicles since it was more convenient than the field cap, which had a large peak and tended to get in the way inside a tank. On the tropical field blouse he wears the insignia from his temperate uniform, while as a quasi-official distinction he wears the death's heads from his black panzer jacket on the lapels. Shorts and high-laced tropical field boots formed part of the basic tropical uniform. Badges are the Iron Cross 2nd Class ribbon and badge on the left breast pocket, above the silver Tank Assault Badge.

ORGANISATION The Africa Corps was originally formed from the 5th Light Division which was later redesignated the 21st Panzer Division and consisted of:
5th Panzer Regiment – two strong tank battalions totalling 150 Mk II, III and IV tanks;
104th (Motorised) Infantry Regiment – two battalions of panzer grenadiers;
3rd (Motorised) Reconnaissance Battalion;
two strong anti-tank battalions;
one artillery battalion.

This division was soon reinforced by the 15th Panzer Division, the two formations becoming the nucleus of the Africa Corps.

In August 1941 the Africa Corps was further reinforced by the German 90th Light Division, the Italian XX and XXI Corps and the Italian Savona Division and was upgraded to become Panzer Group Africa. The 90th Light Division was organised from units already in

Right: Captured Panzer Grenadiers in tropical uniform. Note the badges on the issue caps, the web equipment and the infantry assault badges.

Africa and comprised a motorised panzer grenadier regiment and three motorised infantry regiments, one of which included Germans from the French Foreign Legion.

Panzer Group Africa developed into Panzer Army Africa in January 1942, being supplemented with 164th Infantry Division (three motorised panzer grenadier regiments) in July 1942 and by the Ramcke Parachute Brigade. Also known as the German/Italian Panzer Army the title of this formation was changed to the 1st Italian Army on 23 February 1943 and was combined with the 5th Panzer Army to form Army Group Africa, the last grouping of Axis forces in North Africa.

The 5th Panzer Army had evolved from the German 90th Corps, which arrived in Tunisia in 1942 after Operation 'Torch', and in March 1943 comprised:

10th Panzer Division (7th Panzer and two infantry regiments);

21st Panzer Division;

334th Infantry Division (three motorised infantry regiments);

999th Infantry Division;

Division von Manteuffel (a mixed parachute and panzer formation).

In addition there were two Luftwaffe AA divisions and units of Italian infantry.

The strength of the Army Group in March 1943 was about a third of a million men, and although the Germans accounted for only a third of this number their superior equipment, training and organisation ensured that they had the major role in the last battles for North Africa.

ITALY, 1943–45

The loss of North Africa, the imminent collapse of the fascist government in Italy and the Allied invasion of Sicily placed the Germans in a difficult position. In order to secure Italy as a buffer against the Allies, German divisions were dispatched over the Alps ready to take over the country when the new Italian government made peace with the Allies, which they duly did on 8 September 1943.

Through dogged rear-guard actions combined with Allied indecision the German Army gained time for the con-

124   125

struction of a series of defensive lines along the Italian peninsula which successfully delayed the Allied advance until April 1945. The outstanding feature of the war in Italy was the skilful defensive fighting of the German Army under the leadership of Field Marshal Kesselring, culminating in the battle for Monte Cassino which brought the American and British armies to a standstill for over six months.

German strength in Italy in 1944 reached 26 divisions (including six panzer and panzer grenadier divisions) and six fascist Italian divisions, but, lacking effective air support, the German Army was forced into a defensive role. Although the Allied forces were starved of men in preference to the main European theatre in France, superiority in equipment and air power ensured the defeat of the German Army Group C which surrendered on 2 May 1945.

ORGANISATION Italian defences in Sicily had been strengthened by the 15th Panzer Grenadier Division and the 'Hermann Göring' Panzer Division. After the

Allied landings, two paratroop regiments and the 29th Panzer Grenadier Division were brought in. General Hube took command of these forces and managed to transport most of them back to Italy when Allied victory became inevitable. 4325 Germans died in the short campaign.

Following the successful takeover of Italy through Operation *Achse*, the German High Command reorganised its defence system. Italy had been divided into two army groups each of eight divisions: Army Group C covering the southern half of the country under Field Marshal Kesselring and Army Group B responsible for northern Italy and France under Field Marshal Rommel.

In late 1943, however, Army Group B was reassigned to prepare for the invasion of France from England, and the whole of Italy came under Kesselring's Army Group C. Reinforcements during the autumn of 1943 brought up the German Army in Italy to a strength of 25 divisions which were organised into two armies: Vietinghoff's 10th Army and von Mackensen's newly-formed 14th Army.

This strength stayed fairly constant: in March 1945 there were still 23 divisions, containing 491,000 men when Kesselring moved to north-western Europe and Vietinghoff took overall command.

Given the German Army's defensive role and the mountainous nature of many of the battlefields, the infantry rather than the armoured formations bore the brunt of the fighting, and specialised forces – such as the mountain troops – came into their own. In particular, the ability of small infantry units to operate independently in difficult climatic and geographic conditions was essential.

The company was the basic tactical unit in the German Army, as it was in all other armies, and its organisation varied according to its function.

The infantry company was divided into three or four platoons each of which would be sub-divided into three or four sections, each section consisting of about eight to twelve men grouped around the general purpose MG34 or MG42 machine gun. In keeping with the German principle of decentralisation each company would have its own heavy weapons section which could include mortars, *Nebelwerfen* and machine guns in a heavy support role. During the course of the war the establishment strength of the company decreased (from around 180 to 200 men in the early 1940s to about 140 men in 1944–45) but its firepower increased, through the widespread introduction of good quality short-range (MP38/40) and long-range (MG42) automatic weapons.

UNIFORM Unlike Britain, France and Italy, Germany had no colonial empire and so when it became apparent that she would soon become involved in a desert war, Germany had to design and manufacture a whole range of tropical clothing and equipment over night. With no practical experience nor time for development it was natural that Germany should copy the uniform of those nations with a colonial empire.

When in February 1942 the first German troops landed in Tripoli they exchanged their field-grey uniforms for tropical versions. With their sun helmets, well-cut tunics and breeches and laced field boots they could not fail to look like pre-war British soldiers in India. The Germans soon found their pseudo-functional outfit looked very smart by European standards, but had little in common with the loose and sloppy clothing developed by the native inhabitants of those parts.

It was not long before the Germans realised the functional limitations of their restrictive clothing and the sun helmet,

laced field-boots, tight-fitting field-blouse and breeches were relegated to the baggage. The soldiers in the field developed their own style of clothing which they found to be the most comfortable and practical. The typical outfit of the German desert fighter consisted of a field cap with large peak which shaded the eyes from the fierce desert sun, a shirt, long trousers gathered at the ankles, or shorts, woollen socks, and canvas and leather ankle boots. The German field-blouse continued to be widely worn, but it was not as comfortable as the Italian *sahariana*, which Germans soon 'procured' for themselves. Armoured fighting vehicle crews received a tropical version of the side cap which was more suited for wear inside a tank than the peaked cap.

With the rapid drop in temperature at night, personnel wore a knitted woollen waist protector next to their skin, and a woollen greatcoat over their other clothing. German supply officers tried to make good shortages of steel helmets and woollen pullovers, both of which were found to be essential in desert warfare.

126 Lieutenant, German Infantry, 1944

The well-patched breeches, worn-out boots and general shabbiness of this infantry officer taken prisoner in Italy in July 1944 draw attention to the poor level of supply of German troops in Italy. He wears an old-style field cap or peaked service cap with chin cords removed and a rush-green drill tunic, in the button-hole of which appears the ribbon of the medal for the Winter Campaign in Russia. Equipment is the standard officers' belt and issue map case. The rank of this officer is denoted by the single pip on the shoulder strap.

127 2nd Lieutenant, German Army, 1944

The combination of tropical and temperate clothing worn by this mountain troop officer was quite typical of the Italian Campaign. On the left side of the field cap and on the right sleeve appears the Edelweiss badge of the mountain soldier (Gebirgsjäger). Trousers tapering to the ankle and ankle boots were also a distinctive feature of mountain troop uniform. The badges worn on the left breast pocket are the Infantry Assault Badge (in white metal) and the World War II Wound Badge. Wound badges were issued in black metal for the first two wounds; in silver for the third and fourth; and in gold for the fifth and subsequent wounds.

126

127

provide support for the ground forces in North Africa and cut off the British supply routes in the Mediterranean. For a time the German Air Force had control of the skies, its Messerschmitt Bf 109s proving more than a match for the RAF's Hurricanes.

In the Balkans the 4th Air Fleet of 1200 aircraft supported the German Blitzkrieg with great success and contributed to the hard-fought victory over Crete. Large numbers of aircraft from both the X *Fliegerkorps* and the 4th Air Fleet were withdrawn for the invasion of the Soviet Union, however, leaving the Luftwaffe desperately short of aircraft in the Mediterranean.

German aerial forces in Africa during the summer of 1941 were disposed thus: Tripoli – one Ju 87 dive-bomber *Gruppe*; Sirte – one Ju 87 dive-bomber *Gruppe*; Gazala – one Bf 109 fighter *Gruppe* and one Bf 110 fighter-bomber *Gruppe*; Benghazi – one Ju 88 bomber *Geschwader*.

The appointment of Field Marshal Kesselring as overall commander in the Mediterranean theatre in December 1941 ensured a better allocation of aircraft, and 11 *Fliegerkorps* was brought in from the Eastern Front as a reinforcement. In the late spring of 1942, there were 660 aircraft available for use in the attack on Malta, but strength declined from then on, accentuated by fuel shortages.

In Italy tropical uniforms continued to be worn by German troops combined with items of temperate uniform, which sometimes gave a rather mixed appearance, as in figure 127.

INSIGNIA Rank badges were the same as those worn on the temperate uniform, although the aluminium NCO lace was replaced by yellow-brown silk lace. Officially all ranks were to wear a standardised collar patch, although many officers and all general officers wore the collar patches from their temperate uniform.

Arm-of-service colour (*Waffenfarbe*) appeared in the form of a chevron on the front of the field and side cap, and as piping or underlay on the shoulder straps.

AIR FORCE

The Mediterranean theatre was never a top priority for the Luftwaffe and its units there were generally deprived of resources relative to the forces engaged on the Eastern Front and in the defence of the *Reich*.

There were four major areas of Luftwaffe involvement. Firstly, in the Balkans during 1941, close support of the Army was essential for the conquest of Yugoslavia and Greece and the invasion of Crete. Secondly, there was the central Mediterranean, where the security of Axis supply routes to North Africa and the defeat of the British fleet were the objectives. Neither of these aims was

Above: German infantry in 1944 in Italy. The right breast eagle of the leading man identifies them as Luftwaffe personnel.

Below right: A Luftwaffe major in tropical dress. His rank is shown by the shoulder straps – interwoven braid without pips.

achieved, mainly because the key stronghold of Malta was never reduced. Thirdly, there was the close-support of land operations in North Africa, which gradually became impossible as Allied material superiority eventually told. Finally, the Luftwaffe played a minor role in the Italian campaign (where it was very short of aircraft), although attacks on shipping – particularly at Bari in November 1943 and during the Anzio landings – were sometimes successful.

While the over-stretched Luftwaffe in North Africa was desperately fighting in the air to obtain superiority and to provide close support for the Africa Corps, it also played an important part in the fighting on the ground. Rommel soon realised that in the vast flatness of the desert his existing anti-tank artillery was far too weak, and began to attach motorised batteries of Luftwaffe anti-aircraft guns to his field formations. Time and time again the great accuracy and velocity of the 8.8cm gun resulted in the decimation of Allied tank attacks.

ORGANISATION The first deployment of the German Air Force in the Mediterranean was the arrival of the X *Fliegerkorps* from Norway in December 1940 to

128

129

130

128 Sergeant, German Air Force, 1941
This Stuka pilot, just shot down over the Libyan Desert, wears the summer flying helmet in canvas, Luftwaffe tropical shirt and trousers. In his right hand he carries a metal container for a thermos flask.

129 Lieutenant-General, German Air Force, 1942
This general officer wears the standard Air Force tropical uniform with the peaked service cap of his temperate uniform. His rank is displayed on both his collar patches and on the shoulder straps. Decorations are the 1939 Bar to the Iron Cross 1st Class, Iron Cross 1st Class 1914, Pilot's Badge and a Wound Badge.

130 Lieutenant-Colonel, German Air Force, 1943
With the Luftwaffe tropical uniform this officer wears the tropical version of the peaked cap which was unique to the Air Force and was equipped with a neck flap à la French Foreign Legion. His shoulder straps combine both his arm-of-service colour and badges of rank. Above the left breast pocket he wears a Front Flight Bar with pendant which bore the number of missions flown, Iron Cross 1st Class, Pilot's Badge and Wound Badge.

In 1941 the Luftwaffe had formed a special staff (*Luftgaustab z.b.V Afrika*) to control and co-ordinate the ground organisation of the Air Force and its supply channels. This staff also controlled the static flak artillery which guarded harbours, airfields and supply depots. By August 1941, Panzer Army Africa had at its disposal six batteries of motorised anti-aircraft artillery.

In September 1942 Luftwaffe ground strength in North Africa was 12,000 men, 3400 vehicles and 70 guns over 4cm.

The material build-up of the British and newly-arrived American forces during late 1942 gave them a general air superiority that the Luftwaffe was never able to challenge, although the German planes regularly scored tactical victories over their opponents. A considerable proportion of the Luftwaffe began to be devoted towards intercepting the African-based Allied bomber raids against southern and central Europe. When deprived of fighter support the Allies suffered heavy losses from the experienced German interceptors.

A further role for the Luftwaffe in the spring of 1943 was the supply of Axis forces in Tunisia. Although desperately vulnerable to Allied fighter attacks the German (and Italian) transport planes kept up a regular supply of men and materials (some 19,000 men and 4500 tons of stores were carried across to North Africa during the December and January of 1942/43).

Desperately outnumbered in the air over Italy during 1943–45, the Luftwaffe could only provide occasional support for the Army in field, most of its resources being devoted to air defence against Allied bomber raids.

Luftwaffe units were withdrawn from Italy in June 1944 following the Normandy landings leaving only one night ground-attack *Gruppe* and a few reconnaissance units: a total of 170 aircraft of various types.

The defence of Italy was left to newly formed units of the fascist Social Republic, which were clearly unable to take on the combined power of the Allied Air Forces (by March 1945, there were over 4000 Allied aircraft in the Italian theatre).

131

132

133

AIRBORNE FORCES

Germany's airborne forces were engaged on all the major fronts during the war but it was in the Mediterranean that they achieved lasting fame, fighting in Greece and Crete, North Africa and Italy. Their major employment was, however, as conventional infantry rather than parachute troops.

ORGANISATION After the success of the paratroopers in Holland and Belgium the XI Air Corps was officially formed in the summer of 1940 under the command of General Kurt Student. The new formation was first employed in action during the German invasion of Greece when the 2nd Parachute Regiment was air-dropped over the Corinth canal in an attempt – unsuccessful as it turned out – to secure the single bridge over the canal.

Control of Greece was not control of the Mediterranean, however, and plans were drawn up for the invasion of the strategically important island of Crete. The XI Air Corps would be the spearhead of the assault: the invasion by some

22,000 men and over 500 transport planes as well as seaborne forces began on 20 May 1941 and after 11 days of bitter fighting, in which the Germans suffered 3250 dead or missing and 3400 wounded, the Allied forces evacuated the island, leaving over 10,000 men as prisoners. The capture of Crete was one of the greatest triumphs of the airborne forces but the very high casualties of this parachute operation so shocked Hitler that from then on these élite troops fought mainly in an infantry role.

The assault on Crete was carried out by the 7th Air Division supported by the 5th Mountain Division. The 7th Air Division was organised as follows:
three parachute regiments each of three battalions;
air signals company;
transport company;
medical company;
light anti-aircraft battery;
anti-tank gun company;
pak gun battery;
motorcycle platoon.

After the invasion, the 7th Air Division

131 Corporal, German Air Force, 1943
This Corporal of the 'Hermann Göring' Division in Tunisia wears the camouflage shelter quarter as a poncho over his Luftwaffe tropical uniform. Members of the 'Hermann Göring' division wore a blue cuff-band on the right cuff which bore in white letters the name 'Hermann Göring'. On his belt he has two pouches for magazines for his sub-machine gun.

132 Sergeant-Major, German Air Force, 1943
For the rescue of Mussolini, members of the parachute unit under the command of Major Mors wore the special helmet with German camouflage net, smock in geometric camouflage pattern and Luftwaffe tropical trousers. The cloth bandolier holds spare magazines for the Fallschirmgewehr (a special assault rifle for paratroopers). The four white cloth wings on the sleeve identify the wearer as a sergeant-major.

133 Private, German Air Force, 1941
This rifleman (Jäger) in Crete wears the parachutist's 'bone sack' in plain olive green cotton duck. The helmet is fitted with a cover which had tapes to hold foliage. The trousers are also standard paratroop issue in field-grey with fastenings on the outside leg for the knee bandages to be removed once on the ground.

was withdrawn and re-posted to the Eastern Front, being replaced by the 22nd Infantry Air Landing Division, an otherwise normal infantry division trained and equipped for air transport, which had been unable to participate in the assault.

In Africa the parachute arm was represented by a mixed parachute brigade of 2300 men under Major-General Ramcke, originally trained for the abortive Malta operations, but dispatched in October 1942 to help Rommel in the desert. The brigade consisted of four battle groups of approximately battalion strength with units of artillery, anti-tank guns and engineers. The brigade fought on throughout the North African campaign until the surrender in Tunis in May 1943.

As the Allies prepared to invade Sicily and Italy the parachute formations were gathered together and formed a highly mobile strategic reserve. Based in the south of France the force, still known as XI

Air Corps, consisted of the old 7th Air Division (newly designated the 1st Parachute Division) and the recently-formed 2nd Parachute Division – in all, six regiments which with corps troops totalled 30,000 men.

The success of the paratroops in Sicily and southern Italy led to their further expansion, ten divisions plus other parachute units being formed before the end of the war. In central Italy the I Parachute Corps was formed in January 1944, comprising the 4th Parachute Division and 3rd Panzer Grenadier Division and later incorporating the 1st and 4th Parachute Divisions. (The organisational structure of the 1st Parachute Division is shown in the accompanying chart.) The I Parachute Corps earned the admiration of the Allied troops during its long defence of Monte Cassino, where its soldiers (nicknamed the 'Green Devils' by the Americans) endured immense aerial and artillery bombardment. The corps was

also engaged continuously in the defensive battles north of Florence during 1945, surrendering to the Allies in the April of that year.

UNIFORM As in other branches of the Armed Forces, Luftwaffe personnel received a special tropical dress which in many respects was much more comfortable and practical than that issued to the Army.

The standard tropical uniform is illustrated by figure 130. Certainly the most distinctive feature of this uniform was the tropical peaked cap with neck flap à la French Foreign Legion. There was no special tropical greatcoat and so Luftwaffe personnel continued to wear the blue-grey temperate model.

This basic uniform was also worn by personnel serving in the ground combat formations of the Luftwaffe, but members of the 'Hermann Göring' Division also received Waffen-SS camouflage smocks

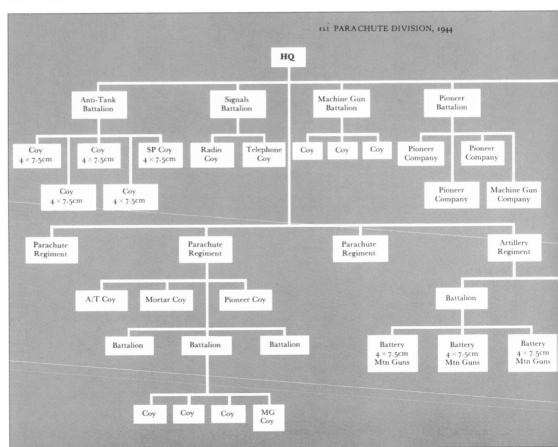

1st PARACHUTE DIVISION, 1944

and helmet covers, and Ramcke's parachutists had a tropical version of their jump smock.

Badges of rank and arm-of-service badges were as for the temperate uniform, although Luftwaffe collar patches do not appear to have been worn very often by troops in the field.

NAVY

In anticipation of the necessity for very close Italo-German naval co-operation in the Mediterranean a German naval liaison staff was established in Rome in June 1940 under Rear-Admiral Weichhold. The principal task of this staff was to keep open the supply lines which served the German troops fighting in North Africa. Losses from Allied air, surface and submarine attacks reached a peak in April and May 1941, and the German Navy was obliged to transfer submarines to the Mediterranean and X *Fliegerkorps*

was ordered to concentrate on convoy defence. As long as Malta held out none of these measures had any decisive effect and sinkings of Axis transports went on unabated, resulting in a German supply crisis in November 1941.

After the beginning of the attack on Tobruk in the spring of 1942, the German Navy established Command Post North Africa on 23 May 1942. This staff conducted naval operations including the deployment of submarines, motor-torpedo boats and mine-sweeping flotillas, and was also responsible for delivering supplies and reinforcements to the German fighting forces in the coastal areas. At the beginning of 1942 there were 24 submarines active in the Mediterranean which, with small vessels and shore establishments, gave a combined strength of about 15,000 men.

Following the collapse of Italy in 1942 there was little the German Navy could do to contest the naval superiority of the British in the Mediterranean, although valuable work was carried out transporting troops in the Aegean.

UNIFORM The German Navy had long experience of the tropics, having raised and equipped expeditionary forces for service in China and German East Africa at the turn of the century.

Before the outbreak of war the German Navy wore a white uniform in Germany and her territorial waters between 20 April and 30 September, or as and when required in foreign waters. Officers and chief petty officers wore a cap with detachable white cover, single-breasted white tunic with stand collar (which in 1938 was altered to an open pattern for wear with white shirt and black tie), long white trousers and white canvas shoes.

Ratings also wore a cap with white cover, or from 1938 with all informal orders of dress, a white side cap with a blue national emblem. The white cotton shirt had pointed blue cuffs and could be worn with either a plain white exercise collar, or with a blue denim collar and the black silk. The white shirt could be worn with either blue or white bell-bottomed trousers, dark blue socks and black shoes or black marching boots.

After considerable experimentation a white sun helmet was introduced in 1938, only to be replaced in 1940 by a light khaki model, which, however, proved to be an unpopular item of head-dress.

On small ships and submarines dress was so informal that it bordered on the slovenly. Officers usually wore a peaked cap with white cover (for the commander only) or a side cap, various types and colours of shirt worn open at the neck

134

134 Chief Petty Officer, German Navy, 1944
This sailor, depicted in the later stages of the war, wears khaki battledress similar in pattern to that of the British model. The three pips on the shoulder strap edged with yellow lace denote the wearer's rank as a chief petty officer. An Iron Cross First Class has been awarded; this medal was reinstituted by Hitler on 2 September 1939; it was traditionally only awarded during wartime and was by far the most common award for valour.

with shoulder straps. Some ratings wore their white sports vest with or without the blue national emblem on the breast. The rest of this 'uniform' consisted of shorts or swimming trunks, canvas shoes with rope soles or sandals.

INSIGNIA Rank badges were of little importance when crews of motor torpedo-boats and submarines knew each other so well. The commander was identified by his white cap cover, and officers and chief petty officers wore shoulder straps, while ratings wore their chevrons on long-sleeved garments.

GREAT BRITAIN

ARMY

The Mediterranean theatre was an area of prime importance to Britain. She had many interests there and the Suez canal was the most important artery of the Empire. British and Empire forces were engaged continuously from the Italian attack in 1940 to the defeat of Germany in 1945, fighting in North and East Africa, Syria, Iraq, Greece, Sicily, Italy and Yugoslavia and garrisoning areas as far apart as Gibraltar and Persia.

After two years of inconclusive fighting, Allied forces took an irreverisble offensive from October 1942, but tenacious defence and the decision of the Allies to give north-west Europe priority meant that the fighting in Italy was prolonged and difficult.

ORGANISATION In August 1939 the land forces in Egypt under Lieutenant-General Sir Henry Maitland Wilson consisted in the main of an armoured division (7th) still in the process of formation, three British infantry brigades, plus a small number of artillery and engineer units. Additional forces scattered through the Middle East Theatre comprised the Headquarters of the 7th and 8th Infantry Divisions and three infantry brigades in Palestine; two British infantry battalions in the Sudan; lightly-equipped locally raised forces in Iraq, Uganda, Kenya and British Somaliland, and small British garrisons in Malta, Gibraltar, Cyprus and Aden. The first reinforcement from India, the 11th Indian Brigade Group, had also recently arrived.

The desert was to be a theatre of war in which an army's success depended primarily upon the quality and quantity of its armoured forces. The British had begun to prepare in earnest in 1938 with the formation of the Matruh Mobile Force from the units of the Cairo Cavalry Brigade. By October 1939 the force had been transformed into a Mobile Division by its commander Major-General P. C. S. Hobart, and the light Mark III, V1A, and V1B tanks and 3.7 inch mountain howitzers were being replaced by A9 cruiser tanks and 25 pounder howitzers. The division's order of battle was:
Light Armoured Brigade: 7th, 8th, and 11th Hussars;
Heavy Armoured Brigade: 1st and 6th Royal Tank Regiments;
plus units of the Royal Horse Artillery and infantry in what was known as Pivot Group.

In April 1940 the armoured formations were reorganised into two homogeneous brigades, the Light Armoured Brigade becoming the 7th Armoured Brigade and the Heavy Brigade becoming the 4th Armoured Brigade. The resulting formation was renamed the 7th Armoured Division and it took over control in May of all troops in the Western Desert until the establishment of Headquarters Western Desert Force on 17 June 1940. In Egypt General Wavell could call on a force of approximately 36,000 men including Indian and New Zealand units, while in Palestine there were 27,500 troops including a horse cavalry division. In essence the fighting troops under Western Desert Force consisted of an armoured division with only two armoured regiments in each brigade, and a British infantry brigade. All units were short of equipment, transport, and artillery, and the 7th Armoured had only 65 cruiser tanks against a requirement of 220. Despite these deficiencies, however, Western Desert Force soon established its superiority over the Italians during operations on the Egyptian-Libyan frontier.

135

136

135 Sergeant, British Army, 1942

The black beret with its silver badge was the distinctive head-dress of the Royal Tank Regiment, and was to be made famous by General Montgomery who wore one as commander of the 8th Army. In fact, the beret that Montgomery wore was 'donated' by this tankman, Sergeant James Fraser, a crewman in Montgomery's command tank. The shirt, shorts, socks or hose tops and short puttees were standard desert wear. The coloured slides or flashes on his shoulder straps and the black lanyard were worn by those soldiers serving in the 6th Royal Tank Regiment. On the 1937-pattern web belt he carries a .38 Enfield No. 2 Mk I revolver in the special holster issued to tank crews, although it was usually worn lower and strapped to the thigh.

136 Captain, British Army, 1940

Cavalry officers in the Western Desert often wore brightly coloured field service caps with embroidered badges as does this Captain in the 3rd Kings Own Hussars. Metal rank 'pips' were fastened to detachable khaki drill shoulder straps. The trousers made of beige corduroy and suede 'chukka' boots with rubber soles were unofficial but often worn. The 1937-pattern web equipment includes a pouch for a compass on the right, and another for ammunition on the left side.

In spring 1941, British forces in North Africa were reduced by the dispatch of a number of units to aid Greece. There were over 50,000 British and Empire forces in Greece, as well as 100 tanks. They were organised as follows:

1st Armoured Brigade;
6th Australian Division;
2nd New Zealand Division;
two medium artillery regiments.

Nevertheless they were soon overrun by the invading Germans, suffering some 11,000 casualties in the process; the remainder were evacuated to Crete and North Africa. The troops in Crete (about 28,000 men) were themselves forced to evacuate by the German airborne invasion, the British Army contingent suffering 612 killed, 224 wounded and 5315 taken prisoner.

The British operations in Italian East Africa were a complete success, however. Two columns of British and Empire troops launched a pincer offensive against the Italians. On 19 January 1941, the first column of two Indian divisions and native troops advanced from the Sudan. The second column, striking north from Kenya on 24 January, had three South African divisions. The two columns totalled around 70,000 men. In the three-month campaign the British and Empire forces captured 50,000 prisoners and the whole of Italian East Africa for a cost of under 500 casualties.

The British faced further trouble in the Middle East from a German inspired uprising in Iraq (soon put down however) and from Syria, under the control of Vichy France. British possessions in the Middle East were threatened by the Vichy forces, some 35,000 men strong, and so a scratch force of 20,000 soldiers was gathered together to invade Syria on 8 June 1941. The Allied forces consisted of:

7th Australian Division;
5th Indian Infantry Brigade Group (plus attached groups including the Transjordanian Frontier Force);
a Free French division.

Damascus was quickly captured but the Vichy French continued a bitter struggle only surrendering to the British and Allied forces on 12 July.

In the late summer and autumn of 1941 the British forces in Egypt prepared for their next offensive. There were changes in both organisation and command, with General Sir Claude Auchinleck replacing General Wavell as Commander-in-Chief Middle East on 15th July. The flow of reinforcements to the theatre had reached 239,000 men (144,000 from the United Kingdom) between January and July, and had included the 50th British Division and Headquarters 10th Corps. On 9 September 1941 the Western Desert Force was reconstituted as the 8th Army with XIII and XXX Corps under its command. The units in Palestine and Syria were regrouped as the 9th Army with the 1st Australian and 10th Corps.

By November, the British armoured forces available to General Auchinleck had also grown in size and strength. The 7th Armoured Division had been re-equipped, the 22nd Armoured Brigade had arrived in Egypt, the 32nd Army Tank Brigade was operational in Tobruk and the 1st Army Tank Brigade was in the process of formation in XIII Corps.

From late 1941 until the summer of 1942, the 8th Army fought a series of engagements which revealed serious deficiencies in its preparedness for desert warfare when compared with the best German units. The fighting during the 'Crusader' battles in November 1941, for example, had convinced General Auchinleck that the British armoured division

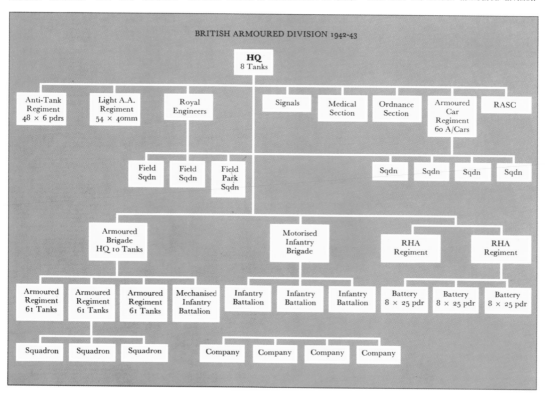

BRITISH ARMOURED DIVISION 1942-43

was an unbalanced formation containing too much armour and too little infantry. He therefore reorganised the armoured divisions so that in future they would essentially consist of one armoured brigade group (totalling just under 200 tanks) and one motor brigade group equipped with armoured cars, supported by artillery, engineers and administrative units. The Army tank brigades, each containing three regiments of about 60 tanks, would continue to be independent formations allocated to larger groupings as the need arose. Auchinleck also reorganised the infantry brigade to achieve a more permanent combination of the constituent arms. Infantry divisions were to consist of three brigade groups each with three battalions, a regiment of field artillery (24 25-pounders), an anti-tank regiment (48 6-pounders), an allocation of anti-aircraft artillery, engineers, and administrative units. Unfortunately these changes had not been fully implemented when Rommel attacked on 26 May, pushed the 8th Army back and captured Tobruk on 21 June.

During the period from November 1941 to August 1942 the British 8th Army had suffered 102,000 battle casualties (of which 49,000 were British) but reinforcements continued to arrive and the Army's

Below: Men of the Queen's Regiment marching into Tobruk in November 1942.

Below Left: Sappers at work mine-detecting, wearing the typical clothes of the desert soldier.

137

137 Soldier, Abyssinian Patriot Army, 1941
A number of Abyssinian soldiers fought with the British Army against the Italians in Ethiopia and were equipped in a European fashion but the figure illustrated here has arms and equipment taken from any source available. In addition to his ammunition belt and revolver he is armed with a German 7.92mm 98K rifle.

138 Guardsman, British Army, 1943
In sharp contrast to the Guard's splendid reputation for smartness, this battered survivor of Monte Camino wears a steel helmet over the woollen cap comforter, and a khaki woollen scarf and standard double-breasted greatcoat. In addition to the basic 1937-pattern web equipment he has a cotton bandolier containing additional ammunition.

139 Lieutenant, British Army, 1943
This officer is from the 2nd Cameronians, forming part of the 5th Infantry Division of the 8th Army in Italy. The head-dress is the Tam o'Shanter which was worn by Scottish regiments with the badge mounted on a piece of tartan cloth. The issue battledress for officers was identical to that issued to the men, but during the war officers were allowed to wear the blouse open at the neck with shirt and tie. His rank badges are the two cloth 'pips' on the shoulder straps while on his sleeve he wears the formation sign of the 5th (Y for Yorkshire) Division above a dark green strip of cloth which indicates his arm of service, namely that of a rifle regiment.

140 Private, British Army, 1944
Of particular interest here is the way in which the typical 'Tommy' in the Italian Campaign carried his personal equipment. On his back is the small pack of the 1937-pattern web equipment. Under its flap he has stowed his 'BD' blouse and a pick head.

138   139   140

strength rose from 88,000 in January 1942 to 126,000 by May. Amongst the 149,800 reinforcements that had arrived in the Middle East between January and August were the British 8th Armoured Division, and the 44th and 51st Infantry Divisions. For the El Alamein offensive General Montgomery, the new commander of the 8th Army, was able to deploy three corps: XXX Corps (five infantry divisions, one armoured brigade group); XII Corps (two infantry, one armoured division); and X Corps (three armoured divisions).

The fighting strength of the 8th Army during the battle was approximately 195,000 men and it suffered a total of 13,560 casualties of which 58 per cent were United Kingdom troops.

As the Axis forces broke away from El Alamein with the 8th Army in pursuit, Allied assault forces were landing in French North Africa. The Eastern Assault Force included the 11th and 36th British Brigade Groups (9000 men) and the mixed Anglo-American 1st and 6th Commandos (2000 men). The British contingent was thereafter expanded to form

the 1st Army, which by 20 December 1942 totalled 189,000 personnel and fielded the 6th Armoured and 78th Infantry Divisions. On 11 April 1943 the 1st and 8th Armies linked up in Tunisia and several of the latter's formations were placed temporarily under the command of the former. By the end of April the 1st Army contained two British corps and one American and one French corps.

It has been estimated that the three years of battle in the Middle East from June 1940 to May 1943 cost the forces of the British Empire 220,000 casualties.

With the surrender of the German and Italian forces in North Africa on 13 May 1943 Allied reserves of manpower and equipment became available for deployment elsewhere in the Mediterranean theatre – in Sicily, for example.

The war establishments of the British formations in North Africa and the Middle East differed significantly from those in the United Kingdom. The scale of movement was considerable, the 51st Division with auxiliary troops totalling 40,000 men with 8000 vehicles.

For the invasion of Sicily on 9 July 1943 the British troops in the 8th Army were organised in two corps:

XIII Corps:
5th Division;
50th Division;
231st Brigade;

XXX Corps:
51st Division;
1st Canadian Division.

On 25 July they were reinforced by the 78th Division, bringing up the total number of British and Commonwealth troops to 115,000 men. After a skilfully fought campaign the Anglo-American forces had control of the island on 17 August, the British suffering 9353 casualties.

The invasion of the Italian mainland commenced on 3 September 1943, with assault landings mounted from Sicily via the straits of Messina by the troops of XIII Corps. On 9 September the 1st Airborne Division was put ashore at Taranto with the task of securing the 'heel' of Italy. By 16 September the 8th Army's strength in Italy had grown to 63,600 men with 15,270 vehicles; only 635 casualties had been suffered.

The US 5th Army, which landed at Salerno on 9 September, was composed of both American and British formations, the latter consisting of the British X Corps comprising the 7th Armoured Division, 46th and 56th Infantry Divisions and the 23rd Armoured Brigade. During the

141 Lance-corporal, Royal Military Police, 1943

This military policeman serving with the 46th (North Midland and West Riding) Division in the Plain of Naples wears a steel helmet with painted band and letters 'MP'. On the right sleeve he wears a blue armlet which also bore the red letters 'MP'. The coat is the special pattern issued to motorcyclists.

battle at Salerno, British units lost 725 officers and men killed, 2739 wounded and 1800 missing. Naples fell on 1 October and on the 12th the long advance on Rome began.

The major problem once the Allies had established themselves in Italy was the need to increase their forces as quickly as possible in the face of German superiority in numbers. In the last week of September 1943 the 8th Army had been reinforced by the 78th Infantry Division (11th, 36th, and 38th Brigades), the 4th Armoured Brigade, the Special Service Brigade (3rd Commando, 40th Royal Marine Commando, and 1st Special Raiding Squadron) and the 8th Indian Infantry Division.

On 9 October 1943 the 8th Army comprised two corps, each of two infantry divisions, one armoured brigade and one army artillery group.

By the end of November British land forces in Italy totalled 351,000 officers and men. The average size of a British infantry division including its supporting units was by now 40,000 men. The problem of finding infantry reinforcements for Italy was thus often acute, particularly in view of the fact that 58 per cent of the 46,000 battle casualties suffered by British Army units between

September 1943 and March 1944 were incurred by the infantry. By February 1944 the infantry battalions of the 1st and 56th Divisions were fighting with only 72 and 68 per cent respectively of their establishment of other ranks, and in March the official establishment of infantry battalions in the Mediterranean had to be reduced from 844 all ranks to 726.

By the end of December the British element of 5th US Army had lost the 7th Armoured Division, which had been withdrawn in preparation for the invasion of Normandy, but was in the process of receiving the 1st Infantry Division as reinforcement. Since its arrival in Italy X Corps had suffered casualties of 1669 killed, 7023 wounded, and 2869 missing. The 8th Army had also changed its complexion and consisted of two British infantry divisions (the 5th and 78th), two Indian infantry divisions (the 4th and 8th), the New Zealand Division, one Canadian infantry and one Canadian armoured division. In the New Year a policy of reinforcing the US 5th Army

Above: Soldiers trudge up a rocky hillside. The caps are the Tam o' Shanter.

from 8th Army and of filling the subsequent gaps with formations newly-arrived in Italy was set in motion, and in preparation for the landings at Anzio the US 3rd and British 1st Divisions formed the US 6th Corps.

For the landing on 22 January 1944 the 1st Division deployed the 2nd and 3rd Infantry Brigades and 24th Guards Brigade, the 46th Royal Tank Regiment and the 2nd Special Service Brigade (9th and 43rd Royal Marine Commandos). By 9th February the Division had been reduced by battle casualties to little more than half its established strength and six weeks after the landing British casualties had mounted to 10,168. When the Allied Armies entered Rome on 4 June 1944 British and Commonwealth casualty figures since the crossing from Sicily had reached 73,122: 14,331 killed, 47,966 wounded and 10,825 missing.

On 30 December 1943 General Sir Oliver Leese had assumed command of 8th Army on the departure of Montgomery for 21st Army Group, and Sir Henry Maitland Wilson replaced Eisenhower as Supreme Allied Commander, Mediterranean Theatre. General Sir Harold Alexander who had been Eisenhower's Deputy became Commander-in-Chief, Allied Armies in Italy.

When Alexander had launched his final drive for Rome, the 8th Army had entered battle with three British and Commonwealth Corps and the Polish Corps. XXX Corps had left for the United Kingdom on 5 November 1943 and X Corps had returned from the 5th US Army on 31 March 1944. 8th Army's

141

order of battle in addition to the Poles was therefore:

V Corps:
10th Indian Infantry Division;
4th Indian Infantry Division;
7th Armoured Brigade;

X Corps:
2nd New Zealand Division.

XIII Corps:
4th Infantry Division;
8th Indian Division;
1st Canadian Tank Brigade;
78th Infantry Division;
6th Armoured Division.

Army Reserve:
1st Canadian Corps;
25th Army Tank Brigade;
6th South African Armoured Division.

By August 1944 8th Army was disconcertingly well-supplied with armoured units for a campaign in which it was almost impossible to employ armour to its full effect. By May 1944 the 8th Army possessed some 1200 tanks, but what it still lacked was sufficient infantry to break rapidly through German defensive lines which used every available advantage of terrain. The V Corps, spearhead of the offensive, did employ four infantry divisions (the British 4th, 46th and 56th and the Indian 4th) but

casualties were heavy: in the three months since July the 8th Army had suffered nearly 20,000 battle casualties with the result that every infantry battalion had to be reorganised. The offensive ground to a halt in the autumn of 1944.

Meanwhile in the Balkans a British force comprising a parachute and an armoured brigade were dispatched to aid the Greek nationalist troops gain control of Greece following the German departure in 1944.

During the winter of 1944–45 the British forces prepared for the forthcoming assault on the German lines. The British Army, supported by a massive aerial bombardment, launched its offensive on 9 April which was a complete success; within three weeks the German Army was at the point of collapse and surrender terms were agreed on 2 May. British casualties during the Italian campaign amounted to 88,790 men.

UNIFORM The regulation tropical dress of the British Army at the beginning of the war in the Middle East was quite a formal affair which required liberal applications of starch and much ironing. As soon as fighting started in earnest a more comfortable and practical outfit was evolved which became increasingly standardised and the differences between officers and men became less pronounced.

Officers wore a tropical version of the khaki service dress which was made of khaki-drill, gabardine or barathea consisting of tunic, shirt and tie, shorts or long trousers which were worn with either khaki socks and shoes or puttees and ankle boots. Mounted personnel wore breeches with either puttees or field boots. The Wolseley-pattern sun helmet was gradually replaced by the steel helmet, peaked cap or field service cap.

On active service all ranks wore the khaki-drill shirt, pullover, shorts or long trousers, while officers in North Africa began to find corduroy trousers and rubber-soled suede 'chukka' boots better suited for wear in the desert.

The rapid changes in temperature which were encountered in the Middle East meant that all ranks had to be equipped with a greatcoat.

INSIGNIA Badges of rank were worn on the shoulder straps by officers, and a slit in the pullover enabled the shoulder straps of the shirt underneath to be worn outside the pullover. Non-commissioned officers wore their rank chevrons in white tape on the shirt and pullover. Formation signs and other corps or regimental insignia were either worn on the shoulder straps or sewn to the sleeves of both the khaki cloth and drill uniforms.

BRITISH ARMY INSIGNIA

Cap — Field Marshal / Generals / Brigadier & Substantive Colonel / Other Officers

Shoulder — Field Marshal / General / Lieutenant-General / Major-General / Brigadier / Colonel (Education Corps) / Lieutenant-Colonel (Infantry) / Major (Royal Engineers) / Captain (Rifle Regt) / Lieutenant (RAC) / 2nd Lieut (Paratroops)

Arm — Staff Sgt-Major (1st Class) / Regimental Sgt-Major (Foot Guards) / W.O. 1st Class / W.O. 2nd Class / Warrant Officer 3rd Class / Staff Sgt (RAC. 7th Armd Div) / Sergeant (RA 50th Inf. Division) / Corporal (REME, 78th Inf. Division) / Lance-Corporal (KOYLI) / Collar Patch: Fld Marshal & Generals / Collar Patch: Brigadier & Subst. Col.

142

142 Flying Officer, Royal Air Force, 1941

Over his khaki-drill shirt with rank badges on the shoulder straps, this flying officer wears typical flying equipment consisting of flying helmet and goggles while in his hand he holds a radio-telephone jack plug. In front hang the oxygen mask and radio-telephone microphones while behind is the seat-type parachute which was worn by RAF fighter pilots.

AIR FORCE

The responsibilities of the RAF in the Mediterranean theatre were complex and wide-ranging, covering a vast geographical area and calling for action in a variety of different roles ranging from ground support work to strategic bombing. Until 1942 the RAF was often short of aircraft and equipment but following the Axis defeat at El Alamein and the arrival of American forces in North Africa the RAF was able to build up a material superiority that was to play a decisive part in securing victory in the Mediterranean.

ORGANISATION The peacetime responsibilities of the Air Officer Commanding, Middle East, encompassed the air forces in Egypt, Palestine, the Sudan, and Kenya, but in the event of war he was also to control the air element in Aden, Malta and Iraq. This vast Command was subsequently expanded to include Persia and the remainder of the Mediterranean theatre up to 100 miles west of Malta. The period between September 1939 and the Italian declaration of war in June 1940 was used to build up the RAF's capabilities in the Middle East within the limitations imposed by the maintenance of the air defence of Great Britain and by operations in France. Yet when Italy declared war the RAF was still greatly outnumbered by the Regia Aeronautica, with the Middle East Air Force comprising only 29 squadrons many of which were equipped with aircraft approaching obsolescence.

The Middle East Air Force was to operate against the Italians in two main theatres, the Mediterranean, and East Africa and the Red Sea; the first attacks being launched on 11 June 1940. By the end of the year a considerable measure of air superiority had been achieved but a further battlefront was created by the Italian invasion of Greece on 28 October, to which the RAF responded by sending nine squadrons to support the Greek Army.

When the German invasion began in the first week of April 1941 the RAF presence in Greece amounted to two detachments of Wellingtons and nine squadrons, a total of nearly 200 aircraft of which 80 were serviceable. During the campaign these squadrons bombed German communications and troop concentrations in Bulgaria and Yugoslavia, provided fighter protection for Allied units, and defended Athens. In the process they lost 209 aircraft and suffered casualties in pilots and ground crew of 163 men.

After the defeat in Greece a new threat was developing in Syria where German aircraft were using Vichy French airfields as a means of subverting British control of the Middle East. In the bitter campaign which developed as Allied troops advanced into Syria the RAF deployed four understrength or re-equipping squadrons and one flight of Gladiators; a total of approximately 50 front-line aircraft. Support was also provided by the Fleet Air Arm from Cyprus and a squadron from Iraq, and subsequently by seven more squadrons of fighters and bombers.

In the Western Desert the first German aircraft appeared at the close of 1940 and when the Africa Corps launched its offensive at the end of March 1941 the RAF had only four squadrons available for the defence of Cyrenaica. The position improved during April and by the middle of the month the units deployed in the desert under No. 204 Group amounted to six squadrons and two squadron detachments. In addition No. 257 Wing of Wellingtons based in the Canal Zone was available for operations in the desert.

The lull in operations in the Western Desert in the summer and autumn of 1941 was used to reorganise, re-equip, and reinforce RAF Middle East. By July 13,000 additional personnel had arrived, and replacement aircraft brought the number of serviceable aircraft in the Middle East to 520. Free French, Greek, and Yugoslav squadrons were also formed alongside the British and Dominion units, and the tenure of a new Air Officer Commanding-in-Chief began with the appointment of Air Marshal A. W. Tedder on 1 June 1941. By the middle of October Tedder had under his command 52 squadrons with 846 aircraft of which 780 could be classified as modern. Tedder created three new subordinate RAF commands in the Middle East: Air Headquarters Egypt replaced No. 202 Group; Air Headquarters Western Desert was formed from No. 204 Group;

Below: Wing Commander Duncan Smith and (left) Group Captain Bryan Kingcombe after a successful day's operations in Italy in November 1943.

ROYAL AIR FORCE INSIGNIA

Air Ranks — Group Captain — Other Commissioned Officers — Other Ranks

Marshal of the RAF — Air Chief Marshal — Air Marshal — Air Vice-Marshal — Air Commodore — Group Captain — Wing Commander — Squadron Leader — Flight Lieutenant (RAAF) — Flying Officer — Pilot Officer

Warrant Officer 1st Class — Warrant Officer 2nd Class — Flight Sergeant (Canada) — Sergeant (Auxiliary) — Corporal (Volunteer Reserve) — Leading Aircraftman (RNZAF) — Aircraftman — Navigator's Wings — Observer's Wings — Greatcoat Shldr Strap Marshal of RAF

Pilot's Wings

and Headquarters Palestine and Trans-jordan was elevated to control the Levant. The total RAF strength in the Middle East was 57,000 officers and men of whom 7000 were committed to the reinforcement routes and 6500 to signal communications.

By November 1941 the squadron strength of the Western Desert Air Force was just in excess of 27, made up as follows:
14 squadrons of short-range fighters;
2 squadrons of long-range fighters;
8 squadrons of medium bombers;
3 squadrons of tactical reconnaissance aircraft;
1 flight of survey reconnaissance aircraft;
1 flight of strategical reconnaissance aircraft.
Of these squadrons, six were South African, two were Australian, one was Rhodesian, and one Free French. During Operation 'Crusader' the Middle East Air Force fought for and gained air superiority, disrupted the Axis supply network, and assisted in the land battle.

Between February and May 1942 the Axis Air Forces made a determined effort to render Malta useless as an air and sea base. Although a squadron of Spitfires flew in from carriers as reinforcements, the number of serviceable Hurricanes had been reduced to 30 by mid-March, and

the majority of the Wellington force was withdrawn from the island. On 20 April 47 Spitfires flew in from the USS *Wasp* but by the evening of the following day only 17 remained in action. A further reinforcement of 62 Spitfires, flown off the *Wasp* and HMS *Eagle* on 9 May, together with the dispersal of German bomber strength to Cyrenaica, Russia, and France, finally marked a turning point in the battle of Malta and the RAF was able to resume offensive operations against Rommel's supply lines.

The RAF was heavily committed during the Battle of Gazala in May and June 1942, and by the middle of July eleven fighter squadrons were at half strength, seven squadrons were still equipped with obsolescent aircraft, and nine squadrons were without any operational aircraft at all.

When the Battle of Alam El Halfa began at the end of August the RAF had 565 aircraft in the Western Desert plus the 165 heavy and medium bombers of No. 205 Group in support. For the loss of 68 aircraft this force harried and bombed the Africa Corps at every opportunity during the week's fighting and their effort contributed significantly to the failure of the German offensive.

The deployment of the US Army Middle East Air Force in October 1942 led to some reorganisation within the

Desert Air Force; the 25 British and American fighter squadrons, for example, being divided between two fighter groups, Nos. 211 and 212. The most modern fighters were allocated to No. 211 Group which was known as Force 'A'. Operational control of the American medium day-bombers was also placed in the hands of the Western Desert Air Force. Altogether 96 squadrons totalling 1500 front-line aircraft were assembled in support of the 8th Army for the Battle of El Alamein.

The RAF participation in operation 'Torch' was numerically smaller than that of the USAAF and it was allotted its own sphere of activity, known as Eastern Air Command, to the east of Cape Tenes. To co-ordinate the Allied air effort in North Africa a unified command structure was adopted on 17 February 1943, combining the three major Anglo-American commands – RAF Middle East, RAF Malta, and North-west African Air Forces – as the Mediterranean Air Command.

Mediterranean Air Command disposed of 267 squadrons, of which 121 were British and Commonwealth and 146 American, and for the invasion of Sicily 2510 of the Command's 3462 aircraft were serviceable. During the campaign the Allied Air Forces destroyed 740 enemy aircraft in the air.

On 10 December 1943 the Headquarters of Mediterranean Air Command absorbed that of Northwest African Air Force to become Mediterranean Allied Air Forces. The Tactical, Strategic, and Coastal Air Forces previously under Northwest African command re-emerged as the Mediterranean Allied Tactical Strategic and Coastal Air Forces.

The pattern of air activity which quickly established itself as the remaining Luftwaffe strength was diverted to France and the Eastern Front became almost a routine for the rest of the campaign. Fighters and fighter bombers provided tactical support and reconnaissance, and interdicted secondary road and rail communications. Medium and light bombers attacked supply dumps and primary communication systems while the strategic bombers ranged into Austria, Germany and Romania. By the close of the campaign in Italy the number of aircraft lost by the Mediterranean and Middle East Commands between June 1940 and May 1945 stood at 5735.

Throughout, the Royal Air Force gave assistance to the Partisan groups operating against the Axis in the Balkans.

In March 1944 responsibility for air operations in the Balkans had been transferred from RAF Middle East to the Mediterranean Allied Air Force and in

June 1944 the Balkan Air Force was formed. By January 1945 the Air Force consisted of three fighter wings, a bomber wing and a special operations wing.

ROYAL AIR FORCE REGIMENT

The possibility of a German invasion of the United Kingdom in 1940 posed a serious threat to the security of the RAF's home airfields. The shortage of manpower had meant that the defence of airfields rested partly with the Army and partly with RAF personnel. This arrangement presented problems of training, fitness, and continuity since Army detachments were frequently changed at short notice. The campaign on Crete in the Spring of 1941 reinforced the need for an adequate local defence of airfields and in February 1942 the Royal Air Force Regiment was formed from the 66,000 personnel serving with airfield defence squadrons.

The normal field squadron consisted of 7 officers and 178 airmen organised as three rifle flights plus support, armoured car, and anti-aircraft flights.

UNIFORM Tropical dress for Air Force officers at the beginning of the war was similar to that worn in the Army with the exception of a black tie and black leather shoes.

The khaki Wolseley sun helmet had a khaki puggree and a flash in RAF colours on the left side. The tunic was single-breasted and worn open with a khaki shirt and had a matching cloth belt with

brass open-frame buckle. Both long and short trousers were worn, the latter with khaki socks. In shirt-sleeve order a light khaki shirt with either long or short sleeves could be worn with an open collar. In the desert campaign a considerable mixture of khaki-drill and grey-blue clothing was worn.

Other ranks also had a formal khaki-drill tunic with brass buttons (later changed to black plastic) khaki shirt, long or short trousers and khaki socks. Sometimes the grey-blue field service cap was worn with RAF badge on the left side, but this was replaced later in the war by a grey-blue beret, particularly in the RAF Regiment. The RAF Regiment served in both the Middle East and in Italy where it received khaki battledress. Badges of rank were worn on the shoulder straps by officers and on the sleeves by non-commissioned officers and airmen. On the khaki-drill uniform the propeller badge for leading aircraftmen was in red, although it soon bleached to almost white.

ROYAL NAVY

The Mediterranean was a traditional focus of British maritime power. In World War II this importance was accentuated after the fall of France in the summer of 1940, because the Mediterranean Sea was now the only theatre left in which British naval and military forces could strike back at the overwhelming strength of the two Axis powers, Germany and Italy.

In 1939 the responsibility for the Mediterranean had been divided between Britain and France but the collapse of France and the loss of her powerful fleet, and Italy's declaration of war on 10 June 1940 placed the Royal Navy in a difficult position.

Out-numbered by the Italian Navy, the British plan was to hold the three decisive strategic points of Gibraltar, Malta and Suez and through them hold open the vital Mediterranean supply routes. Although untennable as a major naval base because of its proximity to Italy, Malta was the linch-pin of the system; a stopping-off point for the convoys and a base from which to attack the Axis supply routes to North Africa.

British planning was expressed on the tactical level by a series of aggressive raids against the Italian Navy. On 11 November 1940, aircraft of the Fleet Air Arm attacked the Italian Fleet at Taranto, crippling three of the five battleships moored there. This success was followed by the Battle of Cape Matapan, a British victory which denied the Axis naval forces control of the central Mediterranean in 1941.

Below: Officers and ratings of the Fleet Air Arm pose in front of a Swordfish. The distinction between the officers' and ratings' uniform in this order of dress is clearly shown.

143

144

145

The surrender of the Italian Navy in September 1943 brought in 700 warships and merchantmen and confirmed Allied naval domination of the Mediterranean. Until the end of the war the Royal Navy carried out routine supply duties as well as providing invaluable artillery support to the Allied invasion forces in Italy (especially the hard-pressed beach-head at Anzio) and to the invasion of southern France in August 1944.

ORGANISATION The Mediterranean Fleet in 1939 was under the command of Sir Andrew Cunningham and comprised: three battleships (*Warspite*, *Barham*, *Malaya*);
one aircraft carrier (*Glorious*);
two cruiser squadrons, each of three ships;
four destroyer flotillas, a total of 31 ships;
four escort vessels;
one submarine flotilla of ten submarines;
one motor torpedo-boat flotilla of ten vessels;
one minesweeper flotilla of five ships.

In addition there was a netlayer, a mine-layer and a repair ship plus other, smaller auxiliary vessels.

The fleet was based at Alexandria although the facilities there for repair and maintenance were far from satisfactory. Two subsidiary bases at Haifa and Port Said were occasionally used to spread the risk of attack from the air but these were too distant from the central Mediterranean to be of very much use.

In the first year of the war the Mediterranean Fleet suffered a number of reductions including the despatch of the 2nd Destroyer Flotilla (five destroyers) to home waters. Following the Italian declaration of war, however, attempts were made to reinforce the Fleet and in June 1940 Force 'H' was formed, based at Gibraltar and comprising the aircraft carrier *Ark Royal*, two battleships and a small number of cruisers and destroyers.

During the fighting in the Mediterranean in 1941–42, Royal Navy losses were heavy but nonetheless the Mediterranean theatre received regular reinforcements so that by the autumn of 1943 the

143 Lieutenant, Royal Navy, 1943
This submarine commander wears the Navy peaked cap with Army battledress and rank badges on the shoulder straps. Under the battledress blouse (which could be worn open by officers) he wears a typical naval roll neck pullover.

144 Lieutenant, Royal Navy, 1943
This officer wears the rig for land operations in the tropics. His rank and Royal Naval Volunteer Reserve status are displayed on the shoulder straps. Over his khaki-drill jacket he wears the 1937-pattern web equipment. The leather leggings were standard issue for officers wearing landing rig. Royal Navy officers played an important part in supervising amphibious operations.

145 Admiral, Royal Navy, 1943
Admiral Sir John Cunningham, Naval Commander-in-Chief Levant, wears regulation Navy whites. The cap was either made with a white top, or a washable white cover was put over the blue cloth cap. Badges of rank were worn on the shoulder straps. On his left side he wears the Order of the Bath, and below that the Norwegian Royal Order of St Olaf, and the Royal Greek Order of George I. The sword is the regulation M1891 naval officers' sword.

Royal Navy had attained an overwhelming material superiority over the Axis Navies. The Mediterranean Station, which included the old Levant Command, was organised as follows:

1st Battle Squadron – six battleships and two aircraft carriers;
12th Cruiser Squadron – five cruisers;
15th Cruiser Squadron – five cruisers;
six anti-aircraft ships;
four escort carriers;
99 escort vessels (destroyers, sloops, frigates and corvettes);
five destroyer flotillas (27 ships);
Levant Command destroyers (11 ships);
two submarine flotillas (24 vessels);
90 minesweepers;
six motor torpedo-boat flotillas (39 MTBs).

This force was supplemented by an armada of auxiliary vessels and a sizeable detachment of French ships which included two cruisers and seven destroyers.

During the war in the Mediterranean 167 British and Commonwealth warships were lost including one battleship (*Barham*), the two aircraft carriers *Ark Royal* and *Eagle*, 14 cruisers and 50 destroyers.

UNIFORM Before and during the war officers wore the white uniform illustrated by figure 145, although this uniform also included a white sun helmet which was only rarely worn during the war. A similar white uniform was also worn by chief petty officers and petty officers, while miscellaneous junior ratings had the same tunic with black plastic buttons. Ratings wore a white uniform consisting of a hat, shirt, jumper with blue denim collar and long navy-blue trousers with black shoes.

In February 1938 another simpler white uniform for everyday wear had been introduced for all ranks. Officers, chief petty officers and petty officers wore a cap with white cover or sun helmet, white shirt worn open at the neck, white shorts, white socks and canvas shoes. Miscellaneous junior ratings wore this uniform with black socks and shoes, while seamen wore a white shirt with blue dungaree binding around the collar which was usually worn under a jumper.

During the war the Royal Navy also adopted khaki-drill, and in 1941 khaki battledress which was worn with naval head-dress. Royal Marines also had a khaki-drill uniform which was basically the same as that worn in the Army, although long trousers were worn with long puttees. A distinctive feature of Royal Marine uniform was the fabric belt in the corps colours.

INSIGNIA Badges of rank were worn on the shoulder straps and sometimes painted on the steel helmet. Chief petty officers and petty officers wore their particular cap badge, and chief petty officers retained the three buttons on the cuffs of the white tunic. Other ratings wore their rank badges on the left sleeve. Royal Marines wore their rank badges in the Army style on the shoulder straps. Officers in the civil branches of the Royal Navy wore coloured backing or 'lights' to the rank lace on the shoulder straps, while cadets and midshipmen had a strip of the same coloured cloth on their shoulder straps. Chief petty officers and petty officers and seamen wore their branch badges on the collar or on the right sleeve.

Officers in the Fleet Air Arm wore the letter 'A' within the curl on the shoulder straps.

ROYAL NAVY INSIGNIA

Cap Peaks

Cuff

| Admiral of the Fleet | Admiral | Vice-Admiral (Surgeon) | Rear-Admiral (Instructor) | Commodore 1st Class (Paymaster) | Commodore 2nd Class | Captain (Engineers) | Commander (Ordnance) | Lieutenant-Commander (Dental) | Lt (RNVR) (Pilot in Air Branch) | Sub-Lt (RNR) (Electrical) |

Shoulder · Cuff

| Warrant Officer (Shipwright) | Midshipman (RN) | Midshipman (RNR) | Midshipman (RNVR) | Cadet | Chief Petty Officer | P.O (with 3 Long Service Stripes) | Leading Seaman (2 L S Stripes) | 2nd Officer (WRNS) | Medical Superintendent (WRNS) |

FRANCE
ARMY

The Franco-German Armistice of 22 June 1940 divided France into two parts. The northern and western area of the country was to be under the direct control of the German armed forces while central and southern France was unoccupied and was given a limited degree of autonomy, being known as Vichy France after the town which became its new 'capital'.

Article IV of the Armistice allowed for a small French army to be kept in being in the unoccupied zone (*l'Armée de l'Armistice*) and for the military provision of the French Empire overseas. The function of these forces was to keep internal order and to defend French territories from any Allied assault while remaining, in theory at least, under the overall direction of the German armed forces.

Vichy forces in Syria, Madagascar and Dakar resisted fiercely Allied attempts to take them over, but the Vichy Army in North Africa hardly resisted the landings of Operation 'Torch'. The defeat of the Axis forces in North Africa and the American 'Torch' landings ensured the demise of Vichy France, and the German High Command set Operation '*Anton*' into action. On 11 November 1942 German armoured columns advanced over the demarcation line and overran the unoccupied zone. Following the German occupation, the *Armée de l'Armistice* was dissolved.

ORGANISATION The exact strength of the Vichy Metropolitan Army was set as 3768 officers, 15,072 NCOs and 75,360 men, all of whom were to be volunteers. In addition the size of the paramilitary Gendarmerie was fixed at 60,000 men plus an anti-aircraft force of 10,000 men. Despite the influx of trained soldiers from the colonial forces (reduced in size in accordance with the Armistice) there was a shortage of volunteers so that initially 50,000 men of the 'class of 1939' were retained until sufficient volunteers came forward to fulfill the quota. At the beginning of 1942 these conscripts were released, but still there was an insufficient number of men, a shortage that was to remain until the Army's dissolution despite Vichy appeals to the Germans for a regular form of conscription.

The Army was divided into two groups each of four military divisions and comprised:
18 infantry regiments;
11 cavalry regiments;
8 artillery regiments;
15 battalions of *chasseurs*.

The Army was deprived of tanks and other armoured vehicles and was desperately short of motorised transport especially in the cavalry units which were supposed to be motorised.

UNIFORM The uniform of the Vichy Army was as that of the Army in 1940.

MILICE

On 30 January 1943 the paramilitary organisation the *Milice* was established by Pierre Laval for the task of maintaining the 'new order' in occupied Vichy France. Inevitably this brought the *Milice* in direct confrontation with the Resistance, and it was to become the bitterest and most detested of collaborationist organisations.

The *Milice* was organised territorially in departments, regions and zones under the overall command of a secretary-general (Joseph Darnand) with his headquarters in Vichy. By Autumn 1943 *Milice* had reached its maximum membership of 29,000 men, but only 10,000 were active, while the rest were either contributors or part-timers.

The military arm of the *Milice* was the *Francs-Garde*, which also had from June 1943 a regular and part-time branch. Regulars were paid, barracked and from

Below: General Noguès (left, with five stars on his arm) and General Juin (with four stars) in Algiers in 1942. The loops on Noguès' pockets are to hold his orders and decorations.

October 1943 increasingly armed, but never exceeded a strength of 2000 men. Like the pre-war German paramilitary formations, the *Milice* adopted archaic terms for its sub-divisions. The basic unit was a five-man *main*, then came a *dizaine*, (ten men), *trentaine*, (30 men), *centaine* (100 men), and a *cohorte* (500 men), four of which formed a regimental-sized *centre* of about 2000 men.

If the military situation dictated, the part-time members were liable for call-up at short-notice and following the D-Day landings 3000 men were mobilised.

UNIFORM The dark blue uniform of the *Milice* was basically that of the French *Chasseurs Alpins* and consisted of black beret, open blue tunic and long trousers which were worn with shoes or ankle-boots and gaiters.

The emblem of the *Milice* was the gamma on the beret, steel helmet and on the right breast pocket. Members of the special units belonging to the *2e Service* (intelligence) wore a metal shield-shaped badge on the left breast pocket. It incorporated the unit's motto '*Devant*' (in front), the death's head and the gamma all in black on a white enamel ground. Equipment was that of the French Army while weapons were either French or came from stocks supplied by the British to the *Maquis* and captured by the security forces.

Rank badges were worn on the shoulder straps by all ranks but were based on those of the French Army.

PHALANGE AFRICAINE

Late in 1942, a unit of pro-Axis French volunteers began to be formed in Tunisia. Under the command of French officers about 300 volunteers (half of whom were Tunisian Arabs) were found for the *Phalange Africaine*. On 7 April 1943 the first contingent with the strength of a strong company arrived at the front at Medjez el Bab. After putting up a reasonably good showing in bitter defensive fighting against British troops the unit was practically annihilated on 29 April. On 8 May 1943 the survivors were paid-off and advised to disappear, while the officers were evacuated to Vichy where some continued to serve in the *Milice* and French Volunteer Legion.

UNIFORM French uniform was worn with the *francisque* on the right breast pocket, and the French national colours on the right side of the German steel helmet.

COLONIAL FORCES

The French territories in the Mediterranean consisted of the Algerian *département*, the protectorates of Tunisia and Morocco and the mandates of Syria and Lebanon. The Armistice called for the demilitarisation of Tunisia – in compliance with Italian wishes – and a general reduction of French colonial troops. Vichy France was permitted 55,000 men in Morocco, 50,000 in Algeria, the Army of the Levant in Syria and Lebanon being reduced from around 100,000 to just under 40,000 men.

The Vichy French Army of the Levant controlled the mandates of Syria and Lebanon and, although it did not mount offensive operations against the Allies, its very presence adjacent to the strategically vulnerable British oil and supply lines posed a constant threat. Syria was invaded by a mixed Allied force on 8 June 1941, the Vichy troops putting up a dogged resistance to the Allied advance, a resistance tinged with bitter ferocity with Frenchman fighting Frenchman.

When the fighting in Syria finally ended on 11 July 1941 the Vichy forces had lost 6000 men, 1000 of whom had been killed. A total of 37,736 soldiers were taken prisoner, but when given the choice of being repatriated or joining General de Gaulle only 5668 availed themselves of this opportunity, the remainder being transported to France.

ORGANISATION The Vichy Army in Syria was divided into the *troupes spéciales* (indigenous native soldiers) and the regu-

lar metropolitan and colonial troops. The *troupes spéciales* were formed by 11 battalions of infantry: 3 Lebanese (*bataillons de chasseurs Libanais*) and 8 Syrian (*bataillons du Levant*). In addition there were two artillery groups and supporting units as well as at least 5000 cavalry organised in squadrons of around 100 men each. Included in this cavalry force were 15 squadrons of Circassian cavalry of which three were motorised. The *troupes spéciales* were led by indigenous officers and NCOs although there was a small French officer cadre.

The regular French troops consisted of the four battalions of the 6th Foreign Legion – the best troops available to the Vichy commander, General Dentz – and the three battalions of the 24th Colonial Infantry Regiment who were brought up to strength by amalgamating them with two garrison battalions of Senegalese to become the 24th *Régiment Mixte Coloniale*.

The African troops were formed from six Algerian, three Tunisian, three Senegalese and one Moroccan rifle (*tirailleur*) battalion, the Moroccan troops being

160

161

160 Private, Vichy French Moroccan Spahis, 1941

The Adrian helmet bears the crescent emblem worn by all Mohammedan troops. The collar patches bear the regimental number, and buttoned to the front of his djellabah is the rank badge of a soldat de première classe. Attached to the special leather equipment is the 1892 knife bayonet.

161 Trumpeter, Vichy French Colonial Infantry, 1941

Viewed from the back one can clearly see the arrangement of equipment on this rifleman. The pack forms part of the 1935 equipment as does the two-litre water bottle. The haversack does not appear to be an issue item; nor does the coat hanger! His bugle hangs by the side of the pack with its red white and blue tasselled cord.

162 Colonel, Vichy French Colonial Infantry, 1942

This officer in Madagascar wears regulation tropical dress with sun helmet on the front of which is the gilt metal anchor, emblem of French colonial forces. The badges of rank are worn on the shoulder straps, and the collar patches, which were rarely worn on the shirt, identify his unit.

162

khaki working, and white undress uniform consisting of sun helmet, tunic and trousers. Other ranks serving in colonial forces had both a khaki drill uniform with shirt or tunic with stand collar, shorts or pantaloons, or a khaki cloth uniform consisting of a double-breasted khaki tunic, pantaloons, and greatcoat while both uniforms were worn with ankle boots and long khaki puttees. Head-dress for Europeans was basically the sun helmet, kepi, beret or side cap, while indigenous personnel wore a red *chechia* (fez) with khaki cover on active duty.

All ranks in all units wore the *Adrian* steel helmet on the front of which was a circular stamped metal badge bearing various devices. For example Mohammedans had the letters 'RF' above a crescent, colonial troops the anchor, and French Foreign Legion and *Chasseurs d'Afrique* (African Mounted Rifles) the same exploding grenade as French metropolitan troops.

Zouaves and *tirailleurs* (rifles) from Algeria, Morocco and Tunisia wore either tropical or temperate uniform with distinctive head-dress. The *chechia* was worn by Algerians and Tunisians, while Moroccans wore a turban which was rolled in a slightly different manner by each regiment. Since in wartime the turban was khaki the pre-war distinctive colours no longer applied.

Below: Loading a Martin bomber of the Vichy Air Force. The men are wearing casual summer working clothes, with a variety of head-gear.

Cavalry also wore the standard uniform but with baggy trousers and special leather leggings. Tunisian *spahis* wore the *chechia* with cover while Moroccan and Algerian *spahis* had their own distinctive turbans.

INSIGNIA Badges of rank were worn in the same manner on both temperate and tropical uniforms, although during the war it was more common to see officers wearing their rank badges on the shoulder straps. Other ranks wore their rank badges on a tab which was fixed to the front of their shirt, tunic, or special clothing.

Arm of service and unit was identified by the coloured kepi or by the colour or combination of colours on the collar patches. The regimental number appeared on the front of the kepi, on the collar patch, and later on the badge worn on the left sleeve of American uniforms.

AIR FORCE

As a result of British aerial assaults on the French fleet at Mers-el-Kébir and the fear of further bombardment against the French homeland the Axis armistice commission permitted the French to retain part of their Air Force. Similarly the French were allowed to keep Air Force detachments in their overseas colonies which were coming under attack from the Allies and, in the case of Indo-China, from the Japanese.

considered troops of the first order.

The artillery available to the French consisted of 120 field and medium guns and numbered about 6700 men. There was also a mechanised element which was provided by the 6th and 7th *Chasseurs d'Afrique* whose forces totalled 90 tanks (Renault R-35s) and a similar number of armoured cars.

The contingent of North African cavalry consisted of the 4th Tunisian, 1st Moroccan and the 8th Algerian Spahis and amounted to about 7000 men, most of whom were either on horseback or in light lorries, with a few equipped with armoured cars.

UNIFORM The French standardised the uniforms of its colonial and African troops on the Metropolitan pattern while retaining certain national features which were only officially to be worn by indigenous personnel. However Europeans also wore them because not only did they go down well in France when on leave, but they were practical for wear in desert or *bled*.

Before the war officers had a light

ORGANISATION In the unoccupied zone of France the Vichy Air Force consisted of:

6 fighter groups;
2 night-fighter *escadrilles*;
6 bomber groups;
2 ground-attack groups;
3 reconnaissance groups.

A group was usually formed from two *escadrilles* which would normally consist of 12 aircraft. The group would consist only of planes of one type, e.g. fighter or bomber, but could be combined to form *groupements* which could be of various types.

Following the German occupation of Vichy France all the remaining aircraft were seized and the French air units disbanded.

In Syria many of the aircraft stationed there had been sent back to France in 1940, leaving only a number of obsolete models. Alarmed by the growing threat of a British invasion, a fighter group was dispatched from Algeria and once the fighting started three groups were flown in from France and three more from North Africa. This brought the Vichy strength up to 289 aircraft organised into:

3 fighter groups;
4 bomber groups;
1 bomber *escadrille*;
1 reconnaissance group;
6 army co-operation groups;
2 transport groups;
1 *flotille* of naval aircraft;
4 *escadrilles* of naval aircraft.

This gave them the edge over the Allied air units until British reinforcements arrived towards the latter part of the campaign. French losses were 179 planes, most of which had been destroyed on the ground.

While the Vichy land forces did little to resist the Anglo-American forces during the 'Torch' landings, the Air Force was hotly engaged. A determined resistance was carried out until 11 November 1942 when a cease-fire was called following which most of the French planes went over to the Allies to join with the Free French.

In Morocco there were two fighter, two reconnaissance and four bomber groups plus two *flotilles* of naval aircraft and two transport groups. In Algeria the Vichy Air Force consisted of three fighter, one reconnaissance and three bomber groups with one *flotille* of naval aircraft. In Tunisia a small presence was maintained by one fighter, two bomber and one reconnaissance group with one unit of naval flying boats.

UNIFORM Uniform and insignia were as before the fall of France.

NAVY

Under the terms of the Franco-German Armistice the French Fleet was obliged to keep its ships under Axis control and be disarmed under German or Italian control. Little attempt to impose this clause of the Armistice was made, however, the Axis being content to leave the French ships in French hands so long as they were withdrawn from the British war effort.

Although the French Navy had no intention of allowing its ships to be used by the Axis, the British and Free French attacks against Mers-el-Kébir and Dakar, ensured that the Navy maintained a hostile attitude towards the Allied cause.

The Vichy Navy came to an abrupt end when the Germans occupied the 'free' zone in 1942. Initially the German Army made no attempt to gain control of the fleet in Toulon, but on 27 November the port was taken over, to which the French replied by scuttling their ships – more than 70 vessels – which included 3 battleships, 7 cruisers, 32 destroyers and 16 submarines.

The attempted German take-over of the Toulon fleet brought the remaining Vichy naval detachments in the colonies over to the Allies and the Free French. The Free French Navy was never an important force, consisting only of a few submarines and escort and auxiliary vessels, although the reinforcement of the colonial Vichy ships was able to provide the basis for a new French Fleet. Thus by the end of the war the Navy had a

163 Rear Admiral, French Navy, 1942

The cap for flag officers had an elaborately embroidered band on which also appeared the five-pointed white metal stars which denoted rank. On his white tropical jacket he wears detachable shoulder straps which also bore the badges of rank.

164 Leading Seaman, French Navy, 1941

The sun helmet and shirt formed part of the tropical uniform introduced in 1925, whereas the cotton duck trousers were part of the working rig. The two bars on the left breast denoted the rank of the wearer.

163

164

strength of 4 battleships, 9 cruisers and 11 destroyers, plus a number of smaller craft supplied by the British and Americans.

UNIFORM Uniform and insignia were as before the fall of France.

FREE FRENCH

ARMY

After the fall of France, various units of French troops in the Middle East preferred to join the Allies. Their position was difficult; many Frenchmen thought them a small group of dissidents, and considered their leader – de Gaulle – a traitor.

In May 1941, as the possibility of operations in Syria became apparent, the scattered Free French Forces were assembled at Quastina in Palestine and formed into the 1st Free French Light Division.

Although the Free French troops fought with traditional *élan* there were understandable problems of morale as former comrades-in-arms and fellow countrymen fought against each other. Altogether the Free French suffered 1300 casualties, a heavy total for such a small initial force.

After their victory in Syria the Free French troops were redeployed in North Africa being reinforced by other French units. Initially Free French forces played only a minor role in operations, their most notable success being at Bir Hakeim when the 1st Free French Light Division maintained a stubborn defence of the desert stronghold during the Gazala battle before breaking out of their surrounding position to rejoin the Allied lines.

The position of the Free French changed dramatically with the collapse of the Axis in North Africa and the refusal of the vast majority of Vichy forces to resist the Allied armies. The Free French commanders were able to persuade the Vichy troops to go over to the Allied cause, a conversion made easier by the German take-over of the unoccupied zone. Thus there was an enormous influx of numbers to the Free French who, with American help in armament and equipment, were now able to make a significant military contribution.

Free French troops fought in the final stages of the Tunisian campaign but it was the war in Italy where the newly reorganised forces were to make their mark. At the end of 1943 units of the French Expeditionary Corps began to arrive in Italy; at first two divisions, the Corps was reinforced by a further two divisions in

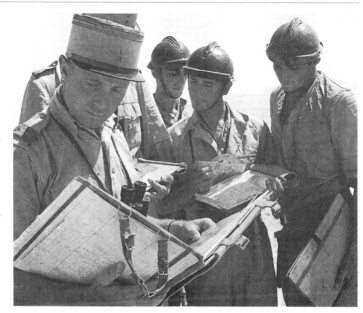

Above: A Free French captain of the 1st Moroccan Spahis gives his men (in armoured crew helmets) instructions. The captain's kepi would be sky blue.

the spring of 1944. The French Expeditionary Corps was heavily engaged in the battles of Cassino and it was its outflanking of the German mountain positions that made possible the Allied victory. After the capture of Rome in May 1944 the French troops were withdrawn from Italy in preparation for the liberation of France itself.

ORGANISATION The 1st Free French Light Division which fought in Syria was divided into two small brigades, the first comprising a battalion of the 13th *Demi-Brigade* of the French Foreign Legion and two Senegalese battalions, the second, a naval infantry battalion (which included two motorised companies) and a further two Senegalese battalions. The division was supported by an artillery battery of six guns; a tank company (eight tanks and armoured cars) and a contingent of naval infantry. In addition there were two squadrons of Circassian cavalry and a squadron of *spahis* (mounted in trucks) under the command of Colonel Collet.

In North Africa, one of the first effective units was the Free French Fighting Column or 'L' Force, a small mixed force of armoured cars, tanks, infantry and anti-tank and anti-aircraft guns under the command of General Leclerc. 'L' Force fought through the desert

campaigns until 1943 when it was withdrawn from the front line to be re-equipped and re-grouped with other French elements to become the French 2nd Armoured Division which then took part in the fighting in Normandy.

After the Syrian campaign the Free French could muster two brigade groups which were known as the 1st and 2nd French Light Divisions and were supported in the fighting in North Africa by a regiment of Moroccan *spahis* who were able to provide reconnaissance detachments for the Free French when necessary.

Following the defeat of the Africa Corps at El Alamein, the brigades were withdrawn from the front and in February 1943 began to be formed into the 1st Free French Division. Its two component brigades fought independently in Tunisia until the autumn of 1943 when they were moved to Tripolitania to be re-organised and re-equipped.

During the short lull in the fighting that followed the Axis surrender at Tunis in 1943 the French forces were re-organised from the old Vichy and Free French troops into the French Expeditionary Corps. Besides the Free French units, French troops consisted of the XIX Corps (three colonial divisions and an armoured group) and three battalions of the *Corps Franc d'Afrique* plus two Moroccan *tabors* which were grouped with the US 2nd Corps. A *tabor* was a unit of Moroccan irregular troops who were known as *goumiers*.

The four divisions of the French Expeditionary Corps under the command of General Juin comprised:
2 infantry regiments;
1 naval infantry regiment;
6 infantry battalions;
3 artillery regiments;
1 mountain artillery regiment;
3 *spahi* regiments;
3 Algerian rifle regiments;
5 Moroccan rifle regiments;
1 Tunisian rifle regiment;
1 *chasseur* battalion;
1 marine infantry battalion;
2 Foreign Legion battalions.

Besides the divisional troops there was a general reserve of three Moroccan *goumier tabors*, two armoured regiments and two regiments of artillery. The forces of the French Expeditionary Corps reached over 100,000 men, while casualties suffered in Italy totalled 7260 men.

UNIFORM Free French troops taking part in the abortive raid on Madagascar and in the campaign in Syria were equipped by Britain with British tropical

uniforms and battledress which were worn with the Wolseley sun helmet. Officers and men in possession of French head-dress continued to wear it as long as possible. With battledress either the sun helmet or British steel helmets were worn.

At first insignia was limited to a flash in the French national colours which was worn on the front or left side of the sun helmet, and 'France' embroidered in white on khaki which was worn on the sleeves of the battle dress blouse. French

165

166

167

colonial infantry wore a metal anchor on the front of the sun helmet as illustrated in figure 162. French rank badges were usually worn on slides on the shoulder straps or in the shape of a tab on the front of the shirt or tunic.

French, African and Colonial troops continued to wear their existing uniforms as long as possible until they were replaced by either British or American uniforms and equipment. American uniform was supplied in vast quantities so that by the time the French Expeditionary Corps landed in Italy it was dressed in American uniforms with French head-dress (when available) and French insignia.

Left: Men of a North African unit of Juin's French corps (the most effective mountain fighters in the Allied armies) move up to the front during the Italian winter of 1944. They have American weapons and equipment, although some have retained the French Adrian helmet. The camouflage netting over the helmets broke up the outline even when (as here) it would have been useless to insert any foliage as an aid to concealment.

165 Private,
Free French Senegalese Rifles, 1941
Serving in Syria, this colonial infantryman wears the chechia with khaki cover, the double-breasted khaki cloth tunic with unit collar patches and lace on the cuffs. The equipment includes the French 1916-pattern ammunition pouches and what looks like a British respirator in its carrying bag.

166 Sergeant-Major,
Moroccan Spahis, 1943
This maréchal de logis-chef of the 2nd Spahis stationed in Tunisia wears cavalry uniform with the Sam Browne belt of a warrant officer. Rank is shown by the three gold chevrons on the arm, and his formation by the collar patches with the Moroccan star.

167 Private,
Fighting French Foreign Legion, 1942
The defenders of Bir Hakeim wore British uniform with the famous white kepi. The collar patches were the same as those worn on French uniform, although the distinctive blue waist sash is not to be seen. Of note are the long shorts here worn folded back.

168 Goumier,
French African Troops, 1943
This Goumier serving with the French Expeditionary Corps in Italy wears a British steel helmet on top of his turban and a djellabah over his American combat uniform. It was possible to tell the tribe by the arrangement and colour of djellabah.

169 Lieutenant,
French Moroccan Spahis, 1943
Although the uniform is basically American, this officer still retains the French motorised troop helmet which he has adorned with an open five-pointed star and the two bars of his rank badge. On his shoulder straps he wears his badges of rank, and on the left sleeve a regimental badge.

AIR FORCE

While most members of the French Air Force accepted the terms of the 1940 Armistice a number escaped with their aircraft to British bases in the Mediterranean where they were re-formed and re-equipped in part with British aircraft. Free French air units fought in the Middle East, Eritrea and North Africa and with the incorporation of Vichy forces from North Africa were heavily engaged against Axis forces in Italy and southern Europe.

ORGANISATION In North Africa and the Middle East it took some time for the Free French units to re-form on a regular basis. By July 1941 there were two bomber groups operating in Africa and two fighter *escadrilles* were united in Syria to form the fighter group 'Alsace' which, equipped with Hurricanes, was actively engaged over the desert during the North African campaign.

The French air units which had gone over to the Allies following the 'Torch' landings were re-equipped with modern British and American aircraft, some groups being transferred to England to conduct bombing operations against Germany but other groups remaining in the Mediterranean to continue the air war against the Axis.

UNIFORM Members of the Free French Air Force cut off from their supplies of French uniforms had to make do as best they could. They tended only to wear French-made uniforms on ceremonial occasions or for walking out, while on duty they wore Australian Air Force blue battledress, or service dress with French insignia. Flying clothing was standard British.

From January 1943 selected personnel from the French Air Force in North Africa were sent to the United States of America for training. They wore French uniform with a 'France' badge on the upper sleeve, and special insignia incorporating three chicks in red, white and blue with the legend *'Ils Grandiront'* (they will grow). Flying clothing and the uniforms for everyday wear were soon supplied by America.

168   169

133

United States
Army

Operation 'Torch' was the first great involvement of US troops in the Mediterranean theatre (and, indeed, the first successful large-scale campaign of the war by the Americans). The landings were followed by the defeat of the Axis forces in North Africa, and then the invasions of Sicily and Italy. The US 5th Army fought throughout the Italian campaign; its men were first to Rome, and were engaged in heavy fighting all the way up the peninsula. US ambitions for the Mediterranean were strictly limited, however (in contrast to the aspirations of their British ally). North-west Europe took precedence, and the 5th Army was weakened in 1944 to provide troops for the landings in southern France (Operation 'Dragoon'). Nevertheless, the 5th Army took a full part in the Italian fighting until the final German surrender there in May 1945. By the end of the war, the US Army had suffered 179,403 casualties in the Mediterranean: 38,741 dead, 107,617 wounded and 33,045 captured or missing.

ORGANISATION Although it is true that the United States mobilised its vast resources in a remarkably short time, American soldiers had ample warning of the coming crisis. In 1940 the Army was divided in three: the regulars, the National Guard and the Organised Reserve. The Regular Army numbered 243,095 and was scattered in 130 posts, camps and stations, the men serving short-term enlistments: the officers numbered 1400. The National Guard was 226,837 strong and was equipped by individual states and received two weeks' training each summer.

There was, in addition, a reserve of 104,228 officers in the organised reserve corps, composed of the Officer Training Camps. The Army received a standard institutionalised pattern of training: the service schools supervised training and the Service Boards tested and developed new equipment.

The continental United States, the Zone of the Interior, was administered by four armies and, in 1940, they only had skeleton staffs of 4400 troops each. There were nine infantry divisions; only three had a complement of regular formations, the other six were only 3000 strong. There was also a cavalry division and a mechanised brigade of 4000 and 2300 men respectively. Responsibility for speeding up mobilisation was given to General Headquarters (GHQ), and in 1941 it was given responsibility for the training of troops under the leadership of General Leslie McNair.

On 17 June 1941 the Army was expanded to 280,000 men and nine days later to 375,000. On 16 September the National Guard units were absorbed into the Army and Roosevelt persuaded Congress to pass the Selective Service Act; by July 1941, 606,915 men were inducted into the Army.

New units were usually formed around the regular or National Guard formations. At first there were 27 divisions, nine regular and 18 National Guard; there were also two armoured divisions and a further three completing their training.

American mobilisation proceeded fairly smoothly before the outbreak of war in December 1941. Thereafter the strain inflicted by the early disasters in the Pacific and the demand for continued

Right: American soldiers move cautiously forward in September 1943 during the Italian campaign. The sergeant in the foreground is carrying the baseplate of a mortar.

170

170 Staff-Sergeant, US Army, 1942
This GI (government issue) disembarking at Oran in November 1942 wears standard American Army combat uniform and equipment. The new steel helmet had a rough sandy finish, and officers sometimes painted their badges of rank on its front. Over an OD (olive drab) flannel shirt he wears a lightweight field jacket, OD trousers, canvas leggings and russet ankle boots. Under the woven equipment can be seen a life jacket and slung round the neck are cloth bandoliers holding extra rifle ammunition. Rank badges are worn on the sleeves and on the left the American flag is prominently displayed. Anglo-French relations in late 1942 were such that Americans were anxious that the French should not mistake them for British troops. The rifle is the US Calibre .30 M1 Garand semi-automatic rifle. This was an outstanding weapon: robust and reliable, it was the Army's standard rifle until 1958.

171 Officer, US Army, 1942
Much more popular than the double-breasted woollen greatcoat among infantry officers was the water-repellent cotton duck M1942 mackinaw lined with khaki cloth and fitted with its own belt as worn by the infantry officer here. Trousers are the standard OD woollen type worn with canvas leggings and ankle boots. On his pistol belt he carries a .45 pistol and a pouch containing two spare magazines. The sub-machine gun is the US Thompson .45 Model 1928 M1 sub-machine gun.

172 Private, US Army, 1942
This engineer clearing mines in North Africa wears the OD cotton fatigue cap, and two-piece fatigue uniform which was issued to all but crews of armoured fighting vehicles, who had a one-piece overall.

expansion proved too much. The War Department originally believed that it could mobilise three or four divisions per month after March 1942, but this rate could not be kept up; by the end of December 1942 only 42 of the planned 73 divisions had been mobilised. Indeed, by September the Army was short of 330,000 men and the ambitious plans laid in that month to create an army of 114 divisions were never realised.

The main factor which limited the size of the US Army, apart from the capacity of the American economy to equip such a large force quickly, was shipping. The shipping estimates showed that no more than 4,170,000 men could be shipped overseas by the end of 1944. In the event the number of divisions shipped abroad did not exceed 88. This fact was an important restraint on Allied strategy. Thus although expansion between December 1941 and December 1943 was unprecedented, with the Army growing from 1,657,157 to 5,400,888, a further increase in the number of units was not undertaken. By December 1944, 4,933,682

Americans were serving abroad in 80 divisions; these were supported by a mere three divisions in reserve.

In 1945 the US Army reached a total of 91 divisions, but three of these were broken up for reinforcements. The remaining 88 were maintained at full combat strength despite the fact that by the end of the Ardennes Campaign in January 1945, 47 regiments in 19 divisions had suffered between 100 and 200 per cent battle casualties.

The American unit organisation had finally been rationalised in 1940. The infantry divisions had adopted a triangular structure which eliminated the brigade, and comprised 15,500 men as a 'general purpose organisation intended for open warfare in theatres permitting the use of motor transport'. The division comprised three infantry regiments and an artillery regiment (four groups each of 12 howitzers), with the normal support of engineers, signals and supply units.

McNair was determined to strip the division of extraneous elements and keep it as lithe and mobile as possible. In 1942

he attempted to cut away the superfluous units and equipment and reduce the size of the division to 14,253 men. Mobility was increased by introducing $2\frac{1}{2}$-ton trucks, 'Jeeps' and $\frac{1}{4}$-ton trailers. The power of both offensive and defensive weapons was increased by introducing the 57mm anti-tank gun and replacing the 75mm howitzer with the 105mm. The infantryman was armed with the M-1 (Garand) rifle and the Rocket Launcher AT 236 (Bazooka) for use against tanks.

Headquarters special troops were set up to coordinate the divisional HQ, and a company each of ordnance, maintenance, quartermaster and signal troops were introduced. Despite a high degree of motorisation (1440 vehicles) a US infantry division did not, however, have the capacity to move all its equipment and personnel simultaneously.

The smallest unit in an American division was the squad of 14–16 men, the largest body of men that could be controlled by a single voice, usually that of a corporal or sergeant; in the artillery the smallest unit was the section. The platoon was composed of several squads or two sections of some 40–50 men commanded by a lieutenant who exercised his control through his squad leaders. The rest of the structure was triangular: three companies formed a battalion and three battalions a regiment.

The armament of the division during the early part of the war (August 1942) included the following:
147 × .30 machine guns;
133 × .50 machine guns;
81 × 60mm mortars;
57 × 81mm mortars;
109 × 37mm anti-tank guns;
18 × 75mm self-propelled howitzers;
36 × 105mm howitzers;
6 × 105mm self-propelled howitzers;
12 × 155mm howitzers.

The armoured division was basically composed of a reconnaissance battalion and four battalions of tanks. In 1942, there were 159 medium and 68 light

173

174

tanks. Accompanying them was an armoured infantry regiment of three battalions all mounted on half-tracks and three battalions each of 18 self-propelled 105mm howitzers. The service troops included an engineer battalion. With 68 armoured cars and over 1000 other wheeled vehicles, the establishment strength of 10,900 officers and men was fully mobile. The novel aspect of the American armoured division was that from March 1942 it was organised in two 'Combat Commands' (each of one tank, one infantry and one artillery battalion) and a general reserve. As all arms were fully motorised, this proved a flexible and very effective system, and in September 1943, three Combat Commands became the rule.

US Army units participating in Operation 'Torch', the invasion of French North Africa were:
Western Task Force of 35,000 men;
1 armoured division;
2 infantry divisions;
Central and Eastern Task forces,
1 armoured division;
3 infantry divisions.

While the Western Task Force was composed entirely of US personnel, the Central and Eastern forces also included British troops.

Activated on 10 July 1943 to carry out Operation 'Husky', the invasion of Sicily, the US 7th Army comprised:
4 infantry divisions;
1 airborne division;
2 armoured divisions.

At the end of the Sicilian Campaign the 7th Army was replaced by the 5th which had been training in North Africa. Elements of the 5th Army taking part in Operation 'Avalanche' the invasion of southern Italy were VI Corps consisting of:
4 infantry divisions;
1 airborne division;
rangers;
1 field artillery brigade and other units.

The 5th Army was an international force, consisting of British, French, Indian and even Brazilian troops, although the majority of its divisions were American. It provided troops for the Anzio landings, but after the fall of Rome was reduced to five divisions when four French and three

US divisions were removed to invade southern France. For the final offensive of April 1945, however, its strength had grown to nine divisions in line with two in reserve. On May 2 there were seven US divisions in Italy: one mountain, one armoured and five infantry.

UNIFORM The Americans experience so many extremes of temperature and climatic conditions on their own continent, that it is not surprising that the American Quartermaster Department had to equip soldiers with a full range of uniforms ranging from lightweight khaki drill to clothing warm enough to wear in Alaska. However American combat clothing, which at the end of the war was the most advanced in the World, looked remarkably outdated in 1941. Figure 176 shows an American officer in a summer uniform worn until the war although it looked out of place anywhere but in Mexico in 1913.

There were three basic classes of uniform; Class A was the winter dress uniform, Class B was the intermediate season uniform with shirt, and Class C was the uniform worn in hot climates which was made of khaki drill or chino cloth as it was known in America.

By the time American soldiers set foot on African soil in November 1942, the uniform was still unproven, and yet it displayed many serious shortcomings. A major change had come in winter 1941 when the old British pattern Mk 1 steel helmet was replaced by a new two-piece American one, which was to prove so successful that it is still in use today. The rest of the uniform was highly standardised and the same for all ranks. The few items of tailor-made uniform reserved for officers were to be found in the service dress.

A new uniform had to be developed for crews of armoured fighting vehicles (figure 175) and the American solution to a problem which faced all designers of combat clothing was a fibre helmet, one-piece overall and olive drab field jacket with zip fasteners and knit collar, cuffs and waistband.

INSIGNIA Badges of rank for officers consisted of gold or silver metal badges which were worn on the shoulders or on the right side (generals both sides) of the shirt collar, on the left front of the overseas cap, and sometimes painted on the front and back of the steel helmet. Non-commissioned officers and men wore their chevrons on both sleeves.

Officers wore metal arm-of-service badges on both lapels, while other ranks wore them on the left side only as well as

173 Private, US Army, 1944

This buck private serving as an infantryman in the US 5th.Army in central Italy wears the M1 helmet, M1941 OD field jacket and OD trousers with canvas leggings and boots. The equipment, consisting of haversack with entrenching tool and bayonet (M1942) with canteen suspended from the cartridge belt, is the standard pattern. The ground sheet is draped over the cartridge belt. The rifle is the US M1 Garand semi-automatic rifle.

174 Officer, US Army, 1945

By the last winter of the war in Italy American troops were beginning to receive suitable winter clothing, although soldiers continued to improvise as best they could to keep themselves warm and dry. This infantry officer wears a hooded snow smock over his field uniform with the special waterproofed M1943 trousers. Over his M1943 combat boots he wears rubber galoshes. On the cartridge belt are a pouch for spare magazines and the M4 knife bayonet. Additional carbine magazines are carried in a special pouch on the butt of the US Calibre .30 M1 carbine.

175 Corporal, US Army, 1942

The fibre helmet with ventilation holes was issued to crews of armoured fighting vehicles, as were the overalls he wears under the lined field jacket, which was so popular that every soldier tried to get his hands on one. Suspended from the woven pistol belt is a russet leather holster for the .45 Model 1911 A1 automatic pistol, a small pouch on the right for a field dressing and on the left a pouch for pistol ammunition.

176 Lieutenant-Colonel, US Army, 1941

This field officers wears the campaign hat with yellow cords for cavalry, 'chino', worsted or gaberdine shirt, cord breeches and russet field boots which were already a rarity by the time America entered the war.

175

176

on the left front of the overseas cap. All ranks wore coloured cords on the campaign hat and coloured piping on the overseas cap which identified the wearer's arm of service. Formation signs were worn on the sleeves at shoulder height and were also sometimes painted on the steel helmet.

AIR FORCE

Prior to June 1941 the Air Force of the United States had comprised two elements, the GHQ Air Force and the Air Force, but through the work of General Marshall, and the Secretary of War, Henry L. Stimson, they were combined to form the USAAF.

For a nation as large as the United States its Air Force was relatively small, consisting in June 1941 of 9078 officers

Left: The crew of a Lee tank cleaning up in November 1942. The man in the foreground is wearing the short tank-crew jacket, and the one-piece overall gathered at the ankle which was standard for armoured vehicle crews. A tank helmet is on the tank itself.

177

and 143,563 enlisted men and about 6000 aircraft. But the next six months saw a rapid expansion of the USAAF, an expansion that was accelerated at a faster rate after the Japanese attack on Pearl Harbor on 7 December 1941. The USAAF reached the peak of its strength in March 1944 with 2,411,294 men while the number of planes used by the Air Force during the war was just over a quarter of a million – a reflection of American organisational and industrial strength.

As part of the reorganisation Major-General Henry H. Arnold was appointed Chief, Army Air Forces and was given a

place on the Joint Chiefs of Staff, which greatly enhanced the prestige and newly-acquired independent status of the USAAF. Indeed, on 9 March 1942 the Army Air Force was made one of the three co-equal semi-autonomous branches of the War Department.

The USAAF was soon involved in the fighting over the Mediterranean in support of the Anglo-American landings in North Africa and once the Axis forces were cleared from Africa, air bases were set up for the aerial assault upon southern Europe. In combination with the British and other Allied air forces the American Army Air Force was able to gain an air superiority over the Mediterranean that was decisive in the successful conclusion of land operations. On the strategic level the industrial centres in northern Italy, Austria and southern Germany were heavily bombed, as were the Ploesti oil refineries in Romania but at the heavy cost of 350 aircraft. Tactically the USAAF played a vital part, acting in an interdiction role preventing supplies and men reaching the battlefronts as well as being engaged in direct battlefield operations.

ORGANISATION The USAAF in the Mediterranean consisted of the 12th and 15th Air Forces, both of which contained fighter and bomber units. The 12th Air Force was established on 20 August 1942 and was soon engaged in active operations in the support of the ground fighting in North Africa. Its initial strength was some 500 planes, a figure that was doubled by early 1943 when it was combined with RAF units to form the Northwest African Air Force under General Carl Spatz. The 12th Air Force acted in support of the Allied armies in Italy and in southern France after 1944 until the conclusion of fighting in May 1945.

The 12th Air Force, flying a total of 430,681 sorties, dropped 217,136 tons of bombs and shot down 3565 enemy aircraft for the loss of 2843 planes.

The 15th Air Force was initially formed from the heavy bombardment units of the 12th Air Force on 1 November 1943, its role being to act as the strategic bomber force for the Mediterranean Allied Air Forces. From airfield in southern Italy this Air Force worked in tandem with the 8th Air Force based in Britain, attacking targets in German occupied Europe. During the winter of 1943–44, however, the 15th Air Force was mainly engaged in support of land operations in Italy and in Operation 'Strangle' (March–April 1944) it was involved in the interdiction campaign to isolate German forces in northern Italy.

Flying 242,377 sorties, the 15th Air Force dropped 309,278 tons of bombs, destroyed 6258 enemy aircraft and lost 3410 aircraft to enemy action.

Before its reorganisation in Great Britain on 16 October 1943 the US 9th Air Force had been stationed in the Mediterranean theatre. The 9th Air Force was officially formed on 12 November 1942 having formerly been known as the Middle East Air Force. The 9th Air Force concentrated on the disruption of enemy supply lines in the eastern part of the Mediterranean as well as acting in a ground-support role in the follow-up to El Alamein. During the period that the 9th was engaged in the Mediterranean 20,080 sorties were flown 20,127 tons of bombs were dropped and 610 enemy aircraft were shot down for the loss of 227 US planes.

UNIFORM As a branch of the Army the United States Air Force did not have its own distinctive uniforms, but continued to wear American Army uniforms throughout World War II. During the course of the war American airmen tried to develop their own particular style of dress, which made them instantly recognisable. For example they removed the stiffener from their peaked or 'vizor' cap which

Below: The basic warm clothing of the American Air Force: sheepskin-lined leather jackets, caps with ear flaps and the A-6 lined overshoes. These were all comfortable and practical items.

gave it a crushed look, they affected a less formal look, and of course the pilots and aircrew tended to have more decorations and 'wings' than ordinary soldiers.

On 21 June 1941 the air forces of the US Army became officially the United States Army Air Force, but this did not lead to new uniforms.

Flying clothing in Europe and North Africa included a one-piece beige flying suit, or a fleece-lined leather two-piece flying suit with helmet and a cap with peak and earflaps. Pilots of enclosed single-seater aircraft simply removed their tunic and donned a leather flying jacket over their shirt with rank badges on the collar.

INSIGNIA Badges of rank were identical to those worn by other branches of the American Army, although a new rank of Flight Officer was created in July 1942.

The arm-of-service badge was the winged propeller which was worn on both lapels by officers or on the left side of the collar and overseas cap by other ranks. Formation signs predominantly in ultramarine, white, red or yellow were worn on the upper left sleeve.

NAVY

The American contribution to the war in the Mediterranean was not enthusiastic and the decision to launch Operation 'Torch', the invasion of French North Africa, was not finally made until July 1942. The American Chiefs of Staff were opposed to it, claiming that the Mediterranean theatre represented a diversion from the vital theatre which lay in north-west Europe, and consequently the American naval contribution to the amphibious landings in the Mediterranean was not large. Another important factor limiting size was the reluctance of the Naval Staff to divert resources from the Pacific.

ORGANISATION US naval operations on the Mediterranean were organised around task forces for particular operations. For the North African landings in November 1942, Task Force 34 was assembled, which included 30 transports with the covering force provided by the Royal Navy. The most important US naval force was Western Naval Task Force whose objective was Casablanca. This was divided into four groups: the Covering Group of one battleship, two cruisers for fire support, covered by a screen of four destroyers. The second was the Northern Attack Group of one battleship, one cruiser, eight destroyers and eight transports. The Central Attack Group, the third, comprised one

armoured and one light cruiser and four destroyers for fire support and fifteen transports. Protecting this force were one aircraft carrier, one auxiliary (later called an escort carrier) and five destroyers. The fourth group, the Southern Attack Group consisted of one battleship, one light cruiser and three destroyers for fire support, with six transports, two tankers, five destroyers and one submarine. Screening these were one auxiliary carrier and two destroyers. This Force totalled 102 vessels including auxiliary ships.

Once the final decision to attack Sicily had been taken at the Casablanca Conference, three task forces were assembled in the North African ports. Task Force 86 transported the 34th Infantry Division with two light cruisers and eight destroyers; Task Force 81 carried the 1st Infantry Division with two light cruisers and thirteen destroyers; and Task Force 85 transported the 45th Infantry Division escorted by one light cruiser and sixteen destroyers. The floating reserve carried two combat teams of the 2nd Armoured Division and one from the 1st. The whole force included 580 ships and landing craft with 1124 shipborne landing craft.

At Salerno, the American contingent formed the Southern Attack Force (Task Force 81). Its main convoy transported US 31st Infantry Division from Oran in thirteen transports, accompanied by three light cruisers and twelve destroyers. Task Force 81 was also called upon to mount the landing at Anzio. The American contribution called 'X-Ray' included four destroyers and one cruiser.

UNIFORM US Navy uniform as worn during World War II was introduced in 1862 and following various modifications and additions was subject to a complete review in 1941

The basic uniform for officers consisted of a peaked cap with both blue or white top, overseas cap, reefer jacket with white shirt and black tie and matching trousers with black shoes and socks. The greatcoat and raincoat were both double-breasted with two rows of four buttons in front. The same uniform with minor differences was worn by warrant officers and chief petty officers (see figure 180). There was also a white version of the basic uniform for officers, warrant officers and chief petty officers, which was sometimes dyed grey for wear as a working uniform. This was found unsatisfactory and a new Army-style light khaki working dress including both long and short sleeved shirts and overseas cap was introduced.

The square rig for ratings is shown in figure 179. In cold weather ratings wore

178

178 Seaman 2nd Class, US Navy, 1942
This rating wears the winter working head-dress to which a face mask could be attached in very cold weather. The lined jacket was worn without insignia, although sometimes improvised rank badges were worn on the head-dress. The trousers are the standard bell-bottoms which formed part of the 'square rig'.

a shortened overcoat or pea-coat with two rows of large plastic buttons bearing the American Eagle in front. Ratings also had plain whites with which the jumper was worn, without the blue denim collar but with the black silk.

Wartime working dress in warm climates was the white cap, blue shirt, and blue jeans, or a roll-neck pullover worn under a blue jean jacket. Winter or cold weather working dress included a padded blue cloth helmet, navy blue version of the Army tanker's jacket with knit collar and cuffs (see figure 178) and matching lined trousers. Foul weather clothing was made of black oilskin, or an olive drab

179

180

181

rubberised material. These working rigs formed the basis for the battle rig with which was worn two patterns of steel helmets (often painted in battleship grey).

Probably the most famous American fighting men are the Marines or 'leather necks' who formed a special corps with its own traditions, uniforms and organisation. The basic service dress was green and the typical head-dress the felt campaign hat with red cords. Combat dress at the beginning of the war was the two-piece olive-drab (actually a pale grey-green) with open patch pockets and the letters USMC stencilled in black above the corps emblem on the left breast pocket. In cold weather a winter combat jacket was worn over the suit.

INSIGNIA The main means of identifying the rank of officers was the rank distinction lace worn on the cuffs and shoulder straps, but officers also wore Army rank badges in metal on the overseas cap (both blue and light khaki) and on the khaki shirt collar. Chief petty officers and petty officers wore their badges of rank on the sleeves, while the three classes of seamen

had one to three white tape stripes on the cuffs of their dress jumper.

The Navy was divided into two basic branches which were the executive or line branch which was responsible for actually operating ships, and the other corps. Line officers had the five-pointed star above the rank distinction lace and rank badges on both sides of the shirt collar, while officers in other corps wore a corps badge above the rank lace, on the right collar only and on the left side of the overseas cap. For petty officers and ratings the system was simpler: they wore their rank badges on the left sleeve if in the corps or on the right if in the executive.

The USMC wore Army rank badges in metal for officers and in cloth for other ranks. The chevrons were in yellow upon red on the blue uniform, red upon green on the green uniform and khaki upon khaki on the khaki uniform. In 1942 it was ordered that chevrons would only be worn on the left sleeve. Certain officers (pay-masters, quartermasters, aides-de-camp and band leaders) wore special Marine branch badges on the collar in place of the corps badge.

179 Petty Officer 1st Class, US Navy, 1942

Overseas the white fatigue cap replaced the unpopular 'Donald Duck' cap and was worn with all rigs. The three seaman grades were identified by the white tape stripes on the cuffs, while this petty officer's rank and radioman badges are worn on the left sleeve.

180 Chief Petty Officer, US Navy, 1941

The uniform is almost identical to that worn by officers except that the peaked cap has a special cap badge, and rank badges are worn on the sleeves of the so-called 'sack coat'. The fact that he wears his chevrons on the left sleeve and has the branch badge of a machinist identifies him as a member of the engineering corps. Each stripe on the cuff denoted four years' service.

181 Captain, US Marine Corps, 1942

With the green service dress, this officers wears the M1917 steel helmet which was originally the first British steel helmet with the A1 modification – an American woven chin strap. The fouragère is that of the French Croix de Guerre awarded to the 5th and 6th Marines for service in France during World War I, while the formation sign was originally that of the British 49th West Riding Division.

NORTH-WEST EUROPE
1941-45

The war in north-west Europe and the Atlantic from 1941
onwards fell into three connected but quite distinct
areas: the Battle of the Atlantic; the bombing offensive
against Germany; and the Allied invasion of France which
culminated in the defeat of the German armies in the West.
On the Allied side, these three aspects of the war
were marked by increasingly practical and sophisticated
organisations and uniforms, while the Germans were forced
to make the most effective use of whatever resources they
could find. By the end of the war, uniform had often
acquired a very modern look, as the experience
of war had made the battle clothing of both
sides extremely functional.

GREAT BRITAIN

ARMY

After the defeat in western Europe of 1940, the British Army's primary task changed from the provision of an expeditionary force for Continental service to the formation of a field force capable of resisting an invasion of the United Kingdom. In June 1940 the Army's manpower stood at 2,221,000 plus 42,800 members of the ATS. Between June and August a further 275,000 men were conscripted and 120 new infantry battalions were formed, but although an eventual target of 55 British and Empire divisions had been accepted by the Government, the losses in weapons and transport occasioned by the evacuation from Dunkirk meant that a considerable period would elapse before anywhere near this number could be fully equipped.

ORGANISATION For the immediate anti-invasion role the resources of the Army and the civil defence organisations were co-ordinated by the Home Defence Executive, initially under the chairmanship of the Commander-in-Chief, Home Forces. This latter post was held by General Sir Edmund Ironside until July 1940 when he was succeeded by General Sir Alan Brooke. The C-in-C, Home Forces commanded all military formations in the United Kingdom with the exception of the anti-aircraft divisions which were subordinated to Fighter Command, and the Free French. The troops at his disposal fell into three main categories: the Home Guard, Home Defence units, and the formations of the Field Force. By the autumn of 1941 there were 27 British, Canadian, and Polish motorised infantry divisions available for the Field Force, each containing a front line strength of approximately 15,500 men. To support these divisions there were 10 corps organisations with 61,000 corps troops. For beach defence eight county divisions had been formed each with a strength of 10,000 officers and men but equipped with only minimal artillery and transport. In addition to the divisional forces there were seven infantry brigades, four motorised brigade groups incorporating artillery, 12 independent battalions, and eight airfield defence battalions. The need to provide flank protection for the Atlantic sea lanes meant that garrisons had also to be maintained in the Faroes, Iceland (24,000 British troops by October 1941), the Azores, St. Helena, the Falkland Islands, and the West Indies.

After the fall of France Britain's

Above : British troops move forward on the back of a Sherman tank in September 1944. They are wearing standard battledress.

armoured forces reached a very low ebb. The surviving units of the 1st Armoured Division and the 1st Army Tank Brigade returned from the Continent with few of the tanks and vehicles with which they had set out. In the United Kingdom an armoured division and four army tank brigades were in the process of formation but they also were short of weapons and vehicles. Despite these weaknesses it was decided to rebuild on the basis of the two existing types of armoured formations; the armoured division for mobile offensive operations on the battlefield, and the army tank brigade for close range fighting and infantry co-operation.

By the end of 1940 the armoured forces stationed in Britain consisted on paper of five armoured divisions (1st, 6th, 8th, 9th and 11th) and three army tank brigades, (21st, 25th and 31st), all of which had reached varying degrees of completeness and training. The planned expansion during 1941 was carried out by converting existing infantry units into Royal Armoured Corps formations, beginning with the establishment of the Guards armoured division and continuing with the conversion of the 42nd Infantry Division. A major change in the organisation of the armoured division occurred in May 1942 when one of the armoured brigades in each division was replaced by an infantry brigade. The HQ Support Group was replaced by an HQ Divisional Royal Artillery and the number of horse or field artillery regiments was doubled. The

resulting organisation was as in the chart on page 117.

Each armoured regiment could deploy 55 cruiser, six close support cruiser, and eight anti-aircraft tanks, which when added to the HQ tanks gave the division a total strength of 201 cruisers and 26 anti-aircraft tanks. Although there were to be further modifications to the organisation of the armoured division – the introduction of an armoured reconnaissance regiment in place of the armoured car regiment for example – its basic structure was to remain the same until the conclusion of hostilities. The division's tank strength however, did increase, to 244 tanks plus 34 AA tanks in April 1943, and to 310 tanks with 25 AA tanks and eight OP tanks in March 1944.

The army tank brigades were henceforth normally assigned to infantry divisions replacing one infantry brigade in each division. The fighting complement of a tank brigade was approximately 1950 officers and men with 178 tanks of which at least 135 were infantry tanks. The 1st, 3rd, 4th, 43rd and 53rd Infantry Divisions each received an army tank brigade during 1942. From 1943 onwards the Army's specialised armour in the form of flail, amphibious, and flame-throwing tanks was grouped in one formation, the 79th Armoured Division.

The successful use of German paratroops during the campaign in the low countries in 1940 led Britain to form her own airborne forces. The first training parachute drop was made on 13 July 1940 and volunteers were quickly raised to form the units which were to become known as the Parachute Regiment. The enthusiasm and professionalism which could be seen in the Army's airborne troops was also reflected in the British talent for raising specialised 'irregular' units. These 'private armies' were trained to fulfil particular tactical requirements, such as amphibious raiding, and to deal with abnormal climatic and terrain conditions such as desert reconnaissance. As there was a surplus of volunteer recruits the units could be highly selective. The Army's principal special forces in Europe were the Commandos and the Special Air Service.

The Home Army's role as the defender of the United Kingdom against invasion was retained during 1943 but with the additional commitment of being able to mount large-scale offensive operations on the mainland of Europe. In terms of manpower the Army continued to grow slowly deploying 2,720,000 officers and men (plus 199,000 ATS) in June 1944 and reaching its peak strength of 2,920,000 (plus 190,800 ATS) in June 1945.

The Army's examination of the problems of a return in strength to France had begun in the summer of 1940 and the amphibious raid on Dieppe in August 1942 had been the logical outcome of that programme of study and assessment. In June 1944 the Army returned to the continent, and it was to the commander of the British forces, Field-Marshal Montgomery, that the Germans offered to surrender their forces in May 1945.

ORGANISATION As the planning for D-Day was finalised the British and Canadian formations assigned to the invasion comprised: 10 infantry divisions; 2 airborne divisions; 5 armoured divisions; (plus a Polish armoured division); 9 independent armoured brigades; 2 special service commando brigades; GHQ Army and Corps troops.

The units, both British and American,

262 Corporal, British Army, 1944
As a dispatch rider this corporal in the Royal Corps of Signals wears a motorcyclist's crash helmet, leather jerkin over his battledress blouse, reinforced cord breeches, and special motorcycle boots. Insignia on the sleeve is the corps shoulder flash, arm-of-service strip, corporal's chevrons and Royal Signals armlet. The sub-machine gun is the 9mm Sten gun Mk II.

263 Private, British Commandos, 1942
This is the 'light raiding order' worn by British commandos on the Boulogne raid in April 1942. He wears a woollen cap comforter, battledress, 1937-pattern web equipment, inflatable life-belt, toggle rope for scaling cliffs, and instead of 'ammunition' boots wears plimsolls. The weapon is the US M1928A1 'Thompson' sub-machine gun.

264 Private, British Commandos, 1944
The critical moment for troops taking part in assault landings was when, heavily laden, they had to jump into water of unknown depth. If the water was too deep a soldier could easily drown if the equipment could not be quickly jettisoned, and for this reason 'quick release' equipment was often issued and lifebelts worn, as here. This soldier wears the green beret, the combined-operations flash, and the machine gun proficiency badge on the left cuff.

262   263   264

in the initial landing were assembled as the 21st Army Group under the command of General Montgomery, to whom the responsibility for the assault and opening stages of the campaign had been delegated. The British and Commonwealth elements in the assault waves were formed into the 2nd British Army.

The 6th Airborne Division with a strength of approximately 12,000 all ranks and comprising two parachute brigades (3rd and 5th) and one airlanding brigade (6th) was dropped in advance of the beach landings to secure canal and river bridges and eliminate coastal batteries. The infantry divisions attacked with their brigades strengthened by the addition of artillery, armoured fighting vehicles, and combat engineers, and the resulting brigade groups had an average strength of 5500 all ranks, of whom approximately 40 per cent were infantry.

On D-Day itself 59,900 troops and 8900 vehicles were landed and by D+50 these figures had risen to 631,000 and 153,000 respectively. The expansion of the Second Army took place on the basis of four corps (1st, 8th, 12th and 30th) with additional formations allocated to the Army Group.

Throughout the campaign the corps organisation remained relatively fluid and units were transferred between corps or attached from the Army Group as occasion demanded. Prominent amongst the GHQ and Army troops were a number of independent armoured and tank brigades which, although still intended primarily for co-operation with infantry, were also expected to be able to slot into armoured divisions as required. Their average strength was 3400 officers and men with a normal complement of 190 medium or infantry tanks (plus 33 light tanks) depending upon the type of brigade. An HQ Army Group Royal Artillery (AGRA) was usually assigned to each Corps and they comprised three medium and one heavy regiment with a total strength of 4400 personnel. The British 1st and 6th Airborne Divisions forming 1 British Airborne Corps were part, along with American airborne units, of the First Allied Airborne Army.

Although the British casualty figures fell short of the level anticipated during planning, the customary shortage of infantry, despite reinforcements of 38,900 from the UK, led to the disbandment of one infantry division (the 59th) and one brigade of the 49th Infantry Division on 16 August. The 50th Infantry Division was also subsequently disbanded.

During the campaign in Europe the establishment of a British infantry division was 18,347 all ranks, but the fighting strength of the divisions in 21st Army

Group rarely exceeded 16,000 officers and men. A further 25,000 personnel were required to support front line troops so that the total strength of an infantry division – or, as it was known to the Army, the 'divisional slice' – amounted to 41,000 men and 8000 vehicles. Thus the 18 divisions serving in the British order of battle on 30 November 1944 had under their immediate command a total of 287,000 fighting troops out of 21st Army Group's gross strength of 805,000. The remainder comprised GHQ, Army, Corps, administrative, service, and line of communication troops.

During its eleven month battle across France, Belgium, Holland, and Northern Germany the 21st Army Group sustained 141,646 British casualties of which 30,276 were killed, 96,672 wounded, and 14,698 listed as missing or taken prisoner.

UNIFORM AND INSIGNIA The uniform of the British 'tommy' remained basically the same throughout the war, but there were certain changes. In 1940 the battledress blouse was simplified by doing

265

266

265 Lieutenant, British Glider Pilot Regiment, 1944

Lieutenant J. F. Hubble of the 1st Glider Pilot Regiment wears parachutist uniform with Denison smock and ordinary battledress trousers. Under his fibre protective helmet he wears a Type C flying helmet with Type F oxygen mask. The wings on the left breast were worn by all qualified glider pilots until after the battle of Arnhem, when so many were lost that trainee pilots had their courses cut short and were made into second pilots, with smaller wings, and a gold 'G' set in a gold ring. The red beret is the type issued to all airborne forces in the British Army; and this mark of distinction rapidly became famous.

266 Trooper, British Army, 1945

The one-piece tank suit shown here was made from water-repellent canvas with khaki cloth lining and had a hood. The black beret was the distinctive head-dress of the Royal Tank Regiment, although many cavalry regiments converted to armour, such as the 11th Hussars, wore their own distinctive head-dress. The British Enfield .38 pistol is in its web holster; the small pouch above it carries spare ammunition. It was not until a late stage in the war that British tank crews were issued with this uniform; previous to this Royal Tank Regiment overalls were worn.

away with the pocket pleats and having all buttons, which were made of vegetable compound, exposed; the field service cap was unpopular and was gradually replaced by the beret, or the 'general service' cap, which looked like a beret but was made from a number of pieces of khaki cloth, and a new steel helmet made its appearance in 1944.

In addition, crews of armoured fighting vehicles, parachute troops and commandos all required special clothing and equipment, and British troops fighting globally in extremes of climate required special clothing to suit the environment.

Despite a number of experimental helmets an ideal head-dress for tank crews was not found. In training crews were issued with a fibre miner's helmet but since this afforded no protection against bullets or splinters it was not worn in action. During the latter stages of the war tank commanders began to wear the rimless steel helmet as issued to parachutists but with a webbing chin strap. Over the battledress tank crew usually wore either a black or khaki overall or denims, and it was only in the last year of the war that crews received a special tank suit (figure 266).

Airborne troops presented another problem which was partially solved when examples of German parachutists clothing and equipment were captured in Holland and in Crete. By October 1941 British parachute troops were receiving a padded rubber training helmet, a smock for wear over the equipment, battledress trousers

with a large thigh pocket and ankle boots with rubber soles. In action 'paras' wore a rimless steel helmet with leather chin strap and chin cup, and over the battledress but under the equipment a camouflage 'Denison' smock (figure 265), on the right sleeve of which were the para wings and rank chevrons.

Badges of rank and arm-of-service strips remained constant throughout the war, although new insignia was introduced for airborne forces and commandos. Coloured berets replaced the old field service caps and new colours (maroon for airborne and green for commandos for example) were introduced as new formations and corps came into existence.

Above: The operations room at RAF headquarters in France, soon after the landings of June 1944. The main features of RAF dress – notably the 'wings' – are clearly shown.

Below: Infantrymen of the King's Own Scottish Borderers using a captured Hotchkiss machine gun in Caen in 1944. They are wearing the new-pattern British helmet.

ROYAL AIR FORCE

Having successfully repulsed the Luftwaffe's immediate aerial threat to the United Kingdom in the Battle of Britain, the Royal Air Force took the offensive as Hitler turned his attention towards the Middle East and the Russian Front. It was the turn of Bomber Command to come into its own and operating almost exclusively by night, and aided by H2S and Oboe bombing radar, the Command pressed home its attacks.

Bomber Command's role in World War II was a controversial one. A sizable proportion of Britain's industrial and military resources were devoted to the strategic bomber offensive and heavy casualties were incurred by the squadrons of Bomber Command for only limited military gains.

By July 1941 the strength of Bomber Command stood at 45 squadrons with a theoretical deployment of 1000 aircraft. In practice, only 37 squadrons could be considered for active operations and not all of these were fully-trained. As a result the tally of sorties over Germany in the last five months of 1941 seldom averaged more than 60 per night. 38 squadrons were operationally effective by the spring of 1942, but of these only 14 were equipped with the new heavy bombers (Stirling, Halifax, and Manchester). The dispatch of reinforcements to the Far East and the demands of

Coastal Command further delayed the growth of Bomber Command, and by March 1943 only 50 squadrons with some 800 first-line aircraft were in commission instead of the planned total of 4000 operational aircraft.

The introduction to large-scale service in early 1942 of the four-engined heavy bombers – such as the Avro Lancaster and Handley Page Halifax – posed a double problem for Bomber Command, in addition to posing one for the German defences. Due to their increased size, the new types required both a mid-upper gunner and a flight engineer in addition to the usual pilot, navigator, wireless operator and gunners. This meant an extra stage in the conversion process, as training aircraft such as the Vickers Wellington were too small to accommodate these personnel. Thus came into being the Heavy Conversion Units or HCUs, which were established alongside the Operational Conversion Units. Runways had also to be lengthened from 1400 to 2000 feet.

Meanwhile, Fighter Command had begun the counter-offensive. While their poorly-equipped night fighters were making halting progress towards stemming the German bombers by night, many 'Rhubarb' intruder sorties were being flown by day over occupied Europe. By 13 June 1941, 104 such missions had been flown, together with 11 'circuses' involving larger numbers of fighters. The RAF intruder force came under the jurisdiction of No. Eleven Group until August 1942, when it passed to Fighter Command HQ. The Dieppe Raid on 19 August, however, was a disaster both on the ground and in the air; the Allies lost about 4000 or the 7500 troops engaged, while the loss of over 100 aircraft compared unfavourably with the Luftwaffe's 50.

A major development in the Royal Air Force's operations over France was the advent of the Hawker Typhoon rocket-armed fighter. These were employed with some success against rail targets, river bridges and airfields, and – importantly – against launching sites then in preparation for the V-1 flying bomb. Some 98,000 tons of weaponry was expended against these so-called 'No-Ball' targets, delaying the V-1's advent until June 1944, considerably later than planned.

As the RAF entered the last year of the war in June 1944, 100 of its 487 squadrons were manned by personnel from the Dominions. Canada furnished 42 squadrons, South Africa 27, Australia 16, India 9 and New Zealand 6. In addition 51 Allied squadrons from Poland, France, Czechoslovakia, Norway, Belgium, Holland, Greece and Yugoslavia were serving in the major theatres of war.

At the end of April 1945 460,000 RAF personnel were serving in the European campaign, the overall strength of the RAF having reached its peak of 1,011,427 officers and men and 174,406 women in July 1944. Between April 1944 and May 1945 the RAF suffered casualties of 23,649 in Western Europe; its total war casualties amounted to 112,296 of which 69,606 were killed, 22,839 wounded, 6736 listed as missing and 13,115 as prisoners of war. In Europe and the Middle East the RAF lost a total of 22,120 aircraft, of which Bomber Command lost 9163 and Fighter Command 3558.

The most spectacular show of strength mounted by Bomber Command was seen on the night of 30/31 May 1942, when 1046 bombers were dispatched to bomb Cologne. Although some 30 per cent of the aircraft on this raid had been culled from training units and thus rendered the raid untypical, the 'Thousand Bomber Raid' was a considerable propaganda triumph and cost only 39 aircraft. Under the leadership of Air Marshal A. T. Harris, the Command progressed to the Ruhr, Hamburg and, in the autumn of 1943, Berlin.

RAF Coastal Command reacted to the threat of the U-Boat in the North Atlantic with the meagre means at its disposal: of the 196 aircraft based in the United Kingdom for maritime reconnaissance, only 12 Lockheed Hudsons and 18 Short Sunderland flying boats could operate further than 300 miles from home base. Despite their lamentable lack of training, the crews registered some success, such as the first aircraft-assisted kill claimed by a Short Sunderland on 30 January 1940 when U-55 was sunk off Ushant. Although conventional bombs proved ineffective, aircraft still proved a deterrent for the U-Boats, and the advent of Air-to-Surface Vessel radar (ASV) in February 1940 proved valuable. It was augmented later that year by the Leigh Light, which illuminated the U-Boat at close range where radar was ineffective.

From August 1942, the increased escort strength of the convoys had driven the

Below: Ground crew bomb-up a Lancaster with a 12,000 lb 'Tallboy' bomb. They are wearing the standard working dress (similar to Army battledress) with side-caps. The bombs on the side of the Lancaster indicate missions flown.

267

268

269

U-Boats into the mid-Atlantic, where they were tackled by the very-long-range Consolidated Liberator, which entered service with No. 120 Squadron Coastal Command in September 1941. Nos. 59 and 86 Squadrons later joined this lone unit, driving the U-Boats into the Bay of Biscay and within range of the RAF's other types. At the peak of Coastal Command's operations in 1944, 52,183 sorties were flown in that year, during which 355 aircraft were lost.

ORGANISATION Bomber Command was organised, like Fighter and Coastal Command, in Groups of varying squadron strength. By March 1943 there were seven Groups (Nos. 1, 2, 3, 4, 5, 6 and 8), of which No. 6 Group was formed of Royal Canadian Air Force squadrons. The expansion of the heavy bomber force during 1943 led to the introduction of a new level of command between the group and the squadron. This was known as a base and it controlled six heavy bomber squadrons or three heavy conversion units, under the command of an Air Commodore. By April 1944 Bomber

Command had a personnel strength of 155,510 and in January 1945 its squadron deployment stood at 95. The total casualties suffered by the Command during the war numbered 79,147, of which 64,780 were battle casualties.

Bomber Command's total of 955,040 tons of bombs dropped during the whole of World War II included 196,335 tons of incendiaries and was delivered in 389,809 sorties. Total aircraft losses sustained numbered 10,688.

Coastal Command was organised in four groups – Nos. 15, 16, 18 and 19 – with No. 17 being designated a training group at Dundee. They corresponded in geographical location to the four naval commands with which they closely worked. The air officer commanding the RAF group would hold the rank of Air Vice-Marshal, while his opposite number in the corresponding Royal Navy command would be a Vice-Admiral or, in some cases, a full Admiral.

For the invasion of Europe the RAF's tactical air strength was deployed as part of the Allied Expeditionary Air Force under two main commands, the Air

267 Flying Officer, Royal Air Force, 1944
This Boston III crew member wears RAF battledress under a US 'flak' vest. Over the British Type C flying helmet he wears a special protective helmet which was lined with strips of manganese steel (its US designation was USM-4). The flying boots are the British 1943-pattern which were so designed that the shafts could be easily removed, leaving a simple black walking shoe which could be worn by pilots shot down in enemy-occupied territory.

268 Flight Lieutenant, Royal Australian Air Force, 1941
Flight Lieutenant Truscott DFC wears the dark blue service dress of the RAAF which continued to be worn throughout Word War II. During the war dark blue battledress was also issued to RAAF personnel on which they wore the usual RAF rank distinction lace on the shoulder straps.

269 Head Officer, Royal Observer Corps, 1944
The ROC was originally formed in 1918 and by 1941 was 30,000 strong with both men and women in its ranks. The RAF-type battledress was introduced in June 1941. The ROC badge was worn on the beret and left breast, while the Spitfire badge was the mark of a master spotter from January 1944.

270

271

ROYAL NAVY

The German conquests in Europe during 1940 placed the Royal Navy in an extremely difficult position. The acquisition of Norway provided the German Navy with deep-water bases for its surface ships which by their very presence, astride Britain's sea-route to the Soviet Union, tied down many Royal Navy vessels. Even more dangerous was the German occupation of naval bases on the French Atlantic coast providing perfect havens for the U-boat packs. This easy German access to the Atlantic was to stretch British resources to the limit.

The Royal Navy had two essential tasks during the early years of the war, firstly the naval blockade of Germany and secondly, the protection of the sea lanes to and from Britain that were vital to the nation's survival. The German threat to Britain's supply routes came from the surface warships and the U-boats.

The surface raiders were less of a problem than the U-boats; after the sinking of the *Bismarck* on 26 May 1941 Hitler was reluctant to risk his remaining battleships in direct confrontation with the Navy and for the rest of the war they spent most of their time bottled-up in safe harbours. Occasionally they were sent out in hunting forrays but with little success: the *Scharnhorst* was sunk in December 1943 and the *Tirpitz* was sunk at anchorage by the RAF in November 1944.

The great threat to Britain's ability to continue to wage the war came from Germany's submarine arm. Prior to the outbreak of war the value of the convoy system was not highly regarded by many Navy experts although it had proved itself during World War I. Only the heavy losses during the early months of the war convinced the Admiralty to reinstitute convoys. Unfortunately lack of pre-war development meant that there were insufficient vessels to escort the convoys and that most of these ships – old destroyers and corvettes – lacked sufficient range to provide a continuous escort. It was only by the end of 1941 that coast-to-coast Atlantic convoys were achieved.

The British convoy system was centred around the three operational bases of the Western Approaches: Liverpool, Greenwich and Londonderry, controlling some 25 escort groups which totalled around 70 destroyers and 95 smaller ships. An escort group was formed of about eight ships (although in practice there were rarely more than six at sea at one time) and, once formed, every effort was made to prevent the group from being broken-up, so that the constituent vessels could operate as a well-oiled machine.

270 Squadron Leader, Royal Air Force, 1941–42

Squadron Leader A. H. Rook commanded No. 81 Squadron, 151 Wing, in north Russia during 1941–42. The units in Russia were intended to familiarise the Russians with aeroplanes they would soon be using (No. 81 Squadron flew Hurricanes), and to cover the Arctic convoys on the last part of their journey; Rook's aeroplanes were based in Murmansk. He is wearing the RAF blue peaked service cap with officers' cap badge, and the M1940 flying suit with fur collar. The web equipment is the 1937-pattern. The life-jacket is the 1932-pattern; this was originally produced in a grey-green colour but was often painted yellow, which produced the buff effect.

271 Sergeant, Royal Air Force, 1943

Sergeant Harold Oliver of RAF Coastal Command here wears flying clothing typical of that of the crews of the aircraft used on the long sweeps over the Atlantic and Arctic. Flights of up to 12 hours were common in the Liberators of which Sergeant Oliver was a pilot, and so the accent was on comfort and practicality. Oliver wears a side cap (with the yellow badge of RAF other ranks) a polo-neck sweater (called the Frock White sweater) and an Irvin sheepskin jacket over a pre-war flying suit.

Defence of Great Britain (formerly Fighter Command) and the Second Tactical Air Force. The main elements of the former comprised four groups (Nos. 10–13) and in the latter four groups (Nos. 2, 83, 84 and 85), one wing (No. 34) and an Air Spotting Pool. The Groups of the Second Tactical Air Force were organised as Wings, each usually of three squadrons. On 16 October 1944 Headquarters Allied Expeditionary Force was absorbed into Supreme Headquarters Allied Expeditionary Force and the units of the Air Defence of Great Britain reverted to the control of the British Air Ministry and were redesignated as Fighter Command. The group composition of the Second Tactical Air Force remained unchanged except for the addition of two RAF special groups, No. 38 (airborne forces) and No. 46 (transport).

UNIFORM The uniform of the RAF conformed to the pattern established by 1940 (see page 73) and remained in service throughout the war. The various styles of dress are illustrated.

272

273

274

Despite the acceptance of the convoy as the best protection against the U-boat, losses rose throughout 1941 (300,000 tons of Allied shipping was sunk in June alone) and continued into the next year. The Battle of the Atlantic was nearly lost by the Allies and it was only won through the massive allocation of Allied resources in developing new anti-submarine techniques, increasing the numbers and quality of escort vessels and introducing escort carriers whose aircraft both inhibited U-boat activity on the surface and destroyed them when submerged. By October 1943 the Battle of the Atlantic was won; U-boat successes were few and in March 1944 they were withdrawn from the North Atlantic.

In addition to its North Atlantic commitments the Royal Navy was heavily engaged in convoy duties in the Arctic Ocean, escorting Allied supplies to the Soviet Union. At first these Arctic convoys met with little opposition: the six convoys which sailed during the autumn of 1941 landed 120,000 tons of supplies for only small losses. But during 1942 casualties

mounted as a consequence of sustained German aerial and submarine attacks, culminating in the P.Q.17 convoy in which, of the 156,000 tons loaded, nearly 100,000 tons were sunk. Despite heavy losses the convoys continued, the Germans suffering high casualties themselves and through their poor performance in the battles of the North Cape and Barents Sea the initiative passed to the British.

Having defeated both the surface raiders and the U-boats, the Royal Navy was called upon to transport the D-Day invasion fleet across the English channel and then to support the landings with battleship artillery barrages. The naval operations for D-Day were a triumph of planning, the British and American troops being put ashore with no interference from the German Navy or Air Force. Altogether some 7000 vessels were involved, which included 1200 warships of all sizes.

Following the invasion of Europe the Royal Navy played a more limited role; the supply of the Allied troops in Europe

272 Petty Officer, Royal Navy, 1941
This petty officer serving in a 4.7 inch gun crew wears the special cap badge for petty officers. The rest of the uniform, consisting of Balaclava helmet, duffle coat and sea socks and boots was drawn from ships' stores when required according to the weather.

273 Gunlayer 2nd Class, Royal Navy, 1942
This is a typical action rig worn by naval gun crews during World War II. Over his clean underwear (dirty underclothing could cause infection in wounds) he wears a one-piece blue overall with a canvas money belt round his waist. His non-substantive badge is worn on the upper right sleeve. The steel helmet is perched on top of an anti-flash hood.

274 Lieutenant-Commander, Royal Navy, 1941
Commander Kimmins, on his return from a combined operation in Norway, wears naval service dress under an Army steel helmet and leather jerkin. The web equipment is the 1937-pattern and the binoculars are marked with the broad white arrow which indicates that they are War Department property. The white lanyard is attached to a folding jack knife. Above the rank distinction lace on the left cuff are the pilot's 'wings' of the Fleet Air Arm.

275

CZECHOSLOVAK
ARMED FORCES

When the fighting in North Africa came to an end, the Czech troops in the Middle East returned to England where, in 1943, they began to be formed into the 1st Independent Armoured Brigade Group. Its 4500 men were organised in:

1st, 2nd and 3rd Czech Armoured Regiments;
Czech Field Artillery Regiment;
Czech Motor Battalion.

In June 1944 the Czech Brigade landed in Normandy where it took over from the 154th Infantry Brigade (British 51st Division) and on 9 October 1944 invested the German position in and around Dunkirk. The Czech Brigade fought with the Canadian 1st Army for a time as part of the 21st Army Group.

A detachment of Cromwell tanks manned by Czech crews was sent as a token force to participate in the liberation and final entry into Prague.

UNIFORM Members of the Independent Czechoslovakian Armoured Brigade wore British battledress with Czech rank badges. The nationality flash, 'Czechoslovakia' was worn on the upper arm.

Below: D-Day casualties are brought on board HMS Frobisher. The sailors in the foreground are wearing the anti-flash hoods and gauntlets (also shown in figure 273), and various overgarments.

Above: The submarine Seraph returning to harbour. The ratings are wearing long sweaters and 'bell-bottoms' – a sharp contrast to the officers' clothing.

**275 2nd Officer,
Women's Royal Naval Service, 1942**
This is the standard women's version of the naval service dress with three cornered hat, reefer and matching skirt. Rank distinction lace in blue on the cuffs had white lights for those in the paymaster branch. Instead of a gold-embroidered cap badge worn by male officers, women had blue laurel leaves.

and the opening up of the Belgian and Dutch ports were its main tasks.

During the period 1939–45 the Royal Navy lost 119 warships in home waters and 84 in the North Atlantic.

UNIFORM As in the RAF, Royal Navy uniform followed the basic pattern discussed in the previous sections. Operations in the extreme temperatures and conditions of the North Atlantic and Arctic required warm, effective clothing. Individuals frequently combined elements of uniform (see figure 272, for example) to combat the hostile climate. Balaclava helmets, oilskins, wellington boots and duffle coats were among the items employed in this respect.

CANADA
ARMY

In direct contrast to the experience of World War I, the Canadian Army which was assembled in Britain during 1939–45 was offered few opportunities for combat during its first three-and-a-half years in Europe. Its role, save for one or two minor expeditions and the single day's fighting at Dieppe, was that of a garrison force.

The initial convoy carrying 7400 troops of the 1st Division arrived in the Clyde on 17 December 1939, and by the end of February 1940 the Canadian Active Service Force in Britain numbered 1066 officers and 22,238 other ranks. The troops were not fully trained for modern warfare, they lacked essential items of equipment such as steel helmets, and nearly all their heavy weapons were obsolescent. The division worked through a crash training course at Aldershot in order to be ready for deployment in France as part of the 4th British Corps. The pace of events was such that the Canadians played only a limited covering role in France and were evacuated soon after landing in June 1940.

In July 1940 the 1st Canadian Division combined with the 1st British Armoured Division and the majority of the 2nd New Zealand Division to form the 7th Corps. Since May 1940, units of the 2nd Canadian Division had begun to arrive in Britain but the divisions' concentration was not achieved until 25 December 1940. From late October the units that had arrived in the United Kingdom joined the 1st Division guarding the beaches of Sussex between Worthing and Newhaven, and on Christmas Day 1940 the 7th Corps was disbanded and the Canadian Corps (later 1st Canadian Corps) was created with nearly 57,000 Canadians serving in Britain.

During 1941 the flow of Canadian units to the European theatre continued, and by the beginning of 1942 the Canadian Force in Britain consisted of four divisions, an army tank brigade and supporting troops, and it had obviously outgrown the bounds of a normal army corps. Accordingly, Headquarters 1st Canadian Army was established on 6 April 1942. In September and October a further armoured force came under its command with the arrival of the 4th Canadian Armoured Division which had been formed by converting the 4th Infantry Division. The armoured divisions adopted the British organisation of one armoured and one infantry brigade and thereby created a number of surplus armoured regiments, three of which tem-

porarily became the 3rd Army Tank Brigade until, in the summer of 1943, they assumed the designation 2nd Canadian Armoured Brigade. At the end of 1942 the Canadian Army Overseas totalled 177,000.

Canadian training for combined operations began in September 1941 and in April 1942 a contingent took part in an abortive commando raid to the south of Boulogne. The failure of this raid only served to add fuel to the frustration felt by the Canadians after two-and-a-half years without close contact with the enemy.

When in April 1942 Combined Operations Headquarters authorised the plan to raid the port of Dieppe, General Montgomery suggested that the Canadians were the troops most suited to the enterprise. The 1st Canadian Army commander General A. G. L. McNaughton agreed to this proposal and the 2nd Canadian Division was chosen for the operation. The selected units were the 4th and 6th Infantry Brigades and the 14th Canadian Army Tank Regiment (Calgary Regiment) of the 1st Army Tank Brigade. They were supported by engineers and artillery detachments from the 2nd Division, by the British No. 3 and 4 Commando, and by 50 rangers of the 1st US Ranger Battalion.

When the expedition set sail on the night of 18 August its military force numbered 6100 officers and men, of whom 1075 were British and 4963 Canadian. The attack, launched at dawn the next day, tragically miscarried and in nine hours of bitter fighting the Canadians suffered 3369 casualties of whom 907 were killed in action or died later in captivity. Only 2211 returned to England and 1944 were taken prisoner.

In October 1943 the 'Canloan' scheme was proposed with the object of meeting the British Army's need for junior officers for the forthcoming campaign in North-West Europe. In all, 673 Canadian officers were provided for British units under this scheme and they saw extensive service in Europe and later South-East Asia. They were paid by the Canadian Government, wore the badges of their British units on their battledress along with a 'Canada' badge and, by the end of the war, had suffered 465 casualties.

On the morning of 6 June 1944 the 3rd Canadian Infantry Division landed on the beaches of Normandy supported by the tanks of the 2nd Canadian Armoured Brigade. As part of the 1st British Corps their role after the initial landing was to advance between Bayeux and Caen, cutting the communications between the two towns. Almost 14,000 Canadians went ashore on D-Day of whom 335 were

276

276 Lieutenant, Royal Canadian Women's Naval Service, 1943

This lightweight uniform was worn by all ranks in the Royal Canadian Women's Naval Service. Officers had the three cornered hat instead of the round sailor's hat worn by women of non-commissioned rank. Ratings had black plastic instead of gilt brass buttons. The regulation bag was also called a 'pochette'. The white lights between the rank distinction lace on the shoulder straps identifies this officer as being in the paymaster branch.

killed in the landing or subsequent advance. The Canadian objectives were reached on 7 June.

The 1st Canadian Parachute Battalion dropped as a unit of the 6th British Airborne Division on D-day and took part in the battle for the bridgehead. In the first week of July the 2nd Canadian Division arrived in Normandy to form, together with the 3rd Division and the 2nd Armoured Brigade, the 2nd Canadian Corps. The 4th Canadian Armoured Division landed in France at the end of the month to relieve the 3rd Division.

277

278

Canadian and British troops advanced.

With the arrival of the formations from Italy there were now two Canadian Corps available for the final offensive against Germany and on 24 March Canadian troops began to cross the Rhine. On 28 April German resistance in western Holland came to an end, but for the 2nd Canadian Corps deployed in northern Holland and Germany to protect the 2nd Army's left flank, bitter fighting continued until 4 May. The eleven-month campaign since 6 June 1944 had cost the 1st Canadian Army 3680 officers and 44,272 men in casualties, of whom 12,579 had been killed.

NEWFOUNDLAND

In the inter-war years Newfoundland maintained no military force of any kind but on the outbreak of hostilities in 1939 her citizens quickly demonstrated their willingness to serve. It was agreed with the War Office that Newfoundlanders should be enlisted for the Royal Artillery and the first draft of 403 volunteers left for Britain in April 1940. By September the number of men had reached 1373. Together with British officers and NCOs these drafts formed the 57th and 59th (Newfoundland) Heavy Regiments Royal Artillery.

The 59th Regiment landed in Normandy on 5 July 1944 under the British 1st Corps and it was soon in action. It supported the 2nd Canadian Division in its advance towards Falaise and covered the crossing of the Seine. Its batteries fought at Flushing, in south-west Holland and in the operations to clear the Scheldt. Early in 1945 half the regiment was in the Ardennes and half on the Venlo-Roermond sector, and in February the whole regiment moved to Grave for Operation 'Veritable'. In March the 59th supported the crossing of the Rhine and from then until the end of the war fought in the British operations around Bremen and at the crossing of the Elbe. Altogether 2327 Newfoundlanders served overseas during World War II and of this number 72 were killed.

277 Lieutenant, Canadian Army, 1942
This private of the Royal Winnipeg Rifle Regiment taking part in the Normandy landings wears the new 1944-pattern British steel helmet and battledress. Canadian battledress was popular because it tended to be made of better quality cloth than its British counterpart, and in a slightly greener shade. The light blue rectangle was the formation sign of the 3rd Canadian Division. The arrangement of personal equipment varied from soldier to soldier. This one carries additional pouches for Bren gun magazines on his back, a shovel, blanket roll and late-war No. 4, Mark 1 or Mark 1* .303. Troops in the first wave of landings had to be sufficiently equipped to maintain a fire-fight with German defences until support weapons or naval fire could be brought in to assist them.

278 Private, Canadian Army, 1944
The greatcoat is the standard pattern for British Army officers, but with the 'Canada' nationality title. The cap, however, is the Canadian pattern with earflaps and regimental badge (Le Regiment de Levis) on the front. There was a winter version of this head-dress with fur earflaps which was called a Yukon helmet. These items of uniform were the most distinctive worn by the Canadian Army, although they soon fell into disuse.

The 4th Canadian Armoured Division was soon heavily involved in Normandy; the Canadian troops played a leading part in the offensive operations around Caen, and they then joined the Allied pursuit of the retiring enemy, pushing north and east towards Belgium and the channel coast. By November 1944 the 1st Canadian Army was rapidly becoming a cosmopolitan fighting force with the following divisions and brigades:
Canadian 2nd, 3rd and 4th (Armoured) Divisions;
British 49th and 52nd Divisions;
American 104th Division (also briefly 82nd and 101st Airborne);
Polish 1st (Armoured) Division;
Dutch Royal Netherlands Brigade;
Czechoslovakian 1st Independent Armoured Brigade Group.

From November 1944 to February 1945 the Canadians stood on the defensive, holding a perimeter which ran for 200 miles from the German frontier through Holland to Dunkirk. On 8 February the 1st Army began its attack against the *Reichswald* meeting German resistance which stiffened considerably as the

UNIFORM Canadian Army uniform was basically the same as that worn by the British Army, and although the pattern was usually identical, clothing and equipment manufactured in Canada did vary slightly in colour and quality. For example Canadian battledress was very popular with British soldiers because the material was not so rough and the colour was a smarter shade of khaki. The winter cap worn by the first contingents of Canadians soon fell into disuse. Badges of rank were the same as the British.

FRANCE

ARMY

The formation and organisation of a French Army to fight alongside the Allies in the liberation of its homeland was an extremely difficult and complicated task. France was still occupied by Germany, equipment and supplies were difficult to find, despite generous American assistance. The legacy of distrust and enmity between those who had sided with de Gaulle and those who supported Vichy still lingered on, and this occasionally tended to create difficulties.

French troops were withdrawn from Italy to take part in Operation 'Dragoon', the Allied invasion of southern France. Known as Army B the French came under the command of General de Lattre de Tassigny as part of the US 7th Army. Operating on the flanks of the Americans the French were hotly engaged against the Germans, following the landings on 15 August 1944. Army B liberated Toulon on the 25 August and played a major role in securing Marseille, France's second city. French casualties during this period were 1444 killed and 4346 wounded.

On 15 September, Army B became the French 1st Army, comprising two corps which included the 1st Free French, 1st Armoured, 2nd Moroccan, 3rd Algerian and 9th Colonial Divisions. During the course of the subsequent fighting the 1st Army received numerous reinforcements so that by 1945 it had a strength of 200,000 men organised into 12 divisions.

One of these divisions was the 2nd Armoured Division which had fought its way through Normandy, inflicting heavy losses on the Germans (13,000 killed or taken prisoner, and 800 vehicles

destroyed) while loosing only 800 men and 57 armoured fighting vehicles in the process. Its organisation at this time consisted of a motorised infantry regiment of three battalions, three groups of artillery, one group of anti-aircraft artillery, one reconnaissance regiment, three tank regiments, one regiment of tank destroyers, a battalion of engineers and supporting services.

The infantry divisions were based around the organisation of three or four infantry regiments with a strong reconnaissance regiment and an artillery regiment plus units of engineers, signals and service troops.

The French 1st Army fought on the southern flank of the Allied line of battle and contributed significantly to the liberation of Alsace and in the invasion of southern Germany. At the end of hostilities on 7 May 1945 the French Army had lost 250,000 men killed during the entire period of World War II.

UNIFORM As the French Army was gradually re-organised and received its American equipment, the heterogeneous uniforms from the former Vichy Army, the French Colonial Army and North African units, and those of the Free French, were replaced by the American uniform (see figure 279).

As and when available (or for as long as they lasted) the various forms of French head-dress continued to be worn with American uniform. These were mainly the *Adrian* steel helmet and the motorised troop helmet, but also included some of the more exotic and brightly coloured head-dresses of the French North

Below: Tunisian troops of the French Army soon after their entry into Germany.

279

279 Private, French Army, 1944

This private of the 2nd Moroccan Division serving in the French 1st Army wears predominantly US uniform and equipment. Above the US khaki wool trousers is the American winter combat jacket with vertical slit pockets favoured by the crews of armoured vehicles. Footgear consists of the French M1917 boots, and he is armed with a British Lee Enfield .303 rifle.

African forces. One of the most unusual combinations was worn by members of the Naval Infantry Tank Regiment who wore naval head-dress and insignia.

Badges of rank were worn in the usual French manner on the head-dress, on the shoulder straps or on a patch on the front of combat clothing.

On the upper left sleeve personnel wore a cloth badge shaped like the patch worn on the collar of French tunics. The colour of the badge, the chevrons and the regimental number or emblem conformed to the old collar patches, but in order to distinguish themselves from metropolitan troops, personnel in units formed in North Africa had three chevrons instead of two.

UNITED STATES
ARMY

American troops had been arriving in England since 1942 as part of the preparation for the invasion of German occupied Europe and by the summer of 1944 over two million Allied soldiers had been amassed for Operation 'Overlord'.

The US 1st Army under General Bradley was responsible for the two western beaches of the Normandy landings and his initial forces consisted of seven infantry and two airborne divisions. Despite heavy casualties on Omaha Beach the American landings on the 6 June were successful and the beachhead was consolidated in order to bring up reinforcements for the breakout from Normandy – Operation 'Cobra'.

During July American troops flooded into Normandy so that Bradley had 21 divisions under his command by 1 August. This entailed a reorganisation of American forces: the US 12th Army Group was created consisting of the 1st Army (V, VII and XIX Corps) and the newly-formed 3rd Army (XII, XV, XX and VIII Corps). Operation 'Cobra' was an American triumph and the rapid exploitation of the breakthrough by armoured elements of Patton's 3rd Army turned the tactical advantage into a major strategic victory. Out-numbered and out-manoeuvered, the Germans were forced back across France towards the Rhine.

Allied progress slowed-up in the late autumn of 1944 as a result of stiffening German resistance and a growing shortage of supplies and manpower. The front-line stabilised along the Franco-German border during the winter of 1944–45. American forces on 1 January 1945 consisted of 31 infantry, 11 armoured and 3 airborne divisions. These formations were organised into the 12th Army Group (1st and 3rd Armies) and the newly formed 6th Army Group which consisted of the US 7th Army and the French 1st Army (these two armies had invaded southern France as part of Operation 'Dragoon' and had joined up with the main invasion force in September). During 1945 a further 15 US divisions (including four armoured)

280 2nd Lieutenant, US Army, 1942
On their arrival in Northern Ireland the first US soldiers wore this uniform. The helmet is the M1918. while the coat is the short version of the officers' greatcoat with rank badges on the shoulder straps. OD trousers are worn inside canvas leggings with russet ankle boots. The equipment consists of woven cartridge belt, braces and gas mask. The rifle is the US Cal.30 M1903 AI Springfield.

281 2nd Lieutenant, US Army, 1944
Equipped for the D-Day landings, this officer wears the special waistcoat with sewn-in pockets for carrying extra ammunition. The basic uniform consists of the M1941 combat jacket and olive drab fatigue trousers. A flotation bag – half inflated – is strapped to the chest and below that is an officer's dispatch case. Rank is indicated by the single bar on the M1 steel helmet. An M1 carbine is carried with an M1911 AI .45 automatic pistol.

282 Private, US Army, 1942
This GI arriving in England wears the overseas cap with light blue piping and OD greatcoat over the Class A uniform. OD trousers are tucked into canvas leggings and worn with russet leather ankle boots over which he has put rubber overboots. The rifle is the US Cal.30 Model 1903 Springfield.

280   281   282

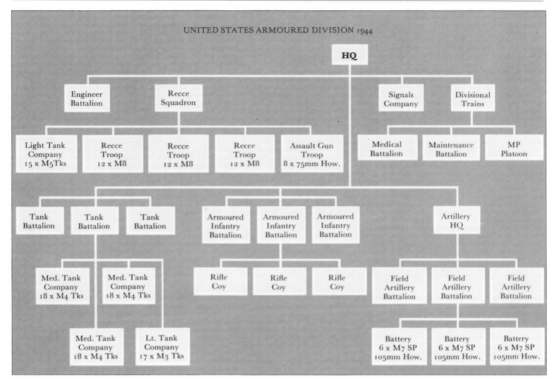

UNITED STATES ARMOURED DIVISION 1944

arrived in Europe bringing the American total up to 60.

Having countered the German Ardennes offensive, the American forces prepared to cross the Rhine and invade Germany itself. The Rhine barrier was breached during March and the 12th Army Group advanced into Germany. In conjunction with the Anglo-Canadian 21st Army Group over 300,000 Germans were taken prisoner in the Ruhr pocket by the US 1st Army. On 25 April contact was made with the advancing Soviet forces and by the first week of May all organised German resistance had ended.

During the eleven month campaign in Western Europe the US armed forces had borne the brunt of the fighting and suffered 591,802 casualties.

ORGANISATION The basic formation in the United States Army was the infantry division. The triangular organisation of three infantry regiments, each of three battalions (see page 135), continued in use throughout the war in western Europe. There were few changes except a general increase in the number and the calibre-size of the division's weapons. The infantry regiment of 1944 consisted of an HQ company; an

infantry gun company (six 105mm infantry howitzers); and anti-tank company (12 × 57mm anti-tank guns); a service company and the usual three infantry battalions (each 860 men strong).

The division's artillery regiment had one medium artillery battalion and three light artillery battalions. The combat element of each battalion comprised three batteries of four towed howitzers; 155mm for the medium and 105mm for the light battalion.

The infantry division of 1944, once in combat, often had its establishment strength of 14,253 men augmented by units of tanks, tank destroyers, anti-aircraft, mechanised cavalry and field artillery.

Besides the artillery units within the divisional system, a considerable number of artillery units were organised outside the division into battalions of medium (4.5-inch guns and 155mm howitzers) and heavy artillery (155mm, 8-inch and 240mm guns). By the end of the war there were 111 heavy battalions with 81 medium battalions authorised. The Army also controlled anti-aircraft units which amounted to 575 battalions in October 1943 but this figure was reduced to 460 in 1944.

During the period June 1944 to May 1945, some 15 American armoured divisions served in western Europe and made a vital contribution towards the Allied victory. The US armoured division was based on the pattern of September 1943 which had three tank, three armoured infantry and three self-propelled artillery battalions with an establishment strength of 10,937 men (see organisation chart). The division was divided into two Combat Commands, 'A' and 'B', each of which could control a varying number of units at the discretion of the divisional commander. An additional Command was introduced which was responsible for reserve elements of the division, being known as Combat Command 'C' or Reserve.

A considerable number of American tank units were formed separately from the armoured divisions as semi-independent tank battalions. During the winter of 1944 there were 65 tank battalions under arms. The organisation of the battalion was that of the armoured division tank battalion, consisting of three medium and one light tank company with a combined strength of 729 men and 68 tanks. Initially the non-divisional tank battalions acted as close support for the infantry, but in the fighting in France they were given a more mobile role, often being combined into groups of five (later three) battalions. When brigaded with armoured infantry units they were termed 'armoured groups'.

A further type of non-divisional armoured organisation was the tank destroyer battalion which had been formed in 1942 as a means of providing a highly mobile anti-tank weapon to blunt the effect of the German panzer divisions. With a strength of about 100,000 men, the tank destroyer force consisted of 80 battalions each with 36 self-propelled or towed guns. The backbone of the battalion were the M10 and M18 self-propelled tank destroyers, lightly armed but equipped with a high-velocity anti-tank gun.

The United States had a long cavalry tradition that continued well into the 20th Century but the outbreak of war signalled the end of the horsed cavalry when regulations for the mechanisation of this arm were issued in 1942. Some cavalry regiments formed the basis of the new tank divisions, while the remainder were broken up to form mechanised reconnaissance units at squadron and group level. Two cavalry divisions remained

Above: US troops of the 89th Division crossing the Rhine in March 1945.

within the American military establishment; one fought as dismounted infantry in the Pacific, while the other was sent to the Mediterranean theatre. Once there it was disbanded, its constituent units being transferred to other formations.

In 1941 the US Army had only one parachute battalion but, impressed by the success of the German paratroopers, a rapid expansion of airborne troops was instigated. By 1944 the 82nd and 101st Airborne Divisions were ready to support the D-Day landings, while the 13th and 17th were still in formation but were subsequently to be involved in the fighting in Europe.

The airborne division was conceived as a small, highly mobile air-transportable formation comprising one parachute infantry regiment and two glider infantry regiments, which with the usual divisional support units came to a strength of 8505 men.

In September 1944 the size of the division was increased so that its strength totalled 12,979 personnel. Similarly, the organisation was modified on the following basis:

two infantry parachute regiments, each of 2364 men consisting of three battalions with a regimental HQ and a service company;

one infantry glider regiment of 2978 men divided into three battalions and a regimental HQ, a service and an anti-tank company;

one anti-aircraft/anti-tank battalion of three machine gun batteries (each of 12 × .50 machine guns) and three gun batteries (each with 8 × 57mm anti-tank guns);

divisional artillery consisting of three batteries of 75mm pack howitzers.

Additionally there were companies of maintenance, engineer and signals troops and a reconnaissance platoon.

A number of other divisional patterns were organised including motorised and light divisions but they played little or no part in the operations in western Europe.

A particular feature of the United States Army was its logistical support services which backed up the man at the front. As in other technically sophisticated armies, the majority of the US Army's soldiers were not engaged in combat but were part of the technical services, namely: engineers, signals, chemical warfare, ordnance, medical and transportation. Thus, although infantry division might have an establishment strength of 15,000 men, with all the necessary supply

283 Private, US Army, 1945
This typical GI at the end of the war wears the M1 steel helmet with camouflage netting, M1943 combat uniform and the new lace-up combat boots. The cartridge belt has pouches for the 42-round Browning automatic rifle magazines. The small pouch on the right holds a field dressing. The weapon is the US Cal.30 Browning automatic rifle Model 1918 A2 which has had the bipod removed.

283

and back-up troops (including assigned Air Force Units) there might be as many as 50,000 men. All these troops were known as the divisional 'slice' and on average needed 1600 tons of supplies a day.

To meet the complex logistical requirements of the US Army in Europe, the 'Red Ball Highway' was introduced, which consisted of a one-way road system reserved exclusively for the transportation of supplies to the front-line. Although the system was a success, the Army was often short of supplies, especially fuel, during the rapid advances of the autumn of 1944. By early 1945, however, the strength of the American logistical system proved itself and the GI was probably the best equipped soldier of any of the armed forces of World War II.

UNIFORM The American troops who landed in Normandy in June 1944 wore the M1 steel helmet and liner, the M1941 field jacket, olive drab (OD) trousers, canvas gaiters and russet leather ankle boots. Equipment was the standard American woven pattern.

But experience in North Africa and Italy had already exposed serious short-comings in the practicality of much of the Army's clothing, and a number of new items, particularly for wear in winter, were developed during 1943. Despite the American reputation for lavishly providing every luxury for its soldiers, the average GI suffered as much as his allies and his enemies from the cold and wet.

In time for the last winter of the war American troops received the M1943 combat uniform, which consisted of a single-breasted tunic with four patch pockets and matching trousers all made from an olive drab water-repellant and windproof cotton. It was issued with a detachable pile fabric liner. The canvas gaiters and ankle boots were gradually replaced by high lace-up brown leather combat boots (see figure 283).

In 1944 the Americans began to wear a wool field jacket (actually a blouse) which was similar in cut to the British battledress blouse. The pattern for other ranks was standardised, but officers wore many different models with different pocket arrangements, and some with concealed and others with exposed buttons. The blouse was worn with either matching trousers or 'pinks'.

284 Private, US Army, 1944

Some US troops were issued with this two-piece camouflage suit for the campaign in Normandy in June 1944, but it was soon withdrawn because soldiers wearing it were mistaken for Waffen-SS men who also wore camouflage uniforms. On his right hip he carries a captured German Walther automatic pistol in its holster. The weapon is the US Cal.30 M1 (Garand) semi-automatic rifle.

285 Major-General, US Army Airborne Forces, 1944

This major-general wears the overseas cap with gold piping and infantry para-glider badge. Artillery para-gliders had the same badge with red edging. The M1944 'Ike' field jacket came in a number of different patterns, while the OD trousers are worn tucked into lace-up para boots. Rank badges are worn on the side of the overseas cap and on the shoulder straps. On the right breast is the unit citation badge and on the left the Army paratrooper badge above an infantry combat badge.

286 NCO, US Army Military Police, 1942

American military policemen dressed like this were to be seen patrolling London's black-out streets during the war and were known locally as 'snow drops' because of their white helmets and accoutrements. The rest of the uniform is the standard (Class A) service uniform.

284   285   286

287

back and a reserve strapped horizontally to the front of the body.

Most of the other additions to the American soldier's wardrobe during the war were connected with improving the weatherproof qualities of his uniform by providing additional warmth, and waterproof footwear for wear over leather boots.

Badges of rank were as illustrated in the insignia chart (page 161) but the two grades of warrant officer were only introduced in January 1942, and it was not until December 1944 that the grade of General of the Army, with five stars as his rank badge, was created.

During the war there was a rapid increase in the number and variety of 'shoulder sleeve insignia' worn, which corresponded to the increase in size and complexity of the United States Army.

AIR FORCE

In June 1941 the United States Army Air Corps became the Army Air Force and was commanded by Major-General Henry H. Arnold. At that time its strength was only a small force of 9078 officers and 143,563 enlisted men. Within six months its strength had risen to 22,524 officers (including cadets) and 274,579 men. The numbers of aircraft had risen from 6102 to 10,329 in the same period. Eight Air Forces were constituted. Four were based within the continental United States and one each was based in the Philippines, Hawaii, Alaska and the

Caribbean. Between 1943–44 the AAF doubled in size and reached a peak strength in March 1944 of 2,411,294 men, of which 38 per cent served overseas. By April 1945 52 per cent of its personnel served overseas. Supplying this sizeable force was a considerable constraint on the number of infantry divisions the US could ship abroad.

Formed on 28 January 1942, the United States 8th Army Air Force was established at Savannah, Georgia, as the air component of the projected invasion of North-West Africa. With the escalation of war in the Pacific, this was cancelled and, re-numbered from its original title of the 5th AF, the 8th was diverted to Britain; an advance party landed in February under the command of Brigadier General Ira Eaker. Initial plans called for a total of 60 combat groups – 33 of bombers, 12 of fighters and 15 of transport and observation aircraft, with a proposed strength of 3500 machines.

April and May 1942 saw the first personnel arrive on British soil. The first raid of major proportions was mounted on 17 August by 12 Boeing B-17 Fortresses, the giant four-engined bombers which, with the Consolidated B-24 Liberator, bore the brunt of the US bombing effort. This raid on Rouen, mounted in daylight, sustained no losses, but this

Below: The crew of a Marauder bomber, having returned from their mission on D-Day, are questioned by the base intelligence officer.

287 Sergeant Grade 4, US Army Airborne Forces, 1944

The special two-piece combat uniform, M1 steel helmet and high lace-up para boots were all developed for wear by airborne troops. Unlike German and British parachutists who wore a smock over their equipment, American paratroopers strapped everything which might become entangled with the rigging lines to their body with lengths of webbing strap. On his upper right sleeve he wears an American flag as an identification for the benefit of the local population, and on both sleeves his rank chevrons. On the upper left sleeve is the badge of the 101st Airborne Division. The carbine is a folding-stock US Cal.30 M1A1.

Americans began to form parachute troops in June 1940 and the first jump dress consisted of a Riddle helmet, a one-piece OD sateen overall, and high lace-up jump boots with rubber soles. Unlike German and British paratroopers Americans did not wear a smock over their equipment; instead, every item that could become entangled with the rigging lines of the parachute was strapped to the body with lengths of webbing. They also wore two parachutes, the main one on the

288

289

290

was not to be the case in the majority of its successors.

Despite the unfavourable weather encountered over Europe, which hindered accurate day bombing, and the inability of escorting fighters to shadow their charges to the extent of the bombers' range, the Eighth continued its campaign. The objectives were, at first, limited to military targets in occupied France, but when the Casablanca directive of January 1943 demanded the strategic bombing of Germany's industrial system, the pattern of operations was changed.

In 107,001 sorties flown by the US 8th and 9th Air Forces from then until 1 March 1944, some 1509 aircraft were lost. On the credit side, however, 92,468 tons of bombs were dropped and 5304 enemy aircraft destroyed. At peak strength, the 8th numbered 40½ heavy bombardment, 15 fighter and two photo-reconnaissance groups. It claimed 20,419 enemy aircraft in a total of 1,034,052 flights, and lost 11,687 planes.

The B-17 carried a crew of ten, consisting of pilot and co-pilot, navigator, bomb-aimer, flight engineer, wireless

operator and four gunners; two at the waist guns, one in a ventral turret and one at the tail. The navigator was entrusted with two window guns, the bomb-aimer with forward-firing armament and the flight engineer with two dorsal weapons. With each aircraft thus armed with some 15 machine guns of varying calibres, a 'box' or formation of Fortresses was not to be taken lightly. Not until the arrival of the North American P-51 Mustang in early 1944, however, could the 8th Army Air Force bombers be assured of a fighter escort at all stages of their mission.

This vulnerability which belied the USAAF's apparent strength in numbers was vividly exhibited at Schweinfurt on 14 October 1943, when 60 B-17s fell victim to the Luftwaffe and 133 were damaged out of a total of 291. This was the 8th Air Force's infamous 'Black Thursday', after which the Mustang's introduction was hastened. The target, a complex of five plants producing bearings vital to Germany industry, was significantly affected, three of the factories receiving considerable damage. Nevertheless, the heavy losses sustained caused

288 Aircrewman, USAAF, 1944

This aircrewman with the 8th Army Air Force wears olive-green flying overalls, brown leather boots and the standard peaked cap. His flak-suit (of which he is holding the abdominal protector) was devised in October 1942 by Brigadier-General Grow, in conjunction with the Wilkinson Sword Company, to cut down aircrew casualties. Its manganese steel plates could stop a .45 calibre bullet at close range. The suit weighed 20lb, but soon became popular, and by 1944 13,500 were in service with the 8th Army Air Force.

289 Major-General, US Army Air Force, 1944

This was the typical service dress of American Army airmen in the ETO (European Theatre of Operations). Badges of rank appear on the shoulder straps and on the left side of the overseas cap. The silver wings were worn by command airmen, and the patch on the left sleeve identified the wearer as being a member of the 9th Air Force.

290 Captain, US Army Air Force, 1944

This pilot of a Mustang (P-51B) wears the overseas cap with rank badges on the left side. Over his leather flying jacket is a life preserving vest. The OD trousers are tucked into A-6 type flying boots, the standard pattern.

Right: Army Air Force men crowd around one of the first Liberators to arrive in Great Britain.

a reappraisal of the 8th Air Force's daylight bombing policy.

The 9th Air Force had commenced operations in the Middle East in mid-1942, disrupting Axis supply lines in the eastern Mediterranean and co-operating with the British 8th Army in driving the enemy westwards. Established on 16 October 1943 as the tactical arm of the US Army Air Force in Europe, the 9th provided its 'big brother' with escort and medium bombing support, as well as being engaged in the Overlord invasion offensive on its own account. The 9th was responsible for a total of 659,513 missions, dropping 582,701 tons of bombs and destroying 9,497 enemy aircraft for the loss of 6,731 of its own.

ORGANISATION The structure of the AAF in each theatre of operations differed with the climatic, geographical conditions and tactical requirements pertaining there. The smallest administrative unit was the group of two to four squadrons. If a group was stationed at a permanent base the various squadrons usually pooled their administrative services; but wherever the squadrons were stationed the group trained together. The air group was the Air Force equivalent of the Army regiment.

The various groups were differentiated by the type of aircraft they flew. For example, a very heavy bombardment group, flying B-29s would comprise 462 officers and 1616 men. But the number of men and aircraft in each group varied. Above this was the wing of two groups which was a non-administrative unit and only concerned with tactical plans and operations.

Two or more wings were usually brigaded together with auxiliary units to form a command – an organization of one kind of air strength, fighters or bombers. If these forces were too large for one man to control, then they would be split into air divisions which rested between wing and command levels. The air force was the largest single unit in the AAF and consisted of three or more commands. If, however, the tactical demands of a theatre required a particular type of air support then an air force would be created within a theatre air force.

UNIFORM United States Army Air Force personnel wore Army uniform with the modifications discussed on page 138. The artwork captions examine the many variations worn in the European theatre of operations.

291 Bomber Crewman, US Army Air Force, 1945

This crewman of the 8th Air Force wears the intermediate wool-and-alpaca-lined flying suit with A-11 helmet, B-8 goggles and A-10 oxygen mask. His flying boots were fur-lined for added warmth.

292 Technical Sergeant Grade 2, US Army Air Force, 1945

Over an OD pullover this ground crewman of the 9th Air Force in the United Kingdom in 1945 wears the one-piece herringbone twill fatigue suit and baseball cap. The rank badges are worn on the sleeves.

291

292

US ARMY/AIR FORCE INSIGNIA

Lapel Badges: Officers

U.S. U.S.

Cap Badge: Officers

Lapel Badges: Other Ranks

Cap Badge: W.O.s

Cap Badge: Other Ranks

Shoulder

| General of Army (Dec. 1944) | General | Lieutenant-General | Major-General | Brigadier-General | Colonel | Lieutenant-Colonel | Major | Captain | 1st Lieut | 2nd Lieut | Chief W.O. | W.O (Junior Grade) |

Pilot's Wings

Arm

Shoulder

Cuff

| Master Sgt 1st Grade (Air Force) | 1st Sgt 1st Grade (3rd Div.) | Tech. Sgt 2nd Grade (4th Div.) | Staff Sgt 3rd Grade (5th Div.) | Technician 3rd Grade (6th Div.) | Sergeant 4th Grade (7th Div.) | Technician 4th Grade (29th Div.) | Corporal 5th Grade (31st Div.) | Technician 5th Grade (32nd Div.) | Private 1st Class 6th Grade (90th Div.) | Flight Off (W.O. Jnr Grade) | Cuff Lace. Officers |

US NAVY INSIGNIA

Cap Peaks

Shoulder

Cuff

| Admiral | Vice-Admiral | Rear-Admiral | Commodore | Captain (Line) | Commander (Medical) | Lieutenant-Commander (Dental) | Lieutenant (Supply) | Lieutenant Jnr Grade (Civil Eng.) | Ensign (Line) | Chief W.O. (Gunnery) | Warrant Officer (Electrician) |

Cap Badge: C.P.O.s

Arm

Cuff

| C.P.O. (3 G.C. Stripes) (Bosun's Mate) | C.P.O. (Machinist's Mate) | P.O. 1st Cl. (Gunner's Mate) | P.O. 2nd Cl. (Aviation) | P.O. 3rd Cl. (Signals) | Branches: Fireman (top) Seaman (btm) | Seaman 1st Cl (3 Gd Condct Stripes) | Seaman 2nd Cl (2 Active Serv Stripes) | Apprentice Seaman (1 A.S. Stripe) | Cap Badge: W.O.s | |

Cap Badge: Officers

NAVY

The US Navy was in many ways un-prepared for war when the Japanese brought America into World War II with their attack on Pearl Harbor. Too great an emphasis was placed upon the battleship to the exclusion of anti-sub-marine warfare, which was essential to success in the Battle of the Atlantic. It was to the great credit of the US Navy that in a remarkably short space of time it was able to re-organise its forces and, in conjunction with the Royal Navy, defeat the U-boat menace.

Even before America's entry into the war, the pro-British Roosevelt govern-ment had provided aid to the British which included the 100 destroyers of the 'lend-lease' agreement and the escort of

Above: A depth charge explodes off the stern of an American destroyer on escort duty in the Atlantic.

293 Ensign, US Navy, 1944

Ensign Roosevelt wears standard officers' service dress with white cap cover. Rank distinction lace and the five-pointed star of a line officer appear on the cuffs. The aiguillette was worn by presidential aides.

293

convoys by US Navy vessels.

As early as February 1941 a Support Force had been set up from the Atlantic Fleet, consisting of three destroyer squadrons and four patrol squadrons of 12 Catalina or Mariner aircraft each. By the end of the following month this force was 27 destroyers strong and was con-centrated on the Argenta to Iceland sector of the transatlantic convoy route. In 1942 the United States Atlantic Fleet consisted of seven battleships, one fleet and seven escort carriers, three heavy and nine light cruisers, and 76 destroyers.

A major problem facing the Navy planners was the allocation of resources: to many Americans the Pacific was the most important area of operations and although the Atlantic was not stinted of supplies, the main effort was justifiably devoted to the Pacific Command. Never-theless, by 1944 seven escort carrier groups had been formed with 7 carriers and 97 destroyers.

In spite of the British example the American Navy, under the direction of Admiral King, was reluctant to develop the convoys system and suffered very heavy losses. During the spring and summer of 1942 the German U-boats decimated shipping off the Atlantic sea-board: during May alone, over 450,000 tons of Allied shipping was sunk off the American coast. Like the Royal Navy the US Navy gained the upper hand over the U-boats by adopting the convoy system, increasing the numbers of escort vessels and introducing new anti-submarine devices such as Asdic and 'Huff-Duff'.

The organisation of the US Atlantic Fleet was initially a hurriedly improvised affair but once was was declared efforts were made to rationalise the Fleet's organisation. Originally, the US Atlantic coast was divided into a number of coastal naval districts, and there were seven of these guarding the vast area of the eastern seaboard stretching from Canada to Florida. These were abolished and replaced by sea frontiers on 1 July 1942. A sea frontier was an area of ocean extending out to sea from a definite section of the coast to a distance of over 200 miles. In all there were four sea frontiers, three of which were relevant to the fight against the U-boat: the Canadian Coastal Zone, the Panama Sea Frontier, and most important of all, the Eastern Sea Frontier. The commanders of each of these areas controlled all the vessels inside them for the duration of their voyage within the sea frontier.

Although the idea of appointing one officer responsible for conducting the U-boat war was discarded, Admiral King set up the 10th Fleet in May 1942 under his own command 'to exercise unity of control over US anti-submarine opera-tions in that part of the Atlantic under its strategic control'. This was a further step in the process of ironing out the series of hasty improvisations created to meet the needs of the moment. The basic function of this force was to destroy U-boats, protect allied and neutral shipping and also to supervise training in anti-sub-marine methods.

By early 1944 the US Navy switched most of its resources to the Pacific, although convoy duties continued and valuable support was given to the Army during the Normandy landings in June 1944.

UNIFORM In the Atlantic theatre of operations US Navy uniforms kept to the basic pattern discussed on page 139.

294

295

294 Soldier, German Army, 1944
This infantryman is equipped with flamethrowing gear consisting of a main cylinder mounted on his back, a flamethrower gun and a protective suit made of a rubberised material which was worn over the standard uniform. The flamethrower worked on the principle of squirting out a liquid or semi-liquid stream of fire at the target. The weapon had four basic elements: a fuel storage system, a compressed gas system, a flame gun and an igniter. The gun element had two triggers, one to release the fuel from the cylinder and the other to ignite the fuel/gas mixture at the nozzle. The flamethrower was not widely used by the Germans, however, being more common in the armouries of Britain and the USA.

295 Private, German Army, 1944
This Panzergrenadier has fitted wire mesh to his steel helmet to hold foliage, and over his field blouse wears an Army camouflage smock, which was reversible to white and was originally issued only to snipers. The field blouse is the 1943 model with plain, unpleated, patch pockets. In his belt he carries a Stielgranate 24 and the rifle is the Mauser 98K.

Below: This crewman of a Panzer Mark IV wears the unofficial dress of the 12th SS 'Hitler Jugend' Panzer Division which consisted of a black leather jacket and the trousers worn by U-boat crews. The 'Hitler Jugend', under the command of Oberführer Fritz Witt, was one of the crack armoured formations of the German Army on the Western Front and sustained heavy casualties in the attempt to drive the Allies into the sea. The tank has been coated with Zimmerit paste, a special anti-magnetic mine solution that had been applied to the external surfaces of most German tanks by 1944. The Mark IV was armed with two 7.92mm machine guns (one visible here) and a long-barrelled 7.5cm high-velocity gun.

GERMANY
ARMY

Following the defeat of France in the summer of 1940 and the abandonment of plans to invade Great Britain, the German Army found itself allotted a defensive role as the occupying force in western Europe. At first France was little more than a retraining and reorganising ground for the battered divisions withdrawn from the Eastern Front but by the autumn of 1943 it had become obvious to the German High Command that an Allied invasion of western Europe was certain. The only questions in doubt were when and where and how the invasion should be countered. Many German commanders thought that the Allied invasion would be directed against the Pas de Calais region and not Normandy, the actual site of the landings.

Although the German soldiers fought fiercely against the Allied invasion forces in 1944, Hitler's refusal to allow a steady withdrawal led to the disaster of Falaise, and the headlong retreat through France during the autumn of 1944.

The retreat cost the German Army heavy casualties but by the end of 1944 the front line had stabilised near the frontiers of Germany itself. Manpower shortages and logistic problems held up the Allied advance, so allowing the Germans a breathing space to mount their last major offensive in the west – the Battle of the Bulge.

Despite some initial success this last gamble ended in failure with the German Army using up its remaining forces.

After the failure of the Ardennes offensive the Germans were forced back to the Rhine and by February 1945 the forces available in the west consisted of 73 understrength divisions. The Army was nearing collapse: the absence of air support and shortages of all necessary war materials made defeat inevitable. On 30 April Hitler committed suicide and the German Army began to lay down its arms, the final surrender being signed on 7 May 1945.

296

297

southern France. Although Rommel had influence with Hitler he had no authority over the armoured divisions which came under direct OKW control and were commanded by Geyr von Schweppenburg (commander, Panzer Group West) an opponent of Rommel's tactical ideas.

Panzer Group West – the German armoured reserve – consisted of four panzer and two SS-panzer divisions, five of them deployed in France with the sixth stationed in Belgium. Allied air power ensured that these formations had less effect than they might have; exposed to aerial rocket attacks, tank units were forced to travel by night and hide by day.

Many divisions were destroyed in the battle for Normandy but by the winter of 1944 there were sufficient troops to consider a further offensive. For the Battle of the Bulge the German Army deployed three armies:
7th Army (one paratroop and three *Volksgrenadier* divisions);
5th Panzer Army (two panzer and four *Volksgrenadier* divisions);
6th SS Panzer Army (four SS panzer, four *Volksgrenadier* and one parachute division).

The composition of these three armies reflected the state of the Army towards the end of the war: the infantry component consisted mainly of the *Volksgrenadier* divisions (examined in detail on page 187) while Army tank strength was greatly reduced compared to that of the Waffen-SS (the 6th SS Panzer Army with 640 tanks had about twice the number of the 5th Panzer Army). Despite the fact that the SS formations had better equipment and armament than their Army counterparts, it was the 5th Panzer Army that had the greatest success during the Ardennes offensive.

By the spring of 1945 the size of the German Army units and formations had been greatly reduced: the infantry divisions averaged around 7000 men each and the eight armoured divisions were desperately short of equipment and fuel. The *Volkssturm* (the German equivalent of the British Home Guard) was called out but, consisting of adolescents and middle-aged men lacking in weapons and training, its influence was minimal. By the end of April 1945 the German Army ceased to exist as a coherent force.

The Army had been at war for nearly six years and had fought throughout Europe and in North Africa. Although the Army had won many great victories during these years the political ambitions of Germany's leaders made victory impossible: the combined numerical advantage of the Allied forces wore the German Army

296 Corporal, German Army, 1944
This Unteroffizier *wears the final version of the World War II German field uniform which was very similar in cut to the British battledress. All insignia was now woven in mouse-grey on field-grey backing. The breeches lined with leather and high riding boots were issued to personnel in horse-drawn units, of which there were still a number in 1944–5. Above the left breast pocket he wears the ribbon for the Winter Campaign on the Eastern Front (often called the 'frozen meat medal'), and on the pocket he wears a wound badge in black.*

297 2nd Lieutenant, German Security Police, 1943
This SS-Untersturmführer *wears the field-grey service dress of the Waffen-SS. Badges of rank appear on the shoulder straps and on his left collar patch. Security service (SD) and security police (Sipo) personnel wore a plain right-hand collar patch and police green piping on the shoulder straps. Those entitled wore the SD badge on the left cuff. The chevron on his right sleeve is not a rank badge but indicated that the wearer had fulfilled certain conditions, such as having been a member of the Nazi Party prior to 1933.*

ORGANISATION Not only did the Army have insufficient men to guard Hitler's 'Fortress Europe', the quality of many of the available divisions was only second rate. A further problem was the fragmented command structure of the German Army in western Europe. Field Marshal von Rundstedt was Commander-in-Chief West but had only nominal authority while Rommel as commander of Army Group B fought with the other Army generals for control of the western defences. This failure to unify German Army command, coupled with inter-service rivalries with the Air Force and Navy, was a fatal organisational error, for when the Allies struck on 6 June 1944 the German response was sluggish and uncoordinated.

Of the 58 divisions available to Rundstedt 43 were under the command of Army Group B (Rommel) which covered northern France and the Low Countries, while the remainder were under the control of Army Group G (Blaskowitz) which was responsible for central and down in a battle of attrition it could never hope to win. The final casualty figure for the German Army during World War II was 3,250,000 men killed.

UNIFORM The German soldier in Normandy in 1944 had an appearance rather different from the typical *Landser* (German Tommy) of 1940. First of all, the various kinds of side and mountain caps had been replaced by the standard M1943 field cap. The steel helmet was no longer shiny and adorned with national emblem and national colours; instead, it now displayed a matt, gritty, field-grey finish or was sprayed in a camouflage pattern, or was worn with camouflage cover or netting. The colour of the field uniform was no longer as green as it had been formerly. It was now becoming increasingly grey, and as the quality of the material was getting poorer so uniforms tended to be baggier. Most insignia were now manufactured in mouse-grey yarn, and *Waffenfarbe* only appeared on the shoulder straps. The expensive marching boot was now a comparative rarity and most soldiers wore ankle boots with canvas anklets, which were disparagingly called 'retreat gaiters'.

A standard field-grey shirt had been introduced to replace the former varieties and colours of shirt; this could be worn without a tunic. New trousers with built-in cloth belt were also produced.

The special black and field-grey clothing for crews of enclosed armoured fighting vehicles and self-propelled artillery were also simplified, while the field-grey uniform began to be issued to all personnel in newly-formed panzer grenadier divisions.

To protect what were becoming increasingly precious uniforms and to improve the protective colouring, various types of overalls, some of which were camouflaged, began to be issued (see figure 295). These were not, however, standardised or as widely issued as those of the Waffen-SS.

Officers were finding it very difficult to obtain uniforms and accessories on the open market because of the widespread shortage of textiles, so they began to wear issue uniforms. Their tailor-made service dress was kept for formal occasions. The rather rigid orders of dress were relaxed to take into account all these difficulties. Some officers, finding the stiff closed collar uncomfortable, began to wear their field blouse open at the neck with shirt and tie, while others had tailor-made blouses which were designed to be worn open at the neck.

During the last winter of the war the typical German soldier was wearing

Above: Taken in Normandy in the summer of 1944, this picture shows part of the crew of a 7.5cm German anti-tank gun. The personnel, who are in an SS division, wear the regulation SS camouflage smocks and helmet covers. The 7.5cm gun was the German Army's standard anti-tank weapon towards the end of the war but its size made it difficult for infantry to handle.

Below: Two soldiers of the Volkssturm *– the German equivalent of the British Home Guard – are pictured in a typical variety of civilian and army clothing. The* Volkssturm *arm-band or brassard is visible on their left arms. The organisation was mainly composed of middle-aged men or youths and, with few weapons and little equipment, was clearly unsuited to play a significant part in modern warfare.*

either the reversible camouflage combat uniform or the standard issue field-grey greatcoat with large matching collar and built-in hood. The coat came in a lined and unlined version.

Since it was impractical to wear shoulder straps on many of the camouflage uniforms (and the various kinds of protective clothing), a new system of rank badges for wear on both sleeves was introduced in August 1942 (see rank insignia chart, page 11).

AIR FORCE

One of the major lessons of the Battle of Britain was the realisation of the vulnerability of the bomber to a well organised fighter defence. The German solution was to turn to night bombing as a means of escaping the fighter menace. Throughout the winter and spring of 1940–41, Britain's major cities were subjected to the Luftwaffe's bomber arm which although causing widespread damage and heavy casualties (50,000 people were killed during the 'Blitz') did not seriously affect

war production or civilian morale, as had been hoped. This attempt to bring Britain to her knees petered out in the spring of 1941 as the German Air Force was redeployed in eastern Europe.

The Luftwaffe moved over to the defensive during the summer of 1941 mainly because the strategic focus had been transferred towards Russia and resources transferred accordingly but also because of the development of a small but growing British bomber offensive against Germany which necessitated a response from the Air Force. The British and later American aerial offensive against Germany was to engage the Luftwaffe in a massive operation to save the *Reich* from destruction.

Below: German soldiers are marched into captivity under Allied guard in September 1944. Their uniform displays the characteristics of late-war German issue, with jackboots having been replaced by marching boots and gaiters in the British style. The soldier to the right wears the chevron of a lance-corporal on his left sleeve, while the leading figure carries the regulation German canteen.

Besides its main function from 1942 onwards as the cutting edge of the Luftwaffe's defensive screen the German fighter arm scored a number of notable successes on the Western Front; these included the intricate fighter umbrella erected to defend the *Scharnhorst* and *Gneisenau* during the 'Channel Dash' and the disruption of the Allied fighter screen over Dieppe in July 1942.

During 1943 the intensity of the Allied bomber offensive increased and the German Air Force was engaged in a desperate struggle against the RAF by night and USAAF by day. Success in this war depended on the application of material resources and technical developments; sometimes the German defenders were in the ascendant and Allied casualties rose and at other the Allies gained the upper hand and Germany's cities were destroyed.

A major turning point was the firestorm raids on Hamburg during July 1943 in which the German air defence was blinded through the jamming of the radar system by 'window' (thin aluminium strips dropped through the air simulating

298 Officer, German Air Force
This figure wears the standard Luftwaffe officers' leather greatcoat. An anachronistic touch is the brown leather Sam Browne belt which is still being worn even though it had officially been discontinued after the Polish campaign in 1939. The officer's rank is not visible from this illustration although the Luftwaffe version of the German eagle can be seen on the peaked cap. Since 1941 the German Air Force had taken on a defensive role on the Western Front as the strategic initiative passed over to the Air Forces of the Allies.

299 Reich Marshal
As the one and only Marshal of the Reich, Göring designed his own uniform, which, since he was also Commander-in-Chief of the Luftwaffe, had a certain Air Force flavour about it. Badges of rank appeared on the shoulder straps and collar patches (see insignia chart). Decorations include the highest Prussian award for bravery, the Pour le Mérite, which is almost totally overshadowed by the highest class of the Order of the Iron Cross, the Grand Cross, of which he was the only recipient. In his right hand he carries an Interimstab which was the everyday version of the field marshal's baton.

300 Corporal, German Air Force, 1944
As a paratrooper, this Oberjäger has the yellow (flying) arm-of-service colour while his rank is displayed on the collar patches and the shoulder straps. The popular flying blouse or Fliegerbluse is the later pattern with pockets and is worn with the field-grey paratroop trousers. Deprived of an airborne role the German paratroops were employed as ground forces and acquitted themselves with distinction in the bitter fighting in the Normandy bocage and against the British paratroops during the battle of Arnhem.

aircraft on German radar screens). Hamburg was virtually razed to the ground: 50,000 people were estimated to have been killed and nearly 1,000,000 made homeless.

New tactics were evolved in this crisis period for the Air Force and during late 1943 British losses rose as did those of the USAAF whose unescorted bombers were appallingly vulnerable to fighter attack. During 1943 the German Air Force tactically defeated the American 8th Army Air Force, which for a time was forced to bomb easier targets in France. But the tables turned to the Allies' advantage in 1944 as the Americans made massive use of Mustang long-range escort fighters which not only protected their own bombers but began to wear down the Luftwaffe's own fighters.

By the summer of 1944 the strain on Germany's industrial and military capacity was beginning to show. Only 419 serviceable German aircraft were able to oppose the enormous Allied deployment of over 10,000 planes to support the Normandy landings.

Although German aircraft production reached its peak in 1944 the Luftwaffe's trained pilots were being destroyed in the daily and nightly running battles over Germany. As serious as the loss of trained aircrew was the growing shortage of aviation fuel in 1944 due to the destruction of oil refineries in Eastern Europe and the systematic attacks on the synthetic fuel industry. In January 1944 Germany was producing 159,000 tons of synthetic fuel a month; by December of that year production was down to 26,000 tons.

During the last year of the war overwhelming Allied superiority destroyed the Luftwaffe which was now unable to either support Army operations or defend German cities from Allied attacks. Despite

Right: A groundcrewman hands night glasses to the pilot of a German aircraft prior to take-off on an operational sortie. Both wear the standard German Air Force overalls. The Luftwaffe conducted both offensive and defensive campaigns by night; in the latter case, 'Wild Sow' and 'Tame Sow' tactics were employed to effect in the defence of the Reich, claiming many Allied bombers.

298

299

300

desperate efforts by the German air crews and the introduction of technically superior aircraft – such as the jet propelled Me 262 – there was little that could be done and only the signing of the peace treaty on 7 May 1945 saved the Luftwaffe from complete destruction.

ORGANISATION The Allied bomber offensive forced the German Air Force to adopt new tactics and organisations to counter this aerial threat. A new and constantly developing system of defence evolved that integrated the various elements of air defence – radar, searchlights, anti-aircraft artillery and interceptors – into a whole.

Originally the defence of Germany was left to the powerful anti-aircraft arm which with its searchlight batteries and later radar controlled height/range finders

301 Captain, German Air Force, 1944
This Hauptmann wears flying clothing typical of the end of the war. The field cap is the standard model introduced in 1943, and the flying suit is a two-piece model consisting of zip-fastened jacket and the so-called 'Kanalhosen' (Channel trousers) which had large pockets containing survival kit. Badges of rank are worn on the shoulder straps.

Below: Crewed by Luftwaffe personnel, this is one of Germany's many 2cm light flak guns employed for anti-aircraft defence. The arm-of-service eagle is visible on the uniform of the soldier to the left, whose rank is that of senior lance-corporal.

301

and predictors was the most numerous element within the Luftwaffe – out of a total of 1,500,000 men in 1939, two-thirds were involved in anti-aircraft duties. And during the course of the war their role increased in importance.

By 1942 it had become clear to the German Air Force planners that an early-warning radar system was necessary to identify enemy planes soon after leaving England so that they could be intercepted before reaching the target. A series of linked radar stations stretching from France to the north of Denmark was built during 1942. Known as the Kammhuber line (after its guiding light, General Josef Kammhuber) this, through a combination of wide and narrow beam radar sets, was able to guide night-fighters on to the bomber streams, often to deadly effect.

The introduction of 'window' in 1943 forced new developments on the German Air Force: *Wilde Sau* ('Wild Sow') and *Zahme Sau* ('Tame Sow') tactics. The 'Wild Sow' method concentrated the German fighters over the target itself where they would search for their prey semi-independently of the radar controller, relying mainly on visual contact. The 'Tame Sow' tactics kept to the basis of the old method: the fighters were directed to where the 'window' interference was the thickest in the hope of picking up the bomber stream and then engaging the enemy in a long running battle over Germany. Improvements in the interceptors' own radar sets, culminating in the 'SN-2' radar, allowed the airborne operators to work on frequencies not so disturbed by 'window' as the old Lichtenstein radar sets had been. The successful use of this new system led to heavy British casualties: during the period 18 November 1943 to the end of March 1944 over 1000 planes were lost and a further 1682 damaged during a series of 35 major raids over Germany.

Against the US day bombers the Air Force attacked in groups of up to 40 aircraft usually concentrating on a certain section of the massed American bomber formation. The lead planes which commanded the formations were a frequent target. Rockets fired from the fighters themselves were highly effective and in certain instances small bombs would be dropped directly onto the enemy plane from the fighters above. The advent of the long range fighter-escort prevented the German interceptors from closing with the US bombers so cutting down their success rate. By late 1944 the German fighter units often found themselves outnumbered and out-fought by the American escort fighters.

The air war in Western Europe was a steady drain on Luftwaffe resources. Hundreds of thousands of men were employed in anti-aircraft duties and in post-bombardment construction work and planes were withdrawn from other fronts, where they were desperately needed, to shore up the German defensive system in the West. Although beaten by the combined Allied Air Forces the Luftwaffe did not waver in its defence of Germany while the physical means to do so remained.

UNIFORM Luftwaffe uniform changed little during the war despite the German realisation that much could be done towards standardising cut if not the colour of the uniforms of the three branches of the Armed Forces.

From 1943 some officers began to wear their tunic and flying blouse closed at the collar, rather than open with shirt and tie. The side cap was changed for the standard peaked field cap, but the greatest uniform changes took place in the Luftwaffe field formations.

The Luftwaffe uniform had not really been designed for ground combat and both the colour and cut were most unsuitable. The first thing to be done was to remove the brightly coloured collar patches since these were far too conspicuous. Tunics, greatcoats and flying blouses were worn without collar patches until the new rifle-green pattern could be issued. These were piped for other ranks in

Above: Officers and men of a German U-boat cluster in the conning tower. Facing the camera to the right is a lieutenant, identifiable as such by the single pip on his shoulder strap. His rank group is indicated by the gold lace on the cap peak.

arm-of-service colour, but the difficulty in manufacturing these collar patches and getting them to the right units at this stage in the war meant that plain green collar patches were eventually issued and the *Waffenfarbe* appeared as piping on the shoulder straps.

Those units in Luftwaffe field formations which were equipped with armoured fighting vehicles also received the special black tank uniform on which Luftwaffe insignia was worn. A blue-grey and later field-grey version was issued to crews of self-propelled assault guns. Finally the Luftwaffe began to produce field-grey uniforms for members of the field formations. The field blouse had plain patch pockets and was worn with blue-grey shoulder straps piped in *Waffenfarbe*, no collar patches and the Luftwaffe national emblem on the right breast.

NAVY

The German Navy, although in the end thoroughly defeated during operations in Atlantic and Arctic waters from 1941 to 1945, threatened to win the war against

Great Britain during the Battle of the Atlantic, and its surface vessels posed a threat to convoys until 1945.

In 1940 Admiral Karl Dönitz, head of the German U-boat Arm, stated that, 'the U-boat alone can win this war', and the submarine was, indeed, the greatest obstacle to Allied success. For the second time in 25 years, Germany almost succeeded in severing Allied sea communications. The German U-boat arm, banned under the Treaty of Versailles, was reactivated after the signing of the Anglo-German Naval Treaty in 1935.

The U-boat arm of the *Kriegsmarine* was organised under the *Führer der Unterseeboote* (Senior Officer Submarines) Admiral Karl Dönitz. In 1939 a total of 55 submarines were organised in flotillas of between five and eight boats each, some of the flotillas being named after U-boat heroes of World War I.

With the introduction of wolf pack tactics in 1941, tonnage sunk rose steadily and the following year proved to be the most successful: U-boats sunk 1160 ships totalling 6,266,215 tons. Gradually, however, the Allies' improved tactics and the use of long-range aircraft and aircraft carriers and radar-equipped escorts began to yield results. Between April and May 1943, tonnage sunk by U-boats began to decline as their losses rose, soaring from 13 to 30 per cent during May, and the remaining 16 or so U-boats were withdrawn from the North Atlantic.

Mid-1943 marked a turning-point in the Battle of the Atlantic; the Allied offensive was beginning to gain momentum and the German attempt to redress the balance had come too late. Nevertheless, German U-boats accounted for the loss of 175 Allied warships and a total of 14 millions tons of Allied shipping throughout the war. Of 1162 U-boats built, 785 were destroyed, 156 surrendered and the rest were scuttled.

Typical German submarines serving in the Atlantic – Types IXC and IXC/40 – had four bow and two stern torpedo tubes and an armament of 41 torpedoes and three anti-aircraft guns. In all, 141 of these types were commissioned with a complement of 48.

Unrelated to the main stream of research were the midget submarines, manned by a crew of up to seven, and deployed to attack shipping in harbours.

In 1941 *Rudeltaktik* (pack tactics) or 'wolf packs' as they were known to the

302

303

Allies, were initiated under the direction of Admiral Dönitz. Groups of 15 to 20 U-boats patrolled the sealanes approaching Britain: when a convoy was sighted it was tracked by the U-boat which radioed its position, course and composition to Dönitz' headquarters, keeping in touch until other U-boats had received their orders and made contact. The boats then

Far left: A petty officer (with binoculars) interviews captured British sailors aboard the German heavy cruiser Admiral Hipper. *Displacing 10,000 tons and armed with 8-inch guns, the vessel operated with the* Tirpitz *against the convoy PQ-17 in July 1942. For most of the war the* Admiral Hipper *was based in Norway and operated against British arctic convoys, but with only limited success.*

Left: Commander Gysae looks through the periscope of his U-boat. He wears the white cap cover adopted almost universally by U-boat commanders. His shoulder straps indicate the rank of Korvettenkapitän. The success of Germany's U-boat fleet owed much to the bravery of their commanders, who considered themselves the élite of the German Navy.

attacked simultaneously, but independently, later reporting their success, or lack of it, to Dönitz who issued the orders for a further attack, or a new patrol line. Admiral Dönitz was thus able to make best use of his forces. However, so much radio traffic had its disadvantages: Royal Navy vessels carrying high-frequency direction-finders were able to pinpoint the transmitting U-boats, enabling escorts to run them down. The efficiency of the wolf pack tactics was further reduced when Allied long-range aerial searches intensified and autumn 1943 saw the final defeat of this strategy.

Despite appalling losses, the morale of the U-boat arm was high and it fought with unrelenting discipline and efficiency. Over 39,000 officers and men served in German submarines and 32,000 were killed in action, the highest proportion of any other force, Allied or Axis, in World War II.

The final defeat of the U-boats reflected not on the ability and courage of the men who served in them, but on the intensive Allied anti-submarine measures and out-

standing technical advances which the Germans were unable to match.

Since in September 1939 there were not enough warships in the *Kriegsmarine* to drive the Royal Navy from the seas, or even to escort any of the merchantmen outside German waters, the best that could be hoped for was to distract or damage part of the British Home Fleet long enough to enable a few blockade-runners to evade its patrols. Meanwhile a handful of surface and submarine raiders were to conduct a campaign against the merchant navies of the British Empire.

Following the declaration of war, the German surface raiders which were already at sea – *Deutschland* in the North Atlantic and *Graf Spee* south of the equator – began to attack commerce. The *Graf Spee* destroyed a total of nine ships during her cruise through the South Atlantic and Indian Ocean, but was herself scuttled following the Battle of River Plate in December 1939.

After the fall of Norway and France, the Atlantic became more accessible to the German Navy. Converted merchantmen

302 Petty Officer, German Navy, 1942
As an Obersteuermann or chief coxswain, this petty officer wears the cap with plain leather peak and lifejacket over his reefer. The latter carries badges of rank on the shoulder straps. He wears leather trousers outside his sea boots.

303 Petty Officer, German Navy, 1943
The black leather jacket and trousers worn here by a petty officer were issued to personnel working in machine rooms, since grease stains were not easily visible against the black. The uniform was worn without insignia, save for the badges of rank on the shoulder straps of the jacket. A cap with plain leather peak is also worn. Regulation uniforms such as this, however, were to become difficult to obtain as the war continued and Germany's position grew ever more parlous.

304 Commander, German Navy, 1943
This officer wears the double-breasted leather jacket which was issued with matching trousers for wear in bad weather. Badges of rank could be worn on the shoulder straps, but often (as in this illustration) no badge of rank were worn. Various kinds of working trousers were worn in preference to the blue service dress trousers.

305 Lieutenant, German Navy, 1942
This Leutnant zur See and U-boat commander wears the peaked cap with obligatory white cover, battered reefer, working trousers and sea boots. Unofficially, crews of submarines began to wear flotilla badges on their head-dresses. He has just been awarded the Knight's Cross of the Iron Cross, while the Iron Cross 1st Class is worn on the left breast of his reefer jacket.

304

305

put to sea: with disguised armament (which equalled that of a cruiser), they were able to approach enemy vessels without attracting undue attention. Between 1940 and 1942 vessels such as *Thor*, *Atlantis* and *Pinguin*, which were engaged in attacking Arctic whaling fleets, accounted for vast amounts of Allied tonnage sunk.

On 18 May 1941 the battleship *Bismarck* departed for the Atlantic on her first and only cruise accompanied by the heavy cruiser *Prinz Eugen*. Although the *Prinz Eugen* escaped the *Bismarck*'s fate, she was put out of action by the RAF in Brest harbour in July, as were the *Scharnhorst* and *Gneisenau*.

In order to prevent further attacks by the RAF, Hitler decided to move the three ships east, where they would be better able to protect Norway. The 'Channel Dash' of February 1942 was one of the most daring German naval operations of World War II in which combined air-sea operations played an important part.

Although the large German warships now turned their attention to raiding the Arctic convoys, they had little initial success, and after the sinking of the *Scharnhorst* in December 1943, surface craft left the convoys alone. The *Tirpitz*, which had almost suffered the same fate as her sister ship *Bismarck* was also damaged and immobilised. She had only once fired her guns in combat when she bombarded a gun emplacement at Spitzbergen.

By May 1945 only three cruisers and a dozen destroyers remained of the surface fleet of the *Kriegsmarine*.

Throughout the war the German Navy was divided between those who wanted a large surface fleet and those who wanted priority given to U-boat production. Fortunately for the Allies, the U-boat arm never received the resources which might have tipped the scales.

UNIFORM There was little change to the blue uniforms of the German Navy after 1940, although the increasing difficulties in replacing worn out clothing led to a lowering of uniformity amongst Navy personnel. At the end of the war it was not uncommon to see an officer wearing a blue reefer with checked or coloured shirt and black tie, simply because it was impossible to obtain the correct white shirts.

Land-based sailors continued to wear field-grey (figure 306). In June 1943 even admirals began to appear dressed in field-grey with blue stripes on their breeches and Army generals' collar patches embroidered in gold or yellow on blue.

INSIGNIA In 1944 Naval officers serving on the Atlantic Wall began to wear shoulder straps which identified their rank on the reefer in addition to the rank distinction lace on the cuffs. This was probably to facilitate inter-service rank identification in a situation where soldiers and sailors were working together.

306 Seaman,
German Naval Artillery, 1944
The field-grey uniform of the German Navy was similar to that worn by the Army, but had different pockets on the field blouse as well as buttons with an anchor on them. Trousers were often worn with ankle boots and canvas anklets (or 'retreat gaiters' as they were known) which began to replace the costly marching boot from 1941 on. Certain field-grey-clad branches of the Navy had emblems on their shoulder straps, such as the exploding shell as illustrated. The rifle is the Mauser 98K.

Right: A group of ratings and petty officers watches a salvo fired from the Admiral Scheer *during a training exercise. The* Admiral Scheer *was one of Germany's pocket battleships and with a gross tonnage of 12,000 tons was armed with six 11-inch guns. The most successful ship in this class, the* Scheer *began the war as a commerce raider in a 161-day cruise which took the ship to the Indian Ocean. Evading capture, the* Admiral Scheer *returned to Germany in 1941 and was dispatched to the Baltic Sea in 1942 to operate against Soviet convoys. In this photograph the sailors are wearing the square rig uniform with white-topped caps, an unusual order of dress for the later period of the war.*

THE PACIFIC WAR

Japanese forces had been engaged
in China since 1937 and, after the Japanese attack
on Pearl Harbor in December 1941, the war was extended
world-wide. Japanese, Chinese, US, British and Empire and
Commonwealth troops were all engaged in a struggle marked
by the vast distances involved, often fighting in
conditions of extreme humidity.
The results were the creation of many
distinctive organisations (especially in the
campaigns in the Pacific islands) and the adoption
of uniforms which were serviceable during weather such as
the Burmese monsoon or in terrain such as the
jungle of Guadalcanal.

JAPAN
ARMY

The Japanese Army was a mirror of Japanese society before 1945. It contained a peculiar amalgam of medieval attitudes and modern *matériel*, for the Army still followed the code of *Bushido* which upheld the virtues of man-to-man combat in a machine age, and demanded that the Japanese soldier die rather than surrender.

The political influence of the Japanese Army had substantially increased in the years between the two world wars. The Army saw Japan's salvation in China: Japan should secure the vast resources of the Asian mainland by carving out for herself a continental empire. The Army consequently viewed the Soviet Union as Japan's most dangerous enemy – a power which had traditional interests in North China. The Navy looked to the Pacific Ocean, and particularly to the South West Pacific, with the rich prize of Malaya and the Dutch East Indies as the means by which the resources vital to the maintenance of Japan as a great power could be seized. The Navy, therefore, regarded the world's two greatest naval powers, Great Britain and the United States, as Japan's most deadly enemies. It was no coincidence that the two services shaped Japan's strategy to suit the exclusive capacity of either the Army or the Navy. Before 1941 the Army had most of its own way.

Japan seized Manchuria in 1931 and the province of Jehol in 1934. Three years later the Japanese Army embarked on a full-scale undeclared war against China. The Japanese aimed to destroy the Chinese Army in the field and thus bring the country to its knees quickly; this would avoid the colossal task of trying to conquer and hold the vast spaces of China. The Japanese generals failed. The Chinese Army was more elusive and remained intact, and Japan's need to keep large forces on the Chinese mainland was a limiting factor on her strategy throughout World War II.

The peacetime strength of the Japanese army was 17 divisions. By 1940 it had 2 divisions in Japan and Korea, 12 in Manchuria and 27 in China. Even in 1943 the commitment in China still amounted to 25 infantry divisions, 1 armoured division, 11 mixed brigades, 1 cavalry brigade and 1 flying division – a total of 620,000 men and 14,000 vehicles. This force, known as the Kwantung Army, was called upon to provide a constant stream of reinforcements for the Pacific War, and by 1945 its units were understrength and too weak to pose any real threat.

307

307 Private 2nd Class, Japanese Army, 1937
The peaked cap with coloured band and piping of this infantryman was replaced by the peaked field cap on active service. The greatcoat is the standard pattern with detachable hood. Rank badges are worn on the shoulders. Equipment includes the waistbelt with ammunition pouches, bayonet for M38 rifle, water bottle and gas mask on right hip. The 6.5mm M38 Arisaka rifle was adapted from the German Mauser and, by 1937, was considered outdated.

308 Lieutenant, Japanese Army, 1937
This artillery officer wears the old-style service dress with stand collar and coloured collar patches with rank badges on the shoulders. The field cap with yellow cloth star on the front was standard issue, but the goggles suggest that his unit was motorised, or that he at least travelled in a car. A pistol is carried in the leather holster on the right hip, and field glasses in a case on the left.

309 Private, Japanese Army, 1941
This infantryman wears the standard M98 field service uniform with full equipment. On the waist belt are two 30-round pouches and at the back one 60-round ammunition pouch. On the left is the gas mask in canvas bag, and bayonet for the M38 rifle. On his back he carries a canvas pack with rolled greatcoat or ground sheet and entrenching tool and mess tin strapped to it.

Below : Heavily-laden Japanese soldiers are pictured while crossing a pontoon bridge in China. They wear M98 field service uniforms and carry bolt-action 6.5mm Arisaka rifles. The enormous distances which warfare in China necessitated were hard to cover, especially for an Army as unmechanised as the Japanese. Logistics were a constant problem for them.

308

309

Military Training and Aviation. The General Staff was composed of five main bureaux: general affairs, operations, intelligence, transport and historical. They prepared for war, trained the troops and researched Japan's strategical requirements. The Chief of the General Staff was officially appointed by the Emperor. The War Ministry – the focus of the Army's political power, for the War Minister sat in the Cabinet and was always a soldier – provided liaison with the Chief-of-Staff and in theory the *Diet* (or Parliament) and handled the administrative, logistical and mobilisation plans. The two Inspectorates undertook the training of the troops.

Once in the field, the Japanese army was divided into army groups, area armies, armies, divisions, and forces with special missions which were not commanded by any particular army or division. Groups of armies represented an entire theatre of war: the Japanese Defence Army, the Kwantung Army and the Southern Army. An area army like the 23rd in Burma was the equivalent of a British or an American field army. The Japanese army was much smaller than its British equivalent, mustering only a strong British corps strength. There were no army corps in the Japanese Army. A Japanese army would vary in size from 50,000–150,000 men. The 18th Army in the south-west Pacific in April 1943, for example, had a nominal strength of 130,000 men, though its actual strength was much lower. This force comprised three divisions and an independent mixed brigade. The artillery component consisted of four independent field artillery companies, two field machine gun companies, one independent anti-tank battalion, six field artillery battalions, six field searchlight companies, and support units, which included engineer, transport and airfield defence troops.

The dominant Japanese organisational weakness, throughout the war, was the splintering of formations. Men were taken from one unit, thrown together with men from another and given a special mission; once this had been undertaken, the unit was either split up again to form another or sent back to its parent formation. There was little continuity and consequently a profusion of independent units.

The typical Japanese infantry division of December 1941 consisted of three infantry regiments, an artillery regiment, a cavalry or reconnaissance regiment and a regiment of engineers. Along with the divisional staff and the signals unit, the division was supported by a transport regiment, a medical unit and field hospital staff, water purification unit, an ordnance

The focus of the war moved away from China to the Pacific when Japan attacked American and British bases in the Far East in December 1941. The Army was involved in a number of amphibious operations in the Pacific Island chains although this area was the Navy's prime responsibility. The Army's greatest success was probably the capture of Singapore and the expulsion of the British from Malaya and Burma. Outnumbered by the British forces the spirit of the Japanese soldiers and the ability of their commanders proved unbeatable: by March 1942 the Japanese Army stood on the frontiers of India. The Army grew to a maximum strength of five million men, in 140 divisions and numerous small independent units.

The summer of 1942 marked the high-water mark of the Japanese advance, however, and when America's vast industrial and military strength was brought to bear the Japanese Army was forced over to the defensive. In the Pacific, US troops waged a bitter island-hopping war

and in Burma the British eventually managed to get the upper hand against the extended Japanese Army.

Although the war was clearly lost for Japan by 1944 the Army fought on as resolutely as ever and continued to do so until ordered to lay down its arms following the surrender on 2 September 1945. The armed forces of Japan suffered 1,700,000 casualties during World War II.

ORGANISATION The figurehead presiding over the Japanese war machine was the Emperor, the titular Commander-in-Chief, who had the power to declare war and make peace. His power was actually merely formal. He was advised by two councils, the Board of Marshals and Admirals and the Supreme Military Council. The real power was vested in the Imperial Headquarters, however. This comprised the Army and Navy Chiefs of Staff, the Army and Navy Ministers and their service advisors. Responsible to these officers were the General Staff, the War Ministry and the two Inspectorates of unit and a veterinary unit. As the war progressed 'comfort battalions' of prostitutes were attached to the divisions. There was, however, a great variation in the organisation and strength of Japanese forces depending on their location and the terrain encountered.

Under the strain of war the Japanese categorised their forces under three headings: 'A' the strongest; 'B' representing the standard; and 'C' the special. Not all Japanese divisions were composed of the same category of men. A standard 'B' division might include 'A' category artillery. Further, there might also have been a variation in strength within the divisional units themselves. In an 'A' class infantry regiment, the regimental gun unit could be either one company of four

Left: Japanese paratroops prepare for action. Note the special helmets with which they were issued. Paratroops were not used in great numbers in their airborne role, although like their German counterparts they were employed as élite ground troops.

guns or two companies of four guns under a small battalion HQ. Despite these variations there were generally four kinds of Japanese infantry division. First was the standard division of 'B' troops, the type most frequently encountered by Allied forces. Second was the strengthened division, composed of 'A' type units which might also include an additional artillery group, consisting of a group HQ and a field or a mountain artillery regiment and possibly a tank unit. Third was the modified strengthened division which included the additional artillery but not the armoured elements. The rifle company strength of this formation dropped from 265 to 205. Finally there was the special division. This was a lighter type of division composed mainly of 'C' troops with two brigades, each of four independent infantry battalions with supporting elements of small units of auxiliary troops (mainly of category 'A'). These divisions were frequently used for garrisoning Japan's small island bases and, in China, for combating guerrillas.

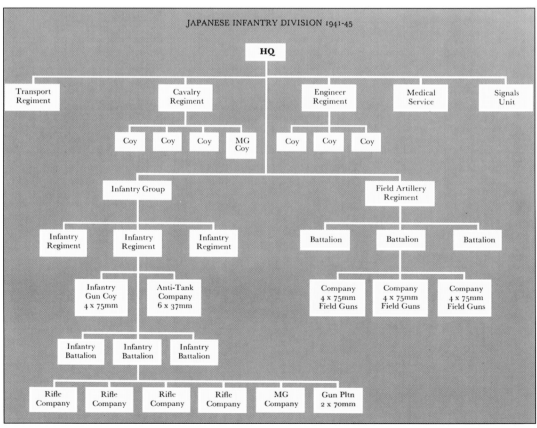

Japanese divisions were commanded by lieutenant-generals, following the German rather than the British model. Each lieutenant-general had a colonel as his chief-of-staff. The divisional staff was divided into two sections: the general staff section and the administrative section. Added to these were five departmental sections and an ordnance, a signal and a veterinary detachment including about 300 officers and men; the division would also have at its disposal 32 telephones and 30 miles of insulated telephone wire, two ground to air radios and eight other radios. It also had pigeons, dogs, helio lamps and semaphores to aid communication. The infantry component of the division – the infantry group – was commanded by a major-general who co-ordinated the three regiments. He had his own HQ and staff of 70–100 officers and men. He might also be allocated tankette companies of 80–120 men with 10–17 tankettes. The group tankette companies were organised into three or four platoons and a company train. Their main purpose was reconnaissance and they were usually sent to divisions which lacked a cavalry or reconnaissance regiment.

The infantry regiment, commanded by a colonel, was formed of the regimental HQ and train, signal company, the regimental infantry gun train and anti-tank company and three infantry battalions with the possible addition of pioneer units. The regimental HQ was composed of 55 officers and men. They were mainly concerned with the tasks of administration, ordnance, and codes and intelligence, with a small detachment reserved for the anti-aircraft section, the headquarters guard and the colour guard. The pioneer or labour units were arranged in seven sections with a strength of 100–200 men. Men from the category 'B' units might find themselves arbitrarily used to build airfields or beach defences. The regimental artillery element consisted of a small HQ staff of 24 officers and men. While one company consisted of two platoons each with two low-velocity infantry guns, the other had three platoons, each with two 37mm and, later in the war, two 47mm anti-tank guns. The machine-gun companies were armed with 12, 8 or 4 machine guns and depending on this number would have a strength of 174, 144, or 73 officers and men.

The forces supporting the division were independent of the infantry group. The divisional artillery usually consisted of a regiment of field or mountain artillery. The guns might be motorised, horse-drawn or pack. There were three battalions with 12 × 75mm guns each, and three gun companies (each with four 75mm

Above: Japanese infantry are pictured in action in south China. This photograph clearly shows the shape of the standard Japanese helmet. The machine gun is the 6.5mm Type 96, which incorporated features of the Czechoslovak ZB.

310 Private 1st Class, Japanese Army, 1942

This infantryman wears typical jungle fighting uniform and equipment. The steel helmet is worn over the field cap with neckflaps. Badges of rank appear on the collar patches. Equipment is the standard infantry pattern, with water bottle, gas mask, waist belt with ammunition pouches and bayonet. Footgear consists of the canvas tabi.

guns) and a regimental train, giving a total strength of 2300 men. The divisional cavalry regiment had three rifle and sabre companies and a machine-gun company, with a total strength of 950 officers and men. The medical units were of poor quality as Japanese soldiers were expected to stand, fight and die and would, therefore, not require an elaborate medical service. A Japanese division might have three field hospitals. Each medical unit consisted of three collecting companies of three stretcher platoons and one ambulance platoon each. In all it would have 180 litters and 45 ambulances. The headquarters train might also include additional carts for carrying the wounded and medical supplies. But these aspects of war were invariably neglected by the Japanese; indeed it was not unknown for their medical personnel to be armed and used as ordinary fighting troops.

310

The Japanese armoured division usually consisted of three tank regiments, and a motorised infantry brigade of 3800 men. The tank regiment would have a headquarters, three or four tank companies and a regimental ammunition train. The strength of the regiment was about 90 light and medium tanks and 800–850 men. In addition, there would be an artillery regiment of eight 105mm guns, and four 155mm howitzers; an anti-tank unit with 18 × 47mm anti-tank guns and an anti-aircraft unit of four 75mm guns and 16 × 20mm guns. There were also supporting engineers, transport and medical units. The whole division totalled 10,500 men and 1850 vehicles. Japanese armoured divisions had some success against poorly equipped Chinese forces, but were in no sense the equal of the tank forces of the other great powers.

The Japanese Army also had a large number of independent units and it was easy to organise special forces for specific missions. Rather than give all of these units heavy elements of anti-tank guns and artillery, these weapons were formed into independent units so that they could be used when needed. This trend reinforced the tendency towards fragmentation. In the first days of the war such combat teams spearheaded the Japanese advance into Malaya, the Dutch East Indies and the Solomons. The heavy losses sustained in 1943 were often due to a careless and haphazard combination of small independent units with little coordination and training. For example, one unit, the

311 Private, Japanese Army, 1941
The helmet of this tankman is the summer pattern made from cork covered in cotton drill with leather chin strap. On the lightweight tank troops' overall rank badges were usually worn on the collar. He carries a bayonet on his left and slung over his shoulders are a haversack, water bottle and gas mask. The Japanese soldier was frequently able to survive in extreme conditions – a trait the Allies found difficult to counter.

312 Captain, Japanese Army, 1939
The uniform of this tank officer is the standard M90 service dress for officers worn here with a tank helmet. This padded helmet came in both summer and winter versions, and later a model with a steel shell was introduced. Equipment is the standard pattern for officers. A pistol is carried in a holster which was worn suspended from a strap over the right shoulder. Other equipment such as binoculars, map case and water bottle was worn over the shoulders.

Right: Cadets at a Japanese military academy are taught how to identify different types of tanks, in this case Soviet models. Officer training in the Japanese Army was thorough and stressed the primacy of the offensive.

313 Superior Private, Japanese Army, 1937

This infantryman wears the special winter clothing for extreme climates with fur cap, double-breasted lined greatcoat, mittens and special felt boots with brown-leather uppers. Badges of rank are worn on the shoulders. The rifle is the 7.7mm M38 long rifle with bayonet.

314 Colonel, Japanese Army, 1944

This officer wears typical service dress as worn during the campaigns in Burma, Malaya and the Pacific. The cork sun helmet came in either white or light khaki. The shirt collar is worn outside the tunic collar, so the rank badges are pinned to the lapels of the tunic. Officers were also allowed to wear shirt sleeve order on active service or on informal occasions. The sword is the tachi style and was worn suspended from a fabric belt worn under the tunic, or from the leather waistbelt.

315 Lieutenant-General, Japanese Army, 1944

This soldier wears the standard general officers' uniform with rank insignia displayed on the collar patches and cuffs. Swords were a common feature in the Japanese Army.

6th Independent Anti-Aircraft Battalion, was rushed from Manchuria to Guadalcanal in 23 days to reinforce the task force thrown together in a hasty attempt to retake the island.

After about 1943 the Japanese also began to use raiding forces (*teishintai*). These were chosen from the infantry, and trained with a particular mission in mind; they were quite independent of larger forces. A typical role was the attempt by Japanese special forces in Burma to destroy British artillery by commando-style operations. The strength of these forces varied with the size of their objectives. A typical example included: HQ group (officer, NCO and orderly); demolition and assault section (15 men); support section (12 men); reserve section (12 men).

There were in addition small groups organised for raids into enemy territory to destroy bridges and lines of communication; to attack pillboxes, and fortified positions; demolition forces and tank fighting units; and also there were suicide squads which would be used to defend a

vital point to the last man.

Within the more traditional army structure, special provision was made for amphibious operations. After 1941, amphibious brigades were created of three battalions with a total strength of 3200 men. Each battalion was 1035 strong and had three rifle companies of 195 men each, divided into three platoons of four sections each and a trench mortar platoon. The 1st Amphibious Brigade had supporting artillery, engineer, machine gun, signal and tank units operating under the brigade HQ which boosted its strength to about 4000 men. During the advance through Malaya each Japanese division was equipped with 50 small motorboats and 100 collapsible launches for the assault on Singapore. All of these were carried on the shoulders of the troops themselves. A first wave of 4000 men and 440 guns (with 20 rounds of ammunition for each) were ferried across in this way.

UNIFORM Japanese uniform developed both together and separately in its two principal theatres of war in China and

JAPANESE ARMY INSIGNIA

Cap Badge Officers

Cap Badge Imperial Guards

Cap Badge Other Ranks

Collar (M98)

Cuff

General | Lieutenant-General | Major-General | Colonel | Lieutenant Colonel | Major | Captain | Lieutenant | 2nd Lieutenant | Warrant Officer

Collar (M98)

Sergeant-Major | Sergeant | Corporal | Lance-Corporal | Superior Private | Private 1st Class | Private 2nd Class | Private | M90 Uniform Artillery | M90 Uniform Airman

Sleeve

Officers | Warrant Officers | NCOs | Corporals | Corporal, acting Sergeant | Private, acting Corporal | Good Conduct Stripe | A of S Chevron (Air-Arm) | Pilot's Wings

the Pacific. The beginning of the Sino-Japanese War in 1937 saw the Japanese Army dressed in uniforms introduced in 1930 which were designated Model 90. Two versions existed in either a yellowish khaki wool for wear in temperate climates, or in khaki drill for summer and tropical wear.

The basic service dress for officers is illustrated by figures 312 and 315. The wool tunic for other ranks was the same as the officers' model and was worn with matching pantaloons, puttees and leather ankle boots. The standard head-dress (a peaked cap) and greatcoat are illustrated by figure 307. Typical winter clothing worn in China is illustrated by figure 313.

On the M90 uniform badges of rank were worn on red passants on the shoulders while the colour of the collar patches on the tunic identified the arm of service.

Two types of steel helmet were in use at the beginning of the war in China. The first model was already on the way out, and was being replaced by the pattern worn throughout World War II which had a metal five-pointed star on the front.

The standard tunic for officers is worn by figure 315. Badges of rank were either on the tunic collar or lapels, or sometimes fixed to the shirt collar which was worn outside the tunic collar. Breeches and long trousers matched the tunic and were worn with either high boots, ankle boots and leather leggings or simply brown shoes with long trousers. Other ranks wore matching pantaloons with puttees tied in a distinctive criss-cross manner, with either leather ankle boots or black canvas *tabi* (a form of footwear with separate big toe). Special uniforms were introduced for crews of armoured fighting vehicles and parachute troops. Figure 312 is a tank officer wearing standard service dress with the padded tank helmet, while figure 311 shows a typical tank man in helmet and overall. There was also a two-piece winter tank suit with short lined jacket with synthetic fur collar and pocket on the left breast. The trousers were cut in the form of a bib and brace overall, like the American tank man's overalls. On the winter jacket badges of rank were worn on the left breast, while on the summer version they were worn on the collar.

Japanese Army parachute troops were first used in Palembang Sumatra in February 1942 and later in Leyte. They wore the uniform illustrated by figure 322. A whole range of infantry weapons had been developed for airborne use, and on Leyte the typical Japanese paratrooper carried the following weapons and equipment: Model 89 (1929) 50mm grenade discharger and four grenades, two small M94 (1934) smoke candles, two anti-tank grenades and a pick and mattock in a specially designed canvas bag strapped to the leg. Strapped to the other leg was another bag containing an M2 (1942) 7.7mm paratroop rifle, a bayonet, four more grenades for the M89 discharger two M97 (1937) hand grenades and 30 rounds of 7.7mm rifle ammunition. A third bag contained demolition material comprising three M99 (1939) magnetic mines and six blocks of demolition explosive. A fourth bag held a variety of canned and concentrated rations, extra socks, an extra shirt, first aid pouch and a length of rope.

INSIGNIA Badges of rank were worn on the shoulders, on the collar of tunics and shirts, and on the front or sleeve of various kinds of special clothing. The rank badges, which were small red rectangles with horizontal yellow or gold stripes and five-pointed stars, were detachable (see rank insignia chart). On the cuffs of the greatcoat officers wore khaki rank distinction lace (one for company, two for field and three for general officers). In 1944 this system was extended to the tunic cuffs (see figure 315).

Arm-of-service colours appeared on the collar patches on the M90 tunic, but in 1938 rank badges were moved to the collar patches, and from this date arm of service was identified by small yellow metal badges worn on the collar behind the collar patches, or by a zigzag strip of cloth in the arm-of-service colour which was worn on the right (sometimes also on the left) breast. The basic colours were scarlet for infantry, and tanks until 1940, green for cavalry, yellow for artillery and dark brown for engineers.

AIR FORCE

There was no independent Japanese air force. The Army and the Navy each had their own air service. Each was nominally controlled by the Emperor. Actual control was vested in the General Staff, the Army and Navy Ministries and the Inspector General of Aviation.

The function of the Japanese Army Air Service was to provide support for the ground troops and to conduct counter-air force operations. It was not expected to initiate strategic operations on its own behalf, as was the case with the RAF for instance.

The Air Service was relatively small at the outbreak of war and Japan's highly-

Below: Japanese bomber crews are lined up on an airfield in northern China in preparation for a raid on the city of Chungking. They are wearing the regulation issue summer flying uniform with rank insignia displayed on the left breast.

trained pilots were soon casualties. Their replacements lacked the necessary flying ability to take on the growing technical and numerical superiority of the Americans. Partly as a response to this shortage *kamikaze* aircraft were introduced. The *kamikaze* aircraft was simply an aimed bomb in which the pilot sat over an explosive charge and aimed the aircraft at the target. First used at Leyte Gulf, these planes caused some consternation to the American forces; but overall their effect was negligible to the final outcome of the conflict.

The Japanese Army Air Service was organised into five air armies with clear areas of operations. Coordination was achieved between the Army and the Air Service by placing the air forces in each theatre under the command of the theatre commander. The largest Japanese tactical organisation was the air division, two or more of which would form an air army. Beneath this was the air brigade; two air brigades formed an air division. The composition of the brigade was flexible. Its HQ was small and concerned primarily with tactical planning. It was usually composed of three or four air regiments; each regiment was equipped with the same type of aircraft (fighters, or light or medium bombers) divided into three or four companies. The company was the most important operational unit; it was normally of nine aircraft, divided into three sections, each of three aircraft.

The total strength of the Japanese Army Air Service in 1940 was 36 fighter, 28 light and 22 medium bomber and 29 reconnaissance companies, with a personnel total of 33,000 officers and men.

UNIFORM As a branch of the Army, Japanese Air Service personnel wore Army uniforms with sky-blue arm-of-service colour which appeared on the zigzag breast badge, and on the collar patches, tunic and shoulder strap piping of Air Force cadets. Qualified pilots wore embroidered 'wings' on the right breast in the traditional manner.

The winter flying suit is worn by figure 316. The two-piece summer version was unlined. The only insignia worn on flying clothing were the badges of rank which were worn either on the breast or sleeve of the winter jacket, or on the collar of the summer jacket. Pilots' wings were also worn on the flying jacket.

316 Captain, Japanese Air Force, 1943
This fighter pilot wears the lined winter flying suit with rank badge on the left sleeve. He carries a short version of the tachi sword, which was symbolically carried in the aircraft. The parachute harness is the standard pattern. He is also armed with an 8mm M94 automatic pistol.

316

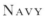

317 Commander, Japanese Navy, 1941
This officer wears the regulation peaked cap with embroidered cap badge and fur-lined watchcoat with badges of rank on the shoulder straps. The binoculars had a strap in different colours according to the rank group of the wearer: flag officers had gold, commanders white and lieutenants blue.

**318 Seaman 1st Class,
Japanese Navy, 1939**
This rating in landing rig wears the Navy pattern steel helmet with the anchor badge on the front which was replaced during the war by the standard Army pattern. With the basic square rig he wears infantry equipment and white canvas gaiters. Badges of rank are worn on the sleeve. The rifle is the 7.7mm M38 long rifle.

NAVY

By mid-1941 the Japanese Navy was finalising its plans for the Pacific war. Firstly, the US Pacific Fleet was to be knocked out and, at the same time, warships would support the Army's southwards drive to gain the oil and raw materials necessary for Japan's existence and military success in China. A defensive perimeter was to be established through the islands of South-East Asia and the Pacific; it was thought that the Americans would grow weary of battering at this impregnable screen.

When war was declared on the United States in December 1941 Japan had made several serious miscalculations. She had underestimated the will of the American people to fight a long, drawn-out war and had, perhaps, been overconfident of her own fighting ability, together with her wartime ship-building capacity. Although the Japanese Command had recognised that fast carrier strikes were the best strategic weapon for the Pacific war (shipboard and land-based aviation had

seen extensive service during the China campaign), her success at Pearl Harbor was somewhat lessened by her failure to destroy even one aircraft carrier.

During the initial run of Japanese victories, however, Allied forces in the Pacific had been building up and in April 1942 there were six American and three British aircraft carriers in the theatre against a Japanese total of ten. The Japanese attempt to isolate Australia in May 1942 in the battle of the Coral Sea was a failure and resulted in heavy losses among aircrew. The following month saw the battle of Midway and further disaster for the Japanese Fleet, which was severely mauled by carrier-based planes: four of her carriers were sunk for the loss of only one US Navy carrier.

The Japanese had lost superiority and naval operations now became concentrated in the South Pacific. After the heavy losses at Coral Sea, Midway and Guadalcanal the Navy began to run short of experienced pilots; squadrons were not rotated so that trainees did not learn from the experience of front-line pilots. An

extensive carrier construction programme was instigated, but Japanese industrial capability was not sufficient for this to change the course of the war. In April 1943 the Navy failed to regain air superiority in the South-West Pacific after launching a concerted offensive, a defeat which indicated the significance of better-trained American pilots flying new aeroplanes from the recently-introduced Essex-class carriers.

In June 1944 the Japanese launched an unsuccessful attack on US naval forces in the battle of the Philippine Sea; this resulted in the loss of around 300 aircraft and the sinking of three Japanese aircraft carriers. Shortly thereafter (in October) the Japanese Fleet finally ceased to exist as an important force in the war when, with the loss of four carriers, three battleships and ten cruisers in the Battle of Leyte Gulf, her surface fleet was destroyed.

Unable to accept the idea of defeat and with no proper defensive strategy, the Japanese Navy now wasted surviving aircrew in *kamikaze* attacks, achieving only a limited measure of success.

ORGANISATION As Prime Minister, General Hideki Tojo presided over Imperial General Headquarters (GHQ) which was split in two sections – Army and Navy. Holding positions at Imperial GHQ were the Navy Minister, Admiral Shigetaro, and the Chief of the Navy General Staff, Admiral Osami Nagano. Other officers and departments handled the responsibilities of staff and ministry.

Executing the naval instructions emanating from Imperial GHQ was the C-in-C of all seagoing warships. In 1941, this was Admiral Isoroku Yamamoto, and following his death in April 1943, his successors were Admiral Mineichi Koga, Admiral Soemu Toyoda (from March 1944) and Admiral Jisaburo Ozawa (from May 1945 to the end of the war).

In addition to the responsibility for implementing strategic moves generally, they were also expected to take tactical command of the most important operation in progress. Admiral Yamamoto flew his flag in the battleship *Nagato* until the superbattleship *Yamato* was commissioned on 16 December 1941. There was a constant restriction on radio communication whenever she put to sea, and at such crucial times, the C-in-C was out of touch with all but the immediate situation. From May to September 1944, the C-in-C's flagship was the *Oyodo*, a command cruiser for combined striking forces of submarines and aircraft. Although permanently anchored first in Tokyo and then in Hiroshima Bay, her communications facilities proved inadequate. The HQ of C-in-C Combined Fleet was finally located at Keio University in the Tokyo suburb of Hiyodashi.

As its name implies, the Combined Fleet (*Rengo Kantai*) was just that – the whole Navy. All other units, regardless of function or size, were designated as *tai* or *butai*, both of which could be translated as corps, force or body. The intelligence sections of other navies assigned the terms fleet, squadron and division for the purpose of description as appropriate.

It was customary for groups of smaller warships to be led by a bigger one. Thus four destroyers made up a division, four divisions a destroyer squadron, plus a cruiser as flagship. A somewhat similar organisation existed for submarines.

For administrative purposes, the Combined Fleet was divided into lesser fleets according to function. At the time of Pearl Harbor in December 1941, its approximate composition was as follows:
1st Fleet (the Battle Fleet) based at Hiroshima – 10 battleships, 3 seaplane carriers, 10 cruisers, 30 destroyers;
2nd Fleet (Scouting Fleet) based at Hainan – 13 cruisers, 32 destroyers;

3rd Fleet (Blockade and Transport) based at Formosa – 5 cruisers, 12 destroyers, 6 minelayers, 1 escort;
4th Fleet (the Pacific Mandated Islands) based at Truk – 4 cruisers, 1 seaplane carrier, 12 destroyers, 2 minelayers;
5th Fleet (Northern Waters) based at Maizuru/Ominato – 2 cruisers;
6th Fleet (Submarines) based at Kwajalein – 3 cruisers, 63 submarines;
Carrier Fleet based at Kure – 10 carriers.

In addition there were base forces located on the islands of Formosa, Truk, Palau, Saipan, Kwajalein, Maizuru and Ominato, and in Indo-China. These and other support units totalled 89 armed merchant cruisers, sub-chasers and patrol vessels, 6 minelayers, 42 minesweepers, 46 auxiliaries and 87 transports. All those which had started life as merchantmen retained their '*maru*' suffix, some being manned by civilian crews. Repair ships and transports had their own special flag.

Vessels did not all operate in these administrative groupings, but were allocated to whatever formation required their presence. Thus the Pearl Harbor strike force consisted of six vessels from the Carrier Fleet, and two battleships, two cruisers and a destroyer squadron from the Battle Fleet. The Southern Force, heading towards South-East Asia and the Philippines, comprised the whole of the 2nd and 3rd Fleets, plus battleships, cruisers and destroyers from the 1st Fleet, as well as submarines, some of which had been allocated to, and then detached from the 1st Fleet.

319 Rating, Japanese Navy, 1942
This rating is wearing the white rig which was worn for clean work, such as clerical and office duties. Note the single blue band around the cap, whereas all commissioned ranks had two blue bands.

320 Lieutenant, Japanese Navy, 1943
This officer wears the cap with white cover and regulation whites. Badges of rank were worn on the shoulder straps. On his left hip he carries an undress dirk which was suspended from a fabric belt worn under the tunic.

319   320

Every force had a scouting and a main body, which was quite separate from the 2nd or Scouting Fleet and from the Combined Fleet main body which concentrated at sea around the C-in-C's flagship. Sometimes these groupings were assembled before departure, sometimes they rendezvoused at sea, and sometimes their routes were so planned that the first time they sighted each other after crossing the ocean, the enemy would be in view.

Such detailed and complicated plans worked well when operating from the centre, as in the first six months of the war, but they could also go seriously awry as they did in the triple Coral Sea-Midway-Aleutians thrust.

Japanese Navy personnel totalled 291,359 in December 1941, rising to 1,663,223 in July 1945. Officers were trained at the Eta Jima Naval Academy. There was further training at various specialist schools, in particular at the main base area around Yokosuka, but it was the cadet's graduation position after three years at the Academy which determined his future career. Those with a first class grade were destined for Staff College and headquarters appointments; second grade – battleships and cruisers; third – destroyers; fourth – submarines; fifth – naval aviation. The sixth grade were regarded as virtual failures, given no further training and consigned to duties in auxiliary patrol and depot ships.

Probably the Japanese Navy's worst mistake was to ignore the merchant marine which in 1939 numbered 2337 vessels, totalling 5,629,845 tons. As indicated by the Eta Jima graduations, commerce protection was uninteresting, and fit only for the unintelligent. Admittedly, in 1939–40 there had been courses for training mercantile masters in Navy procedures, but they had not amounted to much. There was no preparation for a DEMS (defensively equipped merchant ships) organisation, nor was much attention paid to combating undersea warfare, whether in the form of mines or submarines. There was not even any convoy system, although the Japanese Navy had assisted in escorting convoys during World War I.

A further 4,250,000 tons of merchant shipping was built or acquired during World War II, but it still could not keep pace with the losses inflicted by American submarines. Convoys were begun in November 1943, and escort vessels laid down, but they were introduced too late and were still vulnerable to attack from submarines.

A total of 2346 merchant ships were sunk during the war, and most of the survivors were disabled or too small for

practical traffic, or were lying idle as Army or Navy transports.

Built to cooperate with the surface fleet, the Submarine Fleet was employed principally in scouting for the Battle Fleet, also deploying seaplanes and midget submarines against coastal targets from Madagascar to Oregon. There were a few notable occasions when submarines successfully interfered in the set-piece air-sea battles, but generally they did little to disrupt Allied supply lines.

Parallel with the warship organisation was the Directorate of Naval Aviation which, in 1941, was organised under Vice-Admiral Katagiri. The General Affairs Department was responsible for both shore-based and ship-borne units, while the Training Department arranged for nearly all training to be done in Japan by the Combined Air Training Command, principally at Kasumigara. The Technical Department prepared designs for new aircraft and equipment, and undertook their storage and repair at Navy air arsenals, including Yokosuka, Kasumigara, Hiro, Sasebo, Kanoya and

321

322

321 Officer, Japanese Navy, 1945
Like their counterparts in the US Navy, Japanese Navy personnel adopted khaki during the war. The Navy emblem appears on the front of the field cap and the two blue stripes denoted an officer.

322 Paratrooper, Japanese Navy Parachute Troops, 1942
The helmet is the steel pattern covered with canvas; this replaced the old fibre helmet which afforded no ballistic protection for the head. The overall was sometimes worn over the olive-drab naval khaki uniform. Clipped to the parachute harness is a special weapons container which held either firearms or a light mortar.

323 Sub-Lieutenant, Japanese Navy Air Service, 1945
This pilot wears the two-piece summer flying suit which was worn both by Army and Navy pilots. The form of rank badge illustrated was unusual, since most pilots either wore naval collar patches or one 'collar' patch on the breast or on the left sleeve. The Japanese Navy Air Service played a crucial role in the sea battles of the Pacific theatre which decided the course of the war. By 1945 the Air Service had few experienced pilots left.

alongside other Navy installations.

Apart from 370 training and reserve machines, the Japanese Naval Air Force totalled 1750 aircraft in 1941. There were 660 fighters (mainly the legendary Mitsubishi A6M Zero), 330 carrier-borne strike aircraft, 240 twin-engined shore-based torpedo-bombers specifically intended for fleet cooperation, and 520 flying boats and seaplanes. It was standard procedure for floatplanes to be catapulted from cruisers for fleet reconnaissance, thus allowing the strike carriers to be freed from that task.

All these aircraft were organised in the Combined Air Fleet, based at Kanoya, and were subdivided into the 1st Air Fleet (the Carrier Fleet) and the 11th Air Fleet (under Vice-Admiral Nishizo Tsukuhura) shore-based in Formosa and Indo-China. The fleets were further divided into air flotillas (each commanded by a rear-admiral), which were themselves composed of two or more air groups. Each air group comprised a base unit and 12 to 36 aircraft with 4 to 12 in reserve, depending on size. The combat formation was the air division of about nine aeroplanes.

Below left: The colour party of a Japanese naval detachment marches through the streets of Osaka before embarkation to the Front in China.

Below centre: A Japanese naval recruit is issued with his uniform.

Below right: A Navy pilot, complete with life-jacket, helps prepare a Kawanishi E7K2 floatplane.

NAVY LAND FORCES

There were no such thing as 'marines' in the Japanese armed forces until after the First World War. Under the *ad hoc* tradition of the Japanese Army, if amphibious operations were imminent, naval landing groups were improvised for individual missions. Every Navy recruit received training in land as well as naval warfare. If a recruit showed any aptitude for this and showed any special skills, such as proficiency with a machine gun or the ability to drive, they were noted on his file for future reference. The fleet commander would nominate several ships to provide troops for amphibious operations and from these crews assault groups were organised. Needless to say, the military training of these sailors was scanty and their casualties heavy. In the 1920s the Japanese Navy began to experiment with special naval landing forces in an attempt to overcome these heavy losses of highly trained naval personnel. These were permanent units and were first used in China in 1932. During World War II they became increasingly involved in the defence of Japan's island bases. To further this defence, the Japanese Navy developed several other land formations: the base force, the ground force, the pioneers and the engineering and construction units. These formations never matched the excellence of US engineers, however.

The special naval landing forces usually stayed in the areas they seized as garrisons. When unopposed their efficiency was high, but their tactical skills were mediocre

323

324

when opposed. At first they were organised
into battalions of about 2000 men of four
companies. The first three companies
were divided into six rifle platoons and one
heavy machine gun platoon. The last
company, the fourth, was composed of
three rifle platoons and a heavy weapons
platoon which was equipped with four
3-inch naval guns and two 75mm regimental guns and two 70mm battalion
guns. Depending on circumstances they
might be supported with tank or armoured
car units. On the outbreak of war they
were used to seize small islands like Wake,
and were used as spearheads by the Army
against Java and Rabaul. In these operations they might be used as mobile
striking forces. They would be employed

with two rifle companies (each with its
own machine-gun platoon) and one or
two companies of heavy weapons in
formations of 1200–1500 men. They might
also include special supporting troops,
engineers, ordnance and signals. Once
Japan lost the initiative in the Pacific these
forces had to adapt to defensive warfare,
particularly when the Army refused to
defend some islands, claiming that they
were a Navy responsibility. Consequently,
formations were adapted to meet this
change. A typical example was the
Yokosaka 7th Special Naval Landing
Force. When first used at the beginning of
the war, this formation had no infantry
for defensive purposes and no heavy
defensive weapons. By 1943 the platoon

**324 Leading Seaman,
Japanese Navy, 1942**

*Japanese Marines took a very active part in the
combined operations during the Japanese offensive in
the Pacific. Marines were distinguished by the olive-
green colour of their khaki uniforms and by black
leather footwear, and other minor differences in
clothing and equipment. Rank badges are worn on the
right sleeve. This Marine is protected by a bullet-
proof vest and is armed with a Swiss 7.63mm sub-
machine gun which was modified by the Japanese.
The rank badges conform to the old style (as compared
to the new style on page 187).*

*Right: Japanese Marines watch the bombardment
of the city of Manila in the spring of 1942. The
fall of Manila was one of the stepping-stones of
Japan's conquest of the Philippines. This
reconnaissance detachment is wearing the regulation
Marine uniform of olive-drab with cloth covers
over their helmets. The bugler in the centre of the
picture is armed with the M98 Arisaka rifle, as are
most of the other Marines. In contrast to the
Marine illustrated above (figure 324) these
soldiers are wearing puttees (and not the black
leather boots and leggings).*

JAPANESE NAVY INSIGNIA

Collar | Shoulder | Cuff

Admiral · Vice-Admiral · Rear-Admiral · Captain (Aviation) · Commander (Pay Branch) · Lieutenant-Commander (Surgeon) · Lieutenant (Engineers) · Sub-Lieutenant (Construction) · Ensign · Midshipman · Cadet · Warrant Officer

Cap Badge Officers

Arm

CPO (Line) · PO 1st Cl (I) (Aviation) · PO 2nd Cl (II) (Medical) · Leading Seaman (I) (Justice) · Leading Seaman (II) (Construction) · Able Seaman (Pay) · *Cap Badge* M'shipman · *Cap Badge* PO s · *Field Cap Badge* (Aviation) · Fighter Pilot s Badge · Bomber Pilot's Badge

rather than the company had become the basic tactical unit and its artillery component had been greatly increased.

UNIFORM Of all the navies of the great powers, Japan's was the youngest and the uniforms worn by its personnel were basically the same as those introduced when the Navy was first formed at the end of the last century. To the pre-war navy blue and white uniforms were added those in various shades of khaki.

Officers wore the peaked cap with embroidered cap badge and undress tunic with stand collar which was trimmed with black lace. On the cuffs rank distinction lace was in black. This tunic was worn with matching trousers and black shoes and socks. In winter officers wore various kinds of double-breasted watch and greatcoats (figure 317). In summer or in tropical waters officers wore the white uniform illustrated by figure 320, which much resembled that of other navies.

Chief petty officers wore the peaked cap with special badge, single-breasted tunic in navy blue or white with five gilt metal buttons in front. It was worn with matching long trousers and black shoes and socks.

Ratings wore the square rig illustrated by figure 318. The basic head-dress was the round sailor's cap with silk tally on which appeared Japanese characters. The matching trousers were worn with either black leather footwear or white socks and sandals. The white version of the square rig was identical in cut to the navy blue one. The dress version was worn with the blue denim collar and was trimmed with blue denim. The working whites were plain, but ratings also received a one-piece white overall.

During the war the Japanese Navy received a peaked field cap in navy blue, white or khaki, which was identical in shape to the Army pattern. The anchor badge on the front was in yellow on the navy blue and khaki caps, and light blue on the white cap.

Sailors serving on land during the war wore a field uniform made of olive-drab cotton drill. The colour was more similar to that worn by American Marines than to the uniform of the Japanese Army. A typical Japanese Marine in service dress is illustrated by figure 324. Officers wore brown leather equipment and short black leather boots. Navy parachute troops wore the uniform illustrated by figure 322.

A khaki drill uniform consisting of field cap, short sleeve shirt with left breast pocket, open necked single-breasted tunic with patch breast and side pockets, and either short or long trousers was introduced during the war for Navy personnel.

INSIGNIA Officers wore their rank badges on the collar and sometimes on the tunic lapels. Shoulder straps were only worn on the white tunic and various kinds of greatcoat. They were occasionally worn on the khaki tunic.

On the peaked field cap officers had one or two stripes (yellow on blue and blue on white and khaki caps) according to rank. Originally ratings had one stripe and officers two, but this was changed so that ratings had no stripes, lieutenants one, and captains two stripes. From January 1944 officers began to wear one to three narrow lace rings above one to three cherry blossoms on the cuffs of both the blue and khaki tunics.

Ratings wore rate badges on the sleeves. The first pattern was in red on the blue uniform, and light blue on the white uniform. These were replaced by a new pattern (see rank insignia chart) in yellow on blue backing, worn on all uniforms.

The branch was indicated by the emblem which appeared in red on a circular blue badge on the right sleeve. On white uniforms the emblem was in light blue. On the new pattern rate badge the colour of the cherry blossom indicated the branch of the wearer. Officers in certain branches had coloured piping on the collar patches, shoulder straps, and possibly also on the bottom of the peaked cap band.

JAPANESE ALLIES

With the exception of the Indian National Army, the Japanese were not very enthusiastic about recruiting non-Japanese to do their fighting for them, and although Japan occupied vast territories she never really attempted to raise coherent military units from amongst the subject peoples. Most units raised from foreigners were employed in construction work, or, as in the case of the White Russians from Harbin in Manchuria, were formed into small units for clandestine operations behind enemy lines. The intense martial code of the Japanese was ill-suited to other nationalities.

Below: Supplies are handed out to troops of the Indian National Army who have just deserted from the Japanese. The reliability of the INA was always questionable and during the course of the war they proved more a liability than an asset to the Japanese. The soldiers here are shown wearing their old regular Indian Army uniforms and equipment.

INDIAN
NATIONAL ARMY

The Indian National Army (INA), inspired by the goal of achieving independence for India from British rule, was raised in January 1942 at Kuala Lumpur. Its recruits were Indian prisoners of war, some only hours out of battle, enlisted by Captain (later General) Mohan Singh, previously of the 14th Punjab Regiment. With the fall of Singapore in February 1942 there were approximately 55,000 Indian POWs available to Mohan Singh and about 20,000 joined the INA in its first months of existence. A further 20,000 POWs enlisted in the summer of 1942 largely as a means of escaping the deprivations of prison-camp life and the brutal treatment handed out to those who stood firm in their allegiance to the British. Some Indian and Gurkha troops joined simply in order to return to a battlefront from which they could regain the British lines, while others joined to sabotage the INA from within. In general very few recruits were pro-Japanese.

In September 1942 one poorly equipped division was formed with three guerrilla units – the Gandhi, Nehru, and Azad Regiments – and three infantry battalions, the No. 1 Hindi Field Force Group. Supporting units included artillery, motorised, engineer, signal, and transport companies, a reinforcement group, and a medical unit with hospital. A second division was planned but in December disagreements with the Japanese led to an

325 Senior NCO,
Indian National Army, 1942
This havildar of the Indian National Army wears the old Indian Army khaki drill uniform with a khaki turban. The rank of this soldier is identified by the cloth coloured stripes on the shoulder straps. No arms are being carried except for the regulation British bayonet.

326 1st Sergeant, Chinese Army, 1942
The sergeant shown here is unusually well equipped for the Chinese Army, whose members were normally badly supplied. This NCO is part of the presidential guard. He wears a German helmet, and his rank is indicated by the three gold triangles on the blue stripe. The khaki uniform is the regulation woollen field service dress with a stand and fall collar and patch pockets on the tunic. Above the left breast pocket is an identification patch bordered in red arm-of-service colour for the infantry. Well equipped, this soldier is armed with the 7.63mm Mauser semi-automatic pistol complete with wooden holster acting here as a butt extension (just visible below his left hand). Used by the German Army in World War I, the Mauser was modified post-war to take a 20-round magazine and a wooden stock and it was this version that proved popular with the Chinese warlords.

326

Japanese uniforms were also issued. On the left side of the side cap was worn a brass cap badge in the shape of a map of India with the letters INA.

INSIGNIA Badges of rank were worn on the shoulder straps which were usually in khaki cloth. NCOs had one to three stripes across the shoulder strap, company officers one to three stripes above the letters INA, field officers one to three stripes surmounted by an eight-pointed star above the letters INA (all in metallic thread embroidery), and general officers one to three bars surmounted by crossed sabres with an eight-pointed star above, once again all in metallic thread embroidery.

BURMESE NATIONAL ARMY

The Minaimi Organisation in Burma was founded in February 1940. Its 50 members carried out clandestine operations in aid of the Burma Independence Movement. With the beginning of the war in the Far East these men provided the cadre for the Burma Independence Army which, by the time Burma had been overrun by the Japanese, had a strength of 50,000 men which rose to about 200,000. But Japanese occupation policies so disillusioned the BIA that it became a centre for opposition to the Japanese and was disbanded.

The Japanese then formed the Burma Defence Army which was organised in seven infantry battalions, and artillery and miscellaneous units. By April 1943 its strength was about 55,000 men.

On 15 September 1943 the BDA was renamed the Burma National Army (*Bama Tatmadaw*), but it was still only used for garrison duties. By the autumn of 1944 a resistance movement had developed and in March 1945 first the BNA in Mandalay and then the rest of the Army changed sides. On 30 April 1945 the BNA was reorganised by the British as the Patriotic Burmese Forces.

UNIFORM AND INSIGNIA The Burmese forces fighting for the Japanese never found a standardised pattern of uniform and insignia, but wore a variety of British, Japanese and native dress, depending on what was available.

From 1938 Koreans were allowed to enlist for military service, but were mainly used as labourers in Army and Navy construction corps. In 1944 Koreans were subject to conscription by the Japanese.

In May 1939 the Japanese recruited a number of Mongolian cavalrymen who served alongside Japanese cavalry units

under Japanese officers. The Manchurian Army proper in 1939 had a strength of some 75,000 men in infantry and cavalry units. The Mongolian Navy was stationed on the Amur and Sungari rivers which it patrolled with eight large and six small river gunboats.

The puppet government established at Nanking in China was allowed to raise its own forces; these were of dubious reliability and fluctuated in size. Although local disputes often took precedence over national issues, few Chinese fought for the Japanese.

In Sumatra, a force of about five to six thousand men was formed for coastal defence. Many of the men had previously served in the Netherlands East India Army, and seventeen Indonesians were trained in the Imperial Japanese Military Academy.

The Japanese allowed the Malays to form a volunteer force of some 2000 men in early 1944. Some personnel had uniforms and captured British firearms. By March 1944 this so-called Volunteer Corps had a strength of about 5000 men and was used for coastal defence and the maintenance of public order. One Malay graduated from the Imperial Japanese Military Academy.

On 8 December 1943 'General' Artemio Ricarte formed the Patriotic League of Filipinos with about 4000 members who were used on guard and construction duties. Both qualified instructors and arms were in short supply. This was followed by a security force of 300 men, also under Ricarte's command, which provided the personnel for his Guard.

In the other occupied territories various forces were raised: a force of some 1300 Dyaks was formed in 1944 for security duties in North Borneo, for example, and in March 1944 the Japanese formed an Indo-Chinese *Giyutai* of about 3000 men.

The Java Defence Volunteer Army was formed on Java, since the Japanese had only very limited forces there with which to resist an expected invasion. By November 1944, there were 66 battalions with about 33,000 men on Java and three battalions with about 1500 men on Bali, although the Japanese did not recruit in the Christian areas from where the Netherlands East India Army had traditionally acquired its indigenous troops.

Another 50,000 men were formed into a Moslem para-military training organisation (*Hizbullah*), but its weaponry was seldom more sophisticated than sharpened bamboos. There were a number of other para-military organisations and groups with a total membership in the region of one and a half million men, but they did not play any significant role in the war.

80 per cent reduction in the strength of the INA as many of its personnel requested that they should be allowed to revert to the status of POWs. Only with the arrival from Germany of Subhas Chandra Bose, the head of the Provisional Government of Free India, did the appeal of the INA begin to achieve any enduring foundation. Bose had already formed the Free India Legion in Germany from 2500 POWs in Annaburg Camp near Dresden.

Bose persuaded the Japanese to bring the INA's second division to a state of operational readiness and he secured permission for the establishment of a third division. The 1st Division was deployed between January–June 1944 in support of the Japanese offensives in the Arakan and against Kohima and Imphal. Of the 7000 men who joined the operations in the Imphal plain only 2600 survived the fighting and subsequent retreat.

UNIFORM The INA wore either Indian Army khaki drill uniforms with puggree or field service side cap in khaki cloth.

CHINA
ARMY

The seizure of Mukden on 19 September 1931 marked the beginning of overt Japanese aggression against China, and from 1937 there was open war. The disorganised Chinese forces were no match on the battlefield for the Japanese armies, but determined resistance prevented a complete collapse. The very size of China precluded a total Japanese victory, and although the Chinese Nationalist government was forced to abandon the major industrial areas and set up a new capital at Chunking, it maintained the struggle, and, in alliance with the communist forces of Mao Tse-tung, tied down enormous numbers of Japanese troops.

Left: A light field gun (a US 75mm howitzer) is brought into action at an engagement late in the war. Short of arms and equipment the generals of the Chinese Nationalist Army placed great value upon artillery, not so much for military reasons but for the prestige it bestowed.

327 Private,
Chinese Nationalist Army, 1942
This soldier wears blue quilted winter uniform, with white stockings and plimsoll-type shoes secured with string or tapes. His personal equipment was made largely of cotton or canvas and secured with ribbons or string. He carries small-arms ammunition in a cotton bandolier round his shoulders and waist, stick-type German grenades in canvas pockets round his neck and a captured Japanese gas mask and helmet.

327

328

328 Colonel,
Chinese Nationalist Army, 1942

The ski-type khaki peaked cap of this Nationalist infantry officer carries the Chinese cockade. The collar patches in the red arm-of-service colour bear the three triangles of a colonel, while his service dress is completed by the ubiquitous Sam Browne belt. The uniform of this colonel, like that of figure 326, has a distinctly German feel reflecting the German involvement in the building-up of the Chinese Army in the 1920s and early '30s. Footwear is European in style and consists of brown leather ankle boots and knee-length leggings.

329 Private,
Chinese Nationalist Army, 1944

Re-equipped and re-clothed by the Allies in Northern Burma, this Chinese infantryman wears British khaki drill uniform, woollen knitted sweater and 1937 webbing equipment. Woollen puttees are worn in typically Chinese fashion, rolled up to the knee, with light plimsoll-type footwear. He carries a water bottle in a Japanese-type web holder and wears an American M1 steel helmet. His rifle is an American 'Enfield' Cal.30 M1917. The 'Enfield' rifle was first issued to United States troops during World War I but was replaced by the Garand M1 before World War II; surplus stock was sent to arm America's allies including the British (see figure 69) and the Chinese Army.

ORGANISATION Central power was represented by the Generalissimo, Chiang Kai-shek, who presided over the National Military Council, but a unified control proved elusive. Chiang's forces were commanded by men who had distinguished themselves by loyalty to the Generalissimo – and not by feats on the field of battle. Obsequiousness, and not valour, was the secret of a successful military career in Nationalist China. There were 12 war areas and these received their instructions from Chiang and his Council through a chief of staff, General Ho Yin-chin. Such military operations as were undertaken were concentrated on one war area at a time.

The prospect of action was not greeted with any enthusiasm locally because the war lords often doubled as provincial governors as well as military commanders and the expenditure of military force detracted from their local political power *vis-à-vis* neighbouring war lords. Military operations received little support from central authority in Chungking because if a provincial governor fought a successful

campaign, he might feel sufficiently powerful to challenge the power of the Generalissimo. To prevent this from happening, Chiang kept loyal divisions in the rear of the war areas to ensure the continued co-operation of the provincial governors. Consequently, there was no central strategic reserve, and the scattered distribution of military power contributed to the growth of petty satrapies of provincial power which, in turn, contributed to the spiral of inefficiency which reacted on any effort to drive the Japanese back and restore the power of central government. Each area commander recruited, trained, and (in so far as it was possible) equipped his own men. If the Japanese attacked one area, then the National Military Council would try to coordinate its defence.

A Chinese Nationalist Division was a heterogeneous organisation with considerable potential; but as an American report

Below: Chinese- and American-crewed M3A3 Stuart light tanks advance down the Ledo road against Japanese-held positions.

329

CHINESE ARMY/AIR FORCE INSIGNIA

Cap Badge
National cockade for all ranks
of Army and Air Force

Cap Badge
Air Force Officers

Cap Badge
Air Force NCOs

Collar Wings
Alternative designs for
Air Force Officers

Collar Army

Cuff Air Force

General — Lieutenant-General — Major-General — Colonel (MP/Finance) — Lieutenant-Colonel (Medical) — Major (Transport) — Captain (Engineers) — Lieutenant (Artillery) — 2nd Lieut (Infantry)

Collar Army

Warrant Officer — Sergeant-Major — Sergeant — Corporal — Superior Private — Private 1st Class — Private 2nd Class — Pilot's Wings

on the Chinese Army in 1941 observed it was ill-equipped, poorly trained and quite inefficient. The nominal strength of such a division was 9529 officers and men. Most divisions averaged only 6000–7000 men, and others were even weaker. They lacked heavy equipment and an efficient supply system was conspicuous by its absence. It had no artillery or heavy weapons because Chiang hoarded the 800 pieces of Chinese artillery so that he could allot a well-behaved war lord some pieces for continued loyalty; thus they were never used effectively in large numbers.

Chinese divisions normally relied upon trench mortars for artillery support, and a reasonably equipped division would field anything from 18 to 30 of these weapons. Firepower was supplemented on paper by 324 light and heavy machine guns (7.92 mm) – though the average number was 200 light and 36 heavy machine guns per division. Because Chinese divisional commanders looked upon their formations as their private property, American aid had little impact on relative inefficiency because once new weapons arrived, they were immediately impounded by the commanding officer and hoarded.

It is an indication of the level of corruption in China that she received between March 1941 and October 1945 $631,509,000 worth of aid, but nothing like an efficient force was ever permanently established.

In nomenclature Chinese divisions resembled the Japanese (and, therefore, the German) system rather than the American. Chinese divisions were arranged in a triangular structure. There were three regiments to a division, but there was no army corps. This was replaced by a land army of three divisions and three of these armies formed a group army – a force which resembled a Western army. On average, each war lord had three group armies at his disposal. Chiang had a total of 3,819,000 men under arms by the end of 1942. 2,919,000 of these were formed into 246 divisions, employed as 'front line' troops, plus 44 brigades (a loose term applied to miscellaneous military formations). In the rear areas there were another 70 divisions and three brigades with a total strength of approximately 900,000 men. In addition, Chiang had another 30 divisions under his personal command to ensure the loyalty of his war area commanders and to keep a watchful eye on the activities of the communists. Against the Japanese he fielded something like 300 divisions. This alignment was only theoretical, however, because serious fighting was not contemplated.

In October 1942 Lieutenant-General Joseph W. Stilwell was appointed Chiang's co-Chief of Staff. In trying to create an efficient fighting force he was faced with insuperable difficulties that

would have taxed the talents of a more tactful and patient man than he. Political and social factors determined which troops fought in which theatres.

Stilwell enthusiastically supported the so-called 'Thirty Division Plan' which attempted to circumvent the usual restraints on Chinese efficiency by allotting 30 divisions for re-training at American training schools and giving these troops the best American equipment; Stilwell planned to use these troops in Burma. Chiang at first seemed to favour the plan and 20 divisions were initially made available to take part in the scheme. The 5th and 6th Armies were also placed under Stilwell's command in Burma. But Chiang gradually turned against the idea because of the dangers of placing such an efficient force under Chinese officers.

Stilwell was ordered not to use his forces offensively, and when he received copies of the orders being sent out from Chungking, he discovered that all the Chinese commanders from Siam to Indo-China were being instructed to stay on the defensive and await an American victory in the Pacific War – the basis of Chiang's strategy throughout World War II.

UNIFORM Between 1937 and 1945 Chinese uniforms underwent a number of changes. Both the Nationalist and communist armies suffered great shortages of clothing and equipment and had to make do with home or locally made items, so that uniformity was never very extensive and uniforms could vary considerably from region to region, army to army, and year to year.

Initially Germany had been instrumental in organising, training and equipping the Chinese Army, and this fact becomes obvious when one looks at figure 326. However, this shows a member of an élite guard unit, and more typical are figures 327 and 328. Uniforms in khaki drill and blue, which faded to grey, were worn concurrently, and during the bitter winters in central and northern China, it was the blue padded uniform which became the most typical form of uniform.

INSIGNIA Badges of rank were worn on the collar (see rank insignia chart). The collar patches were originally made of cloth, but during the war metal and plastic patches were most common. The colour of the collar patches differed according to the arm of service. On the left breast soldiers wore a cotton label on which was printed in black characters the soldier's name and unit. Some labels had a border in the arm-of-service colour.

AIR FORCE

During the 1930s, the Chinese Air Force was composed largely of foreign volunteers, at first Americans but later Italians.

330   **331**

330 1st Lieutenant, Chinese Nationalist Air Force, 1943
The gilt badge on the left breast of this Chinese officer identifies him as a pilot. His officer's peaked service cap with light khaki band bears a winged badge which, in other ranks, was white. The cuff markings are those of a 1st lieutenant. Non-flyers wore blossoms instead of eagle badges.

331 Pilot, American Volunteer Group, 1941
Enrolled in the Chinese Air Force as civilians, US personnel wore an amalgam of American and Chinese uniform. The US peaked service cap with light khaki crown bears the Chinese Air Force officers' cap badge. The zip-fronted flying jacket is very similar to the US Army tankman's windcheater, with the Nationalist emblem on the left breast. The patch (inset left) was sewn onto the back of the jacket and instructed any Chinese to safeguard the pilot should he force land or bale out. The pistol in his shoulder holster is the US Cal.45 Model 1911A1, a very powerful military pistol.

Right: Chinese ground crew work on a US-supplied Curtiss P-40 of the 76th Fighter Group at Kunming. Clothing is a mixture of native Chinese and American government issue.

By 1937 the strength of the Air Force stood at 500 aircraft, but few of these were serviceable, and the remainder were destroyed by the Japanese in the air battles of 1937.

Chiang Kai-shek and his wife Madame Chiang called for further foreign aid to form an international force to fight the Japanese. At first an international squadron was established of mixed membership, mainly British, American and Dutch pilots. It only had 36 aircraft and had been destroyed by 1938. The international squadron was replaced by six Russian squadrons, two of bombers and four of fighters provided under a clause of the Sino-Soviet Non-Aggression Pact of 1937. The Russian force was totally self-contained and provided all its own supplies and ground crew. It allowed the Chinese Air Force to regroup in the north around Kunming and the Russians sent it 400 aircraft, and a number of new and more efficient flying schools were set up. The kernel of the postwar Chinese Air Force was very largely Russian-trained.

Although efficient, this Russian contribution was too small to provide an overall air defence of China, and in January 1939 after extensive Japanese raids on Chungking, Madame Chiang searched for reinforcements. The American Volunteer Group (AVG) filled the

breach. In October 1940 Major-General Mao Pang-tzo, the Director of the Operations Branch of the Chinese Air Force, was sent to the United States to buy aircraft. Though the Chinese wanted 650, they eventually got 100 P-40s discarded by the British. The recruitment of pilots was much more difficult. Chennault enthusiastically agreed to head the AVG. To get round the Neutrality Acts two corporations were set up as go-betweens, the Central Aircraft Manufacturing Company (CAMCO) and China Defence Supplies. All AVG recruits were considered as 'employees' of CAMCO, and General Chennault was named as their 'supervisor'.

In June 1941 the AVG consisted of 100 pilots and 150 mechanics. The following month the AVG was allotted 269 new fighters and 66 bombers and a scheme was considered to extend the AVG to a second group equipped with Hudson bombers, though the entry of the US into the war after Pearl Harbor pre-empted this.

The opening of the official war against Japan found the AVG in the midst of its worst crisis. The cumulative strain of countless missions, a sense of isolation and lack of adequate equipment – the neglect and incompetence of Chinese ground crews ruined most of their aircraft – led to a catastrophic drop in the morale of

AVG pilots and 24 resigned. Chennault persuaded all but four of these to withdraw their resignations or face charges of desertion. But this kind of disagreement poisoned the atmosphere of the AVG and when it was absorbed into the China-America Task Force, commanded by Chennault in July 1942, only a handful volunteered to join the USAAF. The CATF inherited 57 fighters from the AVG. In turn the CATF was absorbed into the 14th US Air Force in 1943 as China's main air defence.

UNIFORM Since they formed part of the Army, Air Force personnel wore khaki uniforms. Those officers undergoing training abroad, or forming part of a military mission wore the uniform illustrated by figure 330, but the majority of officers wore whatever items of Army uniform they could find, and in general were not as well-dressed.

Other ranks wore Army uniforms. In hot weather all ranks wore the field cap with khaki shirt and shorts, or overalls.

Aircrew and ground crew wore various kinds of flying suits and overalls either of Chinese manufacture, purchased from the United States, or taken from the Japanese. Americans serving with the Chinese Air Force wore the uniform illustrated by figure 331.

CHINESE NAVY INSIGNIA

Cap Peaks

Shoulder

Cuff

Admiral — Vice-Admiral (Engineering) — Rear-Adml (Major-Gen. Flying Branch) — Commodore — Captain (Navigation) — Commander — Lieutenant-Commander (Medical) — Lieutenant — Lieutenant jg (II) (Shipbuilding) — Ensign

Arm

Warrant Officer (Line) — Petty Officer 1st Class (I) — Petty Officer 2nd Class (II) — Petty Officer 3rd Class (III) — Seaman — Seaman Apprentice — Seaman Recruit — Trainee 1st Class — Trainee 2nd Class

INSIGNIA Air Force personnel wore the sunburst badge on their head-dress, and sometimes the same badge was worn on the service dress or flying jacket. Rank badges were worn on the sleeves by officers and on the collar patches by other ranks.

NAVY

In 1937 the Chinese Navy was very small by Western standards and totalled 59 vessels. The largest vessels were six light cruisers, none of which exceeded 3600

Below: Two high-ranking Chinese Navy officers confer with their British counterparts. Their rank insignia is clearly visible in this picture.

tons. Supporting these were 30 gunboats and a miscellaneous collection of 23 gunboats, sloops and transport vessels. Most of these were sunk in the Yangtze, at Shanghai, Tsingtao and Canton during the Japanese attacks of 1937 and fell easy victim to Japanese bombing and artillery fire. Some vessels that were beached were salvaged and repaired by the Japanese, but for all intents and purposes the Chinese Navy had ceased to exist. The great stream of Lend-Lease aid was diverted (when it did not find its way into the pockets of the generals) into military rather than naval uses. In 1945 it was discovered that one torpedo boat and 13 river gunboats were still operating. Five of these gunboats were former

British, American and French craft, transferred when their Western crews had crossed overland from Burma.

UNIFORM The Navy of the Chinese Republic received a standardised Naval uniform in 1913, which followed closely the European pattern.

The uniform for officers is illustrated by figure 332. The greatcoat was double-breasted and was worn with shoulder straps. Summer whites were in the same cut as the Navy blue uniform.

Ratings wore the traditional square rig with British-style cap. The white version of the jumper had blue denim cuffs.

Badges of rank are illustrated in the rank badge chart.

332 Commander, Chinese Nationalist Navy, 1943

Based in London as Chinese Naval Attaché, Commander Chow Ying-tsung wears a single-breasted tunic with concealed fly fastening, trimmed at the edges and collar with black lace.

332

333

COMMUNIST FORCES

In north China, the communist forces of Mao Tse-tung were the main opponents of the Japanese. Like the Nationalists, however, they preferred to maintain a low level of operations, saving themselves for the coming struggle for the control of China. After Pearl Harbor, they decided that Japanese defeat was inevitable, and in any case the major communist offensive of the war up to 1941 (the 'Hundred Regiments' Campaign' of 1940) had been very costly.

ORGANISATION After the losses of the Long March, communist forces had begun operations against the Nationalists from their new base in Yenan in 1936, but in 1937 a truce was patched up to meet the Japanese menace, and the three communist Front Armies under Chu Teh were designated the 8th Route Army; this had an official strength of 45,000 men but was probably 80,000-strong, including guerrillas. After the losses of the 'Hundred Regiments' Campaign', the communists set about expanding their forces and creating a tightly knit army. By the end of 1943, the 8th Route Army was probably 325,000 men strong, of whom two-thirds were guerrillas, but the core was the regular force, which had a very precise structure. The basic organisation was quite standard: three squads (each of 10 to 16 men) made up a platoon; three platoons a company (with its administrative troops about 120 men strong);

three companies a battalion; three battalions a regiment; three regiments a division and three divisions an army. Support weapons were whatever was available, and the communist forces were woefully lacking in machine guns and artillery until the Japanese surrender.

The cohension of this ill-equipped army was enormous, however. The basic squad of 10 to 16 men was composed of three small teams, and the team leaders were often either members or aspirant members of the Communist Party. The platoon leader was invariably a member of the Party. This arrangement cemented loyalty at a very basic level, and was to give the communists a priceless advantage.

In April 1945, Chu Teh, the communist commander, addressing the 7th Party Congress, claimed a total of 910,000 regulars, organised in the 8th Route Army, the New 4th Army, the South China Anti-Japanese Column and the Anti-Japanese Allied Forces. He estimated that two and a half million communist guerrillas were operational.

UNIFORM Chinese communist troops wore the same khaki uniforms as the Nationalists, and, while they were united against the Japanese, they wore the same 'white sun and blue sky' emblem and rank badges. Once civil war broke out again, however, the communists began to replace the army field cap by either a round peaked cloth cap or the so-called 'Mao cap', on the front of which was sometimes worn the five-pointed red star.

**333 Guerrilla,
Communist Chinese Forces, 1944**

This representative Chinese guerrilla wears a rudimentary bandolier fashioned from cotton or canvas, in which is stored the small-arms calibre ammunition for his Chinese-made 'Chiang Kai-shek' rifle. Also of note are the two easily-accessible stick-type grenades slung over the shoulders of his blue jacket. Communist guerrillas often wore a red star on the front of their caps, but this was by no means invariable. Diversity rather than uniformity was the order of the day amongst the Chinese communist armies of World War II.

Right: Chinese communist regular troops stand on guard over captured Japanese Type 97 medium tanks. The Type 97 with a top speed of 25 mph and a 57 mm gun was the mainstay of Japan's tank force and although not comparable with the armoured vehicles of the European theatre, was a considerable bonus for the Chinese communist forces. Often short of equipment and heavy armament, the communists made up for this with the discipline of their organisations. The soldiers depicted here with padded jackets and trousers are well equipped for the cold Chinese winter which could bring military operations to a virtual halt.

GREAT BRITAIN

ARMY

The troops fighting in Burma considered themselves to be the 'Forgotten Army' of the Allied war effort, and theirs was arguably the toughest campaign, certainly in terms of terrain and climate, in which British units were engaged in the whole of the war. Supply and medical problems assumed an importance which at times relegated actual battle to a secondary consideration, while the enemy they fought made up for an inadequate logistical system with a ferocity and tenacity of purpose seldom equalled.

The campaign in the Far East fell into three main phases: first the loss of Hong Kong and Malaya and the retreat from Burma; secondly a period of defensive consolidation with minor offensive operations in the Arakan and the deployment of Chindit columns, and thirdly a victorious advance through Burma. The initial period of defeat owed much to the deployment of inadequate forces, to an underestimation of the enemy and of the problems of jungle warfare, and to the process of milking units of their experienced officers and NCOs in order to provide a cadre for new formations.

When the Japanese attacked, the long argument between the three British services over the strategic deployment of their forces still rumbled in the background. Despite the creation of a new appointment of Commander-in-Chief, Far East in November 1940, the defence was still far from adequately coordinated. There were two commanders-in-chief in Singapore; General Officers Commanding in Burma, Malaya, and Hong Kong who reported to the War Office, and the Governors of Hong Kong, Burma, and the Straits Settlements who were responsible to the Colonial Office. The forces in India were controlled by their own commander-in-chief who was not made responsible for the defence of Burma until 12 December 1941. The sphere of command was further complicated by the creation of the ABDA (American-British-Dutch-Australian) theatre command spanning the South-West Pacific area on 4 January 1942.

ORGANISATION The main deployments of British troops in the Far East, outside India, were in Malaya, Singapore, Ceylon, Burma, and Hong Kong. The two battalions forming the North China garrison at Shanghai had been withdrawn in August 1940. The forces in Malaya

included three British infantry battalions in Singapore Fortress and one battalion in each of three Indian infantry brigades (6th, 12th and 15th). There were two infantry battalions in the garrison of Hong Kong serving with the Mainland and Island Infantry Brigades under Headquarters China Command. The two British battalions in Burma could muster only two companies each in December 1941 and they were deployed in 1st Burma Brigade and the Rangoon Garrison.

Reinforcements of British troops did arrive in Malaya and Burma, notably the 18th Infantry Division and the 7th Armoured Brigade (with only two of its three regiments). Of the 38 battalions defending Singapore until its surrender, 13 were wholly British. The forces which retreated nearly 1000 miles across the length of Burma were organised as Burcorps, comprising two divisions – 1st Burma and 17th Indian Infantry and in April 1942 they included approximately 13,700 British troops, with detachments from the Empire and the Dominions.

334

335

334 Lance-Corporal, British Army, 1945

With his new boots round his neck, this infantryman stands in jungle-green twill shirt and felt bush hat with light khaki puggree. The hat also bears the formation sign of the 19th Indian ('Dagger') Division – divisional signs were only worn when out of the line. His rifle is the British .303 SMLE Rifle No. 4 Mk. I. The No. 4 was the standard British infantry rifle of the war and with a 10-round magazine and a muzzle velocity of 2400 feet per second was one of the best bolt-action rifles of its day. A lighter and shorter version, the No. 5, was introduced for use in the jungle but the violent recoil of the weapon made it unpopular with the front-line troops.

335 Brigadier, Indian Army, 1945

Brigadier Denham-Young of the 5th Indian Division, 14th Army, wears the divisional sign press-studded to the sleeve of his bush jacket. His felt bush hat carries the badge of a brigadier, while the gorget (collar) patches were also worn by colonels. He carries British-pattern web equipment and a leather bandolier with small-arms ammunition. The rough terrain and atrocious climate encountered by the British Army in Burma encouraged a more informal approach to uniform which was facilitated by the introduction of the jungle-green uniform worn by this officer.

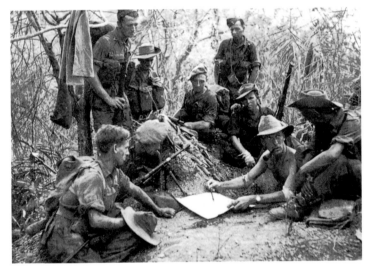

Above top: A group of Chindits awaiting transportation to 'Broadway', the invasion airfield behind Japanese lines. British, West African and Indian troops formed the backbone of the Chindits who paid little attention to parade ground 'spit and polish' and instead emphasised battle and field craft skills. The transport planes in the background are Douglas C-47s, better known to the British as the Douglas Dakota.

Above: A section of British soldiers of the 14th Army in Burma are briefed by their company commander. A wide variety of weapons can be seen, including the Sten sub-machine gun, the Bren light machine gun and the SMLE rifle. The soldier (left background) carries ammunition pouches for Bren gun magazines. The dishevelled appearance of the troops reflects the harshness of the Burmese terrain.

Central Command, containing the majority of training depots and establishments, and three armies: Southern, Eastern, and North-Western. The major operational command was Eastern Army with responsibility for the defence of Assam, Bengal, Bihar, and Orrissa, and it was largely from the formations of this command that the 14th Army was formed in October 1943.

The direction of operations which were based on India and Ceylon was transferred from the C-in-C India (General Sir C. Auchinleck) to a new appointment, filled by Acting-Admiral Lord Louis Mountbatten, of Supreme Allied Commander, South-East Asia (SEAC). The land forces in SEAC, consisting of 14th Army and the Ceylon Army Command, were brought under the new Headquarters, 11th Army Group. 14th Army was composed of XV Corps (5th, 7th Indian Divisions and 81st West African Division) and IV Corps (17th, 20th, 23rd and 26th Indian Infantry Divisions and 254th Indian Tank Brigade). The XXXIII Corps (2nd British and 36th Indian Infantry Divisions) was allocated to South-East Asia Command but remained for the time being with India Command, as did the 19th and 25th Indian Divisions and the 50th Tank Brigade. The major formations within Ceylon Army Command were the 11th East African Division and the 99th Indian Infantry Brigade.

A number of special force units were attached to SEAC, among them 44 Royal Marine Commando, 5 Commando, and 3 Special Service (SS) Brigade. The largest special force was the '3rd Indian Division' which provided the Long Range Penetration Groups (Chindits) commanded by Major General Orde Wingate. The initial LRP groups had been formed as the 77th Indian Infantry Brigade in July 1942, but these were expanded to a strength of six infantry brigades (14th, 16th, 23rd, 77th, 111th and 3rd West African) by breaking up the 70th British Division and appropriating a brigade of the 81st West African Division. Each Special Force brigade consisted of a number of columns, either British or Gurkha in composition, the former with a strength of 306 all ranks and the latter a strength of 369. Each column had an RAF section, a medical section, signallers, sabotage group, a Burma Rifles platoon, an infantry company, and a support group. At full strength and including divisional and attached troops, the Chindits amounted to the equivalent of almost two divisions.

In the spring of 1945 Allied Land Forces South-East Asia comprised one command HQ, one army HQ, three

The defence of India and Ceylon and particularly the need to maintain internal security tied down a large proportion of the troops available in the Far East; in August 1942, for example, 57 battalions were involved in containing civil disturbances. The threat of political unrest was the more alarming since after the outbreak of war in Europe many of the British regular units stationed in India had been transferred to the United Kingdom and the Middle East, their place being taken by Territorial units who were obviously unfamiliar with the sub-continent and its peoples. The Army in India was divided into three commands, Northern, Eastern, and Southern, until 21 April 1942 when India Command was re-organised as a corps HQs, a combat area command incorporating two Chinese armies, two British, two West African, one East African, and seven Indian divisions. In addition 14th Army had three independent brigades. The successful occupation of southern Burma and the requirements of the proposed amphibious operation against Malaya necessitated a command reorganisation in May and June. The headquarters of 14th Army was brought back from Burma to supervise the Malayan operations, its place being taken by a new formation, 12th Army, which became operational on 28 May 1945. The 14th Army which, with nearly 1,000,000 men serving in 1944 and early 1945, had been the largest single army of the war, finally stood down on 1st December 1945. At various periods it had controlled four corps (IV, XV, XXXIII and XXXIV) and 13 divisions had served with it (2nd, 36th British; 5th, 7th, 17th, 19th, 20th, 23rd, 25th, 26th Indian; 11th East African; 81st, 82nd West African). British casualties in Burma between 11 December 1941 and 15 September 1945 amounted to 25,170 officers and other ranks, of which 6921 were killed, 15,585 wounded, and 2664 listed as missing or prisoners of war.

In World War II as a whole the British Army suffered 569,501 casualties consisting of 144,079 killed, 239,575 wounded, 33,771 missing, and 152,076 taken prisoner.

UNIFORM At the beginning of the war in the Far East, British soldiers wore the same khaki drill uniform which was worn in the Middle East, but sandy yellow was found an unsuitable colour for jungle warfare, and the uniform was both uncomfortable and impractical.

In 1942 a new jungle-green uniform (figure 334) began to be introduced and by the time of the 1943–1944 campaigns it had become universal.

The basic uniform was made of a jungle-green cellular material and consisted of a bush jacket and shirt with both long and short sleeves, and long and short trousers. Various kinds of regimental head-dresses were worn when out of action, while on active service the most common headgear was the steel helmet or the slouch hat.

Web equipment was often painted a dark green or black to improve its protective colouring and to make it more impervious to moisture. Much of what is written about the Australian jungle fighter applies equally to the other British and Dominion forces (see page 206).

INSIGNIA Badges of rank were the same as worn on the temperate uniform except for the fact that metal rank badges were often painted black, and the chevrons for NCOs were made of a plain tape.

Regimental and formations signs were sometimes worn as illustrated in figures 334 and 335.

ROYAL AIR FORCE

By 1941 the prime responsibility for the defence of Britain's possessions in the Far East lay with the Royal Air Force. But the RAF was beset with problems, not the least of which was the difficulty of constructing and operating airfields amidst a terrain which gave scant consideration to the need for flat, open, and defensible spaces. In October 1940 it was estimated that the Far Eastern Theatre would require 566 aircraft. When hostilities began, however, there were 362 aircraft available of which only 233 were operational. Moreover, the demands made by the air defence of Britain and the Middle East meant that modern bomber and fighter aircraft were dispatched to South-East Asia in woefully inadequate numbers. The Brewster Buffalo fighter and the Vildebeest torpedo-bomber could

336 Pilot Officer, Royal Air Force, 1945

Pilot officer Alasdair Campbell, Unit Adjutant of the RAF Mobile Repair and Salvage Unit in Burma, wears a jungle-green tropical shirt, on which rank is indicated by slip-on khaki tags on the shoulder. The bush hat was of British, rather than Australian origin, while the overall trousers and anklets were standard RAF issue. The role of maintenance and back-up troops was never more vital than in Burma where vast numbers of men were needed to keep the fighting man supplied. In the case of the Royal Air Force this was especially true as airfields had to be hacked out from the jungle.

337 Squadron Leader, Royal Air Force, 1941

This officer of the Royal Air Force Volunteer Reserve displays the service's tropical dress, but has retained the cap from his blue-grey service uniform. Squadron leader rank badges are worn on the shoulder straps, while his reserve status is indicated by the letters 'VR' on the collar. He wears the observers' 'half wing' qualification badge on the left breast. This smart khaki drill service dress typical of the early period of the Pacific War contrasts markedly with the generally relaxed appearance of the British armed forces by 1945.

336

337

not match the speed and manoeuvrability of the Japanese Zero. The transfer of Hurricanes to the Far East did little to redress the balance and it was not until the arrival of the Spitfire and the Thunderbolt that air superiority began to be firmly established in the 1943–44 campaigning season. Thereafter RAF squadrons aided by the Royal Indian Air Force and by Dominion squadrons, provided every form of aerial support to the forces on the ground, from strategic bombing and air supply, to reconnaissance and casualty evacuation.

ORGANISATION Headquarters Royal Air Force, Far East, directly controlled the stations and squadrons in Malaya, Burma, Ceylon, and Hong Kong from its formation in 1933 until the establishment of the first group (221 Group) in 1941 to command the units in Burma. In the same year additional groups were formed in Ceylon (222 Group) and for the air defence of Singapore (224 Group). By December 1941 22 airfields with either concrete or grass runways had been constructed in Malaya with a further four airfields on Singapore. The RAF, RAAF, and RNZAF units operating from these bases comprised four Blenheim, two Hudson, two Vildebeest, one Catalina, and four Buffalo squadrons. During the retreat from Burma three bomber, three fighter, and two army co-operation squadrons supported the campaign waged by the land forces. The Royal Indian Air Force (RIAF), which had been formed in 1933, was entirely Indian in composition and it began the war with one army co-operation unit and 285 officers and airmen.

In September 1942 the RAF and RIAF squadron strength stood at 31, of which 25 were operational, and by June 1943 the total had grown to 52 squadrons with 34 operational. The number of airfields available in India had increased to 285, of which 140 were fully operational, and the RAF Regiment deployed five field squadrons and 50 anti-aircraft flights in their defence. India Command comprised one bomber group (No. 221), a tactical group (No. 224), a reconnaissance group (No. 222), two training groups (Nos. 225 and 227), one composite group (No. 223), and a maintenance group (No. 226). With the creation of South-East Asia Command the operational RAF squadrons in north-east India were integrated with the United States 10th Army Air Force as Eastern Air Command, forming a Tactical Air Force, a Strategic Air Force, and a Troop Carrier Command. By May 1944 the Combined Air Forces could call upon 64 RAF and 28 USAAF squadrons.

The personnel strength of the RAF and RIAF in the Far East had risen by July 1945 to 207,632 officers and men, of which 13,225 were RAF officers and 118,582 British other ranks. The Royal Indian Air Force strength in August stood at 29,201 officers and airmen and nine squadrons.

UNIFORM AND INSIGNIA The Royal Air Force also made use of the jungle-green clothing, as well as the tropical dress as described in the section on the Mediterranean. The normal head-dress was worn with the jungle-green uniform, together with the appropriate badges and other insignia.

ROYAL NAVY

The fall of the British naval base at Singapore effectively prevented the Royal Navy from participating in the Pacific war until the closing stages of World War II. With the loss of the *Repulse* and the *Prince of Wales*, the Royal Navy was in danger of being driven from its bases in the Indian Ocean. Nevertheless, British leaders were determined to play some part in the war in the Pacific, not only to avenge a catastrophic blow dealt to the prestige of British arms, but to ensure that they would be in a position to protect their colonial possessions that had fallen into Japanese

Below: Admiral Sir Tom Phillips in naval whites. He went down with his ship, the **Prince of Wales** *on 10 December 1941.*

338

338 Groundcrew, Royal Air Force, 1945
Designed to provide the wearer with the maximum possible protection from the heat and flames generated by burning kerosene, this asbestos suiting was issued both to RAF aerodrome fire-fighting units and to Royal Navy ships carrying aircraft. Vision was provided by the tinted reinforced glass plate; otherwise the fire-fighter was totally enclosed in his asbestos suit. Fire aboard ships had always been a hazard of naval warfare but was especially so in the Pacific due to the Japanese kamikaze attacks on the decks of the Allied aircraft carriers.

339 Sub-Lieutenant, Royal Navy, 1945
An officer of the Royal Naval Volunteer Reserve, Sub-Lieutenant A. Lloyd Morgan served aboard HM Submarine Shakespeare *of the East Indies Fleet. He wears khaki drill shirt and shorts, with rank badges on shoulder strap slides. The Royal Navy officers' peaked cap is worn with a white cover. The Royal Naval Volunteer Reserve, instituted in 1903, was distinguished by the square curl of the rank lace which can be seen on the shoulder strap slide of this figure. The Royal Naval Reserve, in contrast, had a star-shaped curl and 'wavy' rank lace. Both types of insignia are illustrated in the rank insignia chart on page 126.*

339

340

341

340 Marine, Royal Marines, 1941

Stationed in Singapore, this Marine wears RM tropical kit of khaki shorts and shirt with full-length khaki puttees, M1908 web equipment and marine service cap with white cover. He carries a British .303 SMLE rifle No. 1 Mk. III with bayonet. The old 1908-pattern webbing reflects the out-dated look of this Marine at the outset of the war. British forces in the Far East were starved of the latest equipment until towards the end of the war and many troops considered themselves to be part of the 'Forgotten Army'. The Mark III rifle was of World War I vintage and although highly-considered by those who used it, was a costly weapon to manufacture and so was replaced by the cheaper No. 4 Mk. 1 rifle. In conditions of active service the distinctive marine cap would be replaced by the steel helmet.

341 Officer, Royal Navy, 1943

Depicted in working garb, this engineer wears the Royal Navy officers' peaked cap with white cover, white overalls and strong gloves. An interesting feature is the absence of shoe laces, which may have been due to the custom of wearing lace-less shoes and boots by those crew members working in confined spaces under the water-line, so that they could be quickly kicked off if the vessel was sinking.

hands. The Japanese had presented themselves as the champions of oppressed colonial peoples; the United States was not sympathetic towards British imperial aspirations and thus British leaders were anxious to preserve British power in the Far East by military and naval action.

At the First Quebec Conference Churchill offered the Chief of US Naval Staff, Admiral Ernest J. King, a British fleet, but this offer was not enthusiastically received. At the second Quebec Conference Churchill repeated his offer of a British fleet. Thanking the United States for its aid during the dark days of the struggle against Germany, he added, 'It was only to be expected that the British Empire in return should wish to give the United States all the help in their power towards defeating Japan'. Roosevelt returned these fulsome sentiments and concluded that 'the British fleet was no sooner offered than accepted'. At last Churchill's dream of a British fleet operating in the Pacific Ocean moved a step nearer reality when it was agreed that it would be based in Australia.

At the beginning of the war against Japan, Admiral Sir James Somerville commanded a sizeable fleet of five battleships, three light aircraft carriers, seven cruisers, and sixteen destroyers. Although fairly strong in numbers, the quality of this fleet was indifferent. The battleships were old and slow, aircraft carriers were no match for the Japanese, and the Royal Navy was inexperienced in the technique of launching large numbers of aircraft from fleet carriers and co-ordinating attacks against a distant enemy. Nevertheless, although Somerville lost one aircraft carrier in his evasive tactics against the Japanese, at least he was successful in keeping the British fleet in being in the Indian Ocean.

Following the defeat of Italy a 'British Pacific Ocean Force' was formed of three battleships, one or two fleet carriers and a number of cruisers and destroyers. This force was broken up because of a decision to re-start Arctic convoys to Murmansk, but by the summer of 1944 Somerville had received two aircraft carriers. HMS *Victorious* and *Illustrious*. He was not, however, to command this force, and in August 1944 was relieved by Admiral Sir Bruce Fraser, ex-C-in-C Home Fleet.

In January 1945 the British Pacific Fleet now comprised one battleship, four aircraft carriers, three cruisers and ten destroyers, and was based at Sydney, Australia. One argument that the Americans employed to dissuade the British from employing a fleet in the Pacific Ocean was the difficulties that the British would have in forming a 'Fleet Train' to support the warships over vast expanses of ocean and, indeed, the Royal Navy did have considerable difficulty in acquiring sufficient merchantmen to carry out this duty. Tankers from the Royal Fleet Auxiliaries were employed, and merchant ships were lent from European navies. Eventually it reached a strength of 60 ships, but the mixed origins of many of the ships did not facilitate easy co-operation.

In December 1944 the United States Navy reluctantly agreed that the British Pacific Fleet should use Manus in the Admiralty Islands as an intermediate base before moving to a more advanced base in the Philippines. By March 1945 it consisted of one battleship, the *King George V*, the fleet carriers, *Indomitable, Victorious, Indefatigable*, and *Illustrious*, five cruisers and eleven destroyers in addition to 218 bombers and fighters. Fine though this force was, by American standards

it was very small, and was only one component in Admiral Spruance's Fifth Fleet of over 1200 vessels. After action off Okinawa in July 1945, the British Pacific Fleet was switched to the US Third Fleet as an additional group of the US Fast Carrier Task Force, initially taking part in attacks on the Japanese mainland.

The Royal Marines were active in the Far East theatre as commandos, quite apart from their normal role as part of the complement of Royal Navy vessels. Their special qualities as élite soldiers were put to good use in Burma where 42(RM) and 44(RM) Commando formed part of No. 3 Commando Brigade.

A typical Marine commando detachment in the later stages of the war would be 100 men strong and consist of a small HQ and three troops of about 30 officers and men, each divided into three sections. Generally, however, the organisation of these units varied according to the operation and to the resources available.

UNIFORM AND INSIGNIA   Royal Navy uniform was basically the tropical issue described in the section on the Mediterranean, although the jungle-green clothing was often worn. As with the Air Force, normal head-dress and insignia were worn with the jungle-green uniform. Royal Marine insignia is illustrated in the accompanying chart.

Above: Royal Marine commandos land on Akyab beach in the Arakan. The Marine in the right foreground wears regulation Royal Marine denims and is armed with a short Lee Enfield rifle. The Marines had an important role to play in spearheading the Army's amphibious operations along the Burmese coast.

ROYAL MARINE INSIGNIA

EMPIRE FORCES

As in the Mediterranean, the forces of the British Empire made a full contribution to victory in the Far East, in conditions which were often extremely difficult and against a redoubtable foe.

INDIAN ARMY

By December 1941 the Indian Army had approximately 900,000 men under arms, of whom almost 300,000 were serving overseas in the Middle East and Malaya. Of the remainder, about 150,000 were deployed in the area of the North-West Frontier and on internal security duty, and a further 300,000 were undergoing training. When the Japanese offensive began, the preponderance of trained and experienced Indian units were in the Middle East, but three divisions were in Malaya and one understrength division was in Burma. This dispersal of strength overseas and the orientation of training towards conditions in the Middle East seriously affected the battleworthiness of the Indian units remaining in the Far East. The rapid expansion of the recruiting programme during 1940–41 compounded these difficulties and led to modifications in the composition of the Indian Army. The martial classes drawn from Moslems and Sikhs of the Punjab and NW Frontier, who traditionally supplied the recruits needed by the army, could no longer provide a large enough reservoir of manpower. In their place new sections of the population were recruited and by the beginning of 1943 the percentage figures of the provincial composition of the Army were as follows: Punjab 50, United Provinces 15, Madras 10, Bombay 10, NW Frontier Province 5, Ajmere and Merwara 3, Bengal 2 and Central Provinces 5. The two largest religious groupings were Hindus who accounted for 50 per cent and Moslems with 34 per cent.

The Indian Army played a major role in the fighting in Malaya and Burma and at one point Indian units amounted to three-quarters of the strength of the 14th Army. After being driven out of Burma by the Japanese in 1942 the Indian Army was able to make a stand against Japan virtually on the frontiers of India itself. The last Japanese attempt to invade India was repulsed at the two battles of Imphal and Kohima in the spring of 1944.

Following these battles, troops of the Indian Army went over on the offensive and successfully cleared the Japanese from Burma in 1945. Casualties in the campaign were high: in the Malayan débâcle the Indian Army suffered 62,175

342

343

casualties (59,000 POWs), and in the fighting in Burma 40,458 men were lost.

ORGANISATION On the outbreak of war in 1939 the Army in India was composed not only of Indian troops but also of British units which formed an integral part of the subcontinent's military forces. The Regular Indian Army consisted of units of native troops commanded by British and Indian officers, but a complete hierarchy of Indian officers was being introduced into a small number of units with the aim of eventually providing a complete Indian division. When sent out to India, British units were transferred from the Home to the Indian establishment.

In the first years of the war, infantry brigades normally contained one British battalion and two Indian (or Gurkha) battalions, although all-Indian brigades and divisions were later introduced in the 14th Army. The British and Indian regulars were supported by a number of irregular and auxiliary formations including the Indian States' Forces, the Indian

342 Sepoy, Indian Army, 1944

Wearing standard issue khaki drill shirt and shorts, this sepoy also displays 1908 webbing belt and equipment. Short puttees are worn over khaki socks. The two large leather ammunition pouches are probably specially-made, and are intended to carry magazines for the Vickers-Berthier Indian Mark III machine gun he holds in his right hand. This was adopted by the Indian Army while the British Army carried out comparative trials between this weapon and the externally-similar Bren gun. Although the British Army eventually adopted the latter weapon as its standard light machine gun, the Indian Army continued to utilise the Vickers-Berthier.

343 Subedar-Major, Burma Rifles, 1942

This subedar of the Burma Rifles is wearing the light khaki service dress with Sam Browne belt; battledress was drill shirt and shorts and 1908 web equipment. The infantry officer's sword had a steel hilt, and the scabbard was of black leather with steel fittings. The two silver badges on the collar were each fashioned in the shape of a peacock. Wool puttees and ammunition boots were also worn. His rank is indicated by the three pips on each shoulder strap. The 20th Burma Rifles had their origin in units formed in World War I.

344

Territorial Force, and the North-West Frontier Province Irregulars.

Many of the problems experienced by the Indian Army in the first two years of the war in the Far East stemmed from the contradictions inherent in an ambitious expansion programme, and a lack of trained manpower, particularly in the fields of artillery and communications. The 1940 expansion programme, for example, was framed for an armoured division, five infantry divisions, and supporting troops; that for 1941 had a similar target of five infantry divisions. The divisional 'slice' in the Far East at 56,000 men was larger than in any other theatre, despite the fact that divisional fighting strengths tended to be lower – largely of course due to casualties caused by disease and to tactical and logistical problems which restricted frontline deployment. In June 1944 the fighting strength of the 7th Indian Division was 10,014 officers and men including 819 British other ranks. Of the Indian Army's strength of 2,000,000 men almost 1,200,000 were ancillary troops.

The original preparation of the Indian Army for service in the Middle East meant that even as late as 1943 divisions tended to be equipped and organised for warfare in that theatre, even though they were due to be dispatched to Assam and Burma. By 1944 there were four types of Indian division plus the British divisions serving in the Far East. The Indian light divisions had a reduced establishment of men and vehicles, the Indian A & MT (animal and motor transport) divisions had a high or low scale of transport, while the 36th Indian Division was organised for amphibious operations and had two brigades each with four battalions. In August 1944 it was decided that the organisation of all

344 Corporal, Indian Army, 1941
This naik *of the 9th Gurkha Rifles is serving with the 11th Indian Division in Malaya. He wears the khaki drill shirt and shorts (the latter nicknamed 'Bombay Bloomers') with short puttees, 1937-pattern web equipment, special web pouches to carry the magazines for his Thompson sub-machine gun and a web binocular case. His* kukri *and felt hat (with rifle green patch on the* puggree*) make him unmistakably a Gurkha. Renowned as fierce hand-to-hand fighters, the Gurkhas were a martial race originating from the poverty-stricken country of Nepal. They had formed a recognised part of the British Army since the 19th Century and had seen action on many fronts. Their most famous exploits were in the Western Desert, in the Italian campaign (especially at the battle of Monte Cassino) and with the Chindits in Burma.*

Right: Indian troops on a training exercise near Singapore. They are wearing the side cap and also the 'Bombay Bloomers' shown in figure 344. The Indian Army provided the bulk of the garrison of Singapore, and the surrender of this great naval base left 32,000 Indian troops in Japanese hands, as compared to the 15,000 British and 13,000 Australians who were taken prisoner at the same time, in this short and (for the British Empire) disastrous episode.

infantry divisions should be standardised on an organisation of three (later four) brigades of three battalions each, a machine-gun battalion, a reconnaissance battalion, and a headquarters battalion. Artillery support would be provided by two field regiments (each of 24×25-pdrs), an anti-tank regiment (36×6-pdrs), and a mountain regiment (12×3.7-inch howitzers). The large establishment of vehicular transport would be reduced and each division would have three animal transport companies.

It had been decided in 1941 that the Indian Army should have its own armoured corps consisting of three armoured divisions. The raising of the 31st Indian Armoured Division had been part of the 1940 expansion programme, the 32nd Indian Armoured Division was included in the 1941 programme, and the 43rd Armoured Division in the programme for 1942. The headquarters and a brigade of the 31st Division were soon dispatched to Iraq but their loss was balanced by the arrival of the 50th Indian Tank Brigade consisting of three Royal Armoured Corps regiments. The Indian armoured divisions were initially formed with two armoured brigades each but in the summer of 1942 their organisation was altered to conform to the British system of one armoured and one motorised infantry brigade per division. The two surplus armoured brigades were thereafter employed as independent tank brigades.

In August 1943 the 32nd and 43rd Armoured Divisions were amalgamated to form the 44th Indian Armoured Division, and this division, together with three tank brigades (50th, 251st, 254th), comprised the Indian armoured strength in the Far East. The artillery element of armoured divisions had been established in October 1942 at two field regiments, one anti-tank regiment, and one light anti-aircraft regiment.

In the autumn of 1943 consideration was given to the question of raising an Indian airborne division and as there was no longer an urgent need for an armoured division in SEAC the 44th Armoured Division was disbanded in March 1944 and its headquarters and divisional personnel used to form the nucleus of the 44th Indian Airborne Division. The establishment of the division was laid down as one air-landing brigade and two Indian parachute brigades each of one British, one Gurkha, and one Indian battalion. The formation of the Indian Parachute Regiment was authorised on 18 December 1944.

In August 1945 the strength of the Indian Army stood at 2,065,554 officers and men, and its major units comprised

Above: Subedar-Major Multon Singh of the Frontier Force Rifles raises the Union Jack at Prome. Lieutenant-Colonel Marks is on the left.

19 cavalry and armoured regiments, 268 battalions of infantry, 207 artillery batteries, and 107 engineer companies.

UNIFORM At the beginning of the campaign in the Far East, Indian troops wore the same puggrees, grey shirts and khaki drill clothing as worn by Indian troops in the Middle East. This uniform was also worn by troops serving in India including those guarding the India/Burma border.

During the war the various kinds of head-dress such as the peaked and field service caps worn by British officers, and the saffa, puggree or slouch hat worn by Indians and Gurkhas gradually gave way to the ubiquitous beret. The puggree was still occasionally worn on ceremonial occasions, or if worn in action was dyed various shades of olive green.

In 1942 jungle-green clothing in various shades began to be issued to Indian troops. On active service it was worn without insignia, except possibly a strip of cloth in a regimental colour on the shoulder straps, or a coloured lanyard. Out of the line formation flashes were worn on the upper sleeves, and a cloth with a regimental designation (for example 6L for 6th Duke of Connaught's Own Lancers – Watson's Horse) embroidered in black. The Indian Army also pioneered the use of knitted cardigans in various colours such as black for Skinner's Horse and brown for the Gurkha Rifles.

INSIGNIA In the Indian Army there were both British and Indian officers. British officers and those Indians holding a King's Commission ranked equally and wore the same badges of rank which were exactly the same as those worn in the British Army. There were also Indian officers holding a Viceroy's Commission who were known as Viceroy's Commissioned Officers or VCOs. These subordinate ranks were jemadar, subedar or rissaldar in cavalry, and subedar major or rissaldar major in cavalry. The jemadar and subedar were usually platoon commanders or in some cases company second in command. The subedar major was the senior subordinate officer and advised the British commanding officer in all matters concerning the Indian rank and file. An important Indian appointment was the jemadar adjutant or 'woordie' major in cavalry. These officers acted as assistants to the British adjutants.

In October 1942 details of rank badges for VCOs were laid down. On khaki cloth shoulder straps VCOs wore one (jemadar), two (rissaldar and subedar) or three (rissaldar major and subedar major) miniature silver pips mounted on transverse bars made up of three strands of braid – red, yellow and red.

MALAYAN FORCES

The Government of Malaya could call upon one regular infantry battalion composed of British and Malay officers and Malay other ranks and a cadre of a second battalion which started to form in December 1941. There were also four volunteer infantry battalions, an armoured car company, and a light artillery battery maintained by the Federated Malay States with a further four battalions raised as the Straits Settlements Volunteer Force. Local flying clubs formed the basis of the Malay Volunteer Air Force which was manned by British residents.

BURMESE FORCES

Until 1937 Burma was part of India Command but with the political separation of the two countries in April of that year the Government of Burma became responsible for internal security, and control of the armed forces passed to the Governor. The Burma Rifles were transferred from the Indian Army and the country's auxiliary and territorial forces became the Burma Auxiliary Force and the Burma Territorial Force. The former comprised the Rangoon Field Brigade RA and four rifle battalions with a combined strength of 11 companies and one armoured car section. The Territorial Force consisted of a Burma Rifles battalion and the Rangoon University Training Corps. On Separation, six of the nine battalions of the Burma Military Police were formed as the Burma Frontier Force.

The outbreak of the war in Europe saw the introduction of an expansion programme for the local forces in Burma. The strength of the Burma Rifles was doubled with the formation of six new battalions and two extra territorial battalions were also embodied; an observer corps was formed, all British subjects resident in Burma became eligible for service in the Auxiliary Force, and four mobile units were raised from the Frontier Force for outpost duty. Several major drawbacks reduced the effectiveness of the expansion programme, among them an acute shortage of transport and equipment, a lack of trained regimental officers and general reserves, and the failure to expand the Army Headquarters staff in keeping with the force they administered.

After the withdrawal of the Allied forces from Burma the Japanese raised the Burma National Army (BNA) in August 1943, but in January 1945 this force informed the Allies of its intention of rising in revolt against the Japanese occupying army. The BNA, with a strength of approximately 8000 men, carried out guerrilla attacks against the Japanese from 27 March 1945.

DOMINION FORCES

The Dominions of Australia and New Zealand were naturally involved in the Pacific War, but whereas the Australian government saw the Far East as its main concern, the bulk of the New Zealand Army remained in the Middle East.

345 Private, Australian Army, 1943
This Australian private in New Guinea in 1943 wears items of equipment from three nations. Typically Australian are the bush hat (the coloured flash stands for the 39th Australian Infantry Battalion) and the Australian 9mm Owen sub-machine gun. He also wears the 1937 British web equipment, large pack and ammunition pouches. Elements of US clothing are the canvas gaiters and bedding roll, while the trousers are the bottom half of a US herringbone-twill fatigue suit.

345

AUSTRALIAN ARMY

As soon as Japan began hostilities the Australian Government decided that a corps of two divisions should be transferred from the Middle to the Far East, and from the end of January 1942 units of the 6th and 7th Divisions began to withdraw from North Africa. Altogether 64,151 troops were to be transferred. The 6th Division was 18,465 strong, the 7th 18,620, with an additional 17,866 corps troops and 9200 base and line of communication personnel. To support this veteran corps there were seven divisions of militia which had been mobilised in December 1941 and the Volunteer Defence Corps which consisted largely of men who had served in World War I.

General Blamey had been appointed Commander-in-Chief of the Australian Military Forces, and in April 1942 he grouped his forces for the defence of Australia as follows:

1st Army in Queensland and NS Wales;
2nd Army in Victoria, South Australia and Tasmania;
III Corps in Western Australia;
one division in Northern Territory.

In troop strengths this organisation embodied about 46,000 experienced combat troops, approximately 63,000 AIF volunteers in various stages of training, 280,000 militia soldiers, and 33,000 Americans with little or no combat experience.

The Australian 8th Division had been engaged in Malaya and Indonesia; its 22nd and 27th Brigades had lost 1789 killed, 1306 wounded and 15,000 prisoners at Singapore. The main Australian effort in the Pacific War, however, was to be in the South-West Pacific. In July 1942, a mainly Australian force had defeated the first Japanese assault on Port Moresby in Papua, and Australian forces bore the brunt of the savage fighting along the Kokoda trail.

By March 1943 the major units of the Australian Army in Australia were grouped as follows:

1st Army – 3rd Armoured Division, 4th Division;
II Corps – 6th (16 and 30 Brigades), 7th and 9th Divisions;
2nd Army – 1st Division, 3rd Army Tank Brigade;
III Corps – 1st Armoured Division, 2nd Division;

Northern Territory Force – 12th
Division;
Reserve – 3rd Brigade, 4th Armoured
Brigade.
Based in Papua-New Guinea were 3rd
Division (17 Brigade), 11th Division (7
and 15 Brigades) and 5th Division (4 and
29 Brigades).

Both of the armoured divisions, whose
original establishment had been two
armoured brigades and a support group,
had by this time been reduced in strength
by an armoured brigade each, but the
independent tank brigades were retained
by the Army. For most of 1943 the
Australian forces in the combined South-
West and South Pacific armies were larger
than those deployed by the Americans,
and in October 1943, for example, there
were 492,000 Australian land forces in the
South-West Pacific and 198,000 United
States troops.

During the early months of 1944,
Australian troops continued to advance
along the east coast of New Guinea, and
in April 1944 the Australian troops in the
South-West Pacific theatre were grouped
as two corps. I Corps consisted of the 6th,
7th and 9th AIF Divisions in Queensland
(the 9th Division had returned from the
Middle East after El Alamein) and II
Corps of the 3rd, 5th and 11th Militia
Divisions which now formed New Guinea
Force.

Since the end of 1943 it had been
envisaged that US Army forces would
progressively take over the operational
role of the Australian troops in New
Guinea. As the American task forces leap-
frogged from island to island their bases
were still threatened by Japanese troops
who had retreated into the hinterland
after losing the battles for the beach-
heads. Although the Japanese were largely
cut off from their sources of supply their
very presence could seriously disrupt
American strategy since the momentum
of the advance would be lost if American
forces had to be constantly detached to
hold the base perimeters. MacArthur
decided that this was a task for the
Australians. Twelve Australian brigades
were to be distributed amongst the bases
in Bougainville, New Guinea, New
Britain, and the smaller islands, thereby
freeing six American divisions. To carry
out this deployment the 6th Division was
transferred to II Corps and together with
the Militia divisions it was to see considerable action against the surviving
Japanese garrisons.

In April 1945 the remaining divisions of
I Corps were given a role in the northern
advance, the 7th Division being allocated
to the conquest of Balikpapau in Dutch
Borneo and the 9th Division to that of

Tarakan in Dutch Borneo and Brunei
Bay in British Borneo. In May and July
the landings were successfully accomp-
lished and Australian forces continued
mopping-up operations until the Japanese
surrender in August.

The gross strength of the Australian
Army during World War II was 727,703,
and of this figure 396,661 had served
overseas. Its total battle casualties
amounted to 61,575 including 18,713
dead. When Japan surrendered, the
Army's strength stood at 385,000 with
167,000 serving beyond the mainland.

UNIFORM During the long hard and
humid campaign in New Guinea, the
Australians found that their tropical
clothing simply rotted and fell apart,
uniforms and equipment were gnawed by
rats and metal fittings rusted.

The Australians began to develop a
new jungle-green battledress which would
stand up to the ravages of jungle warfare.
Buttons had to be made of a material
which did not rust and shirts and trousers
had to be both rat and mosquito-proof.
The felt slouch hat, although popular was
expensive, and had to be replaced by a
much cheaper and more practical jungle
beret.

Footwear was a great problem, and a
new jungle boot which gripped in mud
and slime, and non-shrinking socks replaced the leather ammunition boot.

During the final stages of the war,
Australian troops began to receive increasing amounts of American clothing and
equipment.

At the beginning of the New Guinea
campaign the average Australian infantryman carried 80 lb of equipment,
but this was found to be far too heavy, so
much thought was given to reducing the
soldier's load to a bare minimum of 35 lb
or maximum of 40 lb. It was also found

*Below : Australian infantrymen of the 42nd
Battalion advancing through swamps on
Bougainville, January 1945.*

more practical to wear the personal equipment as high up the body as possible (see figure 345) since this prevented items of equipment swinging and making a noise. The Australian jungle veteran carried his personal possessions in a waterproof wallet and his ammunition and extra rations in special large pouches, while the haversack had an extra pocket for clothing. The blanket roll was made up of a special lightweight blanket, half shelter tent, and either a gas cape or light waterproof poncho which was termed the 'Brown Special'.

AUSTRALIAN AIR FORCE

Australia provided four units to help defend Malaya; these were Nos. 1 and 8 Squadrons with Lockheed Hudson bombers and Nos. 21 and 453 Squadrons with Brewster Buffalo fighters. The latter suffered badly, however, at the hands of superior Japanese fighters.

As the war in the Pacific brought hostilities closer to home, two further Hudson units were established on the islands of Timor and Ambon. After the all-but-unopposed attack on Darwin, Nos. 75 and 76 Squadrons formed for home defence, while Nos. 452 and 457 were recalled, with No. 54 Squadron RAF, in January 1943 for the same purpose.

By mid-1943, nearly 144,000 personnel were serving in the RAAF, of whom over 127,000 were in Australia or the Pacific Islands. No. 9 Group was to play a vital role in the American attack on Rabaul, New Britain, with its amphibious aircraft and bombers. No. 10 Group, now known as 1st Tactical Air Force, forged north to the Philippines.

The RAAF's total wartime enlistment had numbered 189,700 men and 27,200 women. Its losses in Europe were 5397 killed and 947 injured, in the Middle East 1135 and 413 respectively, and the totals in all theatres 10,562 and 3192.

UNIFORM Uniform and insignia were basically similar to those of the British forces, although later in the war American items of clothing became more common.

AUSTRALIAN NAVY

In 1939 the Royal Australian Navy comprised seven cruisers, 17 destroyers and 74 escort and minesweeping vessels. Up to 1941 it had supplied vessels to the Allied war effort in the Mediterranean (where the cruiser HMAS *Sydney* had sunk the Italian cruiser *Bartolomeo Colleoni* before being herself sunk with all hands by a German raider) and to convoy escort.

The main thrust of Australian naval effort after 1941 was naturally in the Pacific, however, and the Navy's vessels were heavily engaged from the battle of the Java Sea onwards, and participated in the landings in the Solomons and at Guadalcanal. Task Force 44 (the Anzac Squadron) was part of the Allied drive back to the Philippines, and its units played their part in the battle of Leyte Gulf. Vessels also served in the Burma campaign, and as part of the British Pacific Fleet late in the war.

UNIFORM Uniform was basically as for the British Royal Navy.

346 Leading Seaman, Royal Australian Navy, 1943

Depicted in an off-duty moment, this Australian seaman wears a white tropical version of the serge temperate uniform. His badge of rank, an anchor on the left arm, surmounts a chevron denoting at least three years' good conduct. The non-substantive badge on the right arm is that of a leading torpedoman.

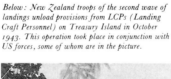

Below: New Zealand troops of the second wave of landings unload provisions from LCPs (Landing Craft Personnel) on Treasury Island in October 1943. This operation took place in conjunction with US forces, some of whom are in the picture.

346

NEW ZEALAND ARMY

The 8th New Zealand Brigade Group arrived on the island of Fiji on 1 November 1940. Its units were brigaded with those of the Fiji Defence Force (one full battalion of Fijian troops plus a number of cadres) and in addition a number of guerrilla groups were formed consisting of 30 New Zealand officers and NCOs and 200 native Fijians.

By the end of November 1940 the 8th Brigade Group totalling 3053 all ranks was established on Viti Levu, the most important island of the Fiji group, in two defence zones 150 miles apart. The 8th Brigade was then joined by the 14th Brigade and eventually became the 3rd New Zealand Division. In July 1942 the division was relieved by American troops.

In November 1942 the division moved to New Caledonia as part of training for the Solomons campaign. A third brigade was formed with two battalions but saw only a short period of service, being disbanded before the division moved up to the Solomons. Nevertheless by the spring the strength of the formation had reached 17,800 officers and men. In August 1943 the division moved to the New Hebrides where final planning and battle training was carried out before it sailed for Guadalcanal. The New Zealanders served in a support capacity for the rest of the war.

UNIFORM AND INSIGNIA New Zealand forces wore uniform based on the British pattern (see figure 347), although later in the war the vast influx of US material meant that American clothing became much more common (for example see the pilot in figure 348). Badges of rank were as for the British armed forces, with formation signs on the upper arm.

NEW ZEALAND AIR FORCE

On the outbreak of war, the Royal New Zealand Air Force numbered some 756 regulars and 404 territorials. It had, however, supplied over 100 fully-trained pilots to the Royal Air Force. The New Zealand Government waived its claim to 30 Vickers Wellington bombers, the first six of which became the 'New Zealand Flight, RAF'. By April 1940, this had expanded to form No. 75 (NZ) Squadron.

The RNZAF in the Pacific was well-supplied with American equipment, and eight bomber, eleven fighter, two transport and two flying boat squadrons were mustered. Final casualty figures were 338 dead, and 58 seriously wounded. For uniform see under Army.

347

NEW ZEALAND NAVY

The New Zealand Division of the Royal Navy was renamed the Royal New Zealand Navy in 1941. At this time, its order of battle comprised: two light cruisers, one minesweeping trawler and one training ship.

The RNZN was dependent to a large degree on assistance from Royal Navy personnel on secondment. The total of 1339 serving men at the outbreak of war included 615 RN, while reserve strength numbered 732. By the cessation of hostilities, the RNZN numbered 5794 persons, of whom only 562 were from the Royal Navy. Additionally, 1086 officers and 2397 ratings of New Zealand origin had joined the Royal Navy.

The two light cruisers *Leander* and *Achilles* were active in support of the American Task Force in the Pacific before the former was holed by a torpedo in mid-1943 and later retired. By this time, four minesweeping trawlers, corvettes and many smaller vessels had been added to the line. A corvette and a cruiser were launched in 1945. Uniform was as for the Royal Navy.

348

347 Lieutenant, New Zealand Army, 1944

This New Zealand officer serving with the 1st Battalion of the Fiji Infantry in the central Solomons wears a British steel helmet with string netting, 1937-pattern web anklets and ammunition boots, with khaki drill uniform and wool puttees. His lieutenant's stars are carried alongside the Fiji Infantry formation sign at the shoulder. His belt, pistol magazine pouch and dispatch case are US Army issue, while he is armed with a US Cal.45 M1911A1 automatic pistol in a russet leather holster. A field dressing pouch is also visible on the belt.

348 Officer, Royal New Zealand Air Force, 1944

This aircrewman has British ankle boots, but his lightweight flying overalls, cap and knife are American. By this stage of the war, the immense output of US industry meant that US equipment was used by nations such as New Zealand which were traditionally supplied by Great Britain. The 'New Zealand' shoulder insignia in red on light khaki remained, however, a distinctive recognition feature. The pictured officer was one of the crew of a twin-engined Lockheed Ventura patrol bomber, a type widely used by the Allies in the Pacific where maritime surveillance was of paramount importance. Normal crew complement of the American-built Ventura was four or five.

in 1944–45 the brigade was able to recruit additional personnel.

The Air Force in December 1941 was controlled by a commandant with an operational headquarters, inspectorate, and services department which dealt with administration and supply.

The flying forces were formed into a regiment with three bomber groups, two fighter groups, and one reconnaissance group. In December 1941 the aircraft strength was 389 planes of all types.

UNIFORM The grey-green colonial uniform, originally introduced in 1916, was worn by both Army and Air Force personnel. The uniform was the same as that worn by figure 349 except that the Army straw hat was worn with the flap turned up on the left and fastened with a circular cockade in a reddish-orange, white and blue. There was also a peaked cap with black band, peak and chinstrap and circular cockade. All ranks wore their badges of rank on detachable collar patches. In 1939 a khaki drill uniform was introduced for Air Force personnel, but it is not known how widely it was worn.

Marines wore the uniform illustrated by figure 349, although the steel helmet was usually worn in action. Officers wore their badges of rank on detachable shoulder straps. Marines trained and equipped in America wore the USMC uniform with either American Marine rank badges or miniature Dutch marine rank badges in metal on the collar.

349

NETHERLANDS

The original Dutch East Indies Army had been formed in 1830, but when war broke out in the Far East, Dutch forces numbered about 1000 officers and 34,000 men, of whom 28,000 were natives.

The island of Curaçao was defended by a reasonably well-trained and armed local militia, while the East Indies had only weak territorial guard units. The Royal Netherlands Indian Army comprised one division and several independent units.

In December 1941 there were 400 marines in the Dutch East Indies. At Surabaia and at the marine barracks at Goebeng there were two companies of 125 men, a motorised anti-parachute brigade and a guard detachment.

On 21 January 1942 a group of Dutch marines left for training in the United States, where it was planned to form an armoured battalion of 1200 marines with 74 tanks to serve in the USMC in the Pacific. With the liberation of Holland

350

**349 Sergeant-Major,
Royal Netherlands Marines, 1942**
This marine NCO wears a lightweight version of the standard Dutch grey-green uniform. His straw hat with tally would have been replaced by the distinctive Dutch steel helmet before going into action. The equipment is natural leather, and the gas mask was the Dutch pattern. His rank is shown by the collar patches.

**350 Aircrewman,
Royal Netherlands Indian
Army Air Service, 1942**
Serving in Singapore during the preparations to withstand the Japanese assault, this airman has been issued with a Dutch 6.5mm M95 rifle. He wears the lightweight grey-green uniform and padded cap with black band and national cockade. The badge on his left breast (a bomb on a winged wreath) is for bomber aircrew.

Left: A captain (recognisable as such by the three stars on his collar patch) checks the equipment of a Dutch bugler. As with the British colonial forces, the Dutch units in the East Indies were noted for their smartness; but they were far too few to resist the Japanese onslaught.

UNITED STATES
ARMY

The rapid Japanese advance across South-East Asia and the Pacific following the attack on Pearl Harbor on 7 December 1941 caught the US Army by surprise. Outnumbered and isolated, America's Pacific island garrisons fell to the Japanese armed forces, although the beleaguered US troops put up a fierce struggle.

By the spring of 1942, the Japanese had achieved their initial war aims and looked to extend their conquests further south; New Guinea and Guadalcanal were the targets. It was here that the Japanese met their first check on land, as combined US Army and Marine forces, with the aid of the Australian Army, repulsed the Japanese offensive.

The battles of 1942 exhausted the Japanese and put them on the defensive, thereby giving the US forces the initiative which they kept throughout the remainder of the war. Given the amphibious nature of much of the fighting, the Army worked in close co-operation with the Navy and the Marine Corps. There was considerable debate within the services as to the conduct of the Pacific War – inter-service rivalries centring on the primacy of their respective roles and allocation of resources – but these conflicts did little to impair the overall American effort.

American strategy in the Pacific involved a two-pronged assault: the one under General MacArthur (mainly the responsibility of the Army) and the other under the command of Admiral Nimitz to capture the Central Pacific islands, this second offensive coming under the control of the Navy but involving Army and Marine troops as the land fighting force.

Although the Japanese held on to their island bastions with a remarkable tenacity, they were unable to stem the American advance. By the end of 1944 the US Army had returned to the Philippines, where the US 6th Army, with the 8th in support, set about the destruction of the 250,000-strong Japanese 14th Army. Parallel with the fighting in the Philippines, the newly-formed US 10th Army undertook the assault on Okinawa, which fell to the American forces on 22 June 1945.

During the summer of 1945, preparations were being made for the assault on the Japanese home islands, but this potentially bloody conflict was prevented by the Japanese surrender following the atomic bomb attacks.

Army casualties were relatively light in the Pacific theatre of operations: 160,454 casualties were sustained, of whom 28,880

Above: The land fighting in Leyte in October 1944. These soldiers, heavily laden with communications equipment, have managed to fight their way off the beach, but are still targets for small arms fire from isolated Japanese strongpoints or snipers who put up a brave defence against the Americans.

Below: While a phosphorous charge explodes on a Japanese fortification on the island of Corregidor in February 1945, soldiers of the 34th Regiment prepare to shoot any Japanese who emerge. The characteristic water bottle pouch of the American infantryman is clearly shown.

351 Major-General, US Army, 1944
*Major-General Innis P. Swift, commander of the 1st
Cavalry Division, is here shown at Los Negros in the
Admiralty Islands in 1944. He wears the light khaki
trousers and shirt, with canvas leggings and russet
brown leather boots. The two stars on the helmet
denote the rank of major-general. The corresponding
service dress of a major-general is depicted in figure
354.*

**352 Officer,
US Women's Army Corps, 1944**
*This officer wears the dark olive-drab cap and tunic
with light khaki shirt. Her cap badge is the standard
officers' late-war pattern of an unadorned eagle,
while the collar badges are the head of Pallas Athene
in gold (a winged propeller was used for USAAF
women officers). Women other ranks wore circular
gold badges on the collar with a similar design
thereupon. The olive braid on tunic cuffs denoted the
wearer's officer status.*

353 Private, US Army, 1944
*This infantryman in northern Burma wears water-
proofed laced boots, two-piece jungle suit and M1
helmet. Apart from water bottle and ammunition
pouches, he carries wire cutters on his belt. His
weapon is the M1903 A4 sniper's rifle, with the
M73 B1 (Weaver 330c) telescopic sight.*

354 Major-General, US Army, 1944
*This officer wears the light khaki service dress worn
from 1943 onwards. The half-inch olive-drab band
on the cuffs were borne by all officers, while those of
general rank wore the letters 'US' in gold on the
collar and had gold piping on the cap. This cap, the
light khaki version of the garrison cap, was known
as the 'chino'.*

351

352

were killed in action. A further 4458
casualties were incurred by US forces in
the China-Burma-India theatre.

ORGANISATION   In 1941 the US
Army was scattered in small outposts
across the Pacific with the exception of the
Philippines, where a substantial American
presence was maintained to support the
US-trained Philippine forces. American
ground troops were formed into the
Philippine Division, which was destroyed
by the Japanese at Bataan, the whole
formation either being killed or taken
prisoner.

Activated in January 1943, the US 6th
Army was the Army's spearhead in the
Pacific island-hopping campaigns. Its
first battle was the capture of Kiriwina
in the Woodlark Islands in July 1943
which marked the opening stage in a
2700-mile advance to the Philippines. For
the assault on the Philippines, the 6th was
joined by the 8th Army which played a
major role in the recapture of these
islands.

By the end of the war, the 6th Army
was organised into three corps of 10

divisions and the 8th Army consisted of
two corps of eight divisions.

The 10th Army originally had been
formed in June 1944 for the proposed
invasion of Formosa, but its target was
later changed to Okinawa. For the
assault on Okinawa, the 10th Army
comprised one infantry corps of four
divisions and an amphibious corps of
three US Marine divisions, a force of
some 154,000 men. Although only activated for one battle during World War II,
the 10th Army lost nearly 50,000 men on
Okinawa.

The infantry divisions which formed
the backbone of the three US armies in
the Pacific were organised on the same
basis as those in Europe (examined on
page 134). What was required for fighting
small last-ditch groups of Japanese in
difficult conditions was a cohesive structure at the section and platoon level and
the Army gave much thought to the
selection of individuals able to lead small
groups of men.

The United States possessed two cavalry
divisions at the outbreak of war, but only
the 1st Cavalry Division saw action as

part of the 6th Army. The division was
organised on the old 'square' (as opposed
to 'triangular') basis of two cavalry
brigades, each of two regiments. In
addition there were two field artillery
battalions which, with the standard
auxiliary divisional services brought the
formation's strength to 12,724 men.

One airborne division was allocated to
the Pacific theatre, the 11th, which fought
in an infantry as well as an airborne role
in the Philippines. The 11th Airborne
Division was organised as the European
theatre divisions, but on the old, smaller
pattern (see page 156), with an overall
strength of only 8505 men. No large
independent tank forces were formed in
the Pacific theatre; only in the Philippines
and on Okinawa were tanks used
extensively.

As well as the main Pacific theatres of
operation, US Army troops were actively
engaged in the fighting in China and
Burma. The most famous US unit involved in the Burmese campaign was
'Merrill's Marauders' which, under the
command of General Stilwell, became the
'Mars' Task Force and consisted of the

353

354

a new M1942 one-piece olive drab overall began to be issued, but it too was found impractical for wear during a campaign in which dysentery was common.

In the meantime the Office of the Quarter-Master General (OQMG) had been modifying the one-piece overall and developing other items of clothing for wear in jungle operations. Towards the end of July 1942 the OQMG received an urgent request from General MacArthur for 150,000 sets of special jungle equipment, and although development was not complete twelve items had to be standardised for immediate procurement and issue. The resulting one-piece camouflage jungle uniform was found satisfactory in the jungles of Panama, but in New Guinea the 'frog skin', as it was known, was found too heavy, too hot and too uncomfortable.

These criticisms led to the development of new materials which, unlike the herringbone twill, did not become so heavy when wet. In this new material a two-piece jungle suit was developed and manufactured and became standard issue in May 1943.

Below: American soldiers examine the damage done by a Japanese air attack on Paranaque in the Philippines on 13 December 1941. These Japanese raids were very successful and crippled the American air defences. General Douglas MacArthur commanded a force of almost 100,000 men in the islands; but of these, only 15,000 were American regulars. The men here are wearing a mixture of uniforms, including British helmets.

US 475th Infantry and 124th Cavalry Regiments, the Chinese 1st Regiment and the US 612th Field Artillery Regiment.

UNIFORM At the start of the war in the Pacific, American soldiers wore khaki drill uniforms which were officially known as Class C uniforms or 'chinos'. The basic service dress for enlisted men consisted of a sun helmet, worn officially until 1942, a side or overseas cap, long-sleeved shirt either worn open or with matching tie and long matching trousers with black shoes and socks. Officers wore the same uniform but in addition had a khaki drill service dress tunic. Both officers and men had a drill version of the peaked service cap with brown leather peak and chin strap.

Combat dress was also the Class C 'chino' worn with either the British pattern steel helmet or the new M1 helmet and canvas leggings with brown leather laced ankle boots. Equipment was the standard woven pattern.

This uniform was immediately found to be uncomfortable and impractical, and far too conspicuous for jungle warfare, so

355 Captain, US Army Air Force, 1944
Captain Benjamin Oliver Davis Jnr. wears the Shearling flying suit with B-3 jacket and A-3 trousers. The B-2 flying cap was fleece lined and had earflaps. Normal dress under the flying suit was either a beige or OD shirt and beige tie, and beige trousers or 'pinks'.

356 Pilot, USAAF, 1944
This pilot with the 1st US Air Commando Force in Burma wears the standard peaked cap, olive-drab shirt and airborne forces' trousers. His weapons are a fighting knife and a M1911 A1 automatic pistol.

355

356

Another problem was one of colour. Reports from the South-West Pacific indicated that the camouflage uniform was fine for stationary snipers, but made men on the move easy to spot. Early in 1944, 400 sets of a new jungle uniform in both poplin and cotton drill were issued for field testing. After various modifications suggested by those who had worn the suit in action, the new two-piece jungle uniform made of 5-ounce olive green poplin was standardised on 11 July 1945.

INSIGNIA Generally speaking no insignia or badges of rank were worn in combat, but various units devised systems of markings which were painted on the helmet or back so that they were only visible from the rear. The 27th Infantry Division painted their steel helmets in dark green with black splodges and a parallelogram. Within the parallelogram was a regimental emblem, on the left was a number which corresponded to a rank, and on the right the company letter. On all other uniforms the same badges of rank and other insignia were worn as on the temperate uniform.

AIR FORCE

In the war against Germany the United States Air Force had a virtual monopoly of aerial operations but in the Pacific theatre the Air Force worked in conjunction with the aviation branches of the Navy and the Marine Corps. Despite this the Air Force's own contribution to the defeat of Japan was far from negligible, some seven air forces being deployed in the Pacific and Far East.

Many American bases in the Pacific were lost to the Japanese in the first few months of the war, a period which revealed the superiority of Japanese aircraft against America's slow and outdated planes. The American recovery was rapid, however, and by the end of 1942 an organisational network had been established in which to deploy the United States' vast industrial resources. The Doolittle raid on Japan on 18 April 1942 was a foretaste of things to come; although the raid did little material damage it was a considerable source of humiliation to the Japanese and a morale-booster to the Americans.

Throughout 1942-43 the Air Force acted in a largely tactical role in support of naval and land forces operations. The Air Force provided transportation and reconnaissance duties as well as carrying out massive bombardments on Japanese island strongholds. By 1944 the air war against Japan was taking on an increasingly strategic aspect as long range bombers attacked Japanese supply centres in China and Indo-China as well as instigating an all-out offensive against the major cities of the Japanese homeland.

During the last months of the war the US Air Force was almost unopposed over Japan and inflicted massive damage on the Japanese urban centres and huge casualties on the civilian population. Tokyo, for instance, had an urban area of 110 square miles, over half of which was destroyed in a series of raids by the USAAF. The war was brought to a conclusion with the dropping of atomic bombs on Hiroshima and Nagasaki.

In the Pacific war the US Air Force flew a total of 669,235 sorties, dropped 502,781 tons of bombs, lost 4530 aircraft and claimed 10,343 enemy aircraft.

Total United States Army Air Force casualties for World War II were 116,501, of whom 32,170 were killed in action.

ORGANISATION The vast distances of the Pacific and the Far East entailed the division of the USAAF into a number of separate air forces stationed in India, China, Australia and the Pacific Islands. Each air force was responsible for a certain geographical area and certain tasks within that area. The seven US air forces were as follows:

5th Air Force – based in Australia, covered the South-West Pacific and was later engaged in the bombing of Japan from bases in Okinawa;

7th Air Force – operated from Hawaii against Japanese targets in the central Pacific and the Japanese homeland;

10th Air Force – responsible for transport and reconnaissance duties as well as combat operations in Burma and Thailand including support for the Chindits and 'Merrill's Marauders';

11th Air Force – a defence and reconnaissance air force based in Alaska, although it carried out attacks on the Kurile Islands;

13th Air Force – conducted independent strategic bombing as well as tactical support for the land forces in the Solomons;

14th Air Force – originated from the 'Flying Tigers' and worked with the Chinese Army against Japanese targets in China;

Above: Groundcrewmen in casual working clothing arm an American fighter-bomber with rockets. Rockets were a useful weapon against enemy communications, and they were highly effective against tanks.

Below: US Army Air Force pilots of the 'Flying Tigers' in China scramble for their aircraft. Curtiss P-40 Kittyhawk fighters painted with the distinctive shark's mouth symbol. Note the seat-type parachutes worn by the pilots.

20th Air Force – activated in April 1944 and equipped with B-29s to act as the main strategic bomber force.

The war in the Pacific demonstrated American organisational flexibility with each air force carrying out its various tasks with considerable success. The Japanese in contrast lacked this flexibility and paid the price accordingly; their failure to adapt to changing circumstances ensured that their meagre resources were wasted and their homeland left unprotected against US bombers.

UNIFORM Air Force personnel wore the same Class C uniforms as the rest of the Army. Officers wore the khaki drill service dress consisting of peaked cap, shirt, tunic, long trousers and brown shoes.

The Air Force winged-propeller emblem in metal appeared on the left side of the overseas cap worn by enlisted men and on the left side of the shirt collar. Officers wore the same emblem on the tunic lapels.

On Class C uniforms rank chevrons were in khaki on blue backing.

357 **Petty Officer 3rd Class,
US Navy, 1943**
This Samoan fita-fita *was a cook with the US Navy
(he wears his speciality badge on his* lava-lava*).
He has a ribbon of the Purple Heart on a standard
Navy undershirt. Note the red turban, waist sash and
four – sometimes three – red bands below the badge.
The US armed forces were obliged to employ numerous
foreign auxiliaries to maintain their long lines of
supply. This was particularly necessary in the Pacific
island chains.*

358 **Lieutenant, US Navy, 1941**
*This naval airman wears the green service dress. The
black lace stripes and star on the cuffs and the silver
bars on the shirt collar denote the rank of lieutenant.
The wings on his left breast are the naval aviation
badge.*

359 **Lieutenant Junior Grade,
Women's Auxiliary
Volunteer Service, 1942**
*This lieutenant's rank is shown by the sleeve stripes
in reserve blue, and the silver bars on the shirt. Her
head-dress is the standard summer cap with Navy
officers' cap badge. The collar badges represented a
white anchor on a blue propeller.*

*Above: The 201st Mexican Fighter Squadron
assembles in front of a P-47 Thunderbolt on
Porac strip, Clark Field, Luzon.*

MEXICAN AIR FORCE

The first Mexican military unit ever to
fight outside Mexico was the 201st
Mexican Fighter Squadron (*Escadrilla
Aguilas Aztecas*) which arrived in Manila
on 1 May 1945.

After a short period of acclimatisation
and intensive training in American fighter
command tactics its 52 officers and 244
men joined in group support missions
against Japanese ground forces in central
and north Luzon. Nine Mexican airmen
lost their lives before the unit was finally
disbanded on 1 December 1945.

UNIFORM Mexican Expeditionary Air
Force personnel wore Mexican uniforms
off duty but American Army Air Force
clothing and equipment on active service.
Some pilots continued to wear the olive
green Mexican Army peaked and side
caps. Mexican rank badges were worn on
flying clothing and overalls.

NAVY

The weight of American naval effort was
directed to the Pacific and, in this theatre
of war, naval power, usually expressed in
terms of carrier-based aircraft, was to be
absolutely crucial. The great influence of
American manufacturing capacity was
nowhere more clearly shown than in the

Pacific naval battles, where the US
superiority in building aircraft carriers
quickly became the decisive factor.

In late 1941, the US Navy consisted of:
16 battleships;
7 aircraft carriers;
18 heavy cruisers;
19 light cruisers;
6 anti-aircraft cruisers;
171 destroyers;
114 submarines.

At the beginning of the Pacific War, the
United States Pacific Fleet based at Pearl
Harbor consisted of eight battleships and
three aircraft carriers. After the attack on
7 December the Japanese sunk four
battleships, severely damaged three
others, and one was beached. In all, 2403
Americans were killed and 1176 wounded.
Fortunately, the three fleet carriers, *Enterprise*, *Lexington* and *Saratoga* were absent
from Pearl Harbor and survived un-
scathed along with five cruisers and
twenty-nine destroyers to form the nucleus
of the new expanded Pacific Fleet.

Naval building had been increasing in
tempo since the 'Two Ocean' Act of 1940,
but the Navy was hard-put to match the
Japanese forces in the aftermath of Pearl
Harbor. The immediate reaction of the
United States was to construct, with great
speed, four fast carriers of the Essex class
(which carried 90 aircraft each) and five
carriers carrying 40 aircraft each.

After the stalemate of the Coral Sea
and the victory of Midway in the summer
of 1942, the initiative lay with the US
Navy, and it rapidly brought into service

357

an enormous tonnage of new warships. The defeat of Japan then became inevitable. The attempts of the Japanese fleet to inflict a large-scale defeat on the American Navy at the battle of the Philippine Sea in June 1944 and the battle of Leyte Gulf later that year, were both disasters and hastened American victory.

There were three basic layers to the US Navy's success in the Pacific. The first was its carrier fleet, and the creation of such organisations as the Fast Carrier Task Forces based upon this strength. A total of 27 new carriers was completed before the end of hostilities, and over 75,000 aircraft were delivered to the Navy as a whole between 1940 and 1945. Naval aviation personnel strength went from 10,923 (2,695 of whom were pilots) in 1940 to 437,524 (with 60,747 pilots) by August 1945.

The second layer was the development of techniques of amphibious landing. Over 66,000 landing craft were built during the war, and the vast majority were used in the Pacific.

Thirdly, there was the submarine war.

Above: During the invasion of Mindoro in December 1944, anti-aircraft gunners on a US Navy cruiser anxiously watch a plane overhead.

By the summer of 1945, Japan had been destroyed economically by the most effective submarine blockade in history. In all, 228 submarines entered service during the war, and 60 were lost; 4,000,000 gross tons of Japanese shipping was sunk.

In December 1941, the Navy had a combined strength of 337,274 officers and men; by 1945, there were 3,383,196 personnel of whom 1,574,614 served afloat.

ORGANISATION Within the Pacific theatre, two commands were set up: the Pacific Ocean Area under the command of Admiral Chester W. Nimitz and the South West Pacific Area commanded by General Douglas MacArthur. The former advocated an advance across the expanse of the Pacific Ocean via the Gilbert, Marshall and Marianas Islands towards Formosa; the latter rejected this in favour of an 'island hopping' manoeuvre based on Australia towards the Philippines. Both strategies would have the effect of isolating the Japanese home islands from the oil resources of the Dutch East Indies. The means differed, however, reflecting the interests of the two services: Nimitz's thrust would give maximum scope for the use of naval power, whilst MacArthur's would relegate the Navy to a supporting role. In the event, such were the resources of the United States that she could sustain both these axes of advance.

358

359

Right: Ordnancemen load 500lb demolition bombs onto a Douglas SBD Dauntless bomber on board the USS Enterprise *on 7 August 1942. This was the first day of the attacks on Guadalcanal – Tulagi, the opening of the campaign which wrested the initiative in the Pacific away from the Japanese. The US Navy, fighting hard in the 'Slot' to keep the US ground forces supplied and to isolate the Japanese, suffered severe casualties; and the* Enterprise *herself was so severely damaged on the night of 24 August that she had to withdraw from the battle.*

Far right: Marine Corps artillerymen operate a field howitzer lashed to a cliff edge on Tinian in the Marianas.

**360 Landing Signals Officer,
US Navy, 1944**

This officer, signalling to the pilot of a plane coming in to land on an aircraft carrier, wears the light khaki cotton or poplin officers' service dress shirt and light khaki trousers, with yellow slipover and helmet.

360

In March 1943 the Central Pacific Force was created as part of Nimitz's Pacific Fleet and commanded by Admiral Raymond Spruance. By the summer of 1943 it had been built up into the largest fleet the world had ever seen and was designated the 5th Fleet in April 1944. There were three task forces: TF50, a fast carrier force with eleven aircraft carriers, six battleships and six heavy cruisers; TF54 which included the amphibious assault force; and TF57 which combined control of all the shore-based naval aircraft, plus the Mobile Service Squadron of repair ships, destroyer tenders and tugs. The whole force totalled 19 aircraft carriers and 900 aircraft.

The fleet was naturally subdivided to suit the operation in hand. For example, the attacks on the Gilbert and Marshall Islands served as models for later amphibious operations. TF52 and 53 formed the attack forces North and South. Each task force was a separate, self-contained force of three escort carriers, a squadron of battleships and a squadron of cruisers with 14 destroyers for bombardment and close escort of the transport ships. The Fast Carrier Force, now redesignated TF58, organised into four task groups sharing six large and five light carriers, each group protected by its own screen of fast battleships, cruisers and destroyers, provided the aerial assault force. TF57 provided land-based air cover (which included over 100 Liberator heavy bombers) under Navy command – an innovation borrowed from Japanese organisation. This vast armada totalled over 200 ships and 1000 aircraft. During the attack on the Marianas, Task Force 58 was divided into self-contained task groups of even greater size and fighting power. TF58.1 comprised the aircraft carriers *Hornet, Yorktown, Bellau Wood,* and *Bataan*; TF58.2 *Bunker Hill, Wasp, Monterey* and *Cabot;* TF58.3 *Enterprise, Lexington, Princeton* and *San Jacinto;* TF58.4 *Essex, Langley* and *Cowpens.* In all, there were 15 aircraft carriers, seven battleships, 13 cruisers and 58 destroyers.

Meanwhile, MacArthur's drive in the South-West Pacific was supported by the South Pacific Force under Admiral Halsey (formed in 1942) which was redesignated the 3rd Fleet in March 1943. MacArthur did not, however, have total control over Halsey's forces. The naval units most closely connected to MacArthur's advance were the Naval Forces South-West Pacific, redesignated the 7th Fleet under the command of Vice-Admiral Carpender in March 1943; Carpender was succeeded by Vice-Admiral Kinkaid in November 1943.

In 1944, as the Americans gradually closed in on the Japanese, the decision was taken to combine the 5th Fleet with the 3rd Fleet and to alternate the command of this vast force between Spruance and Admiral Halsey. When the one Admiral commanded the other would retire with his staff to Pearl Harbor to plan his next operation. When Halsey commanded it became the 3rd Fleet, and when Spruance returned it reverted to the 5th; thus the task forces became 38 and not 58; the ships' names, however, remained the same.

This arrangement worked very well; it was one of the most novel solutions to the organisation problems of this vast theatre.

UNIFORM During the war the service dress of US Navy officers and chief petty officers was the khaki drill Army uniform. It consisted of peaked cap with khaki cover, open single-breasted khaki tunic, shirt which could be worn open or closed with black tie, matching long trousers and black shoes. Other forms of head-dress were the khaki drill overseas cap and a drill baseball cap with peak. The pre-war white uniform continued as a dress uniform.

The khaki drill uniform was not totally satisfactory, however, and its colour was found to be conspicuous, so it was sometimes dyed grey, or officers acquired a grey working dress on which black rank distinction lace was worn on the shoulder straps.

The Navy blue and white square rigs were retained for dress or undress occasions, and the most typical form of everyday wear in wartime was the white fatigue cap, white T-shirt, blue denim shirt and blue jeans. In action all ranks wore the grey-painted M1 steel helmet, and a blue canvas lifejacket. In many ships during the war helmets were painted in bright colours which indicated special duties, so that, for example, fire control men wore red-painted steel helmets.

INSIGNIA Rank badges not only identified rank but also whether the wearer was a member of the executive (or line branch) or one of the other Navy corps. Officers and warrant officers wore rank distinction lace in gold on the sleeves of the navy blue reefer and on the shoulder straps of the khaki tunic. On the shirt they wore Army rank badges on the collar (both sides for executive officers and on the right side only for other officers), as well as on the left front of the side cap. Petty officers had a special cap badge and wore their rank badges on the sleeve. Ratings only wore rank badges on the cuffs of the blue dress jumper.

MARINE CORPS

During World War II the US Marine Corps built up a reputation as one of America's toughest combat services; they were continuously engaged in the Pacific War from Wake Island in 1941 to Okinawa in 1945.

The Marines' first major campaign began with the assault on Guadalcanal in the Solomon Islands on 7 August 1942. With little naval and air support the

Marines fought a desperate battle against the Japanese who launched a series of fanatical, but ultimately unsuccessful, attacks in an attempt to dislodge the Americans. After their victory on Guadalcanal the Marines were involved in the fighting in the central Pacific, most notably on Tarawa. The Marines' war continued with the capture of the Marianas Islands, and Iwo Jima and Okinawa.

361 Gunnery Sergeant, US Marine Corps, 1941
This sergeant is in full dress uniform. His rank is shown by the chevrons on the upper sleeve; the stripes on the lower sleeve are service stripes, one for each four years of service. The three medal ribbons are (left to right) that for service in Nicaragua (at some time between 1926 and 1933), the Marine Corps expeditionary badge and a Purple Heart. Below these he has two proficiency badges; the expert rifleman's badge (with four requalification bars) and the pistol competency badge.

361

Marine Corps casualties for World War II were 91,718 men of whom 15,161 were killed in action with a further 4322 dead through other causes.

ORGANISATION The Marine Corps performed two basic military functions, firstly, to act as land combat troops for the Navy and, secondly, to carry out autonomous amphibious operations of their own. It was this latter function that expanded enormously during World War II within the branch known as the Fleet Marine Force.

In 1939 the strength of the Marine Corps stood at just under 20,000 men; by the outbreak of war in 1941 this had grown to 65,881 and by the end of the war there were more than 450,000 officers and men in the Marines. To some extent the Marine Corps was an army within an army, possessing its own aviation units.

In February 1941 the USMC was organised as two brigades which were then redesignated as the 1st and 2nd Marine Divisions. The process of bringing the new divisions up to strength was a slow one and it was not until the middle of 1942 that the formations were ready for action.

The Marine division was organised as a reinforced infantry division with three infantry regiments each of three battalions, and artillery, engineer and pioneer regiments. The size of the division was a little under 20,000 men and was often strengthened further for particular operations. Specialising in amphibious landings against fortified Japanese strongholds the Marine division had a large compliment of pioneers to clear the way for assault troops.

The two Marine divisions were combined into the First Marine Amphibious Corps (or IMAC), although because of the dispersed nature of the fighting in the Pacific this was more an administrative than a tactical grouping.

During 1943 a further three Marine divisions were raised followed by the activation of the 6th Marine Division in September 1944. A new corps was formed in 1943 and was called V Amphibious Corps (or VAC). This corps was engaged in the struggle for the Gilberts and the Marshalls and later the Marianas Islands. The 4th and 5th Marine Divisions led the assault on Iwo Jima, supported by the 3rd Marine Division, and suffered 23,303 casualties in the bitter struggle for the island.

The III Amphibious Corps, which had replaced IMAC, supported Army operations on Okinawa and consisted of the 1st, 2nd and 6th Marine Divisions. Some 15,000 Marine casualties were sustained out of a combined American total of nearly 50,000 men.

The Marine Corps aviation consisted of two air groups and 10 squadrons at the outbreak of war. Once at war the aviation branch underwent an exceptionally rapid expansion, however, so that by January 1945 there were five aircraft wings made up of 132 squadrons plus other auxiliary units. Personnel strength rose from a figure of 11,000 men in 1941 to 135,000 by 1945. The function of the Marine Corps aviation was to provide tactical air support for Marine land operations.

362 Lieutenant, US Marine Corps, 1945
Equipped for action in the Pacific theatre, this Marine officer carries two water bottles, a pistol in the leather holster, an M4 knife bayonet and pouches for field dressings and ammunition. He has a camouflage poncho strapped to his pack. Rank is denoted by the silver bars on the collar.

363 Lieutenant-Colonel, US Marine Corps, 1942
Lieutenant-Colonel Harold W. Bauer (shown here during the Guadalcanal campaign) was one of the first aces of the Marine air service. When he died in action in November 1942, he had scored eleven victories. He wears the one-piece herringbone-twill olive-drab overall (rather than the lightweight flying overalls) and a lightweight flying helmet. His parachute is the seat type for pilots of single-engined aircraft.

362

363

Above left: Marines using an advanced field telephone during the fighting for Kwajalein Atoll in January 1944. They are wearing helmets with the camouflage cover.

Above: A wounded Marine is brought off Iwo Jima by Coast Guardsmen. The landing craft which went in at Iwo Jima came back with the wounded, who were transferred to hospital ships. The speedy evacuation of wounded personnel was considered essential to maintain morale.

364 Private, US Marine Corps, 1943

This private in the New Guinea campaign has the M1 steel helmet with webbing cover. The two-piece herringbone-twill fatigue suit was introduced in 1942. The woven belt was normally worn only by officers, but is here seen with magazine and field dressing pouches affixed. The latter were very necessary in the hot and humid climate of New Guinea, where even minor wounds could quickly become infected without immediate attention. The herring-bone-twill suit was later discarded, as it became very heavy when wet.

365 Private, US Marine Corps, 1943

The basic clothing of this Marine is the two-piece USMC 'dungaree' uniform, which differed from the Army pattern in having a flapless pocket on the left breast. His M1 helmet has the 'beach' design of camouflage cover, and above the russet brown boots his gaiters are worn under the trousers. He has two captured Japanese trophies (sword and water bottle) hanging from the woven belt. His standard US-issue water bottle has been relegated to his left hip, while the badge is the USMC 'globe and anchor' design stencilled onto his uniform; the cherished symbol of this famous corps.

364

365

INDEX

Numbers in italic refer to illustrations